Hokkaido Dairy Farm

Hokkaido Dairy Farm

Cosmopolitics of Otherness and Security on the Frontiers of Japan

PAUL HANSEN

SUNY
PRESS

Cover Credit: Former Kobe school teacher Matsumoto Keiji's idealized depiction of a Hokkaido dairy farm after living in Tokachi. Used with permission.

Published by State University of New York Press, Albany

For information, contact State University of New York Press, Albany, NY
www.sunypress.edu

Library of Congress Cataloging-in-Publication Data

Name: Hansen Paul, author.
Title: Hokkaido dairy farm : cosmopolitics of otherness and security on the frontiers of Japan / Paul Hansen.
Description: Albany : State University of New York Press, [2024] | Includes bibliographical references and index.
Identifiers: ISBN 9781438496474 (hardcover : alk. paper) | ISBN 9781438496481 (ebook) | ISBN 9781438496467 (pbk. : alk. paper)
Further information is available at the Library of Congress.

10 9 8 7 6 5 4 3 2 1

I dedicate this book to the memory of
Edward, Eileen, and Siobhan O'Toole
for never giving up on a willful, hyper, and dyslexic kid.

Contents

Illustrations

Figures

Tables

Acknowledgments

The duration of this project has been spread over two decades, three countries, six universities, and truly countless conferences, couch stays, conversations, and cocktails. The gratitude I feel toward interlocutors, colleagues, students, family, friends, and SUNY Press is immense and would approach the length of an additional book chapter were I to list everyone involved. So, my apologies to those who do not find their name in the following list, it is due to my battle with concision in a book already spilling over the margins and not the value of your contribution.

I thank the town of "Gensan" and "Grand Hopes Farm" (though these are pseudonyms) for the years they have put up with my presence, persistence, and awkward questions. I am especially grateful to the Abes, the Babas, the Hiraos, the Oguras, the Tanakas, and the Toshimas. I am grateful to the Japanese Society for the Promotion of Science, the Japan Foundation, University of London's SOAS, University of Tsukuba, and Hokkaido University for funding aspects of this research. I was very lucky to have dedicated advisors for my MA and PhD. Thank you, Ian Reader, Delores Martinez, and Johan Pottier. Kuwayama Takami, Ikeya Kazunobu, and Nakamaki Hirochika have been hosts and mentors at Hokkaido University and the National Museum of Ethnology (aka Minpaku). Offering comradery, advice, and critique on all things Hokkaido, my friends Jeff Gayman and John Mock are deeply appreciated. And another pair of Hokkaido-based friends, Susanne Klien and Richard Siddle, both kindly read the manuscript in its entirety offering incisive and insightful comments.

Many thanks to Melanie Rock, Alan and Josie Smart, and Ann Toohey for their friendship and support at the University of Calgary and the Cumming School of Medicine, which provided an office and time to think through some of this book. Robin O'Day, "Master No," Kikuchi Mari, Rafael Munia, Gülin Kayhan, and Nara Masashi, alongside Uchiyamada and Kimura sensei I thank for the *good* parts of Tsukuba life. At Hokkaido University, outside the former colleagues noted above, I thank Stephanie Assmann, Paul Capobianco, Emma Cook, James Letson, Nozawa Shunsuke, Caitlin Coker, and Phil Seaton for their support and friendship over the years. I thank Chiba Kaeko, Judit Kroo, and Omori Hisako at Akita International University and Evan Cacali, Goto Manami, Miyamoto Ritsuko, Miyake Yoshimi, and Nawata Hiroshi at Akita University my current academic home. Thank you to my constant confidant, friend, coeditor, and coorganizer Blai Guarné and others with whom, in no order, I have worked alongside in various capacities: Kawamura Hiroaki, Gordon Mathews, Glenda Roberts, Joy Hendry, Numazaki Ichiro, John Ertl, Laura Dales, Andrea De Antoni, Dan White, Katsuno Hirofumi, Patrick Galbraith, Nishimura Keiko, Iza Kavedžija, Harry Walker, Gergely Mohacsi, Émile Saint-Pierre, Kondo Shiaki, Yoshida Mariko, Don Wood, Peter Matanle, Wolfram Manzenreiter, Sonja Ganseforth, Hanno Jentzsch, John Traphagan, William Kelly, Nancy Rosenberger, Sugimoto Ayumi, Ksenia Kurochkina. And there are so many others with whom I have met and who have kindly discussed research with me at the AAA, AJJ, CASCA, or at other events: please forgive me if you do not find your name above. With much love I thank Jim Hansen, Mike O'Toole, Caleb and Vicky Blankert, Steve and Joanne Poffenroth, and Albert and Brenda Siebert—alongside many four-legged friends among them—for making returns from "the field" to "home" pleasurable and possible. Of course, I want to thank the two anonymous peer reviewers of this book, their critical yet kind comments made revisions actually enjoyable, and the staff at SUNY Press. And finally, love and thanks to Kumi and Seamus "the beast" Hansen for tolerating an often absent, physically and mentally, family member over the years.

Introduction

Yōkoso Hokkaido

Yōkoso Hokkaido simply means welcome to Hokkaido. *Yōkoso* is a catch-word that pervades everyday advertising culture in Japan, especially in places of transit such as airports. It is a word that takes on a different nuance in Japan's northernmost region. Flying into Hokkaido's Tokachi airport from the major population hubs of Kanto, the region around Tokyo, or Kinki, the area surrounding Osaka, is indeed like arriving in another country.[1] Looking down, none of the symbols of a stereotypical Japanese landscape are seen. Urban sprawl and sky-scraping neon are absent. There are no bamboo forests, stratified paddy fields, or elongated hamlets clinging to the walls of lush valleys. There are no picturesque temples with meticulously manicured gardens. If arriving in midwinter as I did the first time, color seems rendered in broad brushstrokes. A choppy greenish sea followed by a vacant rock-strewn coast, then occasional collections of red and blue rooftops surrounded by pure whiteness. This gently undulating snow-blanketed land is only broken by the sparse geometrically calculated roads and fences that cut through it. From above, fences, roads, and the carefully plotted wind-breaking tree lines are evocative of stitching and the land a gigantic patchwork quilt with clearly separated square and rectangular sections stretching into the horizon. Each patch of homesteaded land has its own story. Every staked-out section is its own living fabric, a singular meshwork of buildings, equipment, and well-worn tracks that betray the daily patterns of life and work. The main historical and ethnographic focus of this book is one such farm—one patch of land, one assemblage of living beings—and how it is woven into relationships within the broader tapestry of the local community, Tokachi, Hokkaido, and Japan.

Northern Tokachi is at the center of Hokkaido, Japan's largest prefecture, and the region is home to numerous physical and ideological frontiers making it a unique and particular location in the context of Japan. For example, this northern environment makes certain lifestyles and livelihoods viable while it assures others are impossible to pursue. Dairy farming is a key industry in the area, an occupation that perhaps seems unusual to many in the context of Japan; when one thinks of Japan, milk is likely low on the list of associations. But one contention of this book is that Hokkaido, and certainly Tokachi, is an anomaly in many ways if contrasted with what is popularly considered typical in Japan. This book outlines many reasons why it differs—in cultural, social, political, and economic terms—but for a start, the most obvious reason is simply rooted in the landscape. *Hiroi*, or vast, is an adjective I have often overheard fellow passengers use emphatically on my countless subsequent flights in and out of Tokachi. It is not a word used often to describe locations in Japan, but vast, spacious, and wide, as noted in what follows, describe many aspects of life on Japan's northernmost island.

Hokkaido is on the northern periphery of the country. It is due east of the Siberian steppes and its regional capital city Sapporo is closer to Russian Vladivostok than Tokyo. The region is distant from both North America and its settlers. Yet, if one focuses on environment and temporality, these regions and people share some surprising connections and similarities. Hokkaido has always been popularly imagined as a physical, political, and social frontier for Japanese people; that is to say, it was viewed as an open space where *kaitakusha seishin* (the pioneering spirit), long defined by an outcast independence, was—and I argue still is—tested and confirmed. It is perceived as a place where newcomers can make a fresh start; a place where personal changes happen or can be made to happen (Hansen 2018a, 2020a). Moreover, throughout Hokkaido's history the region has been viewed as a distant place, a locus of capital O Otherness, or alterity, in relation to a hegemonic Honshu as the political and population center of Japan (for Ainu as historically Othered see Bresner 2009; for Tokachi see Hansen 2014a; and for Hokkaido in general see Saunavaara 2018). No place fits this description of Hokkaido as Other more than the plains and foothills that comprise Tokachi (see figure I.1).

The objective of this book is to add to the historical and anthropological record of Hokkaido as a "frontier," a locus of Otherness, and a place rife with concomitant individual and collective security searching. I specifically focus on the north of Tokachi, the largest subprefecture, and

Figure I.1. Looking south over the Tokachi region in January 2008. Photo by the author.

dairy farming as a core industry that embodies these notions of Otherness, security, and frontiers in Japan. I do not presume that the reader has knowledge of either Hokkaido or dairy farming: I describe both in detail. It is easy to find Hokkaido, past and present, intriguing. And having lived, researched, and written about this area for nearly twenty years, and having used this framing of frontier, security, and Otherness in previous academic publications and presentations, I must head off some potential misinterpretations. I am not using the term *frontier* as a general geopolitical claim regarding a buffer or periphery alone. As the second chapter highlights, the term, and its metaphoric baggage, is carefully chosen. Hokkaido has a particular and peculiar place within the context of Japan and the global history of settler colonialism. Indeed, it is Japan's only remaining settler colony. As such, it is a place where the search for micro, meso, and macro security (or individual, community, and national projects of securing) have played and continue to play a central role in defining people and place. It is home to a distinct history of Japanese colonization: a history that can and should be compared to the colonial projects of other nations at the end of the nineteenth century, for example, the settling of the North American West, Alaska, New Zealand, Australia, or East Russia (Irish 2009; Mason 2012; Russell 2007; Seki et al. 2006; Shigematsu 2004; Thompson 2008).

Despite being a relatively ignored region within the context of global colonial history, Japanese history, and anthropology, the story of central Hokkaido is essential to understanding Japan as a modern-cum-postmodern project. Without its resources, from expansive forests to indigenous Ainu lore and, of course, its dairy industry, contemporary Japan would be a considerably more impoverished place financially and culturally. More to the point of this book, the region's history sits parallel to a shared global history of colonization and empire building, subduing native plants, animals, and humans, alongside encouraging the migration of marginalized people to marginal locations at the expense of indigenous life (Povinelli 2016; Shapiro 1997). I argue that this history, one of entwined alterities on a so-called frontier, has sown the seeds for ongoing exploitation of Tokachi as a peripheral region far from external nodes of political and cultural power via centralized governmental agricultural agencies (Hansen 2010a, 2014a). And as highlighted in this book, connections can be made, compared, and contrasted with other colonial acquisitions past and present, from Japan's troubled imperial history with Korea to contemporary identity politics in Okinawa. Again, while Hokkaido, and Tokachi in local terms, has played the role of periphery and buffer, this book is primarily concerned with its role as a frontier, literal and figurative, and the macro to micro security concerns that, past and present, continue to define a livelihood that is imagined and positioned, pragmatically and politically, as Other.

Northern Tokachi and its dairy industry are an important case study in these regards but also, simply, they are an ideal example of agrarian settler history. Important because, first, there is no history of the area in English and, as such, there has been little work contrasting or comparing it with other nineteenth-century colonized regions inside Japan or outside. In looking at the evolution of Tokachi's dairy industry from a comparative historical and anthropological perspective, I suggest that the concepts of Otherness, frontier, and security arise as essential conceptual tools in understanding this region and industry enabling, I hope, future comparisons. My use of these concepts as an analytical tool is clarified in the following two chapters. Second, despite its central role as an industry, a regional identity, and its deployment as an imaginary and image central to the prefecture, there has been no substantial anthropological research conducted on the diary industry in Hokkaido, let alone its northern Tokachi heartland. The reasons for this could be many. First is the engaged nature of such fieldwork. In order to conduct an ethnographic study on livelihood, locality, and labor a researcher needs to commit to working and living long-term in areas that can be challenging on a number of fronts, personal and professional, points made obvious in what follows. Second, any notion of a "unified and unique" Japan needs to be abandoned from the start to recognize that this region and topic fit extraordinarily poorly with many popular, and even academic, presumptions about rural Japan, a central theme in this book (Hansen 2021a). Third, it is often not pleasant to grapple with an industry that is dependent upon innumerable human and nonhuman lives; it inevitably opens the way for discomforting reflections on contemporary practices and social theory issues. For example, how has it come to be that a rural periphery of Japan is in many ways more cosmopolitan than its urban metropoles? Or is it possible to produce a posthuman story that defines the particularity of place, a narrative that allows for the inherent phenomenological interplay and agency of human and nonhuman inclusive of the slippages and blurring of these seemingly secured categories? In this sense, this book is in conversation with other works of an ethnographic ilk, a growing list, that examine the impacts of industrialization on food production and local identity (cf. Blanchette 2020; Gillespie 2018; Kondo and Yoshida 2021; Pachirat 2011).

The Groundwork for Fieldwork

Anthropology, the discipline in which I am trained, has long been mired in internal struggles over reflexivity. For better or worse, it is common to attempt to place oneself in an ethnographic text as the key researcher and narrator. What follows is not intended to be narcissistic self-exploration but a way of sharing with the reader some insight into how this research topic was chosen and what biases might enter the work. In 2005–2006 I was employed for a year as a full-time laborer on one of the largest industrial dairy farms in Hokkaido and I spent a further eight months in 2008 doing follow up research while based at Hokkaido University on a postdoctoral fellowship. This period of research constitutes the core of my ethnography and it is a rather standard fieldwork tour of duty within the discipline of anthropology. A confluence of factors made me choose Hokkaido dairy farming as a topic: a chance encounter in a bar in Hiroshima with two women who had volunteered on a dairy farm in Hokkaido and a wise academic mentor who pointed out that—beyond studies of indigenous Ainu—very few anthropologists have done long-term fieldwork in rural Hokkaido. But the main reason was purely pragmatic: I needed money. I needed to do self-supporting fieldwork and working on a farm was a viable option in that I had plenty of family ranching experience in Alberta, Canada. I applied for dairy jobs across Hokkaido as a laborer through websites. Many Hokkaido farms were and remain desperate for seasonal workers, so almost immediately two farms encouraged me to come and volunteer. However, working for free was not possible, certainly not for a year. Luckily Mr. Wada, a man I introduce below, agreed to hire me under the same conditions he would offer any other worker.

In 2009–2010 I made several return trips while based in Osaka doing research on dog–human relationships (Hansen 2013, 2018b, 2020a). In 2011 I was hired by the Graduate School of History and Anthropology at the University of Tsukuba. And soon after this, I got married in the northern Tokachi town where I conducted fieldwork, and I later became a father. When I started writing this book, my Kyoto-born wife, a prior interlocutor, was a nurse at a clinic in the town and my Tokachi-born *dosanko* (Hokkaido born) son attended a local school for grades 1 and 2 before we moved all moved to Sapporo, making weekly journeys to "home" in Tokachi less onerous for the Canadian in this familial triad. The writing of this book also coincides with the slow restoration of a local house. Thus, my experiences of Tokachi life and dairy farming are professional, as an anthropologist of Japan living and working there, and personal, as my family and I are part of the community that I study. Consequently, I have come to see the area progressively as a visitor, worker, and resident and have gotten to know former interlocutors and coworkers as friends and, on occasion, foes.

Given this background, the ethnographic material presented herein enters a number of ongoing debates in anthropology and social theory. One key issue is in regard to what I have argued is anthropology's too frequent compliance with the objectives and methods of other more meta- or macro-oriented social sciences, notably the social constructivism of Pierre Bourdieu (among others), neo-Marxist paradigms, and the notion of a long-term "objective" participant observer, in homogenizing individual narratives, anomalies, and agencies (Hansen 2015 as a summary).[2] In what follows, I suggest that the people I have come to live with are inimitable individuals; each is a unique and singularly embodied agent (Guarné and

Hansen 2018; Rapport 2012). As a result, the way that I write is a clear and conscious attempt to reduce what Bruno Latour calls "the default social" in the social sciences, or the notion that action and identity are bound to categories (Latour 2005, 4). Strands of anthropology have long argued against such reductive trends, notably Fredrik Barth (Weller and Wu 2020). In short, the goal of this book is not to manufacture reductive human typologies for the reader.[3] I am not interested in producing (or reproducing as the case may be) localized generalities about *the* Japanese, *the* dairy farmer, *the* full-time worker versus *the furītā* (part-timer) nor pitting ethnic or gender identities into competing or comparative binary categories. In this ethnography I present people with their clashes, confusions, and contradictions accounted for in what, lifting from Donna Haraway and Jacques Derrida, respectively, I see as their "significant" (Haraway 2008) "particularity" (Derrida 2008). Or what might be considered their extreme "intersectionality" in a classic social scientific and less philosophical framing (Crenshaw 1989). All of the people discussed in this book are clearly, and profoundly at times, self- and socially aware actors working and living within a rapidly changing industry and area. And importantly, they come and go. It might be surprising for some readers to learn that dairy farmers in Tokachi are an extraordinarily cosmopolitan collection of people. They are young and old, Japanese and non-Japanese, rural and urban born, many have traveled, some widely often to learn about dairying, and each one of them has life course–specific reasons for engaging in farmwork and living in the region, related to their personal demons, dreams, desires, and goals. Unsurprisingly, this human diversity, when packed into the strict regime of dairy farming as a livelihood, alongside the increasing competitiveness of the industry, leads to many conflicts, overt and covert, verbal and physical, that radically displace the aforementioned commonly held stereotypical notions of harmonious agrarian homogeneity in Japan; or as Hannah Arendt once quipped, the "rural communistic fiction" (Arendt 1998, 44). In this area and industry, the Otherness of Hokkaido and the fragmented searches for security played out in it are filtered down to represent an ethos of individual "each otherness" over group belonging. There are ample titles and examples of particularistic quests for personal security in times of rapid change in Japan: a post-1990s "Japan after Japan" (Harootunian and Yoda 2006), a burgeoning "transcultural" (Willis and Murphy-Shigematsu 2008), or "precarious" (Allison 2013) Japan, and indeed there are those who attempt to "escape Japan" altogether (Guarné and Hansen 2018; Ertl and Hansen 2015). I hope this book finds its way onto shelves with similar titles, albeit coming from a rural perspective. But given the novel history of the region and its contemporary lure for highly individualistic, even maverick, people, the final chapters of this book focus on how the shift to industrialized production alters relationships shared between human, animal, and technology. This final objective combines the aforementioned historical and ethnographic data and analyzes it with a combination of social theories derived from the posthumanities and cosmopolitan studies.[4] These are the examinations and issues at the core of this book, but like most ethnographic accounts, perhaps the best place to start telling an ongoing story is where the narrator enters.

Tokachi, Hokkaido: Arrival

After making my way out of the New Chitose airport, forty minutes from Sapporo, Hokkaido's 150-year-old capital city, I collected my bags, decoded the train schedule, and stood outside waiting—body tensed and exhalations visible on a frigid February afternoon. Japan sells itself as a tourist destination by referring to its four distinct seasons. Yet the climate where the majority of Japanese live is quite moderate, and while areas such as Akita are famed for heavy snowfall, they are not prone to winter temperatures of thirty below zero Celsius as in the Rikubetsu area neighboring Tokachi or ice floes like those to the north. In north-central Hokkaido winter is long and cold with a late spring, short summer, and early autumn. If a Hokkaido winter is a test of one's *gaman suru*, or perseverance, then surely the payoff comes in the summer. Hokkaido lacks a proper rainy season and it is not humid like Tokyo or Kyoto, but dry, warm, and usually sunny, teetering in the mid-twenty-degree Celsius range. Japanese have many religious and cultural celebrations such as *hanami* (cherry blossom viewing season) or *o-bon* (festival of the dead) to mark the shifting seasons. Hokkaido's climate, seasons, and differing dates of celebration are ways to mark the distinctiveness of the region.[5]

There is no *shinkansen* (high-speed train) to Obihiro, let alone from Obihiro to Gensan, the town of five thousand I was to first call home for a year of research in 2005–2006, and there likely never will be.[6] In fact, in 1987, due to lack of demand and despite the town's protests, Japan Rail stopped servicing the area. So, not knowing my way around the sporadic train times to Obihiro yet, I took local trains. One three-car train rocked and snaked its way over the Hidaka mountain pass that separates the Tokachi plains from the more densely populated Ishikari plain and Sapporo. Throughout the three-and-a-half-hour journey east I sat reflecting on the landscape, my preparatory pre-fieldwork research, and what might lie ahead. Heading into Tokachi the train slowed as snow had to be cleared from the tracks to progress. While the train crept along, I saw rotting hand-hewn log barns sagging through a combination of neglect and age, but in more affluent areas, these relics of Hokkaido's pioneering past yield to newer galvanized metal structures. Similarly, colorful new tractors sat alongside ones rusted and abandoned after years of toil in the dark volcanic soil of the Tokachi district—a district wherein, like neighboring Kushiro, rice, popularly viewed as the basis for *washoku* (Japanese cuisine), still cannot be commercially grown (Hansen 2014a). Indeed, Tokachi is famous for several products that may not, at least at present, seem particularly "Japanese" to some readers, though they are as Japanese as rice and fish. And such products, alongside those who produce them, serve as indexes of politicized Otherness; potatoes, beets, lamb, beef, milk, and recently wine and artisan cheeses, are all produced and widely consumed in Tokachi. American-style houses with metal or shingled roofs are also part of the landscape. They are mixed in with polyurethane greenhouses, cows, horses, dogs, and occasionally people. Having, until that point, only lived in large cities in Japan (Hiroshima for a year and Osaka for four months), I was struck by how few people I saw from the train, not to mention on it. In Hokkaido, not everyone lives in town and automobiles, preferably four-wheel-drive ones, are a necessity. Passing by modern farms that sprung from original isolated homesteads staked one hundred years ago one can literally see the material culture of historical change (see also Fujita 1994; Mock 1999; and Takata 2004 for similar examples of material culture histories in Hokkaido).

These relics and living remains of early settler life exist alongside newness and novelty. They are tactile reminders of the location's history and are immediately available reference points to anyone looking out the window of a car or train in Tokachi. Homesteading was only a century old when I arrived in my fieldwork area and, as in any "frontier" region, security (the interplay of *to* secure and *to be* secure) remains a clear desire. Tokachi's pioneer settlements mirror, quite intentionally as will also be discussed in detail, both North America's past and present. At first these settlements were geared toward survival. Japanese migrants who were successful at clearing land, building a modest dwelling, and surviving their first winters gradually became families of farmers with horses for traction, tuber crops, and cows or other domesticated mammals like pigs or sheep for sustenance. Though regions near urban centers commercialized after the Second World War through selling agricultural products to city dwellers, a mixed farm model—largely self-sufficient with some crops and some livestock—remained the norm until only forty years ago. However, from the late 1980s, change and Otherness have returned with a renewed vehemence to the area (figure I.2). Industrial dairy farming, with its ever-increasing technological separation of human and nonhuman (ranging from bovine to the environment) and dismantling and reforming human relations is rapidly replacing earlier symbiotic practices on the family farm. There is increased tourism and economic migration, both into the area and out of the area. As working-class Japanese sojourners, and increasingly foreign contract laborers, enter, local young people, particularly women, seeking a more urbane lifestyle leave, underscoring the interplay of Otherness and the search for security found in the north of Tokachi.

Figure I.2. An example of material culture on an ever-changing frontier. Everywhere in Tokachi one can see old barns give way to newer structures. Photo by the author. See the cover of this book for an interpretive and romanticized painting of this photo by the late Matsumoto Keiji.

With changes coming so quickly there is a nostalgia attached to the relatively recent past. For locals, this past is only distanced by immediate family memories; recalling, for example, a time only fifty years ago when the town's population was triple its present declining size. For outsiders, those from Honshu or further afield, nostalgic longing is often of an idyllic rural past. The art on the cover of this book is a case in point. I asked a retired Kobe school teacher, an amateur artist and historian who chose to relocate to Tokachi when he discovered he was dying from cancer, to paint a picture for my book. Figure I.2 is the photo I gave him to work with. Clearly, the image he produced on the cover of the book is a more romantic and impressionistic image. It is a painting from a different perspective, animated with cows, and without the new galvanized barn. It is the rendering of an imaginary space, not the lived-in place of Hokkaido dairy farmers. For many Japanese from outside Hokkaido, Tokachi represents an escape to a safe and secure pastoral past, a past that is invented. It is a complex mixture of domestic and imagined nostalgia, the affective resonance of a transplanted *furusato* (hometown) of Otherness—of a foreign and pastoral ilk—alongside a tactile *akogare* (desire or longing) for a simpler time and lifestyle (see also Klien 2020). For locals however, their image of home is more concrete, often seen as a place of past struggles that is increasingly viewed in terms of present tense uncertainty with an ever-impending insecure future.

This feeling of insecurity felt by many rural Hokkaido residents is not without foundation. The population of the entire prefecture of Hokkaido (Japan's largest prefecture by far in terms of geographic area at 22 percent of Japan's landmass) is home to less than 5 percent (5.2 million) of Japan's approximately 126 million people. Further thinking through these numbers, nearly one-third of Hokkaido residents live in Sapporo, Japan's fifth most populated city with approximately 1.9 million people. Accounting for other Hokkaido cities like Obihiro, the capital of the Tokachi district and Hokkaido's fourth largest at around 170,000 people, one quickly realizes that despite popular imagination of Hokkaidoites as largely rural dwelling, the majority of Hokkaido's population is decidedly urban. But statistics aside, northern Tokachi is rural in the way one might think of rural North America's Midwest or more northern reaches of Finland, Sweden, or Norway. In Hokkaido, locals and tourists alike refer to this location as *inaka* (countryside), although it will become apparent in what follows that the use and interpretation of this term varies widely among individuals. Tokachi is an expansive fertile plain surrounded by mountains on three sides and the Pacific Ocean on the fourth. Given this topography it is often referred to with an expressive *hontō ni inaka* (really countryside)—the implication being that given Hokkaido's location on Japan's periphery, Tokachi's margins mark it as the proverbial middle of nowhere, all the more removed as an area physically cut off within Hokkaido by its rugged perimeters. Gensan as a destination prides itself as a point of isolation (Hansen 2020b). In Tokachi, mountains like towns are usually seen in the distance; one does not feel hemmed in or enclosed. Anyone who has widely traveled in Japan can attest that this contrasts with much of Honshu, Shikoku, or Kyushu with perhaps perceptions of the sea being equivalent in Okinawa.[7] However, in Tokachi one seems forever bordered or shielded by the mountains, heading toward or from them, but always somewhere between them. To use a macro-level metaphor, when traveling one feels as though they are in an expanse of open space with towns as nodes between mountain ranges. In much of Japan, one is enclosed within cities, cities that often give way to indistinct suburbs and then to indistinct towns meandering through green valleys along-side train lines and roadways. For many elderly Gensan residents this would not describe home. Instead, it accurately describes an alien space occasionally and interestingly referred to as *naichi* (literally, inside land, the term for Honshu in the colonial period) in contrast to the colonies (*gaichi*). To them Hokkaido is *gaichi* and Japan, in this popular imaginary, is a place presumed to be clearly distinct from home, perhaps a place seen on television or one they have briefly visited. For locals Hokkaido is outside, open, and on the periphery of the envisaged "primordial" entity known as Nihon or the more politically charged Nippon. Nevertheless, in over a decade of my asking bumbling and earnestly confused questions, no equivalent all-encompassing counter reference point has ever been offered; simply, Hokkaido is Hokkaido. For those who are born to it, it can never be *naichi* and it is never considered to be *gaichi* by insiders. It is the spatial and cultural Other within par excellence.

Meeting Wada *Shachō*

Returning to the story of my arrival, the *shachō* (company president) of the dairy farm I was to work at met me at the station. This caught me somewhat off guard as I arrived in Obihiro about two hours ahead of schedule and was hoping to look around the station and have something to eat. I had dug out the phone number of the *bokujō* (farm), just called, and was in the process of describing my early arrival to a somewhat bewildered and slightly panicking staff member when I heard a voice from behind: "Sumimasen ga . . . Po-ru san desu ka?" (Excuse me, but are you Paul?).

Startled, the best stammering response I could muster was: "Ahh . . . sou desu" (Err, it's true).

A short and slender, clean-cut, smart looking, casually dressed Japanese businessman was peering at me overtop of thick glasses. He replied, nodding: "Uhn . . . Yes, OK, OK."

There was a pause, silence for a few seconds, when time seemed to stop. Then, adding nothing else but a few more nods, Mr. Wada handed me a business card and quickly walked off with one of my bags. I uttered something into the receiver to my soon-to-be coworker along the lines of: "Ima daijoubu desu. Hito ikimasu" (Now it's OK—man goes), with the grammar and meaning being as confused as this English translation.[8]

I hung up the phone and shuffled after Wada-san, trying first and foremost to decipher the Japanese name on the card he had just placed in my hand, while at the same time attempting to pull my stuff, and self, together. Whoever he was, it was clear he was intent on taking me somewhere, but from the look of him I silently reasoned he could not be a farmer. At the station exit, I scanned the parking lot for him. Searching the horizon for the ubiquitous *kei torakku*—a small, usually white, boxy 660 cc mini truck used by farmers across Japan—I spotted Wada-san waving, palm down with a strained smile on his face, ushering me toward a new white Toyota Crown, the emblematic conservative, middle-management luxury sedan, complete with doilies on the headrests. At the time, I had no idea who this middle-aged Japanese stranger was, but later I would discover that he was one of the owners of the farm. I was also to learn that Wada-san had hired me against the will of two other owners, but he was *the* boss. He was also to become a key research interlocutor.

We were soon outside of Obihiro proper. The city's streets are laid out in a highly functional and none-too-interesting grid pattern, betraying Obihiro's late nineteenth-century colonial beginnings. In sum, it is a town like several others in Hokkaido. The streets and avenues heading north and departing from the station lead past a rundown shopping arcade followed by stores mixed together with auto centers, pachinko parlors, convenience stores, and the odd derelict warehouse—a common theme of Japanese postwar midsize city sprawl (Richie 2003). However, after crossing a four-lane bridge spanning the wide Tokachi river val-ley, we entered a new shopping suburb reminiscent of an overgrown American-style strip mall. Unlike Obihiro the stores across the river are booming and bustling. Do-it-yourself home stores, a McDonald's, large supermarkets and drugstores, a Mister Donut, and family restaurants, with names like Victoria's Station, attract both farmers and city dwellers alike. The town is an area famous for its hot springs and it is also the main Tokachi area crossroads, as well as being a conduit for traffic south to Obihiro and north to the Daisetsuzan National Park, Hokkaido's larg-est. It is also near the main thoroughfare that connects to the highway that links Sapporo to the west, with numerous tourist attractions and the Pacific Ocean to the east.

Continuing north through town for four kilometers there is another important intersection where one can choose to either head south back to Obihiro via a more scenic route, passing a famous bakery that has become a major tourist attraction, or head further north toward land pioneered one hundred years ago. As can be seen in figure I.3, the road sign in both Katakana and English reads Furontia dōri (Frontier Road). In northern Tokachi it is a common practice to have names in Katakana, a script further underscoring their foreignness as pointed out in other contexts

Figure I.3. A road sign outside of Obihiro with the winter landscape in the back-ground. Photo by the author.

in the research of Blai Guarné (2018, 90–121); Great North Farm or Big Field Farm might serve as good examples, but Grand Hopes Farm, with a bit of interpretive license, is similar to the real name of the dairy farm I was to spend a year working on. Mr. Wada turned north toward the foothills and Gurando Hōpu Bokujō (Grand Hopes Dairy Farm).

Mapping the Road Ahead

In his study of settler communities in the Russian far north, Niobe Thompson builds off of anthropologist Tim Ingold's call for a new focus on *all* the people of the North (Thompson 2008). In rural locations, anthropologists have long focused primarily on indigenous people in order to better understand what it means to live, or dwell, in northern colonized regions. Research trends in Hokkaido are similar: with a focus on Ainu as a singular indigenous Other and a focus on "proper" Japanese agriculture as something confined to Honshu, for example, a predominance of studies on part-time rice farming (Jussaume 1991; Moore 1990) with rural life equated with local isolation only occasionally critiqued (Kelly 2006; Hansen 2020b, 2022; Klien 2020). This research is not about agriculture in general nor is it about Ainu, though both enter as parts of the story. In this book I hope to convince the reader that Tokachi's dairy industry, though marginalized, is an inextricable part of contemporary Japan's engagement with modernity through a history that is intimately intertwined with Japanese macro, meso, and micro security interests. I suggest that in large part Hokkaido, certainly Tokachi and its dairy industry, are "uncomfortable truths" or alternatively "comfortable myths" for those seeking a unique, shared, and timeless Japaneseness (Chomsky and Herman 1988; Gore 2007). Hokkaido and its dairy farms represent extremes in this sense—extremes because they are so clearly part of what is acceptable as typical contemporary Japan and yet so clearly outside of its "epic" or hegemonic discourses (Bakhtin 1981; Foucault 1970; and specifically in the context of Hokkaido, Hansen 2010a, 2021b; Mason 2012, 2017).

The following chapter, "A Conceptual Scaffolding," and chapter 2 "Toward Modernity: The Forming and Reforming of a Northern Frontier" define how the concepts of Otherness, security, and frontier are used in this book to examine Hokkaido's history from a macro perspective, from an imagined open space to a particular place progressively secured, domesticated, and internalized. Chapter 3, "From Traction to *Teishoku*:

Tracing the Human-Bovine Trajectory," briefly outlines the history of the domestication of cows and the emergence of beef and dairy farming in Japan. The next chapter, "Problems Protecting the Japanese Dairy Industry," focuses on the ubiquitous images and imaginings of Otherness in terms of dairy farming as a specific form of agriculture and livelihood. Hokkaido's settlers formed mixed farms with a symbiotic and symbolic—and in retrospect certainly iconic—relationship to dairy cattle in their attempts to secure new lives on what was interpreted as frontier space. However, facing the contemporary pressures of neoliberalism and globalization, dairying as a way of life in Hokkaido has rapidly changed over the last twenty years. The chapter argues that Otherness in the context of Japan and Hokkaido is well represented by the dairy industry, the policies and products associated with it, and the community tensions and security projects, group and individual, that such international and domestic changes have produced.

Building from these chapters, chapter 5, "Farm Structures," narrows the scope of analysis. Culture and social structures in Hokkaido, and specifically in the Tokachi region, differ from those found in other lasting Japanese colonialist projects such as Okinawa. This chapter maps particular shifts in Tokachi's population and industries over the last century, for example, the introduction of new technologies to these rural communities, such as electricity, tractors, automobiles, Holstein cows as a created breed, and most recently genomics and automated milking technologies. In chapter 6, "The Birth of Grand Hopes," the scope of analysis is reduced further from a social history of Hokkaido and Tokachi to an in-depth ethnography of Gensan and to the workings of Grand Hopes Farm introduced above. This farm, and the social relations on and around it, are then utilized as a core case study of the recent move to incorporated, industrial, mega farming.

Chapter 7 acts as a hinge. "Dairy Farmers: Being, Becoming, and Making" marks a shift from what is heretofore a macro and historical study to an ethnography of particular people in the present tense, to individuals being, becoming, and making themselves in the community of Gensan and on Grand Hopes Farm circa 2005–2020. The ethnography includes a host of interrelated work roles from the head office to the farthest extremities of the farm and details shifting human relationships rooted in Otherness, security seeking, and personal frontiers on the farm and the broader community. Chapters 8 through 10, "From Teat to Tot: Following the Flows," "Producing and Pumping," and "Keeping It All

Working," draw together individuated historical and ethnographic stories underscoring how these changes in production methods and the concomitant increase of Otherness (human, animal, and technological) currently impacts the security of the region, the industry, and people residing in it.

Chapter 11, "Locals, Lo-siders, Outsiders, and No-siders," and chapter 12, "Assembling Communities: Two Genders and One Religion," discuss how farm industrialization and the personal and community security debates that surround it have affected the former insularity of Gensan, opening multiple perspectives regarding, paths to, and negotiations of local belonging. Some individuals are keen to stay while others are eager to leave but many remain in precarious social and employment positions described as "liminally liminal" or suspended liminality.

The book concludes with "On the Frontiers of Animal-Human-Technology" and brings three frontiers in the community and the dairy industry front and center: the shifting macro imaginary of rural Tokachi as a frontier space, the technological meso frontiers of rotary dairy technology as forming a particular place of production, alienation, and anomie, and the micro embodied and affective frontier of human and animal Otherness. The rotary dairy parlor, as an animal-human-machine, is used as a case study crossing these levels of analysis by focusing on issues of how people find security, physical and ontological, at the bounds or frontiers of Other thinking, Other bodies, and Other ways of being and belonging. These have become key issues for the people of the local town, dairy owners, and the workers they employ. The brief epilogue underscores that this region and industry continue to unpredictably evolve, remaining sites of Otherness, frontier, and searches for security. As a final case in point, it highlights recent changes in the lives of some of the ethnography's main actors.

Chapter One

A Conceptual Scaffolding

Introduction

This chapter highlights how the concepts Otherness and security are used in this book. The point is not to forward a definitive exegesis of these terms or concepts. On the one hand, their use is simply an aesthetic choice: common transdisciplinary metaphors used with the aim organizing and making the focus of this book widely accessible and relatable to readers coming from different backgrounds. I contend it constitutes a clear way to thematically organize data that spans anthropology, area studies, food studies, settler history, rural studies, and philosophy or social theory in a manner that allows for open and easy micro, meso, and macro future comparisons. In short, and in this sense, Otherness and security are concepts chosen for their ubiquity across research fields and human–nonhuman experiences. From a more reductive perspective, however, a secondary goal in utilizing these terms is to assist in understanding the settler history of Hokkaido and its dairy industry alongside what influences and motivates contemporary Tokachi dairy farms and the wide variety of dairy farmers and workers like the aforementioned Grand Hopes Farm and Mr. Wada. After over fifteen years of research in the area and countless discussions, formal and impromptu, these workable concepts have emerged in one guise or another.

An ethnographer must grapple with the particularity of location and the contemporary day-to-day lives of individuals. A historian or social theorist must think about how these conditions are comparative over time or across sociocultural assemblages. Anthropologists try to do both. This tension is obvious, likely discomforting for some readers, and one I will discuss further along in this book. One aim is a very particular area studies analysis, be it Japanese studies, ethnography, rural studies, while another more general aim is opening the way toward future detailed comparative historical and ethnographic research on regions and industries that fit within the politically charged definition of a "frontier" colony as discussed in detail in the following chapter. The intention here is to better enable a future relational analysis of Hokkaido dairy farming outside the rubric of Japanese or even Asian studies, viewing the area and industry as a particular example, one case study among many, of a shared historical moment of global settler colonialism (cf. Azuma 2019; Povinelli 2016; Storey 2018; Thompson 2008; van Herk 2001, 2007; Zuehlke 2001). Any meaningful attempt at comparison, however, requires that concepts remain malleable enough to be adapted to different cultures, societies, and people. Toward that end, running through the book is a pliable conceptual triad of Otherness, securities and frontiers (plural intended). Such a research focus is ambitious and taken in its entirety would clearly stretch beyond the confines of a single book. It is in this spirit that the use of these terms might best be thought of as "metaphoric" (Lakoff 1999; Lakoff and Johnson 2003). They are intended to invite loose comparisons and gloss details that might make a meticulous historian or Japanese studies expert uneasy at times, but their use enables the example at hand to be comparatively addressed without eliding the influence of affect, embodiment, and description essential for ethnographic accounts and engaged social theory (Jackson 1995, 1996, 2005, 2013; Stoller 1997, 2009). This framing will not please everyone, but it is, I contend, utilitarian.

Anthony Giddens, in discussing the role of metaphor in social research, has coined the phrase "double hermeneutic" (1984, 374). He suggests that terms used in the social sciences often emerge as vocabulary used in everyday vernacular discussions and vice versa. Researchers use metaphors, hopefully evocative ones, precisely because they are an easy-to-understand shorthand (Hansen 2021a). Moreover, communication is often not transmitted through language alone, but through actions (Jackson 2005; Ram and Houston 2015; Stoller 2009; Wenger 1998). Given this interpretive path to knowledge (as acts do not literally "tell" observers anything) the analysis of nonverbal performances and interactions are kinesthetic and metaphoric revelations, a form of understanding through embodied and affective mimesis, an active and physical grappling with the hermeneutics of phenomenology whereby experiences must be interpreted in order to be effectively described. Similar to the double hermeneutic, Carrithers outlines what he coins conceptual "slippage" in ethnographic research (Carrithers 1992). This occurs when words have changing meanings or can be multiply interpreted depending on the context of their delivery or when an individual's actions convey a message that is not articulated in language or may not even be intended as a message—as in Geertz's classic example of trying to decipher a wink from a twitch (Geertz 1973). Indeed, even using the term *slippage* itself as an explanatory metaphor represents all the above points; words don't physically slip, but through the everyday and experiential meaning and imagery of slippage, its metaphoric resonance is likely clear to the reader.

Most social sciences have traditionally focused on social structures and cultural explanations—both modes of representation being amorphous, hotly debated, and difficult to define perhaps most notably in anthropology. These points of contention are beyond the scope of this chapter.[1] But in sum, I submit that social sciences such as anthropology have, in the main, tended to focus on groups and structures in favor of the analysis of individuals, their inimitable interactions, and their individual interpretations. In this way, thinking about both human and nonhuman relations, group-centric explanations have unsurprisingly become the lingua franca of most *social* sciences and humanities. However, I suggest that tracing the lineage and interplay of Otherness and security provides a less structurally static and determinative starting point to think about the individuated and inimitable relations shared between particular humans, nonhuman agents, the environment, and indeed the frontiers that separate them. Some disciplinary purists or area studies specialists might prefer a different delivery than a conceptual triad running from chapter to chapter, alongside a shifting register of actors (from state to group or community, to the individual or self) ending in a discussion of Otherness, security, and frontiers beyond the human—this, I admit, is a fair enough critique. But a singular, concrete and micro starting point that places agency, creativity, and choice first and foremost opens the potential for a more comparative and varied mode of analysis and frees up future interpretations by not starting from the usual presumptions of myopic group belonging, and it enables utilizing insights from various disciplines like psychology, history, philosophy, and social theory in order to understand individuals *as individuals* and a place *as particular* first and foremost before categorizing and reducing person and place to typologies (cf. Barth 1959, 1969; Hansen 2020a, 2020b; Ortner 2006; Rapport 2012). These ideas are fleshed out, quite literally, as the reader progresses through the following pages. However, in sum it means that while sociocultural history and location are essential components in the story, individual actors, environmental contingencies, and personal choices are also brought to the forefront in the recent historical and ethnographic data. This often outstrips more socially oriented explanations and arguments as to what motivates people to act or to form shifting alliances with persons and places. In starkest terms, the claim being made herein is that in Tokachi's dairy industry the thinking and choosing, particularly embodied individual agent, human or nonhuman in fact, often plays a central role over and above the usual collective or socially constructed subjectivities utilized to describe human belonging and motives such as ethnicity, social status, or gender (Hansen 2015, 2018a, 2020a). In short, though focus on the social verses focus on the individual may well be a classic 'chicken or egg' dilemma, my goal herein is on highlighting the individual first because it is the road far less traveled and this might lead readers to new conclusions, or at least provides a less predictable journey.

Tokachi Dairy: When Otherness Meets Each Otherness

If one decides that they want to leave or to be part of a group, or on the other hand when a community collectively or through meso coalitions denies or accepts an individual, Otherness is formulated, enacted, and entrenched. Who belongs and who does not? What is considered to be the core and at the periphery of a place and for a people? And importantly in what follows, whose story or what grand narrative is popularly (and politically) accepted as truth or fact? These questions define insider and outsider, empowered and disempowered. In Tokachi, this interplay of Otherness has resulted in the ever-shifting social and individual searches for security that can be traced throughout the history of the region into the present workings of dairy farming as its key local industry. For example, as is detailed in this book, over the last three decades there has been a rapid and steady shift in dairy production from pastoral mixed family farms to joint shared industrial mega farms and monoculture practices. The creation of such farms requires obvious material changes, high overhead and technology for a start. But, far from local affairs alone, the emergence of such farms has been profoundly influenced by public wants and macro political policies played out at the local level. While the current image of the region and industry is promoted as a positive one for tourists—they see the projection of a cooperative rural idyll underlying *michi no eki* (roadside stations) selling local products with photos of individual smiling farmers for example—for many locals it is an industry where social alienation and the individuation of workers, animals, and technology have come to play an increasingly central role in rural Tokachi life. Farmers, certainly farm owners, have become progressively more individuated in their actions and individualistic in their thinking, a situation fostered, necessitated even, by the swelling adoption of an industrialized and automatized mode of competitive production.

Otherness is at the center of understanding the move away from older community structures based on mixed farming to this corporate mode of production. This is not only found in Tokachi, of course, one can see this in a number of recent ethnographies focused on the industrialization of pork (cf. Blanchette 2020; Weiss 2016) or beef (cf. Gillespie 2018; Pachirat 2011) production. This shift has not led to security or rekindled solidarity, for example, systems of shared values or a new consciousness of group identity among community members at large or farm owners or workers. A point made clear in this book is that there has been no emergence of a "we the dairy workers" mentality as a result of these changes. Solidarity is cast aside. Dairy farming has become a site of acute social, cultural, and individual confrontation. Indeed, the change in production from mixed to monoculture and from family to corporate agriculture is concomitant with a need for workers from outside the local community, Hokkaido, the agriculture industry, and even Japan. As a result of this influx, those working in the dairy industry frequently act in ways not in concert with those around them, with their peers, families, respective communities, or macro expectations. As a result of such changes and increased Otherness, the local dairy industry, and Tokachi more broadly, is a site of intense micro security searching for young people and even for some local elders, as well as for Japanese and non-Japanese alike. In short, industrial dairy farms are places where regional Otherness or alterity in the context of Japan (Hokkaido and the Tokachi dairy industry in this case) and individuality and individualism in the context of what it is to be Japanese (defining what constitutes us, them, self, and each other) are challenged and questioned amid shifting town demographics, farm policies, and rosters of coworkers that are ever in flux. The present for these individuals in this industry, let alone the future, is profoundly uncertain, from constantly shifting state policies to the contingencies of bovine and human health. And in this environment of unrelenting change and risk, questions of how, and to what degree, Hokkaido dairy farmers desire to fit into any notion of a shared national, prefectural, or even local agricultural community have become a central concern. These concerns are novel in dairy farming as a way of local livelihood, but are not new. They are inherent in the region's very historical formation and its alterity.

From the 1300s until today the islands now called Hokkaido have been marked as a spatial, human, and animal periphery by those dwelling in Honshu (Walker 2001). Elaborated upon in the following chapter, contemporary Hokkaido's popular image is as a "frontier" zone. It has historically been perceived by Japanese as a place of Otherness, progressively and often violently incorporated into contemporary Japan (Saunavaara 2018). Nevertheless, this notion of being outside or peripheral has never been an unvarying or homogeneous condition. Who is and is not considered Other has constantly shifted and blurred depending on time, perspective, and who has the power to narrate belonging (Mason 2012): from the land of Ainu, to land of colonial pioneer, to land of dairy farmers; from miserable backwater to land of opportunity; from a space of escape to the site of a particular individual's hometown. All such notions are an intricate and individuated lattice of how a given person and the group(s) they identify with (or how they are identified by others) link to the contingencies of power, positionality, context, experience, and interpretation: read individual and individuated cases of extreme intersectionality and contingency!

Underscored in every chapter that follows are the largely unspoken ironies that underlie Hokkaido's, Tokachi's, Gensan's, and even the domestic dairy industry's Otherness in the context of Japan. For example, dairy farming is not simply a modern practice imported from "The West," a common misconception. In fact, dairying has had a long history in Japan, as the reader will see, dating at least back to the Nara period (710–794 CE). And, whether self or externally ascribed as Other, and the reader will learn dairy can be both even in the same moment, Hokkaido and its dairy industry are actually central, not marginal, to material culture and daily life in contemporary Japan from the milk in children's nationally supported lunch program to milk in the corporate warrior's canned coffee. Indeed, domestic dairy is everywhere in ways few other products are. Alongside the diversity of the Othered politics and products that Hokkaido dairy farming produces, the island and industry can *only* be viewed as both modern and Japanese. To be a Hokkaido dairy farmer—and more specifically a Tokachi or Gensan dairy farmer, exceptions aside like Vietnamese or Chinese temporary workers I discuss elsewhere (Hansen 2010a, 2010b)—is to be a *Japanese* dairy farmer. Yet, taken all together, there is an extraordinary paradox at work here when one considers the fact that dairy farming is a form of employment and lifestyle that has historically been viewed, and is presently promoted, as Other, even outrightly foreign, in Japan when taken as a national whole.

Today dairying is an industry that is deeply dependent on global markets and international know-how to produce domestic products that are constantly indexed (if not labeled) as foreign foods, as *yōshoku*, in Japan. Hokkaido, also often referred to as *mirukurando* (Milkland) in tourist promotions, is the heartland of the industry and the northern Tokachi region is simply the center that pumps out the most milk. Producing such products in such a location, I will argue, marks modern dairy farmers with an identity external to essential notions of Japaneseness. But clearly this is quite unlike being singled out as Ainu, Okinawan, or for one's hybrid ethnicity or indeed choosing to single oneself out as Other (see Hook and Siddle 2003; Martin 2018; Siddle 1996; Watson 2014 for discussion regarding the sliding scale of indigenous Otherness in Hokkaido). Tokachi dairy farmers are not rebelling against their Japaneseness. They are Othered by proxy, practice, and proximity, much in the way, for example, workers in Japan's meat and leather industry are (Hankins 2014). It is for such reasons, their daily social, historical, economic, dietary, and cultural belonging in the fabric of contemporary Japan while remaining juxtaposed with its essentialist discourses, that make Tokachi and its dairy farmers a particularly interesting focus of study in regard to identity. That is, dairy, Hokkaido, and Tokachi are key to understanding the contemporary Japanese conundrum of the *Other within*, what being a Japanese individual means while remaining clearly external to many of the nation's dominant, essentialist, and group-centric discourses (Befu 2015; Guarné and Hansen 2018; Willis and Murphy-Shigematsu 2008).

Dairy Farmers as Other

Regarding Ainu, Burakumin, Okinawans, and more broadly racial and ethnic others, such as Brazilian, Korean, or Chinese hyphenated Japanese, Roger Goodman writes: "There is a long tradition in social anthropology of studying the margins of a society in order to understand what happens at its core. The study of minority groups in a modern industrial society exemplifies this tradition very well; looking at the way that these groups are defined, excluded, and incorporated by mainstream society provides important insights into the changing nature of what constitutes the core values of that society" (Goodman 2008, 325). In this sense perhaps, dairy farmers, alongside the meat and leather laborers noted above, also have more than a passing similarity to the *ama* (women divers) of Kuzaki investigated by Dolores Martinez (2004). They are treated as external in spite of a given group's productive efforts being central in Japanese daily life. In the case of the *ama*, their "exotic" image and the sea goods they harvest are tied, *via* historical links whether embellished or not, with the Ise shrine. This is a complex that is central to both native Shinto, common seasonal ritual practices, and the Japanese state. Correspondingly, Hokkaido dairy farmers produce government-sponsored products that are consumed in some form by nearly every Japanese consumer in a market that continues to grow. Yet despite the *ama*'s link to nationalist tradition or the dairy or related meat industry's wares being culturally and materially daily consumed—again from publicly funded school lunches to coffee mixer, to popular after-work *izakaya* (pub) snack foods, to baby formula—all groups, though clearly Japanese, are excluded from fitting into the carefully constructed categories of Japan and Japaneseness. The vast majority of these individuals are, of course, ethnically and legally Japanese—nobody questions this. Although some dairy farmers and other residents in the region rebel against an image of what many have called *futsū no nihonjin kangaekata* (typical Japanese thinking) as a social-cultural proclamation of difference to or defiance of social conservatism, this does not mean that they are proclaiming themselves to be something other than legally or ethnically Japanese (Hansen 2018a, 2020a, 2020b, 2022). They simply feel that the tropes long used to represent what is *typically Japanese*, or what Harootunian calls the "'bureaucratic fantasies' of abolishing the historical" in the history of Japaneseness (Harootunian 2019, 306), does not represent them. As such, the reader will find that dairy farmers and their industry, due to its alterity, are central to understanding something new about contemporary Japan and Japanese identity. They are, I suggest, a powerful internal critique to homogenizing drives, and often unabashedly vocal ones. Augmenting Goodman's claim, these people are marginalized, yet they are also at the core of current Japanese material and political culture. One intriguing paradox in Japan is how often key groups at the core of the Japanese national narrative are in fact the most marginalized within it, for example, members of the Imperial family or "international" Japanese salaried workers who, after promoting the nations interests abroad, find that they (*kikokushijo*), along with their returnee children, are treated as outsiders.

I argue that dairy workers are essential pieces in this contemporary sociocultural jigsaw puzzle. Faced with a popular and essentialist image of Japan as an "epic" (that is to say, unchanging and accepted) identity counter to a "novel" (that is to say, an individuated and processual) one borrowing from Mikhail Bakhtin (1981), these farmers and laborers from the periphery of Japan but who are at the center of its daily consumptive culture comprise pieces that cannot be made to fit the dominate narratives that are popularly promoted in media, education, or government policy for example (Befu 2001; Ertl and Hansen 2015; Willis and Murphy-Shigematsu 2008). And their absence leaves gaping holes in any complete story of present-day Japan. From history to production, to consumption, or from imagery and imaginary to official state policy, the facts remain: the majority of Hokkaido's dairy farmers are undeniably Japanese all the while being outside popular essentialist *ware ware nihonjin* (we Japanese), *gaikoku* (foreign), *buraku* (undercast), or *otaku* (internal and yet Othered by self and/or society) categories, identities that are never-endingly promoted and juxtaposed in domestic media, for example, in the attempt to secure spaces of ethnonational separateness, trumpeting an essential Japan and Japaneseness versus any alternate typology or hybridization (Guarné and Hansen 2018). The long exclusion of this place and these individuals, intentional or not, has offered us an incomplete at least, distorted at worst, narrative of Japan and notably Hokkaido as a settler state (Mason 2012).

Beyond macro conceptualizations, the later chapters of this book highlight that Otherness is also represented in the Tokachi dairy industry at the level of any given individual's day-to-day interactions with and engagement in biopolitics, what Didier Fassin calls "the biopolitics of otherness . . . based on the recognition of the 'difference of bodies' which have . . . race, sex, ethnicity, and genes as their foundation . . . internal frontiers founded on physical difference" (2001, 3–7). Such differences have been the subject of what are now classic ethnographies of Japan at the level of the individual interacting with social groups such as day laborers (Gill 2001; Ōyama 2000), the upper classes (Hamabata 1986), preschool children and their mothers (Hendry 1989), female gender (Kondo 1990; Rosenberger 2001), male gender (Dasgupta 2000; Roberson and Suzuki 2003), hetero- and homosexuality (Allison 1994; Darling-Wolf 2003, 2004; Ito and Anase 2001), nationality and/or ethnicity (Fukuoka 2000; Tsuda 2003; Ueunten 2008), whether marginalized nationals (Amos 2011; Chapman 2008; Hankins 2014; Watanabe 1998; Watson 2014) or foreign nationals (Lesser 2003; Roth 2002), company employees (Plath 1983), and artists and actors (Richie 1982; Robertson 1998a). All highlight particular case studies wherein individuated Otherness is an inescapable—indeed visceral and embodied—experience. This book introduces many inimitable characters, dairy farm workers, young and old, male and female, who come from every part of Japan: Okinawa, Shikoku, Honshu, and Hokkaido. They do not, to be sure cannot in any way, separate themselves from a contemporary pan-Japan identity. Many may disagree with what they perceive as the relentless conservatism of *futsū no nihonjin no kangaekata*, but they are not seeking to form a shared or collective socio-cultural identity rooted in this reactionary view. The reader will encounter rich youth from Tokyo proving their mettle, local kids from the wrong side of the tracks, aging owners who choose to stay in the business, others who opt to get out, and recently beyond Japanese farmers, Chinese and Vietnamese economic migrants (Hansen 2010a, 2010b) with promise of other nationalities to come. They all must communicate and often cooperate in ways that two decades ago would have been hard for many of them to imagine. Human Otherness must be confronted as particular and significant, as "each Otherness"—with individuality, interpretation, and agency being played out often with only a surface patina of shared goals in this shared location. And it will become clear to the reader that Holstein cows and technology have and continue to play key roles in enhancing, negotiating, and erasing Otherness at different points in time. Indeed, in the closing chapters of this book the reader will see how individual cows are also a kind of frontier, at the affective and embodied boundaries, of a daily balance between particularization and Othering through technological processes of bio-power and security.

(In)security: Relations of Being and Becoming

Security is perhaps a more complex conceptual device than Otherness; in its everyday vernacular use, there is an inherent play between subject and object as well as states of being and becoming. This notion of capturing both as an act and as an adjectival description of existence has made the term attractive to social theorists. As the *Oxford Dictionary* defines it, to secure is "to actively fix with certainty, to protect, or to succeed in obtaining a desired goal" and to *be* secure is "to experience the certainty of safety, to feel unthreatened, or to be free from fear or anxiety."[2] Security is central to the social theorization of Zygmunt Bauman, Ulrich Beck, and

Michael Dillon whose concepts of "liquid modernity," "risk society," and "(in)security" all work to underscore the instable and uncertain nature of what has been called second modern, postmodern, or indeed post-post-modern society (see Bauman 2000, 2007; Beck 1992, 2002, 2009; Dillon 1996, 2015, respectively). Humans, and I will add nonhumans, are always (in)—actively inside or involved—relations and attempts to be or become secure. In what follows, security and securing are utilized as key concepts in examining and explaining the macro politics of contemporary Japan, community connections in Tokachi and Gensan, and the elaborate, and at times contradictory, motivations of individuals who choose to be employed in the local dairy industry. In sum, I suggest that security and securing are central both to place making and identity politics. Generalizing about Japanese history and its link to "a cultural personality," the all-time bestselling Anglophone anthropologist of Japan Ruth Benedict noted: "The Japanese, more than any other sovereign nation, have been conditioned to a world where the smallest details of conduct are mapped and status is assigned. . . . The Japanese learned to identify this meticulously plotted hierarchy with safety and security . . . [and if such rules and proprieties were followed] . . . the Japanese loved and trusted their meticulously explicit map of behavior, they had a certain justification. It guaranteed security so long as one followed the rules" (Benedict 1946, 70–73).

To be clear, "bestselling" is not equated with qualitatively the best, and Benedict's work on Japan is controversial; for a start she spoke no Japanese and the majority of her interlocutors were interned Japanese Americans or prisoners of war. However, I would argue that her early interpretations of "the Japanese character" have often been misunderstood and essentialized in ways that defy her position in the broader stable of her work and politics (Hansen 2015). *What is undeniable and important here* is that her writings have been central to the development of contemporary notions of Japanese identity. Whether one considers them historically or culturally accurate or inaccurate is another matter; the overarching influential impact is my point. Harumi Befu goes so far as to say that he "is tempted to claim that the post-war anthropology of Japan is in large made up of footnotes . . . [in agreement and disagreement] . . . to Benedict's classic" (2001, 51) and Sonia Ryang in *Japan and National Anthropology: A Critique* (2004) expounds a similar view. And Benedict's work has been influential both outside and inside Japan, seen for example in psychologist Doi Takeo's classic *Amae no kōzō* (Dependency Structure) (2007), wherein he claims to have formulated his original work as a reply to Benedict or the obvious indebtedness of Takie Sugiyama Lebra's *Japanese Patterns of Behavior* (1976) and later *The Japanese Self in Cultural Logic* (2004).

The importance of security, broadly speaking, in Japan is not merely an etic/emic issue of interpretation from outside Japan. Chie Nakane (with the same provisos about Ruth Benedict above equally applicable here) is one of the most frequently cited native Japanese anthropologists of Japan and she uses the word *security*, without defining or operationalizing it, *no less than eighteen times* in her seminal work on Japanese society discussing social security, psychological security, emotional security, and so on (Nakane 1973, 19, 20, 44, 76, 83, 109, 118–120, 127 136)! Of course, all people whether Japanese, Jamaican, or Jordanian have societal norms and security concerns. Again, these terms Otherness and security have been chosen for their comparative ubiquity not because they apply only to Japan. But the point hopefully made here and in what follows is that security has been and remains a common, though I will argue uncommonly common, concern in Japan (and notably on the "frontier" Hokkaido). The salient point here is that, if we put stock in classic social-cultural readings of Japan, the value of *securing and security* has been held in high regard over the previous century according to the anthropologists Chie Nakane and Ruth Benedict and the many academics, native and nonnative, who have made them among the most cited social science scholars of Japanese society.

Moving past these emblematic studies of Japan, it is important in what follows to consider Anthony Giddens's classic and more general notion of "*Ontological Security* . . . a sense of continuity . . . [of space, narrative, and self] . . . and order in events, including those not directly within the perceptual environment of the individual" (Giddens 1991, summarized 243, and detailed 35–62). Simply put, one's sense of self is influenced by the time and place that one lives in. Historically, Hokkaido has been the site of intense macro security concerns be they political, military, ecological, or economic. Throughout the history of modern Japan, and certainly in the context of frontier Hokkaido, one can witness the shifting of security concerns regarding the nation, the community, and the individual.

The region was a site of macro struggles for political security and economic security in the premodern and early modern periods (Blaxell 2009; Irish 2009; Kawabara and Kawagami 2018; Walker 2001). And in its early modern history Japan sought to secure a position for itself in the world order of nation-states with Hokkaido playing a central role in defining an emergent imperial nation-state (Bix 1986, 2001; Gluck 1985, 1998). American incursion in 1854 led to a crisis of national security and identity followed by a sense of superiority (over security) leading to war first with China and then the allied forces (Harootunian 2019; Victoria 2001). And after the Second World War, again, securing communities and identities became key concerns along with issues of food, ecological, and physical security (Dower 1999, 2014; Morris-Suzuki 2011).

While the 1950s to 1980s were periods of *general* stability and economic growth, today, Japanese exist in the wake of a turbulent 1990s that still impacts well into the 2000s. The ethnography and immediate history at the core of this book, roughly looking at 1990 to 2020, engages with a Japan that can be summed up with aptly titled books of the period: *Japan after Japan* followed by *Precarious Japan* (Allison 2013; Harootunian and Yoda 2006). This most recent period is one heralded by the economic recession from which the nation had been slowly recovering until another crash in 2009, with no hope of the return to the rapid growth and securities it fostered and no escape from the insecurities produced (Genda 2009). Indeed, the Abe administration's (2012–2019) revitalizing neoliberal program of "Abenomics" has not caused its expected goal of heightened security (economic or political) but has increased individual uncertainty and precarity augmented by a losing gamble on stronger trade liberalization with the American government pulling out of the TPP (Trans-Pacific Partnership) talks in 2016 and subsequent wavering about rejoining in post-Trump 2020, alongside the UK and Japanese regional rivals South Korea and China voicing an interest in joining the agreement, nearing time of publication, political and economic precarity and the search for security remains a central national issue alongside battling the COVID-19 global pandemic. Security is always a concern.

Underscoring this play in security, the economic and job security brought about by rapid industrialization and mass manufacturing in the late 1950s and 1960s created lesser discussed insecurity spin-offs that Japan is dealing with today such as environmental insecurity, such as polluted water created by this rapid development (Walker 2010) along with dense urban crowding, increased employment insecurity brought about through a rise in urban competition and declines in the birth rate and in the availability of full-time employment after the affluent 1980s. These are very real and palpable insecurities discussed by young people in Japan, theorized by some as a form of ontological insecurity and a lack of "hope" among some youth (Genda 2005; Kosugi 2008). Beyond the early 1990s economic crisis and the end of the Cold War (with the sudden realization that Japan was no longer the only regional player in a US-dominated world), two traumatic watershed events occurred in 1995:

the fatal terrorist gas attacks by a religious cult in Tokyo along with a massive earthquake in Kobe (Reader 1996, 2000, 2001). These events shook the nation and its collective and personal sense of security. To citizens used to depending on the state and feeling safe under its strictures, these events underscored the popular notion of the complete inability of the Japanese government to prevent, prepare, or contend with these situations of extreme insecurity (Leheny 2006; Yoda 2006, 16–53). This does not begin to address the list of security concerns inherent in terms of location itself: Japan's natural environment as an island nation with few natural resources. It has frequent earthquakes and tsunami, 3/11 tragically hammering home coastal Japan's immediate vulnerability with insecurity felt on a national scale. Beyond the risk of natural destruction, the nation has tense relationships with all of its immediate neighbors, which include a now nuclear-ready North Korea, a China that has usurped its role as *the* major economy in the region, and Japan and Russia, largely owing to disputes over the island territories off the coast of Hokkaido, still lack a Second World War peace agreement as of 2022. Given this history, I suggest that the lion's share of Japanese, but perhaps even more those in marginalized areas and industries like Hokkaido and dairy farming, deeply question their societal and individual security. More to the point, influenced by recent events young Japanese, particularly those under the age of forty, have questioned their ontological security in ways that their perhaps more group-centered Japanese forebears (the informants in the aforementioned classical area studies of Japan) did not have cause to (Kato 2009). For example, the lack of societal goals such as those of the past, the building of the nation (1868–1932), the expansion and defense of the nation (1933–1945); the rebuilding of the nation (1946–1970), and the promotion of the nation (1970–1990) all ring hollow to many young Japanese. Globalization has brought unprecedented numbers of foreign Others, and so foreign lifestyles, ethics, aesthetics, expectations, and worries, into Japan especially in areas considered to be peripheral (Arudou 2006; Ertl and Hansen 2015; Faier 2007, 2008; Hansen 2016, 159–175; Ryang 2000; Tsuda 2003; Yamashita 2015 could all serve as sample publications among many more).

Added to all of these security concerns, and commented upon in detail in the body of this book, are an endless parade of present-day food security scares alongside public confidence scandals, concerns about the aging population, a perception that crime has increased (often equated with the change and Otherness inherent in the rise of foreign residents), and the growing awareness that Japan's neighbors—nations with whom Japan has "normalized" relations after a history of war and colonization—are growing in cultural, technological, economic, and political power and influence while Japan's greatest ally and protector, the USA, is arguably in decline, prompting the Japanese state's attempts to "rearm" in order to defend itself.

In short, contemporary Japan is an increasingly risk prone and risk weary society well aware of its (in)securities. That is to say, Japanese people are constantly reminded that they are "in" or a part of macro to micro projects of security building. These issues of security and securing have been, and are increasingly becoming, central concerns to individuals in Japan. As a noun or verb security can be fruitfully applied to understanding the Tokachi dairy industry and the lives of its workers. But perhaps beyond this, this analysis can shed some light on broader existential conditions of anxiety in contemporary Japanese society. The following chapter underscores how this marks a number of changes in the way Tokachi's frontiers have been remade and reformed over centuries.

Chapter Two

Toward Modernity

The Forming and Reforming of a Northern Frontier

Introduction

This chapter draws the themes of Otherness and security together to discuss the making and maintenance of Japan's northern colonial frontier from premodern times to the present. Premodern in the context of this book focuses on attempts at settlement and the eventual colonization of Hokkaido. It largely concentrates on connections made during the Tokugawa era (1603–1867 CE). During the Tokugawa period, Japan was to become increasingly unified, the seed of the nation-state recognized today. This is a complex, and in many instances debated, cultural, social, and political history; indeed multiple histories evolving as research continues. Thus, what follows is not intended to be an exhaustive historical account but to serve as a brief and pointed précis constructed from the scholarship of archaeologists and historians. The purpose is to offer readers with little knowledge of Japanese history a glimpse into the development of colonial Hokkaido as a distinctive place, adding context with which to understand how modern ranching and dairy farming began on the island and on the Tokachi plains specifically. It explains how and why macro security concerns continue to be central in this location, how these concerns have changed, and how shifting conceptualizations of Otherness have played a constant role in quests for political, economic, and personal security.

Frontier is a loaded term. Historians might initially bristle at my presenting Hokkaido as a frontier—as though it is a region of bounded space and conquest separate from Honshu (Bay 2005; Guo 2005; Traphagan 2006; Walker 2001)—for good reason. Most contemporary historians and archaeologists describe the north of Japan similar to anthropologist Fredrik Barth's classic discussion of politicized space in the Swat Valley, Pakistan, a region of historically contested and shifting boundaries with populations that were mixing and melding for centuries (Barth 1959, 1969). One could very well see a similar contemporary categorical ambiguity in the (mis)representation of Métis in Canada or Creole peoples in the southern US (personal communication with Michele Mason, August 2015). The need to question the historical construction of geopolitical frontiers is undeniable. However, use of the term *frontier* for the case at hand differs. The main focus is on the idea and ideology of the frontier stretching across the last 150 years at the level of the state, community, and individual. The emphasis on a macro geopolitical usage is one reading of how frontier space can be conceptualized. But, in the broader sense, an individual living body can be viewed as a frontier, a buffer and receptor, to the outside world, which is also an important reading of frontiers in the later chapters of this book.

The key point brought to the fore here is that what the political elite of the Meiji period (1868–1912 CE) came to call the "north sea route" in 1869 had long been permeated by the migrations, cooperations, and conflicts of native peoples and Japanese or *wajin* (neither being culturally or ethnically homogeneous). As such, the colonization of Hokkaido greatly differs from many other imperialist colonial projects, such as the British colonization of North America, India, or South Africa, insofar as the Japanese colonizers did not need to travel great distances and they had previous prolonged contact with the native inhabitants before intensifying sustained attempts at colonization. Moreover, Tohoku and notably the Tsugaru region, the northernmost area of Honshu, was considered a country within a country by many Tokugawa scholars, and Ainu people also inhabited this area in the late Tokugawa (Fujiwara 2021). In addition, premodern Japan also shared close proximity with another enduring conquest, the islands of Okinawa. But, as outlined below, this entails a very different history. These islands formed the Ryukyu kingdom and are not considered a frontier in terms of ideology or popular imagination in the same way (Furuki 2003; Siddle 1998). Moreover, the early modern Japanese nation-state colonized regions that are no longer part of contemporary Japan, for example, present-day Korea, Taiwan, and Manchuria. Aside from colonization or annexation alone, Hokkaido or, as it is popularly known today *kita no kuni* (north country), differs from these other regions in that at the time of colonization it was construed and constructed much like North America's early modern West or Alaska. At times consciously mimicking settlement in Australia and North America, Hokkaido stands out and is made to stand out in being home to similar experiences and images and imaginaries (Azuma 2019). It is in this context of material culture meets ideology meets ecology that I use "frontier" in a macro context. Hokkaido is analogous with other modern settler states. Though Japan borrowed from other colonizing empires and its ideas and actions ought to be viewed in a comparative light, Hokkaido is home to narratives with decidedly Japanese twists and turns. The naming of a location as a frontier is not an objective reality. It is a subjective and political stance to make what is populated seem unpopulated and to impose a "violent cartography," usurping place names and attempting to eradicate human or nonhuman populations and memories in order to lay claim to a location with those of the colonizer (Shapiro 1997).

Whether the use of "frontier" is politically correct or even historically accurate is a separate matter for a contemporary interpretive anthropologist than it is for a meticulous archaeologist or historian. In sum, the climate, landscape, and history of Hokkaido alongside the enduring industries and practice found there today are comparable with, for example, Australian, Canadian, or American settler history and so too are the vernacular discourses or narratives used in description. This mode of representation is dissimilar compared to the ways other Japanese colonial endeavors are remembered and referenced. Specifically, Hokkaido houses images, ideas, and ideals of *kaitaku*, or "frontier," space, incongruous with the previously settled conception of Okinawa or Korea for example. This is perhaps most readily pop culturally apparent when Hokkaido is promoted in domestic tourist media as looking like, and even being akin to, a foreign country, usually the American West, or less often northern Europe. Importantly, such domestic promotion is quite unlike other efforts to promote domestic tourism discussed by anthropologists Theodore Bestor (2004), Marilyn Ivy (1995), and Jennifer Robertson (1994, 1998b) where the search for an "essential," "real," "premodern," and "nostalgic" Japan is at the forefront—places where the romantic imaginary, often itself invented (Guarné 2018; Vlastos 1998), of "true" Japan takes center stage. Hokkaido is popularly Othered, and that Otherness takes on a particular nuance as frontier space (Kawabara and Kawagami 2018; Miyajima 1998; Saunavaara 2018).

The use of "frontier" in the context of this book is historical and geographic in a popular sense, Hokkaido as a separate place often envisioned as security buffer zone. But it is also intended to draw attention to the present-day comparative similarities of representation, whether actual or concocted, marking a particular moment of global imperialism (1867 on) while accounting for associated and persisting popular ideologies alongside the actions influenced and influential. The intention is not to induce contemporary amnesia with this term—one that is certainly no less fanciful than the common Japanese vernacular notion of the "reclamation" (*kaitaku*) of Hokkaido. Rather, it is helpful to think of Hokkaido and its popular image in terms of a historical time frame alongside a physical and social landscape that can be viewed in tandem with other global colonial settler states. The creation of Hokkaido marks a specific point in world history and not just a part of a "uniquely unique" Japanese history. The region was officially incorporated into the new modern Japanese nation-state the same year the western Canadian "frontier" was incorporated by the central Canadian government into the new Canadian nation-state. Hokkaido's becoming Hokkaido is sandwiched between the Alaska Purchase in 1867 and Australia's Aboriginal Protection Act in 1869. Consequently, many frontier tropes in Hokkaido are shared with the conceptualization and enactment of other colonial frontiers. For example, Hokkaido is depicted as pastoral on the one hand, with foreign domesticated animals (sheep and dairy cows especially), while at the same moment it is viewed as "wild" and natural, in reference to the region's nonhuman and human indigenous populations, notably the *Ezo higuma* (Hokkaido bear) and, as tragically as on other imagined frontiers, its native people, collectively referred to as Ainu.

These shifting images have blurred into distinctive contemporary Hokkaido frontier imaginaries. It is a location popularly promoted and viewed in terms of its perceived alterity—from wild, to natural, to domesticated, shifting back and forth between these markers depending on context or perspective—and is at the forefront of the searches for national, community, and personal securities. Of course, the meaning ascribed to a place, frontier or not, is dependent upon *who* does the looking and *what* they are looking for, a central point in Mason's *Dominant Narratives of Colonial Hokkaido and Imperial Japan: Envisioning the Periphery and the Modern Nation-State* (2012) just as it is in *Challenging Frontiers: The Canadian West* (Felske and Rasporich 2004 ed.) or *Looking West* (Dorst 1999) outlining competing perspectives of the North American frontier. On the other hand, Kitano Shu's *Space, Planning and Rurality: Uneven Rural Development in Japan* (Kitano 2009), Susanne Klien's *Urban Migrants in Rural Japan: Between Agency and Anomie in a Post-growth Society* (2020), Odagiri Tokumi's *Nōsanson wa shōmetsu shinai* [Farming and Mountain Villages Will Not Vanish] (Odagiri 2014), John Traphagan's *Cosmopolitan Rurality, Depopulation, and Entrepreneurial Ecosystems in 21st-Century Japan* (2019), or Don Wood's *Ogata-Mura: Sowing Dissent and Reclaiming Identity in a Japanese Farming Village* (2012) all focus on the here and now and the individuated making and remaking of rural locations in Japan, including multiple perspectives of particular locations and histories. Hokkaido, Tokachi, and Gensan can be added to this list. It is a location that for a century and a half has been home to some familiar Japanese rural images, yet it also houses many unfamiliar lifestyles and livelihoods in the broader context of Japan. Tokachi, dairy farming, and dairy cattle mean many things to many people, both to those working in the industry, be they locals or newcomers, and to tourists passing through. If my arguments give fact its due justice, then one contribution of this book is the deployment of Tokachi, Hokkaido, as a counternarrative, a case study that unsettles the long-dominant and Honshu-centric, if increasingly strained, group-oriented "rice as self" metaphor of rural Japan (Ohnuki-Tierney 1993). And important to highlight is the fact that macro, meso, and micro notions of frontiers, from geopolitical location, to community belonging, to the living body are always shifting as, for example, political identities emerge or evolve or research changes what were previous certainties into new common understandings.

From Ezo to Hokkaido:
A Periphery of Barbarians, Exiles, and Outcasts

The first recorded documentation of Hokkaido is as *watari shima* (island across the water) during the Heian period (794–1192 CE). The region then became known as *Ezo ga shima* (barbarian island) when Japanese from northern Honshu (then the unsettled northern fringe) began to cross the Tsugaru Straits, forming spartan trading settlements. Importantly, these settlements included political prisoners of the Kamakura (1192–1333 CE) military government sent into exile. These southerners essentially stuck to the shoreline near the present-day Hakodate and Matsumae, as they were vastly outnumbered by indigenous peoples whom they considered dangerous. Indeed, skirmishes between Ainu and *wajin* have been a common historical theme in multiple regions north of Sendai, not just Hokkaido (Guo 2005; Siddle 1996; Sjöberg 1993, 2008; Walker 2001). In short, the Japanese and Ainu did not lead separate and isolated lives, with the former in Ezo and the latter in Honshu, yet this modern myth of precolonization separation and exception is a popular and persisting frontier nationalist/ethnic discourse.

When Japan was unified under the Tokugawa shogun from 1603 CE, a strict system of official residence was enforced. Feudal leaders from across the loosely affiliated polity were expected to reside in the capital Edo (Tokyo) for half of the year with their families remaining as "collateral" for the other half. This was not the case for every Tokugawa domain ruler, however. Occupying a fraction of southern Ezo, the Matsumae were the *only* feudal family exempt from this policy of voluntary hostage offering (Harrison 1953; see Siddle 1996 for maps of this region of approximately eighty square kilometers).

From the perspective of the Tokugawa *bakufu*, Ezo was clearly considered a hinterland. First, the lion's share of the area, which had not yet been accurately mapped and was thus only dimly understood, was still primarily occupied by Ainu who were not recognized as Japanese or even properly human. Second, from the Kamakura period onward, scattered coastal areas had been occupied by locally powerful leaders, including cast-off political dissidents, who were not recognized as supporters of the newly unifying Japanese polity (the burgeoning Japanese nation-state). They were, in fact, legally recognized as outcasts. Thirdly, "outlaw" Ainu, Japanese, and indeed Ainu-Japanese traders engaged in unregulated trade (made illegal through disregarding *bakufu* seclusion policy). And finally, Ezo was home to the Matsumae domain, rulers who, though clearly related to the southern Japanese, were just as clearly perceived as peripheral (Mason and Craiger 1997, 202–209).

Thus, even at this early stage of modern history, frontiers went beyond geographic borders to the borders of physical embodiment. The Ando family, originally at the heart of this tiny empire, professed to be of mixed Ainu and southern blood and claimed they were heirs to a separate kingdom, one reason behind the particular treatment of the Matsumae domain. Beyond the fact that the Matsumae were not required to maintain a household in Edo as did other *daimyō* (lord of a feudal fiefdom) or could break seclusion rules with few negative repercussions or sanctions, they also did not contribute taxes in the same form as other *daimyō*. While all others pledging allegiance or paying tax did so with rice, the lords of Ezo did not. The prehybridized cereal simply did not grow there. Moreover, they were not required to pay a yearly homage but only required to do so once every five years. Thus, while the Ainu occupying this space were clearly considered "Others" by Edo, even the Matsumae, essentially *wajin* emissaries in the region, were viewed with considerable ambiguity, as not quite Japanese yet not quite foreign (Morris-Suzuki 1996, 1998, 12–13), offered numerous distinctive rules and regulations, and existed clearly betwixt and between any simple categorical binary of Japanese/not Japanese. This early Tokugawa allowance for ambiguity would gradually change, however.

From the late 1700s, the Ezo hinterland became increasingly important to the *bakufu* due to its significance for both economic and military (mostly naval) security. Owing to these concerns, the colonization of the northern land moved beyond banishing political exiles and appeasing self-proclaimed sovereigns of seemingly dubious heritage to early attempts at full-scale occupation. One reason was that by the 1780s the *bakufu* was slipping into bankruptcy. However, in stark contrast to the declining economy of Edo, when they were not warring with Ainu, the Matsumae were becoming wealthy from fisheries as well as trade in salmon, skins, and natural medicinal goods, among other things. Moreover, Russians were establishing trading operations in Sakhalin and the Kuriles and making trading overtures in Ezo itself despite strict *bakufu* regulations countering "domestic" let alone foreign trade.

Rapidly going bankrupt and progressively angered by the rising affluence of the northerners, in 1799 the *bakufu* attempted direct control of all Ezo land including the lands outside of Matsumae's officially demarcated southern territory. The Matsumae's authority had already been weakened ten years previously when Ainu had mounted a large revolt on Kunashiri Island after the Japanese running fishery operations on the island were rumored to be poisoning Ainu. When the Ainu took up arms the Japanese were outnumbered and called for reinforcements from the south under threat of being overrun. This shock and threat also prompted a push to settle and secure the region as a buffer. By 1798 money was set aside for "Ainu education . . . [and] . . . laws were promulgated for the administration of *Yezo*, and the area was recognized as a colony" (Harrison 1953, 29–30). Powerful samurai in Edo, such as Honda Toshiaki, were vociferous in their support of colonization through agriculture in Ezo, as well as in what are the present-day Sakhalin and Kuril Islands

(Cullen 2003, 138), a theme flowing well into the modern period. Upon usurping Matsumae's control, the first waves of militia settlers were sent to the island. Most settled around the former Matsumae domain on the southern peninsula, but some were garrisoned as far away as the Soya cape, the island's northernmost point. They attempted to establish farming homesteads and fishing settlements, and military outposts were set up beyond Soya in Sakhalin and the Kurils. Climatic conditions this far north, however, proved to be devastating for the farming they were accustomed to. Many died and most abandoned inland areas opting to work in fishing settlements. Thus, the earliest attempt at full-fledged colonization failed miserably, indeed it ended in more local Japanese-Ainu mixing than separation, and the land of Ezo was returned to Matsumae jurisdiction in 1821.

Nevertheless, these tremendous failures in agricultural occupation aside, the *idea* of subjugating the north found fertile soil in the capital. Japan's *sakoku*, or closed nation policy, made securing the frontier even more of a key priority and an issue broader in scope than economics alone. It concerned the security of the entire Tokugawa state. Though the quest for enhanced economic security was initially the most important factor in sending settlers north and attempting to dominate trade, there was also a growing awareness of the military power of other seafaring nations. While the protracted conflicts with indigenous Ainu underscored a unified Japan's vulnerability to its north, Russians also attacked Japanese settlements in 1806 (Cullen 2003, 147). Moreover, the Dutch, who were in perpetual conflict with England, relayed their own nation's interest in expanding trade relations with the "closed country." Using the fresh and pertinent example of the French and English defeat of the Chinese in the Opium War (1840–1842), the Dutch argued that stronger relations with their nation would be more benign and in the interest of the *bakufu* in Edo. Adding to this political instability, English ships occasionally tried to dock in Hokkaido for trade, and American ships, notably commercial whaling vessels, were frequently spotted off its coasts. As noted above, the Matsumae had already flirted with illegal trade with the Russians, possessors of the most formidable navy in the Northwest Pacific at the time, and by the early nineteenth century Russian ships frequently sailed freely past Ezo, not only into the Pacific, but unchecked in the Sea of Japan.[1] In short, the *bakufu*'s secured and closed world was already rife with cracks in its façade. But Ezo was increasingly viewed more like a gaping hole in the north that exposed a carefully crafted Nippon to the world.

Given the actual permeability of *sakoku*, when Commodore Perry's four famed gunships arrived in Edo Bay in 1853, as shocking as this brazen display may have been, the writing had long since been on the wall, certainly in the north. Japan could not remain the relative hermit kingdom its samurai elite had attempted to create. And, important for the points that follow, it was clear that the national security of the soon-to-be modern nation-state of Japan was intimately linked to Ezo. The northern island became a key site in attempts at shoring up economic security for a financially faltering *bakufu* and military security for a nation increasingly in fear of, and seemingly ever on the cusp of, domestic divisions and foreign invasion. It also became a failed testing ground for political security as the Tokugawa *bakufu* could not recover from these external and internal threats. Such fears as much as threats prompted the fledgling nation-state's engagement into unequal trade agreements, buying immediate safety from potential (probable) invasion and time to plot a response to new "barbarians" from farther afield than Ezo (Perez 1997). These trade agreements would "open" Japan and it would take three decades for the Japanese to gain more favorable trade terms. The opening of Hakodate in 1859, Japan's second international port, isolated as it was, underscores that all of these economic, military, and political factors were linked with a north conceptualized as Japanese frontier space, a dangerous and porous periphery bare to the rest of the world. Indeed, proto ethnographer Hirao Rosen upon visiting in June of 1855 before its official opening highlighted the already cosmopolitan alterity of this outpost. As Fujiwara notes, Hirao was shocked that "Westerners had blended into the local scene in Hakodate and the nearby villages of Kameda and Arikawa, such that they could 'rub shoulders' with local residents without locals batting an eyelid. He discovered an international society within Hakodate where encounters with foreigners had become mundane" (Fujiwara 2021, 56). Fujiwara goes on to note that in documenting such encounters "Rosen emphasized the more distinguished and superior sensibilities of the Japanese and expressed prejudices rooted in cultural chauvinism, not uncommon in those days in Japan" (57).

The Meiji revolution or restoration, depending on one's side of alliance, brought about watershed changes in Japanese social and political life as a transition from military-dominated feudal nation to modern imperial nation-state. Here Ezo and its Otherness was again to play a key role. Many samurai, remaining loyal after 250 years of family service to the defeated and fragmented former Tokugawa *bakufu*, fled the capital and nearby provinces to lead insurrections across the new nation-state. The final rebel was Enomoto Takeaki, the head of the *bakufu* navy. Refusing to submit to imperial Meiji authority, Enomoto fled with his retainers to the recently opened Hakodate port.

In December 1868, the Meiji troops under the command of twenty-eight-year-old Kuroda Kiyotaka gave chase and defeated the forces of Enomoto, who had for a short time attempted to form an independent republic on the island. But rather than this rebellion being quashed outright, Fujita points out the somewhat peculiar twist in this story that was to be the formation of modern Hokkaido. "In August 1869 the Meiji leaders reorganized the central government and created the department called *Kaitakushi*, which would be in charge of developing Yezo. . . . Yezo was renamed Hokkaido, meaning the "Northern Sea Road." . . . The irony was that Enomoto and several other rebels were soon to occupy high positions in the *Kaitakushi* through Kuroda's good offices, and they worked for the regime that they had once so desperately fought" (Fujita 1994, 2–4). In short, the last holdouts of the old *bakufu*—defeated but not loyal to the new Meiji government—were ironically to play key roles in the Meiji colonization of this newly named frontier of Hokkaido. This also represented a shift in the image of Otherness—a place of barbarians, exiles, and outcasts was now headed by former rebels charged with the securing and security of the country's north.

From the birth of Japan's modern period, two levels of government, regional and national, have played a central role in the "development" of Hokkaido and the promotion of occupation and agriculture on the island. What had long been the home of many independent thinking exiles and outcasts now became home to a new breed of ambitious ex-samurai. Cut off from their former prestige, not to mention hereditary financial stipends, by the establishment of a conscripted military in 1876, many from former samurai families came to Hokkaido as *tondenhei* (farmer warriors) to work alongside criminals doing forced labor and later impoverished pioneers from depressed areas of Japan—all sponsored, at first, by the *kaitakushi* (Fujita 1994; Mock 1999; Russell 2007; Shigematsu 2004; Takata 2004). And as Japan's colonial empire grew, Korean and Chinese forced labor would also arrive.

This would be the first wave of Hokkaido's contemporary or modern colonization, a location that was envisioned as a frontier, as unoccupied, and so unclaimed as attested to by the new Hokkaido prefectural government or *dōchō* being established in 1886 (and again betraying their core/periphery externality, the prefecture could not elect members to the national assembly until 1902!). By 1899 the *tondenhei* program ended and large tracts of land, especially in the east of Hokkaido, were auctioned off by the government to well-heeled adventures and entrepreneurs. They, in turn, would recruit tenant farmers from poorer areas on the mainland to engage in primary industries such as agriculture, working for fisheries, and mining. This did not just attract new desperate citizens, many of whom were promised a percentage of land ownership provided they could make it workable, but established companies sponsoring "reclamation" projects leading to the establishment of a "colonial bank" (*Takushoku Ginkō*). By the outbreak of the First World War, Hokkaido had become a resource extraction hub and the population increased through steady work and internal migration until the late 1920s when natural population increases overtook incomers at least until the end of the Second World War.

While it is tempting to compare and contrast many of Japan's colonial acquisitions up until its Occupation period (1945–1952), as noted above only Hokkaido and Okinawa have remained part of the contemporary nation-state. And as such, it is important to briefly outline why Okinawa is not comparable to Hokkaido, at least in being considered a frontier. Sidestepping the obvious differences in climate and size, Okinawa is subtropical and Japan's fourth smallest prefecture. It also has an over seven-hundred-year-long history of documented trade relations with China and thousands of years of exchange among neighboring islands (Kerr 2000). Hence it was never considered to be *terra nullius* by the Tokugawa or Meiji elite but was perceived as an established and independent kingdom that needed to be "modernized" by the Japanese. This is a very different notion from a frontier as outlined above. Moreover, with the exception of sugar cane, Okinawa has not been exploited in terms of island resources flowing from this periphery to the mainland core. Finally, life in early Hokkaido was generally a hard and miserable existence in an unforgiving landscape where, certainly in the winter season, death could come quickly. Yet, thousands migrated north for opportunity, perhaps given a lack of other options. On the other hand, though Okinawa had no comparable natural dangers, poisonous *habu* snake aside, it was impoverished, and many chose to leave it, most famously for Hawai'i or Brazil but also cities in Japan such as Osaka. In sum, Hokkaido's early modern history is notable for people from *naichi* entering, not Hokkaido's population migrating to the mainland let alone farther afield (Siddle 1998).

Thus, much like migration to the "new world" of North America, the new prefecture of Hokkaido was, generally speaking, the chosen route of very few well-to-do individuals. In an interview I conducted while researching this chapter I asked Professor Soda Osamu, a respected scholar and founder of Kyoto University's somewhat unusually named Department of Agricultural Philosophy, why people *chose* to move to Hokkaido and I was promptly corrected. "Even fifty years ago things were very different. Nobody *chose* to move to Hokkaido. People went because they had no choice" (interview with Professor Soda at Fukui University on September 13, 2007). They were leaving one known insecure situation, often a life of poverty, to face Otherness and a search for security on a newly imagined and established frontier.

Like the West and Midwest of Canada and the United States, Hokkaido, and all the more Tokachi, was built on stolen land via the trial and error of some fiscally adventurous elites and the blood, sweat, and lives of the desperate. It was also the route taken by, or thrust upon, exiles and ambitious (and often ruthless) merchants and military men. It was thus, very clearly, a violently imposed settler state, usurping the land and subjecting the local population to extract resources that moved from this periphery to the core while acting as a strategic buffer zone. Thus, the history of Hokkaido's coming into being and its early population ultimately relates to early modern and modern issues of military, political, and economic security that can be viewed at a global, national, community, and individual scale. Ezo changed into Hokkaido. Contained within the parameters of the modern Japanese state, it continued to be on the political periphery, an imagined frontier rooted in a history of Otherness and security concerns both national and personal.

Identity, Modernity, and the Construction of Contemporary Geocultural Frontiers

As noted above, the modern period is usually divided into the early modern period, roughly the Tokugawa period, which includes the first ideological underpinnings and systematic attempts at Japanese occupation of both the Ryukyu islands (contemporary Okinawa) and Ezo (contemporary Hokkaido) (cf. Bellah 1957; Bix 1986; Harootunian 2019; Toby 1984; Totman 2000; Walker 2001; Wigen 1995), and the modern period, which is generally accepted as starting in the Meiji period to the present day (cf. Bix 2001; Tipton 2002; Ziomek 2019). While "modernity" is more descriptive of ideological influences as opposed to a clear-cut marking of time, it is perhaps even less clear cut in the context of Japan. What is offered here is a skeletal depiction of over one hundred years of political, philosophical, and social thought and its interweaving relationship with Japanese identity and frontier spaces, including Hokkaido.

The early Meiji-era leaders, fearful of Western imperialism, wanted to develop Japan into what they considered to be a modern and comparative nation-state. They sought to form an imperial power, both freely borrowing from and wanting to be on par with colonial European nations and America. This shift, from a feudal and fragmented collection of regional identities into a unified state, complete with a directed political will (beyond the local), necessitated much "inventing" and "imagining" at the national level (Vlastos 1998, in Japan; Anderson 1991 and Hobsbawm and Ranger 1983, in general). National identity and agriculture are, I suggest, particularly important to highlight among the other modern concerns in the context of Japan as they are central to understanding what underpins essentialist *nihonjinron* (theories of distinct Japaneseness) images of the nation still very much alive today, the contemporary point revisited in detail in chapter 7.

From the early modern period Japanese elites were torn between *sakoku*—the xenophobic exclusion of Otherness related to nativist scholarship—and *rangaku* or Dutch studies—the desire to open the nation, within limits, and learn from foreign experience. This division came to a head with the above-noted shift from Tokugawa to Meiji rule. The Japanese government needed to unite the people it now governed. Stephen Vlastos, among the others in a now-classic edited volume, argues that this was accomplished through inventing—"valorising" and "historicizing"—elements of national belonging and identity (Japan as harmonious and agrarian most notably) (Vlastos 1998, 1–18, 79–94). Beyond ideology alone, top-down national projects of unification were also attempted through force at this time with certainly one of the best-known examples being the persecution of Buddhist sects and the development of Shinto as the state-supported religion (Hardacre 1989; Heisig and Maraldo 1995; Victoria 2001).

The benefits and costs of modernity were debated, most notably in terms of the influences of modernization coming through foreign (Euro-American) channels (Akamatsu 1972; Pedlar 1990). For instance, Yokoi Tokiyoshi (1860–1927), considered the father of modern Japanese agricultural sciences, the publisher of *Nihōnshugi*, and the founder of Tokyo Universities' Agriculture Department, was steadfastly against rapid modernization in terms of agriculture policy focusing on the negative effects on security (national, social, and economic) of the new nation-state in its drive to modernize and industrialize. This prompted a search for (even then viewed as salvaging) distinct Japanese socio-ethno-cultural origins through ethnology underpinned by an opposition to the rapidly shifting technological and sociocultural norms being brought about by Japan's drive to modernize. In terms of anthropology, this is reflected most famously in the school of ethnology as practiced and promoted by Yanagita Kunio (1875–1962) (see Christy 2012; Ivy 1995; Kuwayama 2004; Kuwayama and Ayaba 2006 for detailed accounts of Yanagita).

Yanagita, whose working life actually started in the Ministry of Agriculture, focused on agricultural production in regions that were becoming increasingly marginalized within a rapidly industrializing nation. His search morphed into what became a quest for the essential Japanese *minzoku* or people—similar to the German Romantics, such as Johann Herder's quest for an essential *Volkskultur* (folk culture). From around 1910, the publication date of Yanagita's influential *Tōno monogatari* or Tales of Tōno, and into the 1930s, his mission, and that of the many influenced by him (a "who's who" of the foundation of Japanese *minzokugaku* or native ethnology), was securing the core of Japanese identity in the face of changes wrought by modernization and alterity, indeed a nascent countermove to globalization. That is, securing "the folk" of Japan from the contamination of "the Other." Looking for the internal rural "self" gradually shifted from a more or less benign, if ill theorized, exploration of cultural survivals to become closely correlated with a rise in Japanese nationalism and an escalation in colonial expansion—ergo a motivation for securing the expanding state (Dower 1999). During this period, the focus of nativist ethnology or folklore transformed from a focus on uncovering Japanese origins as representations of an "untainted" rural folk, to increasing attempts to locate Japan's place in terms of both a regional and global "center to periphery" notion of civilization and culture and retrenching notions of bounded sociocultural and biological frontiers (Figal 2000; Hashimoto 1998, 134–143).

Moreover, influenced by nation building and colonial expansion, newly internalized Others such as Okinawans or Ainu (and also it could be argued Chinese and Koreans) could no longer be viewed as external and barbarian peoples (the *i*) from the perspective of policy (in practice prejudice remained rampant however). These citizens needed to be transformed into placeholders in the extension of a geographical discourse moving from the center of Japanese culture (the *ka*) ever outward from the center radiating out past frontiers of belonging to the periphery based on the notion of *bunmei kaika* (civilization). In sum, the external *i* and the internal *ka* needed to be brought into relation, meaning that the periphery (outside Honshu) was "reinterpreted in *temporal* rather than *spatial* terms, as 'backwards' rather than via its 'foreign-ness'" (Morris-Suzuki 1996, 90). This is because the newly colonized places and peoples needed to be incorporated into the expanding nation-state and its civilizing discourse. In sum, a burgeoning nationalism needed a central "folk" to rally around and the agrarian core of Japan, the *minzoku*, were invented as the key to understanding the essential and "natural" soul of Japan and notions of Japaneseness (Vlastos 1998, 79–94). The *minzoku* as category could later be utilized in propaganda forwarding Japanese imperialism through the Daitōa kyōeiken (Greater East Asia Co-prosperity Sphere), seen as liberating Asian nations from Western hegemonic modernity through Japanese rule and, as explained below, a discourse focused on what was constructed as an inherently Asiatic mode of modernity.

This securing of a reductive and singular Japanese identity in the face of the Othering processes of modernity, of which Hokkaido was a prime example, can be readily seen six months into the Pacific War. The Kindai no Chōkoku (Overcoming the Modern) symposium was held in Kyoto wherein key Japanese intellectuals debated what modernity meant for Japan and by extension its colonial possessions and aspirations. Its provocations: How could modernity be incorporated into a particular Japanese context, or how could its Western guise (or in many cases should) be resisted (Harootunian 2019, 303–325; Heisig and Maraldo 1995)? The symposium built upon a long discomforting discourse regarding East (Japan) and West (an ever-changing monolith, then Europe and America, but after postwar Occupation it took on a decidedly American flavor). In sum, the debate was that there was a "premodern" East, a "modern" West, and somewhere between these poles the need for a uniquely modernizing Japan. This was a particularly timely identity politics, a search for a distinct and well-defined localized patent on modernity, and so too security (economic, social, and political), in local/national terms. It was an internal protest to what was seen as a legacy of Western domination through supplanting a lucid (if factually flawed) history and vision of progress and modernity in and of Asia. Throughout the Pacific conflict, Japan as Asia's self-appointed moniker of light and liberation held, but by the end of the Second World War this narrative needed to be radically reevaluated in terms of military defeat and physical, political, and economic domination and occupation. Imperial nationalism, the "premodern," the *minzoku*, and the centrality of agrarian values needed to be reinvented in order to, borrowing from historian John Dower, "embrace defeat" (Dower 1999). And with a largely American-based occupying force from 1945 to 1952 Japan began down the path of framing a new "us" and "them," new ideological and geographic frontiers.

With Japanese post–Pacific War prosperity in the 1960s to 1980s these lofty nationalist tropes began to reemerge with a newly buffed veneer. By the 1980s a popularized notion of "Conquering of Modernity" emerged that viewed Japan as home to a unique patent of modernity, one that was trumping the West in terms of economic growth, with agrarian and communal values at its heart (Harootunian 2019, 303–325). Excellent examples of this type of thinking are offered in analyzing Ezra Vogel's *Japan as Number One: Lessons for America* (1979) or Watanabe Shōichi's *Peasant Soul of Japan* (Watanabe 1989). In this version, the notion of Japanese modernity that was promoted was not that of farmers being innately good soldiers due to their tight link with the land and respect for the cooperative structures that working it underpin, but as good national citizens who embody the collective values of *ware ware nihonjin* (we Japanese) and respect for traditions (rooted above all in essentialized ideas of shared blood and ethnicity). *Ka* equating with "proper" Japanese as opposed to *i*, meaning identities/ethnicities beyond the national frontier and generally viewed as lacking Japan's innate social, cultural, even genetic qualities. This popular cultural/genetic essentialism was undergirded by Japan's regional, and it was pontificated soon to be global, economic domination. With such an ideology as a backdrop, unsurprisingly in the 1970s to 1980s "Othering" became somewhat a national pastime and discourse as "we Japanese" came to emerge as a singular (and superior) collective entity "in which the agents are linked together in a national subjectivity devoid of regional, class, or even gender distinctions, let alone individuals . . . by being deprived of any mark of their opposition to one another" (Harootunian 1989, 89). Simply, this contrastive and ever-evolving discourse is an attempt to secure the state and an idealized sense of self from the social and cultural changes imposed by an engagement with what was constructed as radical Otherness, internal or external.

Yet, not all citizens of the Japanese state belonged in the *nihonjin-ron* camp. For one, the aforementioned centuries of mixing and melding at Japan's geographical bounds, and in Japan itself as a former imperial power, obviously problematize this imagined uniformity of ethnocultural

Japaneseness (Morris-Suzuki 2011). For example, regarding the northern frontier, it must be noted that while many who self-identify as Ainu do actively separate themselves from essentialist epic discourses of Japaneseness, some *could-be* Ainu have no desire to do so. That is to say for some, "the goal of the Ainu people is not only to revive old traditions and pass them on to new generations, but also to recover their identity and rights as indigenous people with a view to achieving a future where they can live a free, human life in accord with their own culture, traditions, and values. . . . The Ainu people are seeking to be in solidarity with other indigenous peoples and oppressed minorities throughout the world" (Watanabe 1998, 4–5).

But for others of a less activist inclination, for example, in Watson's *Japan's Ainu Minority in Tokyo: Diasporic Identity and Urban Politics* (2014), though they identify as Ainu, their goals are more diverse and individualistic. This is a situation loosely mirrored in Okinawa with the Uchinānchu movement, people searching for genealogical and cultural origins and identities. Spokespeople for both groups claim that they form a *minzoku* (a people or nation) separate from "Japaneseness" (Allen 2002). A commanding 72 percent of Okinawans claim there is a difference between Okinawan culture and Japanese culture (Hook and Siddle 2003, 133). In short, it is not simply a case whereby those of Japanese ethnicity are free to label Otherness. Many Japanese citizens proclaim themselves to be something other than ethnically uniform. Thus, the majority of those demarcated as outsiders, for example, both Ainu and Okinawan, are also often choosing to distinguish themselves via cultural difference. For some it may not be an issue at all—they are unconcerned with identity politics—and even for those engaged in the process it can go unidirectionally or bidirectionally. Individuals can separate *themselves* from typical Japanese categories *as well as being separated* out through the homogenizing discourses of Japanese identity. Taking Ainu activists as an example again—despite their acquisition of a contemporary non-Japanese identity through prolonged activism and courting foreign pressure finally becoming legally recognized as an indigenous people in 2008 (see Lewallen 2016 for a detailed ethnographic account)—whether self-declared as Other or self-declared as Japanese, their identity is clearly not solely that of a socioculturally uniform Japanese people and this can be compared with the aforementioned long history of Okinawa (Ryukyu) as a kingdom dating from the thirteenth century (Furuki 2003, 21–38) and individuals who identify with that culture. Again, these diverse peoples and their cultures were premodern fixtures in the southern and northern regions of Japan

(Gou 2005; Howell 1994), not some newly emergent Other. Put simply, if an Ainu claims their origin to be ethnically Japanese or non-Japanese, then they do so as modern subjects. No Ainu is likely to claim that their distinctiveness based on language, narrative stories of hunting grounds, salmon fishing, bear worship, or indeed genetics, is an identity centered in Shikoku. It is inescapably a *contemporary identity* of Otherness, one *bound to the creation of a frontier* and the security and insecurity that creating it, literally and imaginatively, has fostered.

Marking the Otherness on the Hokkaido Frontier Today

A visit to a museum such as the Obihiro City Centennial Museum, Abashiri Prison Museum, Sapporo's Historical Museum of Hokkaido, or Sapporo Agricultural College Model Dairy Farm at Hokkaido University serve as a vivid testament to the distinctiveness of a frontier identity described above, again not only a buffer zone or social, political, cultural periphery, but a conscious construction of a modern settler state often mimicking other settler states. Displays convey the political considerations and aspirations, conflicts of interpretation, desperation, visionary spirit, and the harsh conditions faced by pioneers, prisoners, and indigenous inhabitants during Hokkaido's early modern history. While museum displays are memetic and symbolic devices unlikely to perfectly render Ainu, Japanese, or indeed hybrid Ainu–Japanese relations untainted by interpretation, ideology, and appropriation, they do provide an embodied way for contemporary individuals to experience a flavor, some affective sense, of the early agricultural history in the region. Numerous scholars have discussed the politics of representation in museums, notably in relation to colonized places and peoples (Clifford 1997; Hendry 2000; Kuwayama 2007, 2009, 2012). My point here is less on understanding violence of contact and the use and misuse of narrative accounts of the frontier than on trying to empathize with the material conditions of settlers, those colonized, and the particular environment they encountered one another in. Through touching tools, the smelling of wood and soil, or viewing an Ainu tapestry the material culture of early Hokkaido is imperfectly but evocatively preserved. One can see, smell, hear, and even touch the equipment used during past eras.

Numerous early promotion posters, pamphlets, maps of the region, and instruction manuals are housed in the Hokkaido University's Northern Studies Collection. These materials also provide tangible access to the frontier nature of agriculture in Hokkaido.[2] And through such historical materials and documents, individuals with a present-day interest in the region can see that Hokkaido was symbolic of competing and even contradictory discourses: of Otherness and of opportunity, of security and of danger, of threats to indigenous ways and the emergence of new livelihoods like dairy farming. For the forbearers of the local dairy farmer owners discussed in this book Hokkaido, and notably Tokachi, was a space where individuals facing dire conditions further south could migrate and possibly find security: make a living, a family, a home, and adopt an emerging identity, if they were willing to face the new and unknown, as seen in figures 2.1 and 2.2.

While the wild image of Ezo remains in terms of being home to Japan's largest national parks, the dominant image and imaginary of regional agriculture is decidedly pastoral, tamed, and domesticated. As such, Hokkaido is a "mangle of practices" and perceptions (Pickering 1995). Pickering uses "mangle of practices" and "dance of agency" to describe the reality of how

Figure 2.1. A Meiji-era manual explaining cows intended for settlers who very well may never have had contact with a cow before. Photo used with permission from Hokkaido University's Northern Studies Collection Archive.

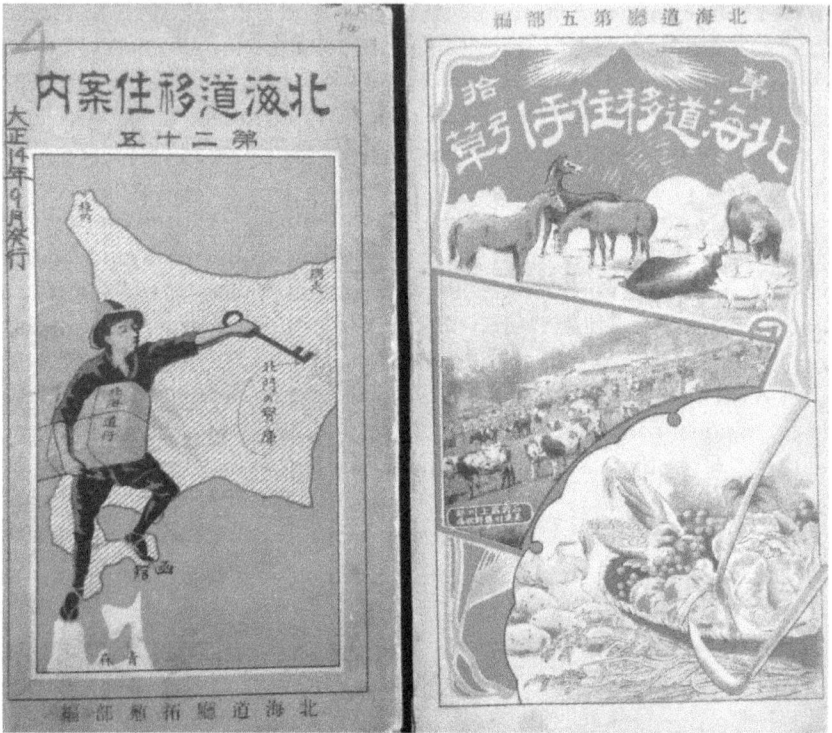

Figure 2.2. An early promotion pamphlet highlighting the Otherness of the region and an invitation to change, opportunity, and hope. In this pastoral imagery there is no rice paddy, and the key feature is a lone pioneer with the key to securing a new future. Photo used with permission from Hokkaido University's Northern Studies Collection Archive.

scientific practices are messy and often contradictory yet retain the patina of uniformity. I suggest these metaphors are extremely apropos in describing the construction of Hokkaido. Tellingly, the bestselling children's book *Hokkaido wakuku chizu ehon* (An Exciting Hokkaido Picture Map) outlines the differing products and practices that identify each of Hokkaido's regional areas via particular practices and environmental proclivities, for example, potatoes in Shihoro, horses in Hidaka, Santa Land in Hirō and, as will be seen below, hot air balloons over dairy farms in Gensan (Horikawa 2006). Though Hokkaido has remained "wild" in the public's perception, in terms of the symbols of a natural environment such as the Hokkaido bear and the various "tourist" Ainu villages (*kotan*), Hokkaido is equally, if not more, associated with a multitude of regional symbols of domesticated rural Otherness. That is to say, with fragmented representations of a real or imagined frontier past, from the aforementioned museums to outright appropriations of the American frontier, to the image of rolling hills, grazing cattle, and fresh dairy products associated with pastoral life. Not relinquishing its history of natural Otherness, Hokkaido, and surely Tokachi, has transformed itself into another dominant frontier of Otherness; between a reimagined Americanesque frontier and Milkland.[3]

Conclusion

This chapter has set the historical frame for understanding Hokkaido and Tokachi as a frontier image, imaginary, and ideology. Specifically, it has focused on the inherent Otherness of the location and the particular vicissitudes, from land of exile, to Ainu, to *tondenhei*, to tourist, to dairy farmer, and the ever-changing politics that serve as a foundation for a multilevel search for security, from state to individual, in the context of Japan. Some key points have been made. First, as a frontier colony the history of Hokkaido, and certainly Tokachi, is quite unlike other regions in Japan (Tokachi kyōdo kenkyōkai 2001). Most importantly in contemporary terms perhaps, Hokkaido is unlike Japan's southwestern periphery, Okinawa, in a number of ways. It can be seen in terms of security and "inter" and "inner" national relations throughout history or the brokering between colonizer and colonized or immigration versus emigration. Second, throughout the long history of social, economic, and political changes in Hokkaido, the indigenous people alongside people drawn to (or often circumstantially thrust into) the prefecture have been demarcated as Others in the context of broader Japanese society: exiles, adventures, indigenous, and escapees. Third, in terms of a frontier metaphor, the settlement of Hokkaido mirrors, and indeed was designed to mirror, North America in many ways, especially in terms of agricultural settlement and practices. This is a point increasingly apparent in the following chapters. And finally, Hokkaido serves as an idealized location that houses particular, specific, and novel narratives that at times combine and at times contrast with hegemonic or dominant discourses of Japan and Japaneseness. Such heterotopic narratives are open to interpretation and they attract Japanese, in particular young Japanese dairy workers, who have their own experiences of these places, good and bad, as documented in the chapters that follow: individuals that can be viewed as micro frontiers on a macro frontier, the individual bodies, individual stories, and individual interactions that, taken together, comprise a contemporary dairying community's being and becoming.

Chapter Three

From Traction to *Teishoku*

Tracing the Human-Bovine Trajectory

Introduction

This brief chapter fleshes out how the dairy and related beef industries were historically introduced and promoted in Japan, with a particular focus on the evolving image of beef and dairy domestically and their relation to national and regional security concerns. It sketches how dairy practices were established and why cattle farming developed at such a late stage in Japanese history relative to Europe, its former colonies, as well as much of continental Asia. Furthermore, this chapter underscores why Japan is an anomaly in regard to its beef and dairy consumption and production. These products are not rare, indeed they have become increasingly central in the typical Japanese diet. Japan is remarkable because—despite the late establishment of dairy production, the relative silence about the domestic importance of it, and the Othering of the industry and its people—in 2005 Japan accounted for 48.5 percent of the East Asian dairy market with Hokkaido prefecture alone accounting for nearly 50 percent of that number. In 2013, Japanese dairy companies Morinaga and Meiji Milk were ranked 12 and 20 globally in terms of holdings and production. Since this heyday period however, Japanese companies have rapidly lost market share, becoming an economic and political concern. By 2020, and at number 17, only Meiji Milk remined in the top 20 with Chinese, North American, and European companies increasing their share inside and outside Japan (BizVibe 2021). Beef and more recently the related dairy industry have become a battleground in terms of economic and food security. Both proved to be a major stumbling block in the 2015 Trans-Pacific Partnership (TPP) trade talks (though they went ahead without the US in 2018). And, as Canada, New Zealand, and Australia are all key players in the dairy industry and China is a quickly expanding market and producer, it will likely be a future issue in international trade negotiations for Japan related to both economic and food security (Obe 2018). Moreover, dairy markets are extremely volatile, compounded by Japan's top-heavy distribution and production systems; indeed, Japan went from a shortage of dairy, notably butter, "crisis" in 2015 (Nikkei Asia 2016) to an overabundance of dairy "crisis" in 2021 (Firstpost 2021).

A History of Japanese Beef Cattle

Although cows are likely not central to the image most people hold of traditional or even contemporary Japan, the history of the relationship between human and bovine in the region is longer than many people may imagine. While it is common to associate Japan with sushi or green tea, calligraphy or Buddhism, in fact the practice of keeping cows far predates the importation and introduction of these and many other well-known "Japanese" practices. Japan's premodern borrowings from the Korean Paekche and Silla (676–918 CE) Kingdoms and Han (206 BCE–220 CE), Sui (581–618 CE), and T'ang (618–907 CE) Chinese dynasties are too numerous to enumerate in any single book. Yet, any discussion of animal domestication or "livestock," even with an eye cast to the modern era alone, must reference the initial impact that these neighboring nations had in relation to the development of animal husbandry and consumption in Japan.

One could accurately say that cows were in Japan before people described as "Japanese" were. Settlers from China introduced cattle and horses on southern Honshu in the early Yayoi period (400 BCE–250 CE). Interestingly, archaeological findings suggest that the initial introduction of these animals was not for use as food. Their importation was linked to the need for their large bones as early Japanese (perhaps better thought of as proto-Japanese) placed great faith in oracle bones and cattle were used for this purpose. Thus, the importation and domestication of the first cattle evidenced by religious or ritual practices was to provide existential security and predict the fates of local elites. But beyond supplying bones, they were initially used as draft animals, as a means of traction to both produce and transport food.

There are some recorded incidents of religious sacrifice and consumption of these animals practiced by peasants at the start of the rice cultivation season during Yayoi times (Ishige 2001, 55). However, these were rituals at annual celebrations and do not reflect a habitual mode of sustenance for the early Japanese. In a similar sense, the Ainu people domesticated bear, and while the animal was consumed after it was sacrificed, the main focus was a form of religious ritual (*iyomante*) and not primarily a form of nourishment. In short, this early link between human and bovine was a commensal or interdependent one; the perspective of human or bovine "work to eat and eat to work" would sum it up. In fact, the Yayoi people strove for relationships of human–nonhuman symbiosis. For example, they also developed a system that ingeniously combined agriculture and fishing, whereby "domesticated" fish lived in and so fertilized the wet rice paddies. The Yayoi occasionally hunted wild game such as boar, still keenly hunted by some people and plentiful in mountainous Honshu (Knight 2003; Pflugfelder and Walker 2005). However, they had no history as organized pastoralists before the introduction of the practice from the Continent. In terms of human–animal relations, Japan's indigenous and eclectic matrix of spiritual beliefs, loosely organized under the rubric of Shinto, contains few examples of animal sacrifice. On the other hand, there is a well-documented history of animal anthropomorphism and deification in the form of shape-shifting foxes or money-attracting cats for example. And, though human and nonhuman animal relations are at the root of many contemporary folk practices (Seki 1963), Shinto's emphasis on *kegare* (ritual purification) made the routine slaughter of animals an undesirable practice for the majority of the population (Nelson 2000).

Buddhism has also buttressed the relative lack of animal husbandry practices, notably of land mammals, geared toward consumption. Buddhism officially entered Japan in 552 CE, during the late Kofun period (250–710 CE), as a gift from the Paekche Kingdom under the guise of being a particularly potent form of practical court-protecting magic and less for any particular philosophical or ethical stance (Ama 2005; Reader and Tanabe 1998). It first flourished under the auspices of the Soga clan but soon after the introduction of Buddhism, continental cultural and religious practices were further reinforced when scores of Paekche loyalists fled proto-Korea to proto-Japan after their defeat by a Silla and Sui coalition. Despite the fall of the Soga in 645, the political influence of Mahayana Buddhism proliferated among Japan's elite, as did the Buddhist precept of *ahimsa* (nonharm). Accordingly, in 675 the Japanese emperor Tenmu declared "an outright ban on hunting . . . [certain fishing traps] . . . and a prohibition during the fourth through ninth months of the eating of beef, horse, dog, monkey, and chicken . . . on pain of execution" (Ishige 2001, 53).

In the Nara period (710–794) the Japanese court began to incorporate continental culture en masse from the T'ang Chinese, often by way of the Silla Kingdom on the Korean Peninsula. Numerous delegations were sent to the mainland to learn everything from language to methods of governance and many Silla and T'ang nobles were devoutly Buddhist and had converted to a vegetarian diet. Rural peasants in Japan, on the other hand, hunted and ate feral meat as well as aged draft animals like oxen. But as Buddhist notions of karma (notably rebirth) began to enter rural consciousness, numerous imperial decrees were also issued banning the consumption of four-legged animals. Thus, red meat–eating practices, even of ritual beef consumption, decreased. The majority of these largely coastal Japanese subsisted on a seafood and vegetable diet while infrequently consuming other forms of animal protein such as wild or domesticated fowl.

Throughout the Heian period (794–1192) hunting was discreetly carried on by the peasantry as was the eating of work-worn beasts of burden. The aversion to eating four-legged animals might be overestimated in earlier academic works, as recent archaeological evidence has uncovered the existence of wild boar hunts and, by the 1600s, domesticated pigs (Pflugfelder and Walker 2005). And for those in society's higher echelons, the consumption of beef for medicinal purposes, called *kusurigui*, was tolerated. Although tying the eating of flesh to therapy may simply have been a ruse for those with money who enjoyed the flavor of domesticated meat to indulge their wants, the official logic was that the consumption of beef cured vague illnesses, such as "weakness" or the disposition of a "delicate nature" (Ishige 2001, 58) and similar ideas were revisited in the Meiji period as detailed below.

In the thirteenth century, and certainly lacking a delicate nature, the Mongols conquered continental Asia and brought with them a long tradition of livestock keeping and eating. They introduced a "barbeque" meat-eating culture including, but not in any way limited to, beef. This culinary tradition has continued in Northeast Asia until the present day, most famously perhaps as Korean *kalbi* (ribs) and *bulgogi* (sliced beef). Although the Mongols made two attempts, first in 1274 and again in 1281, to invade Japan, typhoons or the *kamikaze* (divine winds) repelled them. The meat-loving invaders and their culinary ways stayed across the seas. However, the Mongols did push their way into present-day Sakhalin. And early inhabitants of northern Japan, reaching into Tohoku, ate domesticated animals such as pig, raised hunting dogs, and avidly hunted wild game.

During Japan's feudal period, from the Kamakura (1185–1333) on through to the late Tokugawa (1603–1868), indigenous adaptations of Buddhism developed that appealed to both the ruling military elite and the lay public. The rigid austerity and emphasis on praxis and experience, over and above the more esoteric ritual pursuits that proved alluring to Heian era nobles, made Zen Buddhism, an interpretation of Chinese Ch'an Buddhism, appealing to the pragmatic rough-and-ready new military rulers.[1] The Jodo Shu and Jodo Shin Shu schools (Pure Land and New Pure Land respectively) were forms of Buddhist devotional belief based on a doctrine of salvation and rebirth provided by Amida Buddha, who resided in a western heaven of light where the Buddha preached for eternity. The primary difference between them being the vison of their founders, Honen and his pupil Shinran, and the respective notions that salvation is worked out via the daily practice of reciting Amida Buddha's name or via submission to the saving grace of Amida. Combinations of forms of devotional Buddhism and magical folk practices appealed to the masses and this also bolstered resistance to habitual mammal consumption. Although hunting game, especially deer and wild boar, grew to be an increasingly popular sport for the minority elite of the *bakufu*, the life of the rural peasant ranged from precarious to dire and the majority of their diet was based on cereal crops such as millet and fish not mammals.

In addition to the religious aversions present in doctrines of karma and purity, the eating of mammal meat remained illegal for common people, and moreover the progressive increase in rice tax levies and decrees that commoners could not carry weapons further aided in curbing clandestine hunting. Indeed, there is some disagreement as to whether disarming peasants had more to do with an attempt to reduce the increasing rebellions or to keep the poor from killing livestock or hunting prized wild game (Vlastos 1986). In addition, a subcaste, known as the *eta*, the harbingers of today's *burakumin*, developed from the negative stigma attached to those who worked with animal by-products, such as leather, rendering them personae non grata and forcing them to live outside of Japanese settlements (Hankins 2014). The above was augmented by another basic political and economic condition: all land was owned by feudal lords who were keen to keep tax monies rolling in and to protect their hunting stock. This too kept would-be peasant hunters toiling in the fields despite the nation's numerous famines (Bix 1986; Walthall 1991). Rebellions during the reign of Tokugawa Tsunayoshi (1646–1709) were directly related to his edicts against the killing of animals (notably dogs as he was born in the year of the dog). While peasants were starving, dogs, in the hundreds, were kept in kennels on the outskirts of Edo and fed rice and fish.

Thus, Japan retained its particular form of religion, a syncretism of Buddhism and what was later to be called Shinto (Kasahara 2001) retaining a reluctance to consume mammal flesh without encountering the radical cultural fissure that Mongol domination, and their roasted meat-eating habits, had furnished on the mainland, in areas such as Korea. With a few elite exceptions, bovines were kept and utilized for traction alone, and only reluctantly was beef eaten. It was not until the modern period, and especially after Japan's defeat in the post–Second World War years, that beef was popularly considered (or affordable) as a food fit for daily consumption.

A History of Japanese Dairy Cattle

Similar to beef consumption and contrary to the popular belief that dairy has not been historically important in the Japanese diet, there are several precedents of dairy consumption in premodern Japan (Ashkenazi and Jacob 2000, 2003). During Nara-period imperial banquets, "'Chinese cakes' (tōgashi) and dairy products were served" (Ishige 2001, 48). Also, a type of milk butter, reduced to semi-solid form through boiling, called so (resembling Mongolian ulm) was produced on the advice of an early Heian court Chinese-born chief medical officer (Yamato no kusuri no omi). Indeed, by the middle of the tenth century the court possessed around 1,500 dairy cows for medicinal purposes (61–62). Hence, like beef, dairy products were associated with the promotion of health and the high culture of the Continent during the Heian period. By the thirteenth century however, many of the effete practices of the imperial court nobles were not embraced by the militaristic and pragmatic incoming Kamakura *bakufu* and, as a consequence, the influence of these health-inducing dairy products waned.

Despite the closed nation *sakoku* policies of the Tokugawa regime, dairy was again to return through a powerful foreign influence, this time not coming from Asia. After initial contact with European travelers, most notably the Portuguese, the *bakufu* viewed European nations and especially their Christian missions as a threat to the security of the country. The *bakufu* issued various edicts expelling, and then eventually executing, early missionaries and traders, with the Dutch being the lone exception to this general rule of xenophobic expulsion. Although unable to officially reside "in" Japan, they were able to reside "beside" Japan on a humanmade island called Dejima near present-day Nagasaki, Kyushu. The significance of this, in terms of dairy production, is twofold. First, the Dutch were, for over two hundred years, the official *bakufu* window to the European colonized world.[2] Through "Dutch learning," or *rangaku*, Japanese rulers were becoming increasingly aware that European nations had been making tremendous advancements, surpassing Japan in technologies including science, manufacturing, economics, nautical know-how, armaments, and medicine. The second, and closely related, point is that the Dutch had a long tradition of dairy production and a taste for beef. By 1727 the *shōgun* had imported milk cows and, under direction of Dutch physicians, *hakugyūraku* (white butter) was produced and consumed as a "scientifically proven" health tonic to combat tuberculosis and syphilis. And so, for the second time in Japanese history the health benefits of diary were promoted by powerful outsiders. As noted below, the modern period would again see the consumption of dairy products promoted, not just as an elite practice mimicking other elites but as a daily dietary element, and this was again brought about through powerful foreign influences.

Modern Beef and Dairy Consumption

Perhaps the food most associated with Japan today is sushi. However, *nigiri* sushi, the well-known vinegary rice ball with raw fish on top, was created in Edo by Hanaya Yohei around 1825. The first Japanese ground beef hamburger, the archetypal American fast food albeit morphed into *hamburg*, a European style dish, was introduced by one of Perry's Black Ship cooks to Japanese delegates in 1853. Thus, tellingly for what follows, both of these modern and quintessential "East meets West" creations emerge a mere generation apart in Japan. This culinary trivia punctuates a less than trivial fact; the Meiji period was a watershed era of change. It propelled a feudal and largely inward-looking nation into one that absorbed the technologies and cultures of other imperialist nations while it imposed its own culture through rapidly developing technological and military know-how on others. When the young emperor Meiji, purported by his supporters to be divine, took control through a protracted coup from below, Buddhism was equated with the "old guard," the defeated Tokugawa regime. The government's new rulers, ill-advisedly in retrospect, pulled regional administrative power from the Buddhist clerics and placed it in the hands of Shinto "clerics" who were utterly unprepared to wield it (Victoria 2001). At the same time, the emperor, the head of the now empowered Shinto religion, proclaimed that in order to have strong bodies like those from "the West," Japanese needed to alter official culinary proclamations and eat beef and drink milk (Watanabe 2019). A clear link can be seen here with *bunmei kaika* (civilization and enlightenment) as a new policy in a broader context of the Meiji period's *wakon yōsai* (Japanese Spirit/Western Techniques). That is the strategic importing of equipment and experts and the "nihonification" of these materials and knowledge to buttress the nation. The thought being that, in vogue, evolutionary, and "you are what you eat" terms, the rich protein and fat content found in dairy and beef produced strong people—a people with whom a modern nation could be built, a people who were up to the task of catching up to the rich nations of Europe and America. The idea was, in essence, that "eating rich" would produce the "desired riches" of the bodies and minds, and so, abilities of a fetishized West. This imperially sanctioned "eat-the-rich to be/beat the rich" promotion was, as noted below, better than any contemporary dairy board could muster. Common Japanese, who could afford to do so, began to increasingly consume beef and dairy—after all, with the imperial seal of approval, it was the proper Japanese thing to do.

At the same time, Japan's drive to import anything deemed modern was insatiable. Everything from armaments to automobiles, along with specialists of every stripe, were brought from America and Europe to Japan. This flow of foreign materials and talents included William Clark who came to Sapporo (then a town of a few hundred people) from the University of Massachusetts at Amherst in 1867. Clark established an animal husbandry program at what is now Japan's Hokkaido University, arguably the contemporary research core of Japan's, and certainly Hokkaido's, dairy industry. In short, American and European outsiders and expatriates, at the behest of the Kaitakushi, were responsible for the development and design of Hokkaido's first cattle, sheep, and dairy farms. Fujita (1994), Irish (2009), Maki (1996), Mason (2012), and Russell (2007) all provide fascinating histories of the prominent American agriculturalists who moved to and, in the case of Edwin Dunn, remained long-term in Hokkaido, that are beyond the pale of this chapter. The point emphasized here is that Japan zealously took up the eating of beef, and later dairy, inventing foods like *sukiyaki* (broiled beef) and copying the building of American-style cattle ranches and European-style dairies, and Hokkaido provided the ideal location for such novel experimentation. But this rapid modernization and the adoption of Western foods had its popular critics, such as Kanagaki Robun, the author of numerous satirical articles including "Eating Beef Stew While Cross Legged" (Ohnuki-Tierney 2002, 64–67). He feared that Japan was losing its identity by "eating up" (literally and figuratively) what came from the outside. One can surely draw similarities, as noted in what follows, between these Meiji period debates and contemporary concerns with Japanese identity, security, and food alongside contemporary commentary on the superiority of and idealized "Japanese" diet outlined in Assmann's "The Remaking of a National Cuisine: The Food Education Campaign in Japan" (2015), Cwiertka's *Modern Japanese Cuisine: Food, Power and National Identity* (2006), and Hansen's "Culturing and Agricultural Crisis in Hokkaido" (2014a), for example.

After colonizing Hokkaido in 1869, annexing Okinawa in 1879, and defeating China in 1895 and Russia in 1905, the country's fascination with all things Western slowed. Japan became more self-confident and progressively involved in its own projects of empire building with a top-down cultivated vision of Japan as the divinely governed liberator of Asia. This led to the annexation of Korea in 1910, the occupation of Manchuria in 1932, followed by other occupations throughout the South Pacific from 1937 to 1945. This self-assurance and aggression led to Japan's attacking Pearl Harbor, entrance into the Second World War, and the nation's eventual surrender in 1945.

Among other changes, the Allied Occupation from 1945 to 1952 had the unintentional consequence of transforming Japanese eating trends radically. First, under the largely American led Occupation, primary school was made mandatory, as were school meal programs serving *healthy* food. And healthy by US standards meant, much as the Meiji emperor earlier decreed, rich foods modeled on a rich nation. For Japanese children it became, as it remains for most today, milk served every lunchtime and the occasional serving of beef. From this point on in Japanese history, it seems reasonable to assume that the introduction to beef and dairy at a young age served to open the Japanese palate to beef and dairy later in life.

After the Occupation, with a more liberal constitution in hand and heavily subsidized by the USA, Japan began to rebuild itself. As soon as the early 1950s, the economy was on its way up as the Korean War brought increased affluence through the manufacture of armaments and services for the American military. This increased foreign investment and cash flow, along with the steady flow of American service personnel in and out of Japanese society, brought about an upsurge in contemporary American trends and a second shift in dietary patterns. The Meiji era *mirukuhōru* (milk halls) were being superseded by "contemporary" *kissaten* (coffee shops). Both had existed across Japan long before the war, and even today quieter and quainter *kissaten* can be found that always serve a snack with coffee—often a Danish-style butter cookie. However, after the war, many such shops began to serve milkshakes, soft drinks, cakes, and American-style sandwiches. These establishments began to pop up everywhere, and by the mid-1950s they offered teens a place to "hang out," a place where they could listen to music, often costly jazz records, and meet with friends (Morasukii 2017) while enjoying their "foreign" (though surely domestic) beef and dairy foods of choice. They were the portents of today's popular Japanese family restaurants such as Gusto or Royal Host—restaurants that sell American-style fast foods—fries, burgers, and "pizza" reworked with the tastes of a (presumed) generic Japanese consumer in mind. In essence, these shops became a place to eat "rich" food—imbibing high calories and the cultural capital of wealthy America—with new riches earned in an economy fueled largely by the booming US economy and that country's consumption of Japanese-made goods.

Indeed, between the mid-1950s and the early 1970s, the Japanese economy grew at an amazing 10 percent annually (Goto and Odagiri 1997, 36–43). By the 1960s, Japan was the darling of America's Asian policy, spurred on not only by the procurement of weapons and services starting with the Korean War (1950–1953) and continuing with the Vietnam War (1954–1975) but as a beacon of Asian democracy and a regional bulwark against the "red menace" of China and the USSR. Riding on the coat tails of the American Dream, Japan was able to produce cheap consumer durables—scooters, refrigerators, and stereos—for sale abroad. When the profit from those sales returned to Japan it instigated similar trends of upward mobility, urban migration, and mass consumption in

Japan much as it had in the postwar US. Japan served as a willing portal for American tastes and trends into Asia (Guarné and Hansen 2018, 3–6). A third dietary influence was hosting the 1964 Olympics and the 1970 World Expo, which introduced people and cuisine from around the world to many in Japan. As had occurred during the Korean War, the conflict in Vietnam brought much needed foreign investment to Japan. In sum, the insecurity of Asia, in part left by Japan's own postwar withdrawal, led to the increasing changes in the macro security of Japan in military, political, and financial terms.

Moreover, throughout the postwar period the USA sold technology cheaply to Japan, allowing the nation to develop a thriving and cutting-edge research and development culture. In 1971, slightly less aggressively than in 1853 perhaps, a final major culinary influence arrived. The "real" American burger was promoted in Tokyo, and soon after McDonald's "Golden Arches" had arrived, local and global competition appeared (Ohnuki-Tierney 2006). The 1980s saw Japan become an economic superpower and, more than ever before, "foreign" foods flooded Japan. From Denny's to TGI Friday's, 7-Eleven to Mister Donut, food chains entered Japan, simultaneously modifying and being modified to Japanese tastes; often this modification involved making portions smaller in size, lower in spicy flavors, and higher in fat.

Today, many Japanese still feel that, insofar as dairy and beef are concerned, the richer the better. Japanese consumers buy buttered fatty steak, whole-fat cheese, and, until recently, finding milk under 3.7 percent fat content was a near impossibility. Today low-fat milk is always significantly cheaper yet less popular, due to the equation rich equals rich: fat equals high quality. This image has recently become a problem as globalization has taken a firmer hold in Japan. In short, to the majority of Japanese, dairy is delicious mainly because of its richness, not only in terms of being a luxury product or through the hazy allure of connections to foreign places as in the past, but simply, in terms of its fat content.

During the Occupation high calorie foods were clearly a necessity for a defeated and undernourished nation, but contemporary Japan has become rich itself. It has been transformed into the world's third largest economy and a postindustrial, civil democratic nation with similar problems to other such countries, one of them being an increasingly overweight population. While fat spells and sells flavor in Japan, unfortunately for the Japanese dairy industry, fat also promotes obesity and other weight-related health concerns, and many Japanese, like their counterparts in highly developed and high calorie consuming nations, are becoming more health conscious. While "eating rich" has not completely lost its attraction, Japanese are consuming less domestic dairy than in the past. And, unlike North America or Europe, low-fat dairy has been slow to catch on, partly for the aforementioned reasons, but also due to the inflexibility and ineptitude of the top-down Japanese corporate structures, a point expanded upon in following chapters.

Conclusion

While this chapter has outlined the entwined history of the beef and dairy industry in Japan and its relationship with broad social changes, the influence of other nations, and the confluence of these influences in terms of security. The following chapter focuses on the structure of the industry in Japan and discusses how and why Japanese people have been, at least until the time of writing, willing to pay dearly for the perception of the safety and security of Japan's food supply. In Hokkaido, as elsewhere in Japan, the agricultural industry has been closely managed from the top down, for example, through agencies from the former Kaitakushi discussed in the previous chapter to contemporary governmental wings such as MAFF (Ministry of Agriculture, Forestry and Fisheries), Nōrin-suisanshō, JA (National Japan Agriculture Cooperative) regionally called Nōkyō or JA Zenchu, including a host of linkages with national insurance and banking, or purely regional cooperatives like Hokkaido's Hokuren. Through this governance, a "cooperative" macro level official discourse promoting security and safety is produced and promoted through government, industry, and the media (Hansen 2014a; Mulgan 2006, 2015a, 2015b, 2017). However, for reasons to be underscored, such policies affect the dairy industry due to its marginalization more than other agriculture industries, most notably the production and consumption of rice.

Chapter Four

Problems Protecting the Japanese Dairy Industry

Introduction

With a declining rural population, high and ever-increasing production costs, and the need for extensive and expensive infrastructure and maintenance, especially in Hokkaido given its the topography and climate, nobody debates *if* the Japanese government, regional and national, plays a central role in agriculture. "[In] Japan's agricultural sector, the question of whether the state intervenes to determine economic outcomes is not contested. Agriculture is the most 'intervened' industry in Japan" (Mulgan 2006, 1). This intervention, usually framed as the need for a secure food supply couched in the lack of national self-sufficiency, is prevalent locally, nationally, and internationally, as subsequent chapters will underscore. But by way of introduction, the example of the Japanese government's intervention in the wake of the North American 2003 Bovine Spongiform Encephalopathy (BSE) crisis and its resolution is a telling case study. The crisis, or the creation of this crisis more aptly put, halted the trade of beef from the North American Free Trade Agreement (NAFTA) countries—Canada, the United States, and Mexico—to Japan. And though this particular crisis has passed, it highlights the present condition of the Japanese beef and dairy industry since the late 1990s. They are industries both of the frontier and at the frontier of state and prefectural relations. These actively Othered industries remain in a constant state of tension with insecurity still on the horizon at the time of writing in 2019–2022.

A Case Study: Creating Constant Crisis

In April of 2003 a Canadian beef cow from Alberta died and was diagnosed postmortem with BSE, a neurodegenerative disease. It was, in fact, quite unusual that the case of a "downer" cow was inspected at all. A downer cow is an animal unable to stand on its own due to being injured or ill and the usual practice was, certainly at the time and in industrial operations dependent for their survival on efficiency, to kill the cow and bury it. In response to the report of a single BSE-infected cow, Japan's ruling LDP (Liberal Democratic Party) government quickly suspended all imports of beef or beef products from NAFTA nations. Japanese trade bloc countries such as Korea soon followed their lead. Sidestepping the numerous political issues that arose within NAFTA itself,[1] in Japan the issue was, *on the surface*, presented as a simple one: food safety and food security was the expressed prime concern of the ruling party. This rhetoric was "on the surface" because the issue was the tip of a larger security iceberg. Food safety and security, as explained below, are intimately linked with a long history of economic, political, military, and environmental security issues in Japan. Thus, despite nine incidents of domestic BSE in Japan to that date; despite numerous Japanese and North American government, industry, and independent scientific studies underscoring the impossibility of contracting "mad cow" disease or the related human variant Creutzfeldt-Jakob disease (vCJD) from many of the banned products; despite beef shortages, price hikes, and complaints from consumers and massive beef-utilizing conglomerates within Japan like Yoshinoya, a nationwide beef bowl chain store; and finally, despite pressure from the World Trade Organization (WTO) outlining that Japan was in breach of the General Agreement on Trades and Tariffs (GATT), membership obligations, and moreover, under the threat of legal sanctions and/or embargos: Japan remained defiant. To Japanese officials (at least the official line of the officials) the bans were *not* a trade issue. They were a food safety and security issue. LDP officials remained clear in their rhetoric. The government was actively protecting Japanese consumers and national borders from a foreign biological threat. Unwaveringly, Japan was not open for business to NAFTA beef.

There is, of course, no coincidence in the LDP taking this hard line. It has traditionally been heavily supported by Japan's rural electorate. The Ministry of Agriculture, Forestry and Fisheries (MAFF), the government's main agricultural policy branch, was quick to coalesce with the official party line. Tellingly, the opening chapter of MAFF's 2004 *Annual Report on Food, Agriculture and Rural Areas in Japan* ran with the title "Ensuring Food Safety and Consumer Confidence: Establishing a System for a Stable Food Supply" (MAFF 2004) in direct response to the beef issue and concerns over Japan's ever-declining rate of food self-sufficiency. While domestic food safety scares and scandals are common, they are quickly played down and vanish with clever marketing. Ones involving international products linger and receive greater media focus. This paradox is at the heart of government food policy and it relates to securing frontiers as much as food. On the one hand, the government claims it must improve its margin of self-sufficiency to protect Japanese farms and jobs from an external threat, cheaper foreign imports. On the other hand, the government must be seen as protecting Japanese health from foreign foods and the presumably lax standards they are produced under. Side by side, both ideas have gained both popular and political support in Japan, for example, in the ongoing Fūdo Akushon Nippon (Food Action Nippon) campaign (MAFF 2020). In this case, the BSE cow provided the perfect foreign bugaboo, a symbol to rally agricultural protectionism for the LDP with the claim that Japanese food was safer and healthier because, simply, it's Japanese.

Given this series of events in 2003, beef and dairy producers in North America were furious at Japan's seeming "ignorance of science." Japanese producers were relieved as they were temporarily freed from the competition of North America's cheaper imports. And in Australia and New Zealand producers were elated by these newly open markets in Japan. Bitter trade negotiations continued between NAFTA and Japan for three years with Japan constantly stalling and balking at decisions. But safety and security are, of course, not only agricultural issues. The issue culminated with US officials' new linking of military security and trade issues through hinting that all US troops might be taken out of Okinawa if beef did not start flowing over borders, a move which would leave Japan with no *legal* military (beyond its Self-Defense Forces, a military in all but name due to Article 9 of the Japanese Constitution) amid fraught histories and precarious relations with all its immediate neighbors: South Korea, North Korea, Russia, and China. Indeed, in the Japanese media the two issues "ping-ponged" throughout my first fieldwork year (2005–2006). Stories about the pulling of NAFTA beef out of the Japanese market would be followed or preceded by stories related to the consideration of the US pulling troops out of Okinawa—raising emotions, unbridled jingoism, and rhetoric linking food, economic, and military security on both sides.

The fact that Japan engages in national and national*ist* agricultural protectionism is not interesting in itself. America, Canada, and many member states of the EU (through Codex, for example) engage in trade that is far from "free" as well (MacLachlan 2001, 326–330; Millstone and van Zwanenberg 2003; Pawlick 2006). Nationalist agricultural protectionism is found in nearly every nation, developed and developing (Pollan 2006; Pottier 1999). And often, as in Japan past and present, it is linked with insecurities brought on after military conflict, perceived isolation, or associated with specific ideas linking a type of food to national identity (Draper and Green 2003; Humphrey 2002; Ichijo, Venetia, and Ranta 2019) such as protecting French beans from "invading" bean types (Freidberg 2004). In short, these are all common concerns and actions outside of Japan. However, what *is* particular about food security issues in Japan is the narrowness and zeal with which the Japanese government protects and promotes national agriculture and the domestic food industry, and the public leeway they are given to do so, *as if* a given crisis was an eminent threat when, very clearly to all involved, there is no existing crisis. Seen, for example, in calling a lack of butter a national crisis (Hansen 2014a). Or alternatively, acting *as if* there is no crisis, when one clearly does exist. Seen, for example, when much of a population's food supply is exposed to high levels of radioactive contamination (Sternsdorff-Cisterna 2019).

For decades rice production has essentially been a part-time occupation, treated much like a hobby by many farmers often producing just enough rice for their family or to give as gifts (Jussaume 1991). Yet the government will protect this form of agriculture, ignoring tangible and devastating risks such as threats of an American military pull-out or trade embargos. This is combined with the popular daily media emphasis, and discourse, on the latest *shokuryō mondai* (food stuff problem) and its *kiki* (crisis or danger). This, I suggest, underscores a particular polysemic relationship between security as noun (prefaced by, for example, economic or food) and security as a value or verb (ensuring safety, predictability, or fixity) that is popularly expressed at a grassroots level with an uncommon passion, certainly post 3/11. While Americans may want to save the heartland, the UK may promote "Buying British," and Albertans may sport a number of United Farmers Association "Back Your Beef" bumper stickers—none of the above seem as willing (or as seemingly "vulnerable" to the perceived risks) to destroy trade relations or unquestioningly pay exorbitant prices. Again, the BSE issue highlights all these points, as does the end of that particular crisis.

In October of 2006 NAFTA beef trade with Japan resumed with much fanfare. In front of the US embassy a flock of pigeon-toed young Japanese women in tight-fitting red, white, and blue low-cut jumpsuits waved silver pom-poms giggling and chanting, "Yakiniku daisuki" (I love barbeque beef). Across Japan McDonald's advertisements had to be changed. This beacon of Americana opted to no longer advertise that *anzen = zero yen* (safety or security = no charge) because, ironically, the American pop-culture icon no longer served Australian beef alone. By the end of the dispute, it was clear to all involved (and to anyone still following the issue in the news three years on) that first and foremost, this was an economic and political security issue with identity construction Othering (of an "us" and "them" variety) playing a key role in Japan. The actual physical safety of Japanese consumers was, in fact, minimal and far from the equation on either side of the Pacific. Knowing the malleability of the crisis, the US had handily turned it into a military issue. Yet, despite the lack of any attestable health risk to consumers, this issue remained promoted by the government, filtered via media, and earnestly viewed by many in Japan as a food security and safety issue: an issue clearly liked to health, but as clearly hitched to ideas regarding Japanese identity. Exactly whose security and safety were at stake in this crisis? Was it the safety and security of the consumer, the government, or the farmers and employees in Japan's many redundant agricultural cooperatives, all of the above, or perhaps the Japanese nation itself?

At the national level one way that protectionism is fostered is through product labeling laws. And Japan has some of the world's most protectionist laws regarding food product imports and labeling (Sternsdorff-Cisterna 2019). Underlying this in the context of Japan are notions of self and other (Lebra 1976, 1985), domestic and foreign (Davies and Ikeno 2002), or *soto* (outside) and *uchi* (inside) (Nakane 1973). In one form or another, numerous studies of Japanese culture have taken as a perennial theme the lateral concepts of insider and outsider, proclaiming the Japanese to be insecure and insular at one pole or xenophobic and racist at the other, with more nuanced comparisons located in between. However, I contend that one way to view the seemingly paradoxical nature of Japanese nationalist agricultural discourse—that is, the ability to accept or reject science as political convenience dictates, or to ignore the voices of the electorate for their own safety (with either heavy-handed approach largely unquestioned by the public)—lies not through examining these many possible parallel dialectics but in looking at the vertical discourses of top-down power relations. Where does information come from and what can and average citizen do with it in Japan?

Nakane Chie's classic notion of "vertical stratification" is a useful starting point to think through such issues (1973, 90), by focusing not only on corporate or family structure but on where public information comes from and how it is filtered to the population. Again, as with agricultural protectionism, there is nothing particular about nations pursuing national interests while disregarding "fact" and using the gatekeeping role of the media it sanctions (Chomsky and Herman 1988). But the mass media alongside public education plays an extraordinarily homogenizing role in Japan. As detailed in what follows, I argue that the reason why science or dissenting opinion can be ignored is related to the end goal: to protect "agricultural regimes" at the top of society (Mulgan 2006). Again, the question is not *if* the ways and products of "the Other" are seen as an ever-questionable security concern, nor is it a question of *if* the government manipulates agricultural industries; as the above history and the examples of the BSE crisis and labeling emphasize, these points are obvious. The questions are, rather: Why is it able to intervene so unchallenged? And how does it actually intervene? The answers to "why" and "how" are intimately linked in a top-down discourse. Broadly put, "why" is related to function and "how" is related to structure, but the two do neatly dovetail.

Why Does the Government Intervene?

"Why?" is the more empiric and simple to answer question, though for the Japanese food producer it is likely the hardest to swallow. Japanese agriculture, and the Japanese beef and dairy industries specifically, as detailed below, simply cannot compete on a global, level, open, or free-trade playing field. These industries need significant structural support from above in the form of import tariffs, production cost subsidies, and considerable nationalist rhetoric and propaganda directed at consumers to spend more for less, or much of the commercial agricultural industry would quickly cease to exist. At the least radical changes would need to be implemented for it to continue, changes that the second Abe administration tried, for better or worse being another issue, early on in its final term (2012–2020) (Mulgan 2015a, 2015b).

There have been, for example, many studies on how and why the Japanese government protects domestic rice markets through subsidies, tariffs, and propaganda (Blaxell 2009; Jentzsch 2021; Moore 1990; Odagiri 2021; Ohnuki-Tierney 1993, 2002). This research is significant in terms of dairy production as well. This is because Japan is self-sufficient in producing only two staple food commodities: rice, for which the Japanese consumer pays up to seven times the world market price, and drinking milk, for which Japanese consumers pay approximately two and a half times the world market price. The key point here, as will be elaborated upon below, are the different prices, domestic and international, and differing tariffs for drinking milk and product milk. Liberalization has recently opened Japanese markets with the EU in terms product milk (for example, cheeses or whey products) but the LDP has managed to negotiate and maintain a domestic monopoly over drinking milk (Meyer 2018). Shockingly, even with these ratios of exchange, the costs of these two foodstuffs are capped because they are deemed essential products, thus disabling market prices to even determine costs *within* Japan. That is, both milk and rice retain inflated world market prices despite the substantial tariffs and subsidies actually designed to bring costs down!

Hokkaido produces a little over 50 percent of Japan's raw milk (MAFF 2017) and is far and away the most important dairy production prefecture in Japan. However, due to central and eastern Hokkaido's relative isolation from major population centers, leading to a combination of high transport costs and endangering the profit margins of smaller southern farmers, only around 15 percent of the prefecture's milk is used as "drinking" milk; 85 percent is used for product manufacturing. This relates directly to the prices milk producers are paid as the drinking milk price is set up to 33 percent higher than the product milk price. Importantly, Hokkaido producers, under strict regulations and regional cooperative quotas, are paid far less for the same output of milk than other areas of Japan. Added to this deflated price, there are the extra costs associated with production in Hokkaido, such as the need for heated milking parlors (an essential system detailed later in this book), transportation distances, or even on farm snow removal. Despite these costs and limitations on milk use, within Japan Hokkaido remains the largest producer of drinking milk, far beyond the capacity of the population of the prefecture to consume. And it simply dwarfs any other agricultural region in the output of milk utilized for dairy products (MAFF 2017). Moreover, as noted at the end of this chapter, the dairy cow plays a central role in the production of images for the tourist industry in Hokkaido—pastoral romance and nostalgia, though largely imagined, is abundant. In short, in Tokachi, dairy production, related industries, and related images are key features of the real and symbolic economy of the region.

Though direct comparisons of diary producing regions (not national averages) are rare, one study directly compares the advantages of the dairy industry in New Zealand to Hokkaido's disadvantages (Ozawa et al. 2005). In New Zealand, production costs for raw milk are 29 percent of Hokkaido's and herd size in New Zealand is roughly four and a half times as large. The climate and landscape of New Zealand allows for year-round grazing, self-sustainable feed production on farms, and a minimum of animal housing facilities. In Hokkaido feed alone accounts for 82 percent of production costs, costs that continue to rise while the price of milk is kept artificially low within Japan. Though dated, the premise remains the same, other studies focus on comparing Japan as a whole with the rest of Asia, the USA, the EU, and Australia and while statistics vary the message is clear (Beghin 2006; Obara et al. 2005). "The order of competitiveness of Asian dairy economies from least to most competitive is Japan, Korea, South East Asia, South Asia, China and India. . . . [With trade liberalization] . . . net imports would increase most of which [in Asia] would come from Australia and New Zealand" (Peng and Cox 2005, 20).

This became a larger issue case with Japanese markets being open to EU dairy products through the Economic Partnership Agreement (EPA) in July of 2018 largely dropping tariffs on many dairy products such as incoming cheeses. It gets worse for Japan. In India and China, the market for domestic dairy products in both, and beef in the latter, are increasing in terms of production and consumption; in sum they are becoming more competitive producers domestically, while in Japan the demand for dairy has remained more or less stable. So, the consumption of drinking milk has slightly decreased while the consumption of imported and domestic dairy products and beef has increased. Taking stagnancy, or worse and more likely, a decline in domestic market shares into account (while adding the aforementioned topographical factors that cannot be easily altered such as the low density of arable land, land suitable for building on, or the climate) and considering the high cost of labor, building, equipment, feed, and transportation, it is abundantly clear that the dairy industry in Japan, and even in Hokkaido, has not been able to survive without significant intervention and this situation is unlikely to improve. Thus, dairy subsidies and import tariffs are a safety and security issue to be sure, but this clearly extends far beyond simply considering the well-being of consumers. The food security rhetoric and intervention support the continuation of the precarious livelihoods of dairy and beef farmers, product producers, as well as the extensive entwined network of governmental bodies from MAFF to JA to regional cooperatives that cater to agriculture in Japan.

Thus, "why" the government intervenes in Japanese agricultural production is a reasonably straightforward issue. It enables the multilevel economic survival for agriculturalists as much as the domestic food business and the levels of government that manage it. It is not just the perception of public safety and food security that matters, the Japanese government *demands* that Japan strengthen its borders, extending political and economic frontiers, in order to be self-sufficient (seemingly at whatever cost), secure in its ability to produce food. Toward this end, it protects Japanese food producers and government agencies at the expense of international relations and spiking consumer costs. Japanese consumers, as noted below, tolerate this for reasons past and present, logical and illogical, personal and popularized. Much of their information about food security issues is filtered via the mass media. In effect they are told, and sold, the idea that if Japan intends to maintain a domestic agriculture industry it presently has no choice but to continue its top-down protectionist agenda. So why do consumers so readily, eagerly even, buy into this nationalist food propaganda? Japan has a history of security and Othering concerns that make this intervention more palatable than it might otherwise be.

There are frequently vocalized reasons why the Japanese public is willing to pay more for less. Japan has a long history of famines. Japan is an island nation with few natural resources and generally poor farming conditions, at least in terms of arable land to population ratio, and these numbers are ever in decline (Matanle, Rausch, with the Shrinking Regions Research Group 2011; Mock 2014). Severe food shortages were experienced during and after the Second World War and general resource shortages during the world energy crisis in 1973 and 1980. More to the point, these events happened within the lifetimes of many of my informants, certainly within family members' lifetimes. In short, food security and scarcity issues are not distant history and the notion of Japan as misunderstood, vulnerable, and an isolated victim is a common media trope— notably during the August 6th A-bomb memorial services in Hiroshima televised yearly on NHK (Pollack 1992). Linked to this popular sentiment of a victimized and socioculturally unique (and distinct) people is the rather dark irony that the archipelago of Japan is surrounded by nations that it formerly colonized (Oguma 2002). As such, Japan has disputes over land, trade, human rights, and reparations with South Korea and China. Such conflictual relations are worsened by the lack of what many in these nations consider to be an acceptable Japanese war atrocity apology alongside their own growing power and rising nationalist sentiment. There is constant North Korean posturing, along with heated debates over former kidnappings and the repatriation of human remains. There are North Korean missile tests over Japanese airspace (some landing off the coast of Hokkaido and killing Japanese fishermen during my fieldwork). Finally, Japan has remained officially at war with Russia since 1945 over the Kuril Islands. In sum, Japan has tangible reasons to worry about its regional security, including a secure food supply. Popular media voraciously reports on all these issues whenever they arise, portraying them from an unapologetically and uncritical right-wing angle; Japan is always right and usually the victim in contemporary regional conflicts (Stockwin 2017). In short, Northeast Asia is a politically insecure area, and Japan has historical enemies and animosities with growing regional powers and, as noted above, recent frictions with its main protector, the US. Thus, the "isolated and resource-poor island" rhetoric is a reliable and powerful one for conservative politicians and it is a perspective easily supported with many historical examples to exacerbate such anxieties in the present.

But beyond the historic and potential political, economic, and military unease, there have in fact also been numerous food safety scares. Some have been major, such as the 1995 seafood *E. coli* 0157 outbreak; the 2001 "Snow Brand" incident, in which the sale of various contaminated dairy products resulted in over fourteen thousand people falling ill; the 2006 "Meat Hope" beef scam whereby a variety of meats were mislabeled beef; and the 2007 "Shiroi Koibito" (white beloved) cookie scandal over misrepresentation of best-sell-by dates with officials acknowledging this practice had been going on for ten years before anyone got sick (Kyodo News 2002, 2007). None of this is lost on Japanese popular consciousness. Every year a religious leader in Japan is asked to produce a *kanji* (a Chinese character) that they feel best represents the year. At the end of 2007 the kanji *nise* (fake or false) was chosen, in large part due to food safety and labeling scandals (Funabashi 2007). And the list of such common infractions continues, from pesticide-tainted frozen food produced by Maruha Nichiro in 2013 to plastic fragments in Coco's curry cutlets in 2016. In short, domestic food security issues are a perennial theme in Japanese popular media.

Though Japanese distrust foreign food safety regulations, domestic ones do not seem particularly effective either; mistrust over domestic foods is a central common issue in post-Fukushima Japan (Sternsdorff-Cisterna 2019). This is because inside Japan cover-ups are the common first response to a domestic food crisis. All of the above scandals were accompanied by attempted cover-ups. When caught, tried, and accused—as there are rarely open admissions of wrongdoing from the start—the result is generally a staged, deep bow performed by the company president and other elites in a wash of clicking cameras and media limelight. Then there follows the predictable political apology: First, the usual claim is that "we didn't know that (whatever infringement committed by those under them in the company structure) was either wrong or had occurred" (with the obvious cover-up attempts before getting caught often sidestepped). This is followed by "now we see our wrongdoing" and the requisite "mōshi wake gozaimasen" (a polite apologetic excuse, literally, "there is no excuse"). Finally, amid more bowing, the apology is likely capped off with a "we will *gambatte* (do our utmost) to set it right" followed by a slap on the wrist, usually in the form of a fine and nominal, temporary salary cuts. Weeks later, with some media promotion, these formerly "dangerous" products, stand-ins for the latest food crisis, are often back on the shelves with consumption resuming as normal. But the issues of insecurity and uncertainty remain. Japanese people are not being hoodwinked, but deep emotive chords are being played in the presentation of these issues.

In interviews and informal discussions with countless Japanese people about food security over the years—teachers, farmers, and random people on trains alongside Japanese friends inside and outside Japan—a common claim is that food product safety is a ubiquitous problem in Japan. But significantly, this proclamation is nearly always followed up with Japan being described as an isolated island country that must endeavor to produce its own food supply. The obvious question, to an outsider, stemming from the above information is why produce overpriced food—produced at an incredible net loss—if you can produce other manufactured products, as the globe's third largest economy, that enable you to buy "safe" food more cheaply? The Japanese consumer could pick nearly any country deemed to have a safe food supply and be economically ahead by importing even more of their food. Why erect borders when crossing them would be a better option?

One common response is that food produced in Japan tastes better because it is grown in Japan. Again, this brand of "nationalist" logic is difficult to understand in nonsymbolic or not purely aesthetic terms (Ohnuki-Tierney 1993). First, it is notoriously hard to define flavor, let alone the "best." But such classification is commonplace in Japan: Aomori has the best apples, Niigata the best rice, Hokkaido dairy is tops, and on it goes. Second, it is also reasoned by many Japanese—whether from the historical factors, the media circus of ongoing food scandals, or anxieties about the nation's political, military, and economic future, noted above—that Japan *must* worry about food security and food safety. Thus, despite the countless internal breaches of food security and safety, many Japanese still prefer to have faith in themselves and provincial systems of classification.

I asked numerous coworkers at the dairy farm I was employed by what they thought about the future possibility of drinking milk being imported from the expanding market in China. Wada-san laughed and replied, "Muri da yo!" (That's impossible!).

"Why? Because of the shipping costs or know-how?" I queried.

"Iya. Iya. Iie!" (an ardent no), he replied, "Abunain dakara, chūgoku wa kitanai" (Because it is dangerous, China is dirty).

He explained that Japanese would never buy milk from outside of Japan even if it was cheaper, underscoring his faith in the quality of Japanese products and loyalty to products "made in Japan." But he was a farm owner and pretty well off I reasoned. He could afford to buy whatever foods he wanted. I asked another coworker, scraping by on the same tight budget as me. He said that he refused to buy food in 100 Yen stores.

"Why?" I asked.

"Zenbu wa chūgoku ga tsukutteiru kara. Abunai yo!" (It's all made in China—it's dangerous I tell you!), was his emphatic reply.

I immediately responded: "I eat food from 100 Yen shops, look at me." He poked my belly and I told him that I did not buy 100 Yen beer. We laughed, and I dropped the subject. However, a few days later at his apartment and unprompted, he recalled our conversation. He showed me a website with compelling photos: a brown lawn being painted green in front of a portrait of Mao, a dried-out river with people collecting thousands of dead fish—presumably to sell or eat, and a two-headed fish in a tin. This was: "Nihonjin no chūgoku no imēji" (the Japanese image of China) and "Kono pēji wa minna wakaru. Chūgoku wa totemo kowai" (Everyone knows this web page. China is scary). Dramatic and overly inclusive perhaps, his opinion on this topic was direct and clear. The danger of Chinese pollution, the danger of Chinese people, and the unsuitability of Chinese products, along with the possible threat to Japan and my health were points that he wanted me to consider seriously and these were worries he felt were widely shared among his compatriots.

In short, most of the Japanese that I have interviewed or informally chatted with are concerned about the fragility and insecurity of the nation's food system through historical, geographic, economic, and political modes of thinking that do not concern the lion's share of North American or European consumers as deeply. And the media and government play an essential, and self-serving, role in filtering this information to would-be consumers. Of course, there are those in the world for whom food security is an immediate and daily life and death concern (Runge et al. 2003). Yet, this is clearly not the case for the majority of even the most marginal of Japanese, though poverty, notably among the elderly and children, is a growing problem (Hansen 2020a; Kimura 2018). There are of course "foodies"—those who engage in "slow food" movements, organic farming, or promote regional diets for personal health and the good of the environment—however, these movements are not shared as a discourse by the majority of Japanese consumers (Assmann 2015; Klien 2020; Rosenberger 2016). But sidestepping the food security concerns of both the extremely desperate and the culinary bourgeois, food is taken as a serious business for many people in Japan. "You are what you eat" takes on an entirely different significance related to financial, personal, and ecological notions of macro and ontological security. Thus, "why" the government intervenes and why this intervention is tolerated—even defended and promoted—by Japanese consumers is clear. And this is intimately related to the more complex question of "how" the government achieves its protectionist agenda filtered to people through popular media.

How Does the Government Intervene?

As noted in the previous section, in a classic anthropological account of Japanese social structure Nakane discusses the top-down vertical hierarchy of Japanese society, particularly in terms of family, corporate, and government organization (Nakane 1967, 1973). One needs to be careful not to overstate the rigidity of these vertical bonds today in an increasingly individualized, interpersonal, and globalized society, a point I return to in discussing personal and work relationships in following chapters. But numerous scholars have both built upon and critiqued Nakane's well-known work, making it a good starting point to think about deeply entrenched issues. It is difficult to find a book on social structure in Japan that does not in some way engage, positively or negatively, directly or indirectly, with Nakane's notion of hierarchies (Ryang 2004). There have been some major turning points in contemporary Japan: the economic collapse of the late 1980s and early 1990s, the dwindling of the salary man ideal, the *Aum* subway gas attacks, the 2005 Hanshin earthquake, the 2011 Tohoku triple disaster of earthquake, tsunami, and subsequent nuclear meltdown, which led to mass death and the displacement of people alongside the contamination of much prime agricultural land and ocean, and, most recently, the global COVID-19 pandemic. These are all watershed moments, but even something as seemingly mundane as the influence of the internet in constructing identities cannot be accounted for in relying on research that predates it (Ertl and Hansen 2015; Guarné and Hansen 2018). However, it is not that classic anthropology got things "wrong," but just that it often needs to be, choosing the word carefully, *reframed* in order to fit a present tense context.

Nakane discusses relations at length using the word *frame* (essentially social structure), while her *attribute* refers to the individual's position acting within these structures. I suggest that while the attribute of many Japanese, certainly young people, is in flux, frames or social structures, whether perceived positively or negatively by individuals, often prove to be more resistant to change. Popular media in Japan ought to also be viewed in this light. More than in many other national contexts it functions as a unifying pop-cultural political tool. For example, media in Japan is, by linguistic default alone, more local than global (Leheny 2006). It is often used to promote "Japaneseness" or the uniqueness of Japanese customs or areas alongside offering commentary on sociopolitical issues, often presuming consensus, thought to be particularly Japanese (Kingston 2018; Martinez 1992, 1998). Regional reporting is as often linked to local news events as it is to banal regional promotion efforts. And this "news creation" (a festival, a music event, the weather) is nearly always linked with "local" foods as tourism and food are intimately linked in the Japanese media with programs on regional foods presented daily, if not hourly (Assmann 2015). This links to a strong sense of localized "nostalgia" for imagined communities, practices, and golden ages (Robertson 1994, 1998b). I do not wish to exaggerate the role of mass media, say the NHK television network or Asahi Shimbun newspaper, as homogenizing agents, much as I do not wish to emphasize hierarchy alone as a structuring factor in Japanese society. Nevertheless, due in part to the limited global use of the Japanese language, general political disinterest, or defeatism in political affairs domestically, let alone internationally, through government ministerial will and the self-policing of reporting, and frankly triviality (as there are simply so many reginal outlets that not enough "newsworthy" news can fill up the airtime) the media, and it has long been argued educational materials and programs as well, serves to unify public opinion and promote cultural conformity in Japan (Ben-Ari 2003, 111–132; Cave 2013; Hendry 1989; Mock, Kawamura, and Naganuma 2016).

Chomsky and Herman propose a propaganda model of the media that underscores the top-down nature of news production leading to disengagement with political action. They discuss how American media "manufacture consent" by "fixing the premises of discourse," "filtering" how supposedly unbiased and factual information is disseminated (Chomsky and Herman 1988, xi; Hansen 2015). The fact that the Japanese media promotes a homogeneous sense of belonging and regional nostalgia or longing is noted in the introduction to this book. However, there are flip sides to what is potentially viewed by many as a harmless, even positive, notion of cultural belonging. First, such populist reporting and education can be alienating for those not included in the "national" discourse, for individuals Othered by media, government, and education. Second, media exacerbates or manufactures popularly shared feelings of anxiety or crisis, most notably for the case at hand about food security (Hansen 2014a).

This collective crisis creation motivates many Japanese to suggest that actions from above (often via the government) ought to be directed toward solving whatever crisis is presently popular. David Leheny focuses convincingly on the frequent media portrayal of "youth culture gone wild" (often child prostitution and violence) and "vague anxiety" directed toward internal outsiders, such as foreign workers, or external threats such as China's growing economic power or North Korea as a military threat (Leheny 2006, 27–49). Genda Yūji and Anne Allison note how job insecurity and precarity are also presented and promoted in media accounts (Allison 2013; Genda 2005). The notion of cultural or racial Otherness as a danger is also a perennial theme in Japanese media (Arai 2006; Arudou

2006; Forero-Montoya 2020). Similarly, the media feeds into and off of related vague anxieties about Japan's food supply. Food security and safety must be added to this top-down media fearmongering (Hansen 2014a). Aforementioned government programs such as Food Action Nippon forward the rhetoric that Japan and Japanese must be self-sufficient and not dependent on the goodwill of other countries. Though frequently disappointed, many expect that the government is looking out for them or they resign themselves to the perennial mantra of *shikata ga nai* (nothing can be done) (Long 1999) about these complex and intertwined economic, military, and food security issues.

Moreover, via the media, the official voices of Japanese nationalist agricultural rhetoric are heard from representatives of what Mulgan calls the agricultural "iron triangle"—MAFF, LDP, and the numerous *nōgyō* (agricultural cooperatives with Hokuren being the most powerful in Hokkaido) scattered throughout Japan (Mulgan 2006). These are powerful bodies supported in large part by votes and funds from rural areas. Obviously, sustaining a constant state of food crisis and maintaining their image as civil protector heightens their profile and importance in terms of reelection or simply self-serving job security. MAFF is the branch of government responsible for the various livelihoods across rural economic sectors. However, the economies under the purview of MAFF are often in conflict; for example, one need only think of conflictual land use in agriculture and forestry or water usage and pollution in agriculture and fisheries. *Nōgyō* associations like JA or Hokuren essentially function as "go-betweens" for producers, MAFF (and so the government), and wholesale buyers such as food processors and supermarket chains.

Given the iron triangle, farmers themselves have virtually no voice in the sale of their products. Government and private corporate interests set the price and quota limits to which farmers must adhere (see MacLachlan and Shimizu [2022] for recent and detailed explanation). Thus, neoliberal rhetoric aside, this really is not a system based on markets, producers, and customers negotiating prices, but top-down governmental and bureaucratic regulations of production, cost, and supply. Farmers rarely sell or produce food independent from government controls, and the ample frustrations that more ambitious agriculturalists feel about this lack of self-determination are detailed in the following two chapters.

Finally, there is a huge variety of agriculture, differing from region to region, in Japan. But, for comparative purposes, it is of prime importance to note that the production and promotion of rice and dairy, two highly subsidized and nationally self-sufficient foodstuffs, require very different processes. First, milk products, unlike rice, spoil quickly. Raw milk, for example, cannot be stored for more than a day. It must be processed and sold soon or rendered into powdered form, which radically reduces its value. As a necessarily fresh product it is more susceptible to rises and falls in the market. It costs to dry milk, and once done it is no longer fresh milk. Its higher market value as "drinking" milk is lost as it can only be sold as "product" milk. Thus, hedging bets on the market is far riskier in the dairy industry. Second, rice production is seasonal and often conducted by families on a part-time basis, whereas dairy production is a daily task and there are very few (if any) part-time dairy farmers.[2] Dairy farm families are usually dependent upon the income brought in from dairy farming alone. They are far more vulnerable to the insecurities of production prices and market limits but moreover unable to work off the farm part-time if the milk market, so to speak, sours (Hansen 2010b).

Conclusion

The consumption of bovine products has increased throughout the history of Japan. Today, milk production is considered an essential industry, at least essential enough to subsidize and include as "cultures" within popular culture; milk is in one's morning coffee, in a child's national school lunch, or in afterwork *izakaya* snacks. Moreover, beef and dairy importation issues are considered central enough to jeopardize international military, political, and economic security in the name of domestic food security. Increases in production and consumption of beef and dairy were always brought on through the acceptance of foreign influences: the Chinese brought milk in as a product of high culture, court aesthetics, and for medicinal purposes and the Dutch promoted the health benefits of dairy as a scientifically proven product of the Enlightenment. Post Tokugawa era, the production and promotion of dairy products under American and European influence was widely promoted as symbolic of modernity itself. After the defeat of Japan in the Second World War, the Occupation forces, among numerous changes regarding Japanese society, sought to feed undernourished Japanese children with school lunch programs including beef and dairy. Nevertheless, though diary has clearly become increasingly important and central to the Japanese diet, the industry in Japan has always been promoted and represented as the consumption of foreignness, the Other, despite the lengthy domestic relationship between cow and human in Japan.

Since the 1980s, globalization has brought a host of new milk products, both imported and domestically produced, to the core of Japanese consumption. Japanese eat the Othered: French brie, Bulgarian yogurt, Mexican burritos, and American-style pizza. Far from exotic, all contain dairy and all are found in contemporary Japanese restaurants and supermarkets. Indeed, such products are often adapted to Japanese tastes and they are often not foreign at all. Yet despite milk being produced in Japan by Japanese, these foods are often not considered "properly" Japanese. They are labeled as *yōshoku* (Western foods). However, they are not "properly" foreign either. Burritos are bland and pizza might have mayonnaise, potato, and seaweed in place of, or terrifyingly alongside, "pepperoni" resembling "American" hot dogs. Yet, I cannot tell one bowl of rice from another. Not so for most Japanese.

Emiko Ohnuki-Tierney claims that for Japanese people, rice is a "dominant symbol . . . rice as *our* food and on the other hand rice paddies as *our* land . . . [and these symbols] . . . reinforce . . . each other" (Ohnuki-Tierney 1993, 4–5, italics in the original). Many feel that this is an overreaching, essentialist metaphor, including, emphatically, one reviewer of this book. And, to be clear, I agree. Yet, it is a telling one. For example, it is undeniable that rice—despite popular trends such as a reduction in rice consumption and production—features first and foremost in why and how JA constructs its agriculture policies (Jentzsch 2021; McLachlan and Shimizu 2022). JA will go to great lengths to sustain foods associated with *their* identity—rice as self/nation. But despite the official, obvious, and comparable importance of dairy products in modern Japan, Hokkaido dairy farmers are at an extreme disadvantage here. The production of rice is popularly linked with the formation of Japanese society and values such as cooperation or "groupism." *Gohan*, cooked rice, is a synonym for the word *meal*. *Mochi* (a chewy pounded rice flower cake) and *sake* (rice-based alcohol) are central features in Japanese celebrations such as New Year's Day. Metaphorically speaking, if rice can be seen as the relation between a traditional Japanese self and Japan—factual or not, the popular representation of *our* land, *our* food, and so, *our* bodies in need of securing and protection—then perhaps milk alongside its production and imagery can be thought of as another type of contemporary Japanese symbol, one of the Otherness inside Japan. That is to say, in the top-down structuring of media representation and government policy, milk is deemed as "essential" in Japan, yet it remains symbolically "Other." Dairy is treated as a marginal industry located on the periphery despite its actual contemporary centrality. Ask a Japanese person anywhere, in Hokkaido or Honshu, California or Canberra, what *represents* Japan, *sake* or milk, rice or cheese? Japanese rice and its products will be the answer, at least it always has been the answer given to me.

Thus, building on Mikhail Bakhtin and his comparison of epic and novel modes of representation (Bakhtin 1981, 16–17), I suggest that rice and its production can be thought of as Japan's epic story. Rice, and the social and political discourses surrounding its production such as respect for four seasons, groupism, rural land, and so forth, is the valorized peak of an unchanging Japaneseness. This is the "epic." It is the unalterable historical tale perceived as the origin of national belonging and identity. This story is the antithesis of change, heteroglossia, and alternative interpretations. It is rooted in pride and a unique story of origins—social, aesthetic, and values—that cannot be altered. Rice and its associated images, I contend, can be viewed as one of the main characters of the Japanese epic. As noted above, it can stand in for the timeless hero of Japanese land, social structure, and culture. However dairy, despite the lengthy outlined history and despite its essential position in the social structure and culture of modern Japan, is not allowed a role in this epic depiction.

Dairy is more like the modern novel. The novel is "the genre of becoming" (Bakhtin 1981, 22) and results in "a radical restructuring of the image of the individual" (35). It is a representation of particularity not generality. Novels focus on individuals who "cannot be completely incarnated in the flesh of existing social-historical categories. . . . There always remains an unrealised surplus of humanness" (37). Consumers expect Hokkaido to be something Other than Japan and Tokachi even more so. *Historically* it clearly is. And so, it is and is so represented through alternative images, products, and histories. Novel stories are essential to any understanding of contemporary Japan, of a Japan, or even just rural Japan, beyond a monolithic representation (Hansen 2020b, 2022).

Herein is the inescapable paradox for essentialist representations of Japan or of Japaneseness examined in all of the chapters that follow. Hokkaido, Tokachi, Gensan, and its dairy industry have been and continue to be key players regarding modern Japan's macro security concerns whether political, military, economic, or food. Yet it is equally clear that frontier Hokkaido, and the ideological and physical frontiers internalized in that location, alongside the *cultures* they produce, human and non-human, cannot be included in an existing "epic" discourse of Japan or Japanese identity.

Chapter Five

Farm Structures

Introduction

The chapter by chapter focus of this book shifts from generality to particularity; from past to present; from macro, meso, to micro in analysis; and narrowing in scope from Japan to Hokkaido, to Tokachi, to Gensan, to Grand Hopes Farm. Accordingly, the methodology moves from an investigation of history, policy, and statistical trends presented in the previous chapters to epistemologies that are increasingly rooted in ethnographic fieldwork and embodied interactions with particular individuals and places. In this chapter the scope narrows further to discuss modern history and interactions at the community level in northern Tokachi, Gensan, and its surrounding dairy farms. For the present, it should suffice to note that in what follows the broader issues of Otherness, the search for security, and frontiers are less couched in terms of Japan's or Hokkaido's history and agricultural policy and more rooted in community perceptions and projects. This serves as an axis point before the focus tapers further still to describe and analyze Great Hopes Farm, a single industrial dairy operation, and the individuals who worked and work there. In sum, the maneuvering is from the historic to the contemporary and from the nation of Japan to specific interactions of select human and nonhumans bracketed within a particular time (largely 2005–2020).

Gensan reached its centenary during my first stint of fieldwork research in 2006. The town's population peaked in the late 1950s and also began its decline within the lifetime of many of my interlocutors. Thus, while I use texts as a touchstone, much of the history offered in this chapter comes from visits to local museums and from the mouths of Gensan's older residents, whether day-to-day gossip and small talk or through extended interviews and prolonged friendships.

The Development of Gensan, Tokachi, and a Modern Hokkaido Industry

There are several parallels between the history of Tokachi and the history of neighboring Kushiro in the eastern part of Hokkaido (Takata 2003, 2004, 2007). For one, Tokachi's capital city was originally an Ainu settlement. In 1883, Yoda Benzō and Watanabe Masaru, both land speculators from Honshu dedicated to the government's project of modernization, arrived in Opereperekepu (an Ainu name they understood as Oberiberi) and renamed it Obihiro. Yoda, having come to Tokachi via the sea from Yokohama, claimed his parcel of land with mixed blessings from the Meiji powers. He started a company called Bansei and was offered land in Hokkaido provided he could make it productive. Blessings were mixed as this raised the ire of the declining Kaitaku office who, despite central governmental decree to open the land to private ownership, saw the vastness of central Hokkaido as their own. However, with the offer of private ownership, adventurous well-off Japanese set out to stake land and later *banseisha* (tenant farmers from poor areas) came to join Yoda. Watanabe was also a wealthy adventurer. He inched his way along the southern coast by foot from Hakodate to do the same. By 1890 the population of Obihiro was only around three hundred people, Ainu traders and some *tondenhei* and their families. Desperate peasants seeking a new start, or at least a way to survive after the collapse of Japan's feudal system, were then brought in by the new landowners. Ill-prepared for the harsh climate, many perished.

A local turning point came in 1895 when construction was completed on a national prison in Obihiro, a branch of the famed prison of Abashiri in Hokkaido's north (Shigematsu 2004). Within three years of its establishment, Obihiro's inmate population of around 1,500 men had cleared an incredible 72 hectares of land and 450 farms were established, including some by former inmates who were now free. Highlighting some similarities with the settlement of Australia and the Americas, as in much of Hokkaido's expanse, prison labor was essential to infrastructural development (Buckley 1992; Robson 1965; Shigematsu 2004). After clearing land, inmates were utilized to build roads and lay rail track. Thirty years later these convicts would be joined by forced labor from the colonized nations of China and Korea to engage in what are now popularly called *san kei* occupations—*kitanai, kiken,* and *kitsui,* maybe best rendered as "three D" occupations: "dirty, dangerous, and difficult" in English (over the years I have also heard *kibishii* and *kane ga nai* (strict and poorly paid thrown in) associated with building, mining, farming, and forestry (Seki et al. 2006). Due to the success around Obihiro, other well-funded elite "settlers" eventually staked out huge territories and then brought peasants to work with the promise of eventually owning their own land.

Another such pioneer closer to contemporary Gensan was Seki Yutaka, whose compelling life history is proudly displayed in the Obihiro museum and catches the essence (at least the elite and official essence) of the Meiji "frontier" spirit in Tokachi. Born in 1827 in Chiba prefecture (neighboring present-day Tokyo), Seki was a middle-aged medical doctor when the emperor Meiji took the throne in 1868. In 1869 he moved to the southern island of Shikoku to start a new modern hospital in Tokushima where he worked until 1902. Then at the age of seventy-four, he made the journey, not just to Hokkaido, an impressive feat to accomplish alone at the time, but through the harsh "new" lands of Tokachi's Rikubetsu region, its northernmost and coldest post (with drops in temperature to minus thirty degrees Celsius). Here he staked his claim and started to clear land by his own elderly hand. He made arrangements the following year for peasants and horses to come from Shikoku. He died in 1910, two years before the end of the Meiji period, happy it is said, at eighty-two years of age—truly having lived a life in the adventurous and ambitious spirit of the times.

Many early pioneers share Seki's story of adventure mixed with individual fortitude, hardship, and determination. The first settlers arrived in Gensan from the mainland in 1906. Many of the initial settlers came from Gifu prefecture in central Honshu with the aid of a well-off farmer named Ogura, a family name still prominent in the area, but soon settlers were coming from areas across Japan. During this period the population of Tokachi rose from 10,852 in 1897 to 147,126 by 1926. Agricultural settlements were progressively established from southwestern Tokachi to the northeastern regions. Most newcomers survived by creating small mixed farms including livestock and various cereal and tuber crops. Hogs, chickens, dairy and beef cattle were primary stock; horses were also essential for traction. Influenced by both the European and American styles of farming promoted early on by the *kaitakushi* and tested in Hokkaido and Tokyo Universities, and due also to the climatic conditions, wheat, barley, and potatoes were harvested in lieu of rice (Dempster 1966; Tanimura 1922).

Thus, in the context of Japan, many forms of borrowed agriculture, or agricultures rooted in Otherness, were being tried and tested in topographic and climatic conditions that newcomers from Honshu had no prior experience of living in, let alone harvesting from. These conditions led to adaptations in forms of dietary sustenance. Put simply, the new forms of agriculture yielded new forms of produce creating "Othered" foodways. In contrast to Honshu, milk, meat, and potatoes became, through necessity, the staple diet of the northern settlers. Even in less climatically harsh regions of Hokkaido, such as the Ishikari region near Sapporo, the harvest of rice, certainly high-yield, was unpredictable until recent decades.[1] In northern Tokachi, corn, potatoes, milk, and lamb are extremely popular foodstuffs. Some people coming from other areas of Japan have told me that they find the regional seasonings off-putting, notably due to their being excessively buttery (or fatty, e.g., *abura*) or sweet. Many go on to link this predilection for tastes with the history of local areas where impoverishment, the need for hard labor, and a cold climate underscore the prior need for caloric intake and so the prominence of these flavors.

Originally Tokachi was one administrative zone. But as the population grew, areas began to segment in rings from the vast north. First Obihiro separated as a region from what was seen as the frontier further north. It was followed by neighboring town Otofuke. Village after village, moving from central Obihiro outward, newly settled regions staked their claim as separate municipalities standing against the vastness of unstaked land. In 1931 Gensan was declared a village, winning its own identity in greater Tokachi. Dairy farming began in earnest in 1933 with the government's promotion of a five-year agricultural development plan implemented across Hokkaido. While forestry and mining were originally the most important elements in the area's economy, dairy farming, as an occupation, rather than for self-sufficient survival, developed slowly. German and Danish farmers came to Hokkaido sponsored by the government in the mid-1930s to teach modern dairy practices to the new pioneers, many of whom had never seen a milk cow until their arrival.

However, as Japan's military machine expanded across Asia, many new dairy farmers turned to the more profitable project of rearing military horses. Even at the end of the Pacific war there was still a market for horses, as they were largely the only form of traction until the early fifties. With the end of World War II, and the destruction of many of Japan's major cities, repatriated soldiers from Manchuria and Korea began life anew in Hokkaido, marking a second wave of Tokachi migration. By 1954 Gensan was officially declared a town. No longer a mere village, it grew rapidly with the massive construction project of a hydropower dam and the population of the town grew to around 13,608 people by the mid-fifties (Kamishihoro Yakuba 1992). While local museums and town archives are great repositories of local history, town elders' narratives supply living testimony that these were colorful, if rough-and-tumble times.

The story of Yūji-san, in his early seventies when I started fieldwork and, to my good fortune, an energetic friend at the time of writing, offers a prime example of the "type" of person who grew up in the Gensan area during this era. His parents had come from Kōchi, Shikoku before the war, as funded settlers who were given ten acres of free land and 350 yen with the promise of title to the land if it was cleared after five years. Yūji-san is quite a character. He is a skilled craftsman, making *tatami* (rice straw) flooring, but his real passion is freshwater fishing. I first met him through his sixty-year-old partner who, after a particularly difficult divorce, had moved from Osaka to Gensan for a change (Hansen 2018a, 2021b). In November of 2007, in order to learn more of the area's history, I arranged a long interview with Yūji-san at his home. In exchange he hinted that he would not protest if I lubricated our discussion with some *imo shōchu*—a 25 percent sweet-potato-based spirit. And he would offer up freshly grilled lake fish and hours of access to his memories and photos.

According to Yūji-san, until the 1960s, after which transportation and production methods improved, there was no money to be made in dairy farming. In fact, nobody he knew was a full-time dairy farmer and he and his peers were uninterested in such work at the time. Then, milk cows, two or a few, were kept to supply the family and local markets and to augment a largely self-sufficient local population. Hunting, and more so fishing, were and continue to be common (Hansen 2020a). There were no tractors until the early 1960s. All draft work in farming and forestry was accomplished through human and equestrian toil (as demonstrated in figure 5.1). Yūji-san spent his entire life in the area. Early in our first discussion he produced photos from his first job working as a laborer for a forestry company and I used photos as the basis to interview and record as a methodology (Harper 2001). As Yūji-san and I viewed his photos, he animatedly recalled and described the area. Some photographs

Figure 5.1. A circa 1950s photo of intensive forestry propelled by horses and hard work. The Daisetsu mountain range, just north of Gensan, can be seen in the background and these cleared foothills would become farmland by the 1960s. Photo shared by Yūji-san.

showed row upon row of muddy streets and snow-covered logs—in fact the logs were even used as makeshift roadways to get across snow or mud to access even more lumber.

There were pictures of young male workers with crew cuts, looking thin and cold, and family photos with children wearing dirty and patched clothes. The images reminded me of Depression-era photos of my own Canadian hometown, and indeed other publicly available photo albums or local museum collections augment this impression (Yonekura 2018). Yūji-san assured me that the times were hard and living was spartan, but there was an air of optimism. At that time, with prefectural construction projects and resource extraction industries, Gensan was a boom town. He could recall the introduction of trucks, rare as they were in the early 1960s—indeed, figure 5.2 shows one of the first trucks in the area and its new owner, beaming with pride—electricity in the late 1960s, and telephones soon after.

During the building of a dam, located about twenty odd kilometers north, the town became home to numerous workers, including many

Figure 5.2. Yūji-san's friend, all smiles, with his new truck circa 1960—a radical technological shift in the then-thriving forestry industry. Photo shared by Yūji-san.

Koreans. As in the frontier towns of the Canadian Prairies, social ills came in tandem with the boons of expansion (Brennan 2002; van Herk 2001). *Yakuza* (gangsters) on the lam from larger centers were frequent visitors, as it had a reputation for having a thriving red-light district, which was right behind Yuji-san's house. However, like all small towns in northern Tokachi, Gensan's population began to steadily decrease after the 1950s (Zandanhōjin Hokkaidō Shinchōson Shinkō Kyōkai 2004). While Obihiro and larger bedroom communities have grown, the populations of smaller towns have steadily decreased. Larger urban centers such as Obihiro or Sapporo lure many of Tokachi's youth—especially young women—where opportunities for nonlabor jobs, education, or attractive romantic partners have long been perceived as being more plentiful (Mock 1999). As a result, various nightspots, indicative of previous prosperity, have disappeared; the town's cinema has closed and a derelict pachinko parlor stands beside another showing its age. While some less than reputable remains of a *mizu-shōbai* district still exist in Gensan, at least in the form of rundown *sunakku* (snack bars), with matron-like owners, catering to well-weathered patrons, remaining town elders like Yūji-san remember better times. And, disappointingly for some, all are aware that many of the young do not see their future in town. In the 1950s it had both a JR and a private rail line. But by the 1980s, the population had dropped over 60 percent since the building of the dam. In 1987, a time when the rest of Japan was still enjoying the fruits of the Bubble Economy, Gensan JR closed the final rail line. Despite continuous efforts to attract newcomers, there was a steady annual decline in the town's population until 2015 when numbers slowly started inching up (Hansen 2021b). Nevertheless, some residents question if the town has a future at all. Coworkers and friends from other areas of Japan, and the "tourist workers" described in the following chapters, would joke about how after seven in the evening it became a ghost town.

Town and Country

Yet, despite this long decline, and maybe even stressed by its recent plateau, there are many attractive features to be enjoyed around Tokachi in any season and Japanese tourists, and increasingly international travelers, flock to the region year-round. Indeed, domestic tourists are drawn to what they see as the "Otherness" of the area. They come for outdoor adventures, to enjoy a cool summer or engage in winter sports, to enjoy the vast *amerika-teki* (US-like) pastoral scenery, and to sample local foods, especially dairy products. Understandably, Gensan's location was viewed as a boon and savvy local employers know it is an attractive lure. *Bokujō* websites, geared to attract would-be employees, generally list the locations of nearby attractions and the estimated time to drive to them. Rustic *onsen*, aging ski hills, national parks, and an expansive and natural land-scape grace the pages of many tour guides and employment websites.

In 2006, the community of Gensan had a population of approxi-mately 5,500 people, as of April 2009 the population declined to 5,229, and by December 2015 the population stood at its lowest to date at 4,886, underscoring a long-term trend of depopulation despite extensive efforts to attract newcomers. However, by 2020 efforts seem to be paying off with a population of 5,002 people (Hansen 2021b). In terms of layout, in many ways Gensan is like a miniature version of the regional capital Obihiro. The streets are set out in a grid pattern with highways angling the town off at its corners. It is home to a large Shinto shrine, three Buddhist temples, and comparatively new Jehovah's Witness and Mennonite churches. Many locals knew nothing about the Mennonite church, and, alarmingly in such a small town, a number of residents did not even know of its existence on the main street! The Jehovah's Witness congregation is more visible, namely through their weekend door knocking. One building often in use is the renovated town library. Due to its open spaces, heated interior, and central location, students from the local elementary, junior high school, and high school frequently congregate there.

The town has a local chapter of JA (the newest and tallest build-ing in town), a town hall (the largest building in town), a post office, a bank, a sports center, an *onsen*, as well as a few small supermarkets, gas stations, convenience stores, medical clinics, and clothing shops. It has a pair of coffee shops, neither attractive or inviting enough to warrant a second visit, a few *izakaya*, one of ill-repute for good reason, and a half-dozen restaurants serving typical fare, from affordable ramen to pricey, but outstanding, sushi. Thus, given its actual population, Gensan has dis-proportional amenities as it also serves the surrounding area of farmers due to the distance from any other major population center. Moreover, the town has a wide range of free programs, from afterschool care, to judo, to seniors' gate ball teams. However, for the average Hokkaido citizen, or even Tokachi resident, the town would be, in a word, "unremarkable."

The surrounding area is remarkable. The town has an expanse of park space, wide roads, and the air is fresh, with an ever-present hint of *bokujō* aroma for earthy effect. The parks were designed for the viewing of the beautiful *momiji* (turning leaves) in the fall and *hanami* in the spring, though both of these seasons are short in Tokachi. There is a mini golf course, a large campground and barbeque area. In the winter there is an impeccably maintained cross-country ski course. The location offers up publicly accessible open green fields in the summer and pure white snow cover in the winter, and in two directions the town had a clear view of the nearby jagged Tokachi Mountains and the more distant Hidaka range.

There is one major tourist attraction within the town itself. In fact, the event drew large crowds from across Japan. Every June the largely self-contained town bursts at the seams, with its campgrounds filled and shops packed, as it hosts Japan's largest hot air balloon show. This bian-nual festival is also held in February. Though the turnout in the Tokachi winter is only for the more diehard of balloon enthusiasts, the summer season draws less intrepid tourists. The festival began in 1974 and today around forty teams annually compete. For three days teams compete in various races testing speed, navigation, and control. This is surely the largest one-shot mixing event for locals and outsiders, as many of the perennial teams are local businesses. The participants and numerous spec-tators are entertained with the usual array of Japanese small-town festival goings-on. There are food tents, beer tents, tents in which cheap toys and T-shirts were sold, and a local talent show, wherein a hodgepodge of entertainers showcase their skills. Numerous discordant *enka* singers croon about heartache, straining their quavering voices while clutching at the air, presumably snatching the time before their imagined dreams lay shattered. Legions of would-be pop stars of varying ages and talents dance, prance, and yelp around the small stage, looking for their break in Gensan. The most intriguing entertainer for me dates back to 2008. A young rapper who furnished the look of "urban gangster" energetically extolled the virtues of eating barbequed lamb, linking this love of lamb to his rural Hokkaido identity. To this day I occasionally hear recordings of his "Jin, jin, jin, ji, ji, jin gisu kan" song in local supermarkets. The annual spectacle is ever presided over by a middle-aged woman with immov-able hair and a penchant for ending every sentence with an extended and overly spirited *neee* (isn't it so). Very few people become absorbed in the seemingly unending entertainment. Local male elders, their stoic defenses temporarily numbed by heat and drink, usually offer the occa-sional hushed *urusai* (shut up) in lieu of applause or the more frequent blank stares and silence. This spectacle is set against the less-than-com-mon background of aerial acrobatics: gliders, parachute jumpers, and the staged swooping down drama of the local helicopter rescue service.

Perhaps, predictably, there is a balloon theme guiding the decor and identity of the town. Having just missed the winter event when I arrived, until my initiation into the world of Gensan ballooning, the balloons painted on, and inside, many of the town's buildings—the balloon manhole covers, the balloon streetlamps, a smiling cartoon balloon on the town's natural gas bills beckoning residents to pay, and the town's entrance sign depicting balloons flying over a field full of oblivious cows—seemed an odd rural aviation fetish beyond my comprehension. However, I joined a balloon team in the summer of 2006 and have attended or volunteered several times until 2019. It is abundantly clear that this event is central to the identity of the town. Given their long work hours few *bokujō* employees attend, but the people of Gensan and hundreds of tourists enjoy the festivities yearly. Some arrive as early as 4:30 a.m. to watch the balloons prepare to take to the sky, and for the three days lunch, with copious cans of beer, starts for many at around 9:30 a.m. Through the balloon festival the identity of the town is secured, at least at the official level, since Gensan is widely known as the "air sport town." However, as depicted on the official town sign, the balloons do not fly over empty fields; rather, they fly over a landscape dotted with dairy cows and dairy farms.

The Range of *Bokujō*

Like the people who own and work on them, no farm is the same. *Bokujō* conditions in the Gensan area of Tokachi vary according to size, ownership, production level, and age of operation. On numerous occasions I discussed work conditions at Grand Hopes Farm. When I subsequently went to interview staff on other farms and mentioned that I worked for Grand Hopes, without any prompting people generally compared the real or perceived attributes of employment in one workplace in favor or against another. Conversations were always carried on outside the earshot of owners and bosses, but of course they too were well aware of typical farm-work conditions and where their farm fit, or conceivably fit, within the continuum of desirable workplaces. Locals often had friends working on other farms, or had come from family farms themselves, and were aware of the work situations nearby. And many from outside of the locality had also come from, worked on, or had friends who had worked on farms elsewhere in Japan. Whether done overtly or covertly, comparing farms was a common practice for owners, locals, and staff alike. Yukiko-san, a tourist worker discussed below whose boyfriend worked at a neighboring farm, and "Between"-san, a good-natured but exploited local worker also discussed in the following chapters, had the following exchange one morning on the way to the catch barn:

Between-san: "Murakami no bokujyō wa totemo ii basho desu yo. Shigoto wa kantan da shi Murakami-san ga totemo yasashii . . ." (Murakami farm is great, the work is easy and the owner is a nice guy . . .)

Yukiko-san: "Ee, sou ja nai yo, ano Ōnā wa henna sekebei na ojisan tte kiita." (No way man, I heard the owner is a sleazy old man.)

Between-san: "Eeee (*giggles*) Hontou ni? Murakami wa toshi-yori . . ." (Come on, really—that old man?)

Yukiko-san: "Un, Ikeya kun wa ne, Biggu Yama no mae, rokk-agetsu gurai Murakami de hataraita. Yappari dame desu. Totemo kitanai shi, pāra wa furui . . ." (Yeah, before Ikeya worked for Big Mountain Farm he worked there for about six months. It's bad, it's filthy, and the parlor is old . . .)

Between-san: (*giggling still*) "Mada genki da na . . . Uso desho! Ore no tomodachi no otōsan no da yo" (He's [still] lively then . . . (you're) joking/lying, come on. He's my dad's friend you know . . .)

Lighthearted banter was common while heading to do tasks that were often done solo with little or no social contact. What did you do on your day off? What is work like on other farms? Do you know so and so on X or Y farm? These questions were frequent fodder for chitchat. For the most part, people agreed that Grand Hopes, despite having the longest hours, was a place where working conditions were fair, if not better than average according to informed regional gossip.

Grand Hopes Farm was less than four years old when research for this book began. It was a product of the shift to "incorporated" or joint stock farms in the late 1990s, described in the following chapter. Grand Hopes was on the grand side of scale and the owners had high hopes for the expansion and profitability of the business. The organizational struc-ture of the farm was, or more precisely *was intended to be*, organized along the lines of a set of clear managerial top-down, or to borrow from Nakane again, vertical hierarchies (Nakane 1973). While the rest of this book is a clear testament as to how in practice the farm seldom functioned this way, it was accurately viewed by its owners as a company run by families.

When I began fieldwork in 2005 there was a fluctuating full-time staff of twenty-eight Japanese and a dairy herd of around one thousand head. By January of 2010 the herd had surpassed 1,700 head and there were thirty-two full-time staff members, including four Chinese workers. While working on the final draft of this monograph in January of 2021, I learned that the numbers were still on the rise with around three thousand head and over sixty staff members, with almost half of this staff hailing from China and Vietnam.[2] I avoid exact numbers to protect sources and avoid superfluous detail, but the key point here is that the farm by any international standard is large. Today it would be impossible for the members of a single family to manage all aspects of running it. The farm has one of the highest milk production outputs in Japan—an output that is, moreover, always increasing. Great Hopes Farm is clearly something other than a typical family dairy farm. But the average family dairy operation in Hokkaido is growing in size and already approximately three times larger than the national average, with numbers that are, in fact, nearer to the EU average of about 114 cows per farm. It is clearly a *mega fāmu* (mega farm). Indeed the founding president of Sapporo Agricultural College William Clark's century-old famous parting words, known across Japan and always in English, "Boys be ambitious," have been realized by two of the incorporated farm's original owners.[3] Echoing this American educator's "ethos," the *shachō* and *kachō* (company president and manager) were ever keen to expand the operation, constantly buying new cattle, diligently inseminating existing cows, and improving the facilities to meet the government's ever-tightening ecological standards.

When the issue of expansion was brought up with the *shachō*, he would invariably tilt his head to the side while producing an uneasy hiss—a Japanese gesture reserved to express something troubling almost to the point of physical discomfort—and reply along the lines of "Sore wa muzukashii yo" (thissss [business of expansion] is difficult, I'll tell you). And sometimes, with time and energy permitting, Wada-san would describe in an uncharacteristically animated fashion, in order to penetrate my oft-cloudy Japanese, how the government—and by this he meant the MAFF, Hokuren, JA, and/or his nemesis the *yakuba* (the municipal or regional government)—ceaselessly frustrated his ambitions.

On one occasion he confided that he had the funds at his disposal to buy many more cattle and that neither labor costs nor equipment expenses were at issue. Although regulated milk pricing described in the previous chapter was perceived as a problem at the time, he had faith that this would remedy itself in 2009 with the lifting of the milk price cap (though it did not). With the TPP in discussions in 2015, while small farmers pondered their existence, Wada-san posited that things would surely get better for Grand Hopes Farm with fewer domestic farms to compete with (though with the US scrapping the TPP in 2016 alongside the aforementioned passing of the EPA trade agreement with the EU much of the *shachō*'s optimism has been tested). The immediate problem then was, as now, land. Not the cost, for one advantage Hokkaido farmers have is the low cost of land relative to other areas of Japan. The problem is that the amount of cropland owned or leased by the farm is not sufficient enough to meet the regulations set by the prefecture to safely spread the manure produced by an increased herd.

This was the key issue holding the expansion of the farm back in 2010. Undeniably, fertilizing croplands by manure spreading is the most economical and beneficial way to use this animal by-product; it replenishes the topsoil with phosphates and nitrogen. In the USA and Canada, farmers often pay to have manure spread on their croplands. However, as noted above, the increasingly intensive nature of dairy farming in Hokkaido means that, in essence, the ratio of cattle to land area is ecologically problematic as in other high-intensity dairy regions. Plainly put, there is too much manure and no ecologically secure place to put it. As noted in the previous chapter 82 percent of feed is imported because there is simply not enough cropland to produce it domestically, ipso facto, there is also not enough land to spread the "post-cow" product in its raw form. Thus, recycling this toxic effluent has become a major issue in Hokkaido and manure output a serious ecological challenge. The logic is simple: as there is a lack of land to produce the feed, there is also a lack of land to safely spread the by-product on crops without causing water table and other toxicity problems. It must be stored and processed, and during my stay at the farm a new manure storage facility was installed at great cost and two more were added in 2012 and 2015. And numerous biomass fuel projects have started in the area (Nishizaki 2002, 2009).

At one point in 2006, Mr. Wada was eager to promote low-fat dairy products to combat the impression of dairy goods as unhealthy, an irony given the aforementioned history of dairy in Japan. One afternoon he had me search for websites instead of working with my cohorts, in order to find information about low-calorie dairy products in Europe and North America. He claimed that he was willing to try his hand at producing such products by starting a subsidiary company. He was enthusiastic, even having workers in the staff room sample various milk products and comment on packaging over a lunch one day. However, his objectives, and our bloated stomachs, were all for naught. He soon found out that MAFF's iron grip regulations would not permit his opening a dairy company related to the Grand Hopes Farm operation (Hansen 2010b, 2014a).

The *shachō* wanted to produce more milk. In 2008, he wanted to hire more staff and buy more cattle and run the dairy on a twenty-four-hour rotation of shifts. But even if he could contend with the manure issue, he found that the production of milk over quota is fully policed by Hokuren in accordance with the inability of smaller producers to keep pace with stable higher output. Indeed, if he wanted to produce products, he would have to sell his milk to Hokuren, who would then mark it up 33 percent and sell it back to him (after he paid the over-quota penalties). As outlined in the previous chapter, like a protective parent might care for their less robust children, MAFF and the various *nōgyō* vehemently protect inefficient and part-time farmers at the expense of more efficient farms with higher overhead costs. Concrete proof of this small farm and price protectionism is easy to find, but few cases are as dramatic as that in April of 2006, when Hokuren opted to dump one thousand metric tons of excess processed milk rather than have it enter the highly regulated market and lower the overall milk price. This action angered many in Hokkaido, indeed many across Japan—where, as detailed in the previous chapter, food security issues hit a raw nerve. Urban and rural Japanese alike thought that this milk could have been put to better use and were rightfully piqued at the lack of consultation and noncooperative nature of Hokuren's action. The milk could have, for example, been converted to dry milk for food aid, stored in dry form for future possible shortages, or even used as product milk, albeit going over quota. Hokuren's action only aggravated the *shachō*'s steadfast contempt of the system he perceives as being set up to penalize the ambitious while supporting smaller inefficient farmers, the latter functioning as obstacles to his vision of progress. In short, his frustration and growing resentment toward the control of JA and Hokuren were palpable and frequently articulated. What is ironic about the situation is that these bodies ceaselessly claim to protect Japanese farmers, a point to which I will return (Hansen 2010a, 2014a).

Again, despite political grievances and the industrious desires of the boss aside, most agreed the material conditions on the farm were good, and, in many ways, they were slightly better than the norm. While the day started earlier, ended later, and the monthly pay was average, due to the large size of the company the employees were given *kaishain* (company employee–like) conditions. Insurance was provided, a bonus of a month's salary was given in June and December for full-time employees, a moderate fuel allowance doled out, and a company car and semi-furnished company apartment—both relatively new—could be leased for a nominal fee. Workers were offered a four-day-on and one-day-off schedule, which amounted to six days off per month—two more than many farms. As of 2019 the farm owns three small apartment buildings, two in town (one for males and one for females), and one on the farm itself largely occupied by foreign workers who are unable to drive.

At Grand Hopes Farm the *shachō* does the majority of hiring and firing, at least for those who are not locals, and the aforementioned topic of government intervention notwithstanding, he gives the impression of being a calm, confident, busy, reasonable, and good-humored businessman. The equipment and buildings are safe and new when compared to most of the surrounding farms. For workers who might be interested in the newest dairy farming methods and machines, the fifty-cow parlor (milking machine) was, in 2005, at the cutting edge of technology, at least in Gensan. When I would describe the situation at Grand Hopes to outside interlocutors actually interested in dairying as a career, the situation at the farm was often commented on with envy.

Numerous examples of contract conditions can be found on the internet or in one of the local or national magazines catering to youth looking for *arubaito* (part-time) employment. Generally speaking, for an entry-level position on a farm, one must be between the ages of eighteen and forty and although experience is not necessary it is preferred. Usually, one must commit to a three-month contract, although in practice this is an impossible regulation to police with regard to Japanese employees, hence the requirement is frequently broken by staff and ignored by employers. Dairy work is a year-round vocation, so even the short but prized Japanese national holidays, such as Golden Week, do not apply to dairy cattle, and so neither to the employees of dairy farms. Shift-work scheduling was adhered to 365 days of the year. Holidays could be negotiated, with short absences (up to two days) made up later, or longer ones without pay prearranged. However, though possible on paper, an employee negotiating for a long holiday was very rare in practice. I know of only one long-term employee who took a week off to return home to Chiba. And a friend from Kyushu who worked at a beef farm near Gensan, a far less demanding position in regard to scheduling as there is no milking involved, claimed that she had taken off only two weeks in her seven years of employment. Thus, the majority of holidays taken were of a short duration and the shifts were scheduled to "catch up" the missed hours either later in the month or the following month, negating the need to alter the monthly salary or do complex calculations. For example, on the schedule at Grand Hopes Farm a "+1" or "+2" was written so that all knew who owed how many days at the month's end or start. Often employees from outside the area would plan to take extended travels around Hokkaido after they quit the *bokujyō* and before they returned to home, school, or commenced their next job.

Securing Employment: Individuals Brokering Their Situations

Although dairy farm schedules are not exactly alike one can speak of "run-of-the-mill" shifts. They start with milking in the early morning, often 5:00 or 6:00 a.m., and run through to the early evening, often 6:00 or 7:00 p.m. For most employees, the last shift generally ends with the completion of the day's second milking and the cleaning of the milking equipment and holding areas. A three-times-a-day milking program exists, but, noted below, this is rare. So, for most in the industry the workday is viewed in two halves: morning and late afternoon/early evening. There is usually a substantial midday break from late morning to early afternoon, commonly spent eating and napping. Workers purchase their own clothing, such as the required rubber boots and rainsuits. Such clothes are necessary for the jobs to be done out of doors in rain, snow, or shine. Coveralls and seasonal hats are often supplied to the farms by local equipment dealers and are emblazoned with their company logos. These are for use by employees inside the buildings or when weather or a task permits or requires their use.

The above are benchmark conditions. Because there exists a shortage of labor caused by a substantial outmigration from rural areas to the cities, and because individual farms, farmers, and their needs differ, a significant amount of leeway is open for present and would-be workers to negotiate for more personally favorable conditions within these base structures.

The brokering of employment situations is highly personal, rational, and individual. During an impromptu interview with a dairy farm owner near Wakanai, the northernmost town in Hokkaido, I was told that his workers alternated in taking lengthy holidays without pay; basically he hired more than needed and then negotiated their coming and going related to season and desired vacation times. In another conversation with a farmer near Hidaka in central Hokkaido, I was told that he had the same student helpers come for the summer and they are not missed in other seasons. On big farms like Grand Hopes, during the autumn silage harvest season help is always required, while over the winter, although the farm remains busy, they can manage without external helpers and the extra overhead. Some farms offer free housing but no leased car, some offer homestay at the farm with meals. By way of a more concrete example, none of the locals at Grand Hopes Farm took advantage of the accommodation or the lease of a car. These perks were offered but employees preferred to make their own arrangements—often living at home and showing pride in their customized automobiles—thus, these deductions were not taken from their paychecks. Some long-term workers chose to live in a larger apartment not owned by the *bokujō*. Although they paid their own rent, in one instance the farm paid ¥60,000 for a larger heater to be installed in an employee's private abode (US$10 equals ¥1,000 as a useful, though inexact, benchmark). And as noted below, one worker and his family lived on the farm on the *shachō*'s old homestead.

Other individually negotiated perks were bargained for. Some employees had a background in agriculture. Small bonuses might be applied to their pay. In theory, workers were offered a yearly raise if they opted to stay on. Moreover, pay increased as additional responsibilities were placed on workers who were deemed capable. Students from an agricultural college in a neighboring town, and also some from the more prestigious national university in Obihiro, worked part-time during the milking hours alone for ¥2,500 a shift. And in the early autumn of 2006, six poor souls from a mechanics training program run by a large international tractor company were "volunteered" by their employer to work 7:00 a.m. to 7:00 p.m. for two weeks. In short, there are many farms, many farmers, and much scope for astute workers to haggle for opportunities and suitable conditions within the general framework of hours and days governed by the nature of dairying and rural life in Tokachi. Unlike the image of a big city *kaisha* (or a national university for that matter), where predictably and seniority guides promotion and some ethic of egalitarianism exists (gender, ethnicity, and actual academic production aside in practice), Tokachi dairy farms were meritocracies, often popularity contests, and/or could be wildly unequal in their employment practices. But they were also open to negotiations by shrewd individual agents, and while employees came and went, those who remained over a couple years often had worked out jobs they enjoyed and for which, when age, education, hours, and so forth, were considered, they were well paid and generally content.

Conclusion

Continuing with the themes of Otherness, frontiers, and security, this chapter has moved from the national register to focus on farms in the Tokachi region, specifically around the town of Gensan. The early modern history of Tokachi saw the arrival of settlers: individuals generally seeking escape from their former lives and seeking to secure a new life on the frontier, on the new margins of Japan. They changed the landscape of the region through facing Otherness—a new climate, crops, humans, and animals. Today this search for security and the concomitant engagement with change and Otherness remains. Dairy owners try to secure the best staff they can and struggle against administrative bodies to manage their own farms, and individual workers are able to broker the best conditions for their employment. Comparatively, and unlike the highly protected rice market, dairy farming is more akin to the work conditions found on other neoliberal-influenced, industrialized livestock operations in the US for example (Blanchette 2020; Pachirat 2011). The following chapter will note how changes are affecting the lives of those seeking security in Tokachi by focusing, in the main, on the individual farmers that came together and then drifted apart marking the creation of Grand Hopes Farm.

Chapter Six

The Birth of Grand Hopes

Introduction

The chapter outlines the birth of the farm and the story of the four families that were at the heart of the formation of this industrial dairy operation from 2000 to 2020. It underscores the reasons why the four owners chose to create a mega monoculture farm and some of the issues they faced. For example, their choice to expand was perceived negatively by some townspeople and dairy farm owners, while to others it was seen as inevitable, laudable, or even visionary. At one extreme people saw Grand Hopes Farm as the way of the future. At the other end of the spectrum, it was viewed as representing the surest way to extinction for Japanese agriculture and dairy in particular. But there were a wide range of nuanced and individual opinions that existed between these alternate poles. While a diversity of individual opinions among locals is unsurprising, what was unexpected, at least by the author, was the divergence of views among the shifting roster of owners within the Grand Hopes operation itself. The search for security amid such changes was a matter of community interest and speculation, but it was a matter of ontological security and livelihood for the individual owners of the farm.

Grand Hopes Farm as a Case Study

Employment conditions are a common conversation topic around Gensan and despite its large size, using Grand Hopes Farm as a point of reference is not unreasonable. The working conditions at the farm, though not identical to other farms, are akin to the majority of dairy farms in Tokachi, with similar hours, salary levels, perks, and to some degree the same daily routine of tasks and divisions of labor.

The base salary was ¥160,000 per month when I started work in 2005 and this had not changed as of 2021. A modest ¥10,000 was deducted for a newer one-room apartment, but internet, phone, electricity, and gas were all paid separately. This came to approximately ¥15,000 per month and ¥10,000 was deducted for the use of a leased car. All told, after taxes and deductions an average worker on the lowest rung was left with just under ¥120,000 take-home pay per month. This was the salary paid to all first-year workers regardless of their education, aptitude, or day-to-day work assignments. While some workers had serious financial problems due to gambling and fiscal mismanagement, others claimed that they were working at the farm in order to save money, in one case for a wedding, in another to continue education, cases I discuss in the following chapters. Although grievances emerged through hushed "shoptalk" on and off the job, pay was not a typical grouse: most workers were satisfied. Also, in general, a farmhand willing to stick it out could expect substantial biannual bonuses (about a month's wages) and a moderate yearly pay increase. Again, employment conditions were negotiated directly with farm owners on an individual level. As on all Hokkaido family farms, industrial or not, there was no union. Dissatisfied workers could leave, and they frequently chose to, including numerous members of the owners' families. Workers also shifted from farm to farm. For those not interested in a career in farming, this might just be for a change of scene, moving from a Gensan dairy farm to work in another part of Hokkaido. For long-term employees and locals however, such shifts were usually rooted in a deeper dissatisfaction with personal relationships or work conditions on a given farm.

One contentious issue among staff at Grand Hopes Farm was the 4:00 a.m. morning milking start for the *hayaban* (morning shift) and *nakanuke* (midday rest or split shift) workers. Many employees clearly waited until the last possible moment to come to work and arrived with tousled hair, red eyes, and less than alert expressions. Some were perennially late and their morning started with a halfhearted scolding by the equally exhausted shift boss. On the schedule, milking lasted until 8:00 a.m., but usually milking and the required cleanup was completed by 7:45 a.m., if not earlier. There was then a break until 9:30 a.m. Some workers would remain in the staff room to eat, watch television, or nap sprawled out on a section of the room's many *tatami*. Exhaustion settled heavily on those sleeping. They were oblivious to the surrounding soundscape of the TV, boisterous conversations, people coming and going from the room, the intrusion of salespeople's greetings, and even the milk truck noisily pumping out the morning's liquid haul in the next room. Other workers chose to return home for breakfast with family or, presumably, just to get out of the building. At 9:30 a.m. the *osoban* (late shift) workers would arrive and all three shifts would work until 12:00 p.m. doing various tasks related to the care of cattle, usually cleaning stalls or transporting animals. At noon all workers took their lunch break, and again, some employees would stay while others would opt to return home or occasionally go to town for lunch. While the *hayaban* and *osoban* workers would return to work at 1:30 p.m., the *nakanuke* workers' break would last until 4:00 p.m. The shift from 1:30 to 3:30 was, like the shift from 9:30 a.m. to noon, dedicated to various maintenance tasks. After this shift there was a half-hour break, usually passed in the "laundry/staff" room attached to the parlor. The time was spent smoking, talking, or enjoying a cold drink; bidding farewell to the morning shift workers after they completed their laundry with an *otsukaresama* (good job, literally: you are a tired person); and welcoming the returning *nakanuke* workers who entered in various stages of drowsiness. The final milking shift began at 4:00 p.m. and usually ended just before 8:00 p.m.

Although dairy farm schedules differ, two-times-a-day milking is the standard practice; often starting an hour later than noted above and finishing an hour earlier. Thus, most farms adopt some form of modified *nakanuke* work schedule, for example, starting work at around 5:00 a.m. and finishing around 7:00 p.m. after having taken a long lunch break. In my final month of work, Grand Hopes Farm instituted a three-times-a-day milking schedule much to the "behind the scenes" chagrin of the workers and to the shock of the neighboring dairy owners. Many workers quietly growled: "Nani o kangateirun da . . . mō, dame da yo . . . taihen da yo ne?" (What are they thinking? This sucks! What a pain, don't you think?).

Indeed, a thrice-a-day milking shift is alienating and exhausting. Workers who drew this shift were often quite bitter and the Chinese workers on the farm were nearly always given this shift. More will be said of these individual grievances in the following chapters.

Many neighboring *bokujō* owners expressed surprise at this move by the biggest dairy in town: "Dame yo, ushi ga sugu byōki ni natchau yo" (It's a bad idea, their cows are soon going to get sick).

One rather outspoken small-scale farmer who I often ran into at a local convenience store simply tilted his head and said: "Kono aida no hanashi oboeteiru? Wada san wa baka da" (I told you the other day, Wada is an idiot).

Under this new schedule the *nakanuke* shift was replaced by a *sankai* (three times) shift. *Sankai* workers did not partake in any form of animal care or maintenance. Working only during milking times, they had no other contact with the cows beyond peering between their legs and attaching milking equipment mediated by a machine. The second milking began at noon and the final milking began at 6:00 p.m. Consequently, *osoban* started at nine in the morning and lunch ran from eleven to noon. The second milking session ended at around 3:30, and the final shift ended at 10:00 p.m. Viewing the following schedule (table 6.1) is perhaps more useful than trying to imagine the routine through prolonged explanation.

There was a certain amount of social alienation inherent in this system. Clearly, if one works a *nakanuke, osoban*, or *sankai* shift followed by a *hayaban, nakanuke*, or *sankai* shift, the morning comes quickly! In essence, finishing work at 8:00 p.m. or even 10:00 p.m., returning home, eating, and then retiring in time to return to work by 4:00 a.m. means that facing the next day presents a mental and physical challenge over a prolonged period of time. Often workers were scheduled for four back-to-back *sankai* or *nakanuke* shifts and some mornings, especially after a night of overtime or moderate carousing, everyone's requisite *ohayō* (good morning) was half-hearted followed by an expressive *nemuiiiii yo* (I am so tired!).

Similarly, as the farm followed a four days on and one day off routine across a range of jobs highlighted in table 6.2, if one finished the week with a late shift and started the new workweek with an early shift, one's day off was effectively eighteen hours. Time off was generally a private affair. Indeed, as will be seen in the chapters that follow, time alone was common both on the job and off. Moreover, due to the nature of the four-day rotation schedule, workers did not get the same day off weekly. As such, scheduling meetings with friends or family on a day off was often difficult to plan especially if they worked on neighboring *bokujō* or had jobs with regular weekends and holidays off. Workers often complained that they seldom saw their friends or families beyond mealtimes and that, due to working such unusual hours, finding or maintaining a romantic

Table 6.1. An outline of the thrice-a-day system that initiated December 2006.

Time	Hayaban	New Hayaban	Osoban	New Osoban	Nakanuke	New Sankai
4:00 a.m.	Milk	Milk	OFF	OFF	Milk	Milk
5:00	Milk	Milk	OFF	OFF	Milk	Milk
6:00	Milk	Milk	OFF	OFF	Milk	Milk
7:00	Milk	Milk	OFF	OFF	Milk	Milk
8:00	Rest	Rest	OFF	OFF	Rest	Rest
9:00	Rest	Work	OFF	Work	Rest	Rest
9:30	Work	Work	Work	Work	Work	Rest
10:00	Work	Work	Work	Work	Work	Rest
11:00	Work	Lunch	Work	Lunch	Work	Rest
Noon	Lunch	Lunch	Lunch	Lunch	Rest	Rest
12:30	Lunch	Milk	Lunch	Milk	Rest	Milk
13:00	Lunch	Milk	Lunch	Milk	Rest	Milk
13:30	Work	Milk	Work	Milk	Rest	Milk
14:00	Work	Milk	Work	Milk	Rest	Milk
15:00	Work	Milk	Work	Milk	Rest	Milk
15:30	Work	OFF	Rest	Rest	Rest	Rest
16:00	OFF		Milk	Rest	Milk	Rest
17:00			Milk	Rest	Milk	Rest
18:00			Milk	Milk	Milk	Milk
19:00			Milk	Milk	Milk	Milk
20:00			OFF	Milk	OFF	Milk
21:00				Milk		Milk
22:00				OFF		OFF
Overtime						

partner was nearly impossible. If the question, "X—san, kinō wa anata no yasumi no hi deshita ne. Nani o shimashita ka?" (Hey X, yesterday was your day off. What did you do?) was posed, the reply, more often than not from locals, was that they watched television, slept, went shopping, or played pachinko. Outsiders generally led solitary but reasonably active

Table 6.2. A list of the jobs and the corresponding kanji or katakana symbols as found on the sample farm schedule below. Subcontractors are not included.

ホ	Holding
ス	Stall cleaning
エ or 育	Feeding
●	Parlor shift boss or teacher
○	Parlor shift worker
二	Tasks in second barn
ハ	In charge of cows in heat
哺	Nursing and caring for calves
/	Day off

lives. While at some point *junbi* (preparation) was always included in the reply to my question (for example: prepare lunches for the week, do my laundry, clean my apartment, etc.), they also often went on solo trips to surrounding tourist areas. For example, it was common to go on a trip to a town for famous local cuisine, visit a nearby national park to hike or ski, or spend a relaxing day at an *onsen*.

On the work schedule for November 2006 (see figure 6.1), each day is represented by a square. Names are removed but would ordinarily be placed at the start of the left-hand row. The actual outline of the jobs and their purpose are outlined in chapters 8 through 10. The square is divided into three sections relating to the time of day the indicated task starts. For example, a mark to the far left would indicate the *hayaban* work shift, meaning the task and start time of 4:00 a.m., while three marks would indicate working only in the parlor during milking. Occasional overtime was not added to the schedule but was instead communicated on the day, by posting a note on the staff room door or the laundry room table.

As noted in the previous chapter, secure or stable work situations, including insurance, predictable bonuses, hours, wages, and job titles, were assured by the careful and reasoned brokering of owners and workers without the aid of intermediaries. Therefore, as independent agents, the workers needed to be confident in their abilities, capabilities, and desires. This securing of personal securities, so to speak, in terms of both conditions of employment and the clear articulation of what was expected of employer and employee was, in theory, unambiguous. However, the

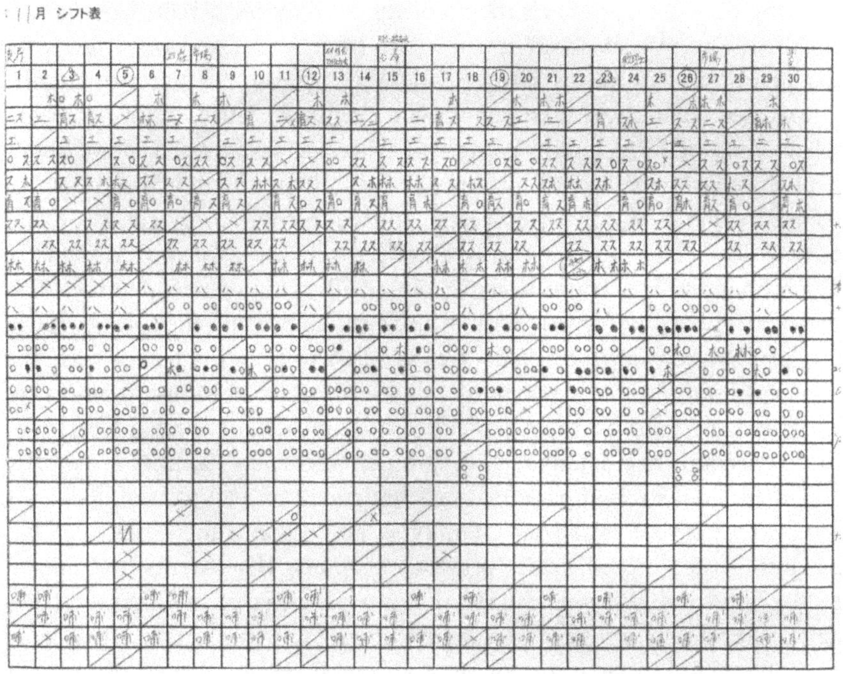

：| | 月　シフト表

Figure 6.1. A copy of the work schedule for November of 2006 after the introduction of a *sankai* milking schedule. Photo by the author.

actual work conditions were often open-ended and undefined. That is to say one's place in the shifting chain of command or unscheduled long hours forcing unhealthy sleep and diet patterns were not part of a contract. Thus, despite a clear division of labor on paper, the actual working out of "who did what with whom and when" was deeply dependent on individual negotiations and on the needs of the farm, which shifted according to daily demands and season. This did little to promote a sense of physical security or well-being; stress, confusion (personal and professional), exhaustion, and as noted in the following chapters, frequent interpersonal and interspecies conflicts were all common.

Grand Hopes: The Farm and Its Families

The following insights into the lives of four families that owned Grand Hopes Farm are gleaned from ethnographic research: that is to say, from working daily with some members of the families for a year; from gossip within the farm and about town; a two-hour structured interview with the *shachō* and countless shorter follow-up meetings; a night of slightly intoxicated chatting with an owner who eventually left the farm; constant discussions of farm family goings-on with Matsuyama-san, a well-connected department head; and, not the least, living in the community of Gensan, on and off, for fifteen years exposed to community gossip on and off the farm. The *shachō*'s family has been selected as a central focus in this ethnographic account because, out of all of the owners' families, it is their story that I know best and, in the end, he became the sole owner of the farm. Moreover, since Wada-san's family had been in Gensan since the area was homesteaded, everybody knows or knows of him. But all owner families have lived on their respective homesteads for three generations. In this account, the details regarding other co-owners' families are mostly added for context, comparison, and confirmation.

The story of Wada-san's family is not unlike the stories of other modern settlers noted in the previous chapters. His parents had moved to Tokachi from Honshu. His father was a papermaker in Gifu prefecture and his mother was from a farming family in Fukui prefecture. They came to pioneer land in Gensan, not yet a village, in 1928, a time before roads or electricity and when horses were used to break land and for transportation. While I was working on the farm, both of Wada-san's elderly parents were still living on the original homestead in a newly built house. His mother was energetic and often seen walking on the roadway, but the father was badly hunched over, perhaps arthritic, from his previous years of work. Generally, he was restricted to the front yard. They had three children: the *shachō*; his younger brother, who worked as an architect in Tokyo; and his sister, who was married to a police officer in Kyoto.

My links with the boss were perceived as tight by most workers. He had hired me, trained me, and would ask me how things were going with work and my research in front of coworkers. He also gave me occasional privileges: for example, I had negotiated time off for research and in return I was asked to look at English websites. Moreover, his closest worker became one of my main interlocutors. Matsuyama-san was close both in terms of proximity, when I was working on the farm he lived with his family across the road in the *shachō*'s old house, and in position, as the *buchō* in charge of cattle welfare. And over the years, Matsuyama-san and his family have become confidants and friends. In sum, it is quite possible that some of my coworkers were reluctant to say negative things about the *shachō* to me, given these connections with both him and his right-hand man. Contrary to this, there were no shortage of complaints expressed about the *kachō*, along with griping about various *buchō* and a few fellow workers. Far from a sense of "groupism" as noted in what follows many relationships were more confrontational than cooperative.

Unlike the wives of the other owners, the *shachō*'s wife did not work on the farm. Nevertheless, she was well known by the farmworkers for her kindness. She often left snacks and cold drinks for us in the staff room. There seemed to be no particular logic governing her acts of generosity, but all recipients were pleasantly surprised. Like a cameo player, she would just appear at work with a bag of treats, ranging from pears to McDonald's cheeseburgers, ask employees to enjoy them, and, bowing and nodding graciously, exit out a side door. She was very fond of gardening and occasionally looked after Matsuyama-san's son when his wife was at work in a local supermarket. The *shachō* and his wife had three children. One daughter was twenty-four years old when I worked on the farm. She was a caregiver for the elderly in a nearby town. The other daughter was twenty-one and worked as a hairstylist in Obihiro. Occasionally, the daughters might be glimpsed in front of the house, but they were never seen on the farm and they had never worked at the farm. The son, discussed below, was twenty-five and lived in Sapporo at that time.

The *kachō* was a short, stocky, loud, impatient, and brash man. With an ever-present cigarette dangling from the corner of his mouth and a hat precariously positioned on his head like a star atop a Christmas tree, he would drive around the grounds of the farm, often stopping to yell at someone or to tell workers to get in the back of the truck—which they would quickly do despite knowing the task at the end of the ride was bound to be unfavorable. While the *shachō* from time to time lost his temper, the reason was generally clear to all involved; a tool had been forgotten or a worker had arrived late. His wrath was largely limited to a tilted head, a disgusted look, a hiss, and inaudible, self-directed grumbling. Often, there was no particular reason for the numerous "Nani yattanda (x) yaro?" (What the "curse word explicative of choice" are you doin'?), doled out daily by the *kachō*. It was accepted as just his way of being and workers' comments underscored that he both demanded, and indeed in many ways commanded, respect, first through fear and loathing and second because he was a bottomless reservoir of resourcefulness and pragmatism. He got things done and it was clear to everyone, including the other farm owners, that he was the most knowledgeable about the practicalities of running a farm. If problems regarding the functioning of the equipment or the logistics of moving cows arose, he was the "go to" man. The general agreement was that he was frustrated by the general incompetence of his staff on what was now an industrial farm with many unskilled workers who knew nothing about farmwork beyond what they learned on the dairy and mostly through trial and error. While human relations were not the forte of the *kachō*, his frustrations with workers, equipment, and cattle, combined with a degree of social ineptness, made him prone to fits of rage that would quickly (and for the most part, harmlessly) pass. Moreover, despite his rather militaristic and despotic approach to management, he had clear ideas about what his workers should, or should not, be doing. All agreed that his job was stressful: to ensure that thousands of costly cows were properly cared for by workers who often did not know—or occasionally did not care—about their safety and security as they moved through the daily regimen of milking.

Countless ethnographic examples could serve to highlight the *kachō*'s drive to control workers and cattle, but a couple will suffice. On one occasion he had nine workers stand outside to watch cows get loaded onto a truck twenty minutes before the end of their shift, because "jikan ga aru" (there is time). There was absolutely no need for workers to be standing in the baking hot midday sun after putting in a late night of unpaid overtime. Nonetheless, most of the workers trotted around sweltering and attempting to look helpful, while three others held on to an immovable gate just in case something might happen. When he was not around, and if the scheduled tasks were completed, workers often left a bit early. Indeed, the *shachō* frequently told workers to go home early if required work was done, with the mutual understanding that occasionally workers would have to stay on an extra few moments to finish a task. However, if the *kachō* was lurking around, there was always a hushed panic, whispers of "Ima nani o shimasu ka, jikan ga aru?" (What should we do, there is still time?). In these moments of transition looking busy was far more important than actually accomplishing any task; washing a manure shovel or picking weeds in an open field would suffice. Often, like a Mr. Hyde to the *shachō*'s Dr. Jekyll, with ten minutes remaining on the clock, the *kachō* would drive up, bark out orders that a twenty-minute task needed to be completed, and drive off. The task was always completed. Summoning the depths of my courage, I once asked why he was so concerned with putting in the scheduled amount of time for a livelihood that defies such rigidity. He had his reasons and rules. From his perspective, for workers not to work the entire scheduled period was unfair to their cohorts: all or nothing without carryover was how he viewed the workday.

The owners of the farm did not always agree. I learned that before my arrival at the farm there had been heated disagreement among the owners over hiring me. The *kachō* was dead set against the idea. The coworker that relayed this information to me also explained that the *shachō* felt obliged to hire me because in his youth he had been hired by a dairy farm in Wisconsin, USA. It was reasoned that I was his penance (or as a different coworker put it, his *giri* or duty) for his previous good fortune. Somehow, behind closed doors they came to an agreement, likely most influenced by the fact that they desperately needed employees. However, the *kachō* made it clear from our first meeting that he was not keen to have me around and would occasionally make comments to hammer the point home. On more than one occasion he entered the staff room and stated that he needed a *nihonjin* (a Japanese person) to help him. This continued when Chinese workers arrived at the farm near the end of my contract. His wife was reserved and seldom worked outside of their homesteaded section of the farm. They had four children. The youngest son, Masahiro, worked on the farm and is described at length in the chapter 8. The older son worked for the main dairy processing company near Obihiro. One daughter worked at a hotel and the other was still attending high school. Only Masahiro wanted to remain on the farm.

Yamamoto-san was another owner. He was in charge of feed and spent most of his working day on a tractor carting feed from point A to point B. He was a quiet man, and, although I saw him nearly every day during my time at the farm, we barely ever spoke, only exchanging bows and smiling cordial greetings and agreements about the weather. He too had four children. Two were working in Obihiro and two were students. His wife was also politely uncommunicative with me, but she joked with the other wives and the women who worked with the calves. None of his children were interested in taking over the dairy farm, which is what prompted him to join the Grand Hopes operation. There was little point in hanging on to a farm that nobody wanted when shares in an incorporated farm like Grand Hopes could be sold off.

The final owner was Katō-san. While the other owners were in their fifties and sixties, he was twenty-seven years old. For weeks I had no idea that he was an owner. It was not until I inquired about the large Jizō statue (a Buddhist deity related to safe passage of living and dead) at a nearby crossroads that I learned his father had tragically been killed in a car accident two years before my arrival. Katō-san did not have any siblings. He inherited his father's share in the farm and soon after he and his mother opted into the incorporated farm. His mother worked in the lower barn area with the calves. He was a reluctant owner, and, quite at odds with the kachō, he was a very jovial and good-natured fellow. He never flew into fits of rage like the manager or some of the department heads. Unlike the affable but silent Yamamoto-san, he would occasionally, boisterously buy a round of soda or canned coffee from the vending machine in the staff room. With his big belly jiggling and an ear-to-ear grin, he would heartily laugh at both his own and others' jokes, steaming up his thick glasses while taking drink orders. He was a mixture of slapstick comedian and sumo wrestler, stuffed into ill-fitting overalls, and an all-around likeable everyman.

Unfortunately, pleasant as he was to be with, he was also notoriously lazy. Unlike the other owners or their spouses, all of whom worked as hard if not harder than their employees, hired hands often found themselves having to work for, or rather, work *around*, Katō-san, who at times seemed like a gregarious and gleeful pylon. He worked holding, milking, and stalls depending on where he was scheduled. If a stall worker was his partner for the day, they might comment, "Kyō wa Katō-san to issho ni hataraiteiru" (Today I am working with Katō-san). The set reply was "Gambatte" (do your best/good luck), but often a look or head tilt would suffice as empathetic understanding of the predicament.

During his agricultural college days, Katō-san had spent three months working as an exchange student on a cattle farm in Colorado, USA, and, similar to the *shachō*, he would occasionally intersperse English into his Japanese when talking with me. At one point, waiting for the delivery of rice husks to shovel out for bedding, I asked him about the chain of command at the farm. He listed the president, the manager, and claimed that Yamamoto-san was also a de facto manager as only he was in charge of the feed. I said that I knew he was also a co-owner, yet noticeably missing from his list. He replied in English, "No Pōru, I am very, very lowly." His meaning was, I suspect, that his position was low on this scale of power, but my impression was that he was uncomfortable being viewed as on the list at all, uncomfortable being positioned beyond an ordinary worker. Truly "lowly," he saw himself out of place, a reluctantly assigned department head of a nondefined department at best.

Katō-san lamented about the large size of the farm. If his personality contrasted with the *kachō*, his impressions in regard to the progressive industrialization of the farm were the mirror opposite of what I had been told by the *shachō*. Katō-san was convinced that he had more free time and a more enjoyable life when he worked on his family's farm, before its incorporation into Grand Hopes Farm. His lowliness had more to do with the added responsibility of being a new owner, with a hazily defined position and the loss of his father, than with the increased farm size alone. Katō-san gave a happy-go-lucky impression, but he clearly had conflicts and worries about the direction of the farm, including his position on it. And as it turned out, the reader will learn in the following chapters that this was a sound worry for him to have.

Before the birth of Grand Hopes Farm in 2002, all four families had managed their own "medium-large" private family dairies, ranging in size from 120 to 180 head. However, in 1999 the government opened the way for the development of incorporated farms. An explanation of these shifts in policy are highlighted in detail by Jentzsch (2021, 46–61) and MacLachlan and Shimizu (2022, 50–81). The upshot was a national effort to encourage consolidation, the expansion of large farms, and the phasing out of small, inefficient farms. The *shachō* explained that the four owners had batted around the idea of incorporating for a year and finally in 2000 they sat down over coffee and discussed the pros and cons of merging their private farms into an incorporated operation. The *shachō* and *kachō* held the most cattle (about 180 head each) and equipment. While Katō-san's father and Yamamoto-san held less stock or liquid capital, they both had a good deal of cropland in the surrounding area. It was agreed that a merger would be beneficial for the following reasons:

1. They would be able to share equipment, for example, tractors and cultivating equipment. They could buy a rotary parlor system difficult to afford for a family farm (though some did purchase smaller models, such as a nearby farm with three hundred head).

2. They would cut down on competition between themselves for resources such as lease land for crops.

3. They would need to hire workers, but this meant more time for family and friends. That is, days off could be arranged, as opposed to working 365 days of the year.

4. The farm would be a business and not a personal venture. Thus, owners could be bought out if their offspring were

not interested in farming. Moreover, with the capital from all the farms condensed they would be able to secure larger loans at more favorable terms.

5. The risks of working together were lower than those facing individual farmers. Sickness in cattle or family would be offset through the assistance of others. Equipment failures would be offset by the use of the others' equipment—and as above—new equipment could be leased or purchased on more favorable terms.

6. The prefecture and the municipal government would be willing to assist with some grants and loans.

7. They would produce more milk of higher quality in less time.

For these reasons, relayed to me during a taped semi-structured interview with the *shachō* and triangulating this data with other conversations, Grand Hopes Farm was formed. However, what was not addressed in the interview became clear over time spent working on the farm and living in Gensan. By undertaking such a large venture in a small town, a certain amount of untold acrimony arose between the owners themselves, and also between the townsfolk and the farm. Put another way, they were staking their future security by setting themselves up as Others within the community and erecting a frontier between industrialized incorporated farms and family farms.

The farm incorporation was not paid for by the owners alone: the prefecture, through a combination of grants and long-term loans, contributed about 25 percent of the start-up cost for the farm. The owners collectively paid around 25 percent, and with their combined equity, they secured a loan for 50 percent to cover the remainder. Depending on one's opinion and on the ever-volatile future of the milk market, this was a courageous and clever or foolhardy move on a grand scale. A point, not contentious to any observer or the owners themselves, was that—as in Fredrik Barth's classic analysis of headman competition in the Swat Valley, Pakistan—this was a rationally thought-out sizable risk taken by the family heads that could end in family success or disaster (Barth 1959). The ethnographies provided in Jentzsch (2021) and MacLachlan and Shimizu (2022) underscore similar local debates in other regions of Japan: some agriculturalist opting to try to stay afloat following the status quo, some opting to expand, others opting to get out of farming altogether in the face of declining profits, a lack of successors, and the perception of limited opportunities for younger family members.

The *shachō* confided in me that the substantial debt they took on was problematic to manage. But, provided that the consumption of milk did not drop further, a second speculative hazard, the move to an incorporated farm system would pay off in the end. This financial situation was one reason why the farm was under pressure to produce and run smoothly. It also explains the *shachō*'s aforementioned anger at government-set production limits. While the government sponsors the move to larger farms, it concomitantly cripples farms that have high overhead costs by setting low quotas, thereby encouraging small and part-time farmers to continue farming where, in a free market, they would surely fail. The building of Grand Hopes was a high-stakes gamble by the four families on a future in which the industry would move toward mega farming and away from smaller family or mixed farms, gambling that Japan's generous small farm subsidies would dry up as consumers demand lower prices.

This raises an interesting point in accord with the financial condition of the farm. There was a great pressure for everything to look good and run smoothly: the promotion of an image of a successful and progressive farming business. This is because a large farm equipment dealer in Obihiro also had a stake in the development and continued functioning of Grand Hopes Farm. At first the owners and *buchō* were reluctant to tell me about these external links. I persisted in questioning, irritatingly so in retrospect, wheedling information from one source, for example, a *buchō*, and relaying it to, for example, an equipment service technician out on call for the day, so that I might then feed his response to the *shachō*, and on and on until what gradually emerged was a series of formal and informal agreements.

The equipment dealer helped to design the parlor and some outbuildings. If there was a problem with the equipment, a team of three or four service technicians would arrive from Obihiro within a couple of hours. They would not only repair the equipment; they would wait until it was in use for a substantial period of time (one night waiting until 11:00 p.m. after repairing the parlor) to be certain that it was functioning as it should. When I asked smaller scale farmers in the area what sort of customer service they expected from their local equipment dealers, the answers ranged. Some seldom called upon dealers, as technicians were an unneeded expense for repairs that they could execute themselves, especially on farms with older or more basic equipment. Others claimed that they received satisfactory service. But all found the description of service at Grand Hopes Farm curiously exceptional. This was true of government subsidized NOSAI veterinarians as well. Grand Hopes was the only dairy in the area to have its own full-time veterinarian on call during the afternoon. However, this high level of service was not strictly financial or due to the size of the farm. That is to say, the farm did not pay more for its services than other farms. Indeed, it was occasionally given a discount due to buying its parts in bulk. What was at stake was greater than direct economic exchange. It was the symbolic capital of being linked with the image of Grand Hopes Farm, that is, being connected to the newest in farming technology and being seen as futuristic (or indeed as having a future). Again, this farm was seen as Other, as a farm that was embracing the frontiers of dairying technology, and the security of local equipment dealers to sell newer equipment was at stake.

Given the rate at which local dairy herds were increasing in size, and small farms disappearing, rotary parlor technology was touted as the "way of things to come" and many Tokachi farmers had their eyes trained on the fate of Grand Hopes. Indeed, the farm had visitors from across Japan and even the agricultural minister of Thailand paid a high-profile visit in 2013. Thus, the fortune of the farm was entwined with the profitable sale of new high-output, and high-cost, farming and dairying equipment and services, from the latest milking technology to the newest advances in artificial insemination. These frontiers of the body and science, widely construed, are detailed in the final chapter of this book. The point made here is that the windowed room overlooking the high-tech milking parlor was frequently filled with the recognizable faces of the equipment salesman and their potential clients, often large to midsized farmers from the area. Grand Hopes Farm was a beacon of the future of farming for those considering the shift to the industrialization, monoculture, and the incorporation of their farms. It functioned as the unofficial showroom for this new equipment, and I daresay this ideology, thus, the great emphasis on appearance and efficiency. The farm had to appear successful and profitable even if it was struggling to pay off debts. This was a key reason why the floors and walls of the parlor were kept impeccably clean; the stall area water troughs looked new; and at one point, amazingly and as seen in figure 6.2, a team of around a dozen workers, myself included, used brooms to sweep dead grass off the acres of lawn in front of the main office. The cleanliness or purity of the milk was important for obvious

Figure 6.2. *Bokujō* Zen? Sweeping the lawn to keep appearances up are Haruko, "the Chinese," and a worker on loan from a local equipment dealership. All workers whose stories are introduced in the following chapters. Photo by the author.

reasons. Price and acceptability are determined, in part, by the pre-pasteurized germ content, but the cleanliness of the publicly visible areas of the farm was critical to sell the image of success, modernity, efficiency, productivity—in short, the farm served as a symbol of its Otherness, the future of mega farming, and the hope of enticing small farmers to get big or get out. However, in a town as small as Gensan, an image that runs counter to local knowledge and gossip is perhaps harder to sell than high-tech equipment.

Whether in a local library, *onsen*, or curry restaurant, past and present, I am asked what I am doing in Gensan. From my first day in town to the present, I have told anyone who asks that I am a researcher and have worked at Grand Hopes Farm. This information is usually met with an "Ah naruhodo nee" (Oh, of course, that makes sense) and then nothing more unless I press the subject, but occasionally this introduction acts as a magnet for occasional approval or disapproval of the farm's direction.

For example, at the town's *onsen* one evening I could not escape the gaze of Sato-san, a well-known local elder, a local clothes shop owner and a near nightly patron of the town's hot spring and *izakaya*. Notoriously friendly, talkative, and opinionated, he knows everybody and everybody knows him. Upon learning about my research, he told me that the farm was bound to fail because of the high turnover rate, the crowding of the cattle, and the debt. This all seemed to be accepted knowledge among his cohort, as the others in the sauna said nothing but nodded their heads in emphatic agreement. Outgoing nature aside, neither he nor they would comment directly on the owners, beyond head tilts and *yoku wakaranai* (I'm not really sure). Of course, he asked me what *I* thought of the owners. I replied honestly that they had been helpful and kind to me and had gone to considerable trouble to arrange my visa. "Gaijin dakara" (Because you're a foreigner), the ultimate label of Otherness and outsider status in terms of being Japanese, was his reply. And again, he referred to this being the case for the image of the farm as progressive: hire a white researcher and you look futuristic. Heads continued bobbing.

There was little room for speculation about the thoughts of another man I met nearing the end of my first stint of fieldwork in October of 2006. After a few comments about the turning leaves, discussion turned to work. He was employed at a nearby beef farm. As it turned out, his wife had worked part-time at Grand Hopes Farm and had left on bad terms. According to him, the owners were fools, they knew nothing about cattle, they mistreated their animals and staff, they were deep in debt, and the whole town hoped that they would fail because mega farming was destroying local farmers and businesses. But of course, *none* of this was new information to me at this point. In Gensan, these sorts of diatribes, pro or anti Grand Hopes Farm, were common, though seldom as vehemently and unambiguously articulated. Usually, the negative comments were more along the line of: "Shakkin wa taihen deshō" ([Such high] loans are difficult [to keep up the payments on I bet]), or less optimistically, "Kono saki ninen de ano bokujō ga mada aru kanaaaa" (I wonder if there will be a farm there in two years, hummm). The patent response was a play on the optimism of the katakana name of the farm—here a pseudonym—but saying something like, "Grand Hopes indeed," "Keep on hoping," or "Hopes won't pay the bills" might be seen as suitable parallels. Eiji-san, a particularly insightful, frequently drunk, and often head-to-toe leather-clad man in his sixties who frequented a friend's curry shop, claimed (prophetically as it turned out), "Four owners will always move in four directions." In his view, Yamamoto-san and Katō-san were weak links that would be cut out of the chain of command at the first chance.

He saw the *shachō* and *kachō* as both *zurui hito* (crafty people). And by 2008 these two original owners had indeed been bought out by the *shachō* and *kachō*, replaced by other neighboring locals with land and a lack of capital, and they soon were bought out too. The *kachō* and his son sold their shares in Grand Hopes in 2014, albeit on good terms as they still lease their land and the son seasonally works on the farm. By 2015, Mr. Wada became the sole owner of this now massive dairy farm.

The owners of other large farms sometimes questioned the utility of certain Grand Hopes practices, such as milking three times a day, but they clearly saw the simultaneous increase in farm size and decrease in smaller farms as desirable, if not inevitable, and they too had, albeit to a lesser degree, cast themselves as Others in the "bigger-is-better" lot seeking their own positions of security. In interviews with more positive interlocutors two words constantly arose in relationship to industrializing dairies and their new technology: *shinpo* and *shōrai* (progress and future), a discourse not so different from those promoting the Japanese drive to modernize in the early Meiji period. However, the future of the dairy market was and remains nothing if not insecure and uncertain and the meaning of progress was not agreed upon by the four original owners of Grand Hopes Farm, let alone their fellow dairy farmers big or small, old or young.

Conclusion

One night over dinner I relayed the generally negative talk about town to Matsuyama-san. He looked perplexed and leaned back in his chair. "Set-sumei wa muzukashii yo" (It's hard to explain), he said, and he asked for my electronic dictionary. He produced the phrase "sour grapes"—"Kore!" (it's this), he said handing it back. His young wife looked over my shoulder and ardently added in a descending singsong tone, "Sou sou sou" (Exactly).

The individual differences in interpretation among the townspeople and the original owners of Grand Hopes Farm highlight individual Otherness or, better put, "each" Otherness, even for those in the same camp pushing the frontiers of how dairying should be done. Yet, most people I talked to were dairy farmers and all were from this small town. Hence, beyond the monolithic group Otherness (being dairy farmers in the first place), or a tendency to view the dairying occupation as a source of shared identity, they did not uniformly agree on what was best for the community, what constituted progress, what the best on-farm practices were, or what the future could, should, or would hold for dairying. In sum, there was no agreement on what practices did or did not hold the promise of social or economic security.

Community agreement, even in terms of what constitutes one's community, such as a "community of dairy farm owners," is surely easier to maintain when changes come slowly. But changes have not come slowly in Gensan or on Grand Hopes Farm. Thus, any notions of group solidarity, of communal, farm, or family relationships, rapidly became relationships of "each" Otherness. Whether cooperative or combative, dairy farmers often were not following well-trodden social paths but, similar to the first settlers literally breaking new ground and trails around Gensan, they were attempting to secure new relationships. If one is careful not to overgeneralize, a similar understanding of general farm cartography, organization, and conditions of employment, as noted above, can be usefully applied to the majority of dairy farms, certainly industrial operations, across Tokachi. And this can be compared with other agricultural areas and industries facing rapid shifts seen for example in the US (Berry 1996; Blanchette 2020; Gillespie 2018; Harper 2001; Pachirat 2011; Pollan 2006), Canada (MacLachlan 2001; Novek 2012), France (Vialles 1994), or the UK (Franklin 2008).

The remainder of this book adds flesh, feeling, and interactions onto the "cartographic stage" of Grand Hopes Farm. These issues will be expanded upon below in terms of a detailed ethnographic study, outlining that at the core of Otherness is a search for security on numerous levels: financial (paying off farm debts or working to save or just get by), physical (work hours or personal altercations), and ontological (for example, questioning the meaning of such work, its future, and one's own future).

Chapter Seven

Dairy Farmers

Being, Becoming, and Making

Introduction

The previous chapter introduced Grand Hopes Farm and its owners as individuals with very different perspectives on what the optimum dairy farm situation was, is, or could be. This chapter will continue with that focus on individuals and individuation. Considering the plurality of farms, one of the foremost essayists of rural ecology, Wendell Berry, notes that "the most insistent and formidable concern of agriculture, wherever it is taken seriously, is the distinct individuality of every farm, every field on every farm, every farm family, and every creature on every farm. Farming becomes a high art when farmers know and respect in their work the distinct individuality of their place and the neighborhood of creatures that lives there" (Berry 2005, 45).

In Gensan, while land is portioned in similar geometric plots, the layout of each farm always differs. This is the case even more so for a farmer in their field. To farm is, in essence, for an individual to attempt to secure biological Otherness with ever-changing conditions. Each farm is a microcosm of agentive being and becoming. It is a particular ecology of farmers and farmhands; neighbors engaged in a variety of agricultural and nonagricultural occupations; nonhuman domestic animals from cows to cats; other nondomesticated animals from pigeons to deer; vegetation, both domesticated and indigenous; waterways, both above and below ground; and bacteria both benign and harmful. At the heart of each individuated plot of complexity called farmland (lives and liveli-hoods that human and nonhuman, animate and inanimate, comprise) is a cosmopolitical search for security, a drive to keep the farm producing, providing, and so, continuing.

Starting analysis from such a micro level is not to suggest that beyond a farm's fences, broader ramifications, whether economic, eco-logical, political, community, among other actors and agencies, are unim-portant. Nor is it to insinuate that generalizations about farms, farmers, and farming are impossible to make. Both of these points hopefully are made obvious in previous chapters. Farmers frequently discuss both com-munity interests and their individual hopes and desires beyond the farm itself. However, in focusing on dairy farming as a collective or shared endeavor there is a danger of creating what Hannah Arendt, in a discus-sion about changing labor patterns and rural life, calls "a communistic fiction . . . [of] . . . social forces . . . that no longer correspond to real-ity" (Arendt 1998, 44), a point echoed in the context of rural Japan by William Kelly (2006). Moreover, the farms discussed herein were built upon actions and ideology of frontier expansion and have existed and continue to exist as homesteads *apart* from other homesteads; they are not villages, nor are they a shared commons. They are bounded plots man-aged by individuals and families independently, a point elaborated upon for the remainder of this book. Simply put, farms are often as dissimilar as the people who work and own them. What can be compared is the desire to secure a livelihood dependent upon a number of contingent, changing, unpredictable, and risky factors—weather, markets, and human and nonhuman health for example.

This chapter sets the framework for a comparison of individuals understood as persons, as selves, and not as generalizations or types. I am not interested in describing social stereotypes writ singular nor do I wish to forward the idea that singular beings ought to be viewed as group representatives. Alex Blanchette, in his ethnographic research on pork production, notes, "It would be hard to find much in common among the coworkers who were . . . around me, apart from the fact that we labored in the same barn . . . it is hard to think of any of these people from the confines of a predetermined class or subject position . . . differences in national origin, education, gender, socioeconomic class, language, age, legal status" (Blanchette 2020, 77–79). This situation is the same, with less emphasis on ethnicity, as discussed elsewhere (Hansen 2010). Thus, in what follows emphasis is made here on plurality, on "each Otherness," and on multiple ways of *being, becoming,* and *making* oneself in this particular location. Just as it is a mistake to categorize dairy farms essentially, without reflection on the very separate essence of each farm under study (due to history, region, climate, size, age, efficiency, and layout), it is also a mistake to neglect the needs and desires that differ for individuals from farm to farm and on a single farm. Moreover, looking at the lives of human workers alone does not begin to plumb the depths of the more animated aspects of farm diversity. Similar to the trial-and-error history of what works and what does not work in any given farm landscape, it is important to remember that there are differences for everybody—*every single body* whether two or more legged—on a farm. To be clear this is a matter of perspective. I am not claiming that "the social" is unimportant or that researchers ought to not make generalizations. In the chapters that follow I do, but I am not starting from them. I am claiming that viewing actors first as liminal, confused, and at times utterly irrational agents, prone to good and ill fortune, to wise and foolhardy choices, to moods and affective motivations, intersectional to the point of contradiction is a far less common path to the forefront in a social science context. If successful, this book is an exception, but not an opposition, to this normative collective portrayal of people and one that has resonance with recent ethnographies of agriculturalists as particular people with inimitable personalities who often defy simple, even intersectional, classification (Pachirat 2011; Weiss 2016).

At the Frontiers of the Social, the Individual, and the Self

The social, the individual, and the self are concepts that have long been debated in the humanities and the social sciences and they are not going to find ultimate resolution here. It is, nevertheless, essential to highlight how they are approached in the remainder of this book. Equally important are the relationships between these concepts and their links to aligned research methodologies and theories.

In what follows, the individual is viewed as being biologically and historically unique, the ontological and phenomenal core of agency, and so the maker and interpreter of meaning over and above the social relations that they are born into and in turn cultivate, sustain, or change.[1] However, despite this theoretical/methodological focus, I do not in any way or at any point deny the inescapable influence of social worlds. It is simply a matter of emphasis, and the emphasis on Grand Hopes Farm, as demonstrated and explained in these final chapters, was and remains decidedly oriented toward individuals alongside a profound respect for individualism that can seem incongruous for people expecting a different side, perhaps a more collectivist side, of rural Japaneseness, a point returned to below.

The division of the social and the individual as a research focus has been at the forefront of anthropological theories and methods since anthropology's inception as a social science. There are researchers and theorists who have tended to focus on the individual as a rational actor at the forefront of making, creating, and interpreting their world. As a counterpoint, others more heavily accentuate that fact that humans come into a ready-made world and so prefer to view social structures as dominating, or largely determining, the actions of individuals. There is nothing new about this tension in the social sciences, and especially comparing anthropology and sociology. The so-called father of American anthropology, Franz Boas, referred to these poles of perspective as the "cosmographer" and "physicist" respectively. He claims

> it is in vain to search for an answer to this question, Which of the two methods is of higher value? as each originates in a different desire of the human mind. An answer can only be subjective, being a confession of the answerer as to which is dearer to him—his personal feeling towards the phenomena surrounding him, or his inclination for abstractions; whether he prefers to recognize the individuality in the totality, or the totality in the individuality. (Boas 1996, 14)

Historically these views can be seen as underpinning and forming a contrast between British social anthropology and American cultural anthropology. The latter is heavily influenced by a concept of the modern individual crafted from Max Weber, Franz Boas, the Culture and Personality school, and interpretive approaches such as that of Clifford Geertz.[2] The former has been strongly influenced by a statistical approach, typologies, and the cohesive function of shared acts such as are found in Émile Durkheim, Alfred Radcliffe-Brown, and the neo-Marxism of the ubiquitous Pierre Bourdieu and his followers.[3] Most scholars are not particularly dogmatic in their theoretical and methodological approach. For example, Peter Berger argues that "the Durkheimian and Weberian ways of looking at society are not logically contradictory, they are only antithetical since they focus on different aspects of social reality . . . they contain between them the paradox of social existence . . . that society defines us, but is in turn defined by us" (Berger 1963, 28).

My focus on the individual is not a dismissal of a social framework. It is a defense of the embodied and affective individual's place as central to it.[4] It is a reassertion of the individual's role in being-in-the-world and also actively becoming-part of it; creatively making, remaking, interpreting, and moving *within* her cultural and material environment (Ingold 2000, 2011; Jackson 2013; Ortner 2006). "The default position of our mental software," as Bruno Latour notes, "is the notion that viewing the social is paradoxically . . . 'casual and material' . . . [giving the erroneous impression that] the social could explain the social" (2005, 1–4). I am working along with this presumption in that the aforementioned social subject of *ware ware nihonjin* has long been the "default" position in *nihonjinron* arguments with counterclaims to this notion of a predominately social self often being framed as, for example, "antisocial": individuals who are *NEET* (not in employment education or training), *otaku* (literally meaning home, but implying social outcasts with obsessive and idiosyncratic tastes), or even minority groups within Japan such as Ainu or Burakumin, who might question the political status quo. I seek a different way to ground the understanding of dairy farm workers' lives. While they are not part of Japan's aforementioned *ware ware* "epic" discourse, they are not positing themselves counter to it in any organized or intentional manner (Bakhtin 1981). Through focusing on the individual first and foremost, and on social relations as malleable and not merely determinative, my intent is to highlight their "novel" ways of being and becoming.

This is because the people I worked, played, and lived with at Grand Hopes Farm and in Gensan were often highly individualistic, world-dwelling, and world-creating people who were involved in social relations both seen and unseen by me. As Jean-Luc Nancy contends, one cannot *be* without *being-with*; that is to say, "being cannot *be* anything but being-with-one-another, circulation in the *with* and as the *with* of this singularly plural coexistence . . . existence *is with* otherwise nothing exists" (Nancy 2000, 2–4, italics are included in the original text). Moreover, human relations are concomitantly observable and unobservable, conscious and unconscious. It is essential then to acknowledge the fact that life as lived is not just being. Becoming is always a part of life, the process of constant change (aging, for example) and engagements with Otherness that can be expressed in conflict or cooperation, in defense, dissolution, or dismissal of hegemonic discourses, and dependent upon individual bodies and intimate singular histories as much as any social milieu.

In the chapters that follow, the book's key themes of Otherness, security, and frontiers are brought down (better metaphorically visualized as "brought in") from the macro level to the community and individual levels. The polysemic play of securing and security and of Otherness ought not to be conceptualized as playing out in binary terms, through *the social* **or** *the individual*, but as *assemblages of individuations*, as actors or agents that independently derive and interpret meanings and pleasures from the interplay of internalities (including embodiments, values, experiences, or histories) and externalities (including environments, nonhuman animals, and things) that form the lattice of individual and social worlds as they are concomitantly created (Hansen 2018a, 2020b; Haraway 2016). Perhaps to some readers this nears what Yamazaki Masakazu calls "the universality of gentle individualism" in Japan (2000, 107–149). The individual is not simply dominated by the social world, not "enveloped" in the social, but is often the "unsung" essence of its making, becoming, and changing.

Unsung because classic interpretations of belonging in Japan have generally been quite different: often focused on group formation or maintenance or the social aspects of being as belonging with becoming frequently interpreted as fulfilling a role or following a predictable path. Joy Hendry notes that the conflation of individuality (as an existential condition) and individualism (as an ideological stance) is common in Japan (Hendry 1992, 56–57). And via such a social-centric framing, individuation and individualisms are seen as secondary, outcast, or not important at all. This is understandable as there has been a long and widely popularized history of framing of the self as primarily social in Japan. Philosopher Watsuji Tetsurō is illustrative in this regard (1996). His conceptualization of human existence, *sonzai no ningen* (the being/ existence of human), is posed as a response to Martin Heidegger's more "Euro-centric" being-in-the-world (often dwelling) or being-toward-death (1988), which Watsuji viewed as an inherently Western and "individualistic" approach. This conceptualization has been extremely influential in defining a modern and particularistic "Japanese" interpretation of self as primarily social and not individual (Oguma 2002, 260–295). This interpersonal *betweenness* is a conclusion arrived at via a Buddhist-inspired, and highly indirect, definitional maze based on negating a myriad of Western philosophical notions of self with its own logic and agenda well beyond the scope of this chapter (Watsuji 1996, 352–354). The key point is an attempt to define nondualistic human being as a uniquely Japanese understanding of existence that is inherently social through interrogating the kanji character for *ningen* (joining human and between).

I build from both Nancy's and Watsuji's notions: *being with* or *being between*. Neither negates the power of agency and becoming. Simply, they firmly write into the equation of individuality the well-worn truth that "no person is an island." Humans are born into ready-made, though increasingly and rapidly changing, uniquely interpreted "fluid" social worlds (Bauman 2007). More to the point, few people, Japanese, French, or otherwise, are concerned with in-depth metaphysical speculation to the degree that they choose to base their careers or spend lives debating it. East or West, the notion that the self is at once culturally constructed while also individuated, in flux, liminal, and becoming is relentlessly haggled over but it is seldom denied, a point made obvious below. Tokachi dairy farmers are concerned with *making*, with making their way through the day and sustaining a secure future, and they can only do this while being aware that life is spent in the presence of, and under the scrutiny of, other lives.

Being between Extremes:
Nihonjinron, Social Others, and Dairy Farmers

Problems inherent with historical claims to sociocultural uniqueness are famously addressed by Eric Hobsbawm and Terence Ranger in *The Invention of Tradition* (1983) and Benedict Anderson in his seemingly ubiquitous *Imagined Communities* (1991). The literature coming after these influential publications in relation to Japan is staggering and space does not enable a full review of it (e.g., Befu 2001; Howell 2005; Hudson 1999; Miyoshi 2000: esp. 11–24; Oguma 2002; Ryang 2004; Sugimoto 1997; Vlastos 1998; Willis and Murphy-Shigematsu 2008). All critique previous studies that view Japanese people as sharing a worldview rigidly structured through a uniformly shared conservative and cooperative tradition often defended in the context of hazy historical arguments or biology. Studies, for example, that mark Japan as a particularly distinctive nation formed and maintained through agrarian social life, "concentric circles" of obligation, well-defined hierarchies of power, notably the *ie* (family system), and/or a lengthy, often mythic, history of linguistic and biological sameness.[5] Concisely put, the epic narrative in such studies is that "the Japanese" were, are, and often in fact self-ascribe as a "unique people" who historically have lived in a natural and functional harmony with each other and nature, a condition induced by the influence of rice cultivation and/or, in the case of much *nihonjinron* scholarship, perceived cultural and genetic similarity. In such studies, social collectivism is attributed to a bond of "Japaneseness" that keeps society harmonious.[6] Ideas regarding Japanese uniqueness like those above have been roundly critiqued in terms of their exclusionist ideology (Kondo 1990; Miyoshi 2000), in terms of genetics and archaeological/historical evidence (Howell 2005; Hudson 1999), in terms of exclusionary political action (Amos 2011; Groemer 2001; Hane 2003; Siddle 2013), and combinations of these three critiques (Dale 1986; Harootunian 2019; Ziomek 2019).

Some readers might be sighing, "Not this again." But my point differs. I am not concerned with the *factuality* of this critiqued research; my focus is the continued *popularity* of the *nihonjinron* genre of literature/research and its astounding resilience (Ertl and Hansen 2015; Guarné and Hansen 2018). A stark, now if dated, example of *nihonjinron* thought that taps into many of the above tropes and is especially relevant given the focus on agriculture and security herein can be found in the book *The Peasant Soul of Japan* (Watanabe 1989).

The author Watanabe Shōichi sets out to discuss how Japan's unique agrarian existence, largely equated with the cultivation of rice paddies, is linked with a shared social contract or ideology of security and consensus (1989, 13–40). After a rather lengthy discussion of the role that night soil played (before late modern methods) in fertilizing Japanese rice fields he states, "Our forefathers' excrement went into this Japanese soil which produced the rice which our parents ate" (25). He notes that the islands of Japan (excluding the othered peripheries of Okinawa and Hokkaido of course) were already mentioned by name in the *Kojiki*, a book of Japanese creation myths dated 712 CE, though his intention in using it seems to be lending credence to his views regarding the book as a sort of factual historical record. Using a socioecological metaphor of recycling, he claims that "biological" Japaneseness (formed in the practice of farming and through the linking of human waste fertilizer to soil to rice) has been passed on from Japanese to Japanese (and to the exclusion of whoever he might consider non-Japanese, or not a part of these "pure blood and soiled soil" Japanese so to speak) from time immemorial. He goes on to lament the "impurity" that contemporary sewage systems have brought to urban Japan and notes that at his university, Sophia University (a prestigious private university in Tokyo), the excrement of foreign professors is mixed with that of Japanese. This melding (indeed once could say the collapse of a frontier of the foreign and the modern for him) has led to a loss of the recycling capabilities of the formerly pure Japanese soil, which he equates with the "peasant soul," the essence of Japan and Japaneseness (ibid. 31). Watanabe continues more philosophically, "In country villages in particular, where people use the same privy as their ancestors, I think there is a deep feeling of inner security. However poor you may be, if you are born on this earth and raise your children on it you are immortal. The most fundamental thing in the spiritual structure of a peasant people is this 'feeling of security'" (32, quotes in the original).

In what he calls "Equestrian Societies," social orders based on mobility and speed, and clearly here opposing Japanese history with Chinese and Korean history—an idea not referenced but likely borrowed from Japanese anthropologist Umesao Tadao (2003)—harmonious and "spiritual" attachment to land is impossible. In Equestrian Societies land merely becomes an acquisition. As an interesting aside, taking his argument at face value, the novel history of Hokkaido is thus de facto excluded from his epic history of peasant society based on land, blood, rice, and excrement; indeed, as noted in the previous chapters, land and excrement on a dairy farm poses entirely different ideological and ecological problems!

To defend *nihonjinron* ideas like this beyond their genetic, historic, and agrarian "glue," other essentialist conceptualizations are also often put forward. It is popular to cite perceived social psychological relationships placed along a continuum, such as *tatemae/honne* (surface/underlying) or *soto/uchi* (inside/outside), or value systems claimed to be shared among the Japanese community as a whole such as *amae* (dependency).[7] These positions are often defended by claiming that a dichotomy exists between the "Oriental" sense of self and the "Western" sense of self (Bachnik 1994; Lebra 1985, 2004). Language is frequently cited as a source of ethnocultural difference. One common focus is on the use of the pronoun "I" in English contrasted with the many "situational and interpersonal" pronouns that exist in Japanese—*watakushi, watashi, boku*, and *ore*, for example—and Watsuji Tetsurō also focuses on the proposed uniqueness of general Japanese pronouns (1996, 49–54). Andrew Miller provides a book-length condemnation of this sort of uniqueness via linguistics theorization (Miller 1982). Indeed, why not go even further than Watsuji does and include the uniqueness of many regional dialects in Japan, for example, in the Kansai dialect *washi*, *wai*, *ate*, *uchi*, and so on. It is because this further incision into *ware ware* itself would even cut at the premise of a unique and singular unified Japanese language, cleaving even more regions and individuals from its epic discourse. Moreover such analysis lacks any phenomenological context that philosopher and linguist Ludwig Wittgenstein has shown is essential to the understanding of any language-game (2001, 31–33). In sum, if the Japanese self is, as D. T. Suzuki infamously commented, able to understand the silences in Zen in ways that the Western mind cannot due to a particular sensitivity of self and the sameness of self and other essences (Suzuki 1970), then one might ask why the use of such cumbersome pronouns in the first place. Why the *need* for several pronouns, and regional variants, in lieu of innately shared communication, *haragei* or through the belly? Why complicate this cultural intuitiveness? More to the point, why is it that Japanese dairy farmers manage to misunderstand one another—and do so frequently as outlined in the following chapters—much like other people do both inside and outside Japan? In short, the idea that Japanese conceptualizations of the world, self, other, lifestyle, and so on, have somehow remained trapped in a formaldehyde mixture of language, agrarian imagery, or ethnic origins has fallen out of academic favor even if popular *nihonjinron* scholarship presses on.

However, as essentialist, functionalist, and structural representations of Japan have waned, at least in academia, a new polemic vision of an unsettled, fragmented, and often dysfunctional Japan has emerged, one that often outlines extreme *social* "Otherness." Such representations build upon this notion of a popularly shared monolithic cultural and social "glue" keeping Japan together, but then subvert this reading of national homogeneity with micro homogeneities. These are intersectional memberships that chip away at the wall of *nihonjinron* one social group at a time. That is to say, focus has shifted to smaller social orders and shared identities of "non-epic" Japanese who will not, or indeed cannot, fit within the confines of popularly accepted Japaneseness (Mathews and White 2004; Willis and Murphy-Shigematsu 2008; Ziomek 2019). As opposed to the aforementioned "cement" of belonging, this counter focus is on tradition "unglued" with scores of studies that focus on Japan as the quintessence of postmodernity and confrontational identity politics envisioning Japan as caught in the eye of a globalization storm in terms of cultural loss, a populace so entrenched in tradition that engagement with the ever-expanding globalizing present is possible for only an outcast few. This is augmented by the aforementioned focus on collections of marginal others in Japanese society, such as Okinawans, Ainu, or "the hyphenated"—Korean-Japanese, Brazilian-Japanese, or Filipino-Japanese for example (Siddle 2013). And there are too many contemporary subcultures in Japan to enumerate. Taking all such groupings into consideration definitely has questioned any *nihonjinron* homogeneity thesis of Japan and I applaud such work. However, there is a danger here. The focus often still steers clear of the individual. Groups are perceived as *collectively* rebelling against Japanese-ness. Indeed, they form easy to identify collectives even if infighting and one outstanding example of such contestation related directly to Hokkaido can be found in terms of contemporary Ainu identity (Hudson, Lewallen, and Watson 2014), precisely because they self-ascribe or are ascribed as collective Others actively distancing themselves (or being distanced from) epic Japaneseness.

In examining these discourses and debates, perhaps condensed as being uniquely uniform Japanese or uniquely nonconforming Japanese, a key reason emerges as to why dairy farmers, with a few exceptions such as migrant workers, are interesting. They are clearly Japanese and identify themselves as such—vehemently so in some cases. Every Tokachi dairy farmer I have met was at most three generations separated from family roots in Honshu, Shikoku, or the Kyushu Peninsula. Moreover, the lion's share of young farmworkers I have met over the years have resided in Hokkaido for less than a year after coming directly from other parts of Japan as varied as central Tokyo and rural Tokushima. Workers are not uniform in a myriad of other ways. They are a mix of young and old, urban and rural born, and come from low-, middle-, and (albeit more rare) upper-class backgrounds. Some stay working at dairy farming permanently while others only last a few weeks. The important observation here is that, beyond being Japanese and working at this job, little unites them. If anything, they provide a rather diverse sample of what politically, geographically, and demographically comprises the contemporary Japanese populace. And again, all are engaged in a mode of agriculture that is sponsored by the government in order to produce a product that is commonly consumed by Japanese with little export potential. Representatively, they are a microcosmic sample of being as "Japanese" as one can get. Yet, what follows ethnographically underscores how they are paradoxically internal Others—imagined as and treated as though they were outsiders.

It is important not to write off the idea that there are particular aspects to being Japanese—that is not my intention—and all but the most jingoistic of *nihonjinron* texts (even Watanabe's toilet musings noted above) offer the reader something about the way many Japanese individuals collectively construct their worlds and are influenced by the world, both in Japan and outside (see also Befu 2001; Clammer 2001; Ertl and Hansen 2015; Morris-Suzuki 1998, 154–160, on this point). These books become bestsellers in Japan for good reason. They tell an epic story that people either do, or do not, agree with, and stories that people do, or do not, want to hear about themselves. For example, Nakane's work on social structure is over fifty years old, but it is still invaluable in its explanatory power of ideal Japanese corporate structuring. Similarly, Doi's 2007 reissue of his classic 1973 text *Amae no kōzō* (The Structure of Dependence) outlines its continued popularity and in it he explains how he could not have predicted the vast changes in Japan that transform contemporary youth cultures (Doi 2007). And today's *otaku* studies, social group studies, or even books of the "Japan is crumbling" ilk are not an indication of poor scholarship; they are an indication of the research climate in ever-changing times. In a simple and aptly titled essay, "Japan Is Not Interesting," Miyoshi (2000) outlines how scholarship in and on Japan has tended to be rather conservative and inward looking, research of the "we Japanese" sort that seldom asks who that "we" really is. The flip side to this is the tremendous amount of money paid to scholars of Japan, notably nonnative ones, to make it seem as if Japan is unique and unusual (Hansen 2015) or "cool" and interesting (White 2015). As Sugimoto contends, perhaps the most unique thing in all this is the unique obsession with finding and authenticating this imagined shared uniqueness (Sugimoto 1997)! Japan and Japanese, like Jamaicans and Jamaica or Jordanians and Jordon, are far from homogeneous or static entities. Japan and the Japanese people are, and always have been, a work in progress.

In sum, nobody at Grand Hopes Farm claimed to be, or acted as, a monocultural conservative conformist, nor did anybody express the desire to become, or seem to be, a complete renegade social outcast. Of course, as individuals, some people were more conservative and others more liberal, some were introverted and others were extroverts, but none were constrained completely by social relations or radically fighting to extract themselves from Japanese society. However, it is safe to say that to some of my more conservative informants, who were often locals, it seemed as though processes were in play that were "ungluing" Japanese society, pulling traditional ways of being asunder. For them, local life was changing fast in circumstances they could do little to control, while it seemed to the more liberal workers, often individuals who were working on short-term contracts from outside the local community, that their move to Gensan marked a point where their social relations were becoming free, "unstuck" from former social expectations that they viewed as constricting.

Farm Individuals and Their Grand Hopes

Living in a small town and working daily with over fifty co-employees means that one's activities or behavior quickly becomes public knowledge. And all farmers and farmhands were aware that the smooth functioning of their work life and social life would be best served if they could "get along" with others, whosoever they were, despite their backgrounds or aspirations, and through weathering whatever political, economic, or social changes occurred. As such, and as the reader will discover in the chapters ahead, ontological security and the securing of a public self were perennial concerns. Nevertheless, in such a close-knit environment fights were frequent, the employee turnover rate at Grand Hopes was high, and malicious gossip about the farm, both on and off it, was rampant. Quite distant from any notion of agrarian harmony or consensus, relations and motivations were more often individual and confrontational than group focused and cooperative. Due to the condition of "betweenness" or "being-with" outlined above, each individual agent interpreted, acted, and strategized how best to cope with other people, the Otherness of Tokachi itself, and the particularities of any given farm; from encounters with cold coworkers, to freezing morning chores, to dealing with a particularly ornery cow, dairy farm life was enveloped in human and more-than-human negotiations on any given day.

Farmers could explain their motivations and convincingly narrate their individual story relationally, rationally, and lucidly, as independent agents with trajectories through time and space dependent upon their choices, desires, and actions to work at Grand Hopes Farm. They were able to narrate an individual "self-construction" or "life-script" (Appiah 2005, 198) accounting for how they engaged in a way of being or dwelling, in what anthropologist Tim Ingold describes as a "lifeline . . . in short . . . understood relationally as a movement along a way of life, conceived not as the enactment of a corpus of rules and principles . . . received from predecessors, but as the negotiation of a path through the world" (Ingold 2000, 146). They ought to be considered as individuals embodying their own agency in selecting their own course of life through the choices they make and the actions they take, over any form of determining habitus, shared class consciousness, or common culture (Cf. Bourdieu 1984; and in terms of labor Charlesworth 2000; Willis 2003). Nobody I met claimed they were inescapably compelled to play a social role, and though each person had particular triumphs and disappointments, these were not necessarily related to broader shared "social" orders, systems, or structures. As anthropologist Gordon Mathews notes in his inimitable style: "Japanese senses of self are indeed culturally shaped . . . yet I have never met a Japanese person, and I am confident no anthropologist has ever met a Japanese person—at least outside of a mental institution or possibly a Zen monastery—who claims to have no coherent, separate self" (Mathews 1996, 721).

Workers at Grand Hopes Farm, much like the young Japanese *ama* divers in the work of Dolores Martinez, were individuals who viewed changes in their lives and interactions with others in active terms: relations of *naru* (becoming) and *tsukuru* (making) (Martinez 2004). Their dairy farm experience was ever in process—fluid, alive and changing, not static, and certainly not socially replicating. Of course, whether in the case of Tokachi, Gensan, or Grand Hopes Farm, some people were born into these places and into particular social positions, say, the son or daughter of a local farm owner. But they could, and as the reader will discover often did, choose to opt out of these locations and choose new relations. Readers will find that workers were attracted to this rural area and dairy farming for a wide, and even contradictory, combination of structural and personal reasons (Hansen 2018a, 2020b, 2022; Klien 2020; Traphagan 2019). While some workers had a short career in the industry, again for reasons structural and personal, they left and they were replaced by new individuals with equally wide-ranging drives and aspirations. Many were constantly in a state of liminality, torn betwixt and between choosing to leave or stay (Turner 1969, 1987).

One reason is because at Grand Hopes Farm both technology and alienation were ever on the rise. This meant that *making* oneself was a central concern for some individuals, a drive to be made a department head or make money, for example, while *becoming* was more difficult, more personal, more processual. It was difficult to become a local for example. One could not simply choose to be socially accepted, or even know what steps might necessarily move one toward that goal. Moreover, I contend that many workers were in a state of *liminal liminality* at work and in the community. Having been misunderstood by some fellow anthropologists before, what exactly I mean by this requires some clarification. Liminality presupposes a known threshold, a known and expected end to the liminal state, for example the final transition to socially sanctioned adulthood in a coming-of-age ceremony. However, in Gensan many thresholds, such as becoming a local, are not clear or implicit. It is often hoped that a path to a threshold, a compulsion to stay or go be it for a relationship or a job promotion, will emerge, but for many it does not. Individuals work with the vague hope that some change in life course will come. Describing such states as being *liminally liminal* captures this evolving process of "self" discovery. Living in, or better through, a state of "indefinite" liminality means that individuals were not reaching sanctioned thresholds of change in ritual processes leading to social transformation. Most workers were not moving through Japan's socially acceptable life's stages of work, marriage, responsibility to community, respect, and retirement (Cook 2016; Mathews 2006; Roberson and Suzuki 2003; Rosenberger 2001; and the classic Plath 1980, 1983). Thus, making and becoming could be a source of great anxiety and frustration in their daily being. Many were in a sort of limbo without reprieve. They did not know when, if, or how they would pass through these rites of passage perceived as normative in Japan. There was, to address the classic framing of liminality, often no agreed-upon threshold to cross. More interesting still, while some did not see this as a pressing problem, a few remained dogmatically opposed to ending their liminal state despite its insecurity. They viewed themselves as completely set apart from accepted community social structures. For them, there was no collective identity, but one focused, by choice or by circumstance, individualistically and through coping with, and the cultivation of, their individual circumstances.

Failing to see this early in fieldwork I went through my own academic liminal state as a process of making and becoming. I spent hours making and mulling over numerous social and group categories. After all, that is what anthropologists are trained to do (Hansen 2021a). However, these typologies became increasingly frustrating due to the constant shifting and overlapping of actual people; whatever box I constructed, people would not fit and if they did, many would soon burst through the sides, spill out the bottom, or overflow the bounds (Rapport 2012). The epiphany came when I understood that the workers *themselves* did not categorize fellow employees beyond their individual relationships. When asked, workers defined no rigid collective or shared identity related to the industry or to one another beyond three exceptions. Females and males often played differing roles on the farm, related to different social expectations. Locals, outsiders, and what might be best called "no-siders" and "lo-siders," formed loose assemblages from which it is safe to make some generalizations about social or collective belonging. And some aspects of religion could mark (however transiently) the threshold of becoming a local, a dairy farmer or a member of the community. All these categories are detailed and expanded upon in the chapters that follow, but to be clear such "social facts" did not *determine* the trajectory of individual lives. People planned trajectories based on a nexus of abilities, interests, luck, determination, goals, desires, and so forth, dependent on the changes and adaptations of their particular perceptions and contingent state of being.

Individuals—liberalist legal structures aside—are, in fact, not equal (Nussbaum 2006). Whatever intersectional, culture, social category, economic strata, or geographic location one may be ascribed to or inscribed with, no single person shares the same experiences, mind, and build: in a word, embodiment. We are all cast into unequal lifeworlds. Yet, in a rapidly changing frontier context, faced with Otherness (Otherness in terms of industry, location, lifestyle, and bodies both human and other than human) few individuals were trapped into structures that were viewed or experienced by them as social inertia. This contrasts with, for example, Bourdieu (2002) who claims to be looking for inertia or what does not change in structures. All beings, uniquely embodied, adapt and animate their lifeworlds through choice and change, contingency and action, and their engagement with Otherness. In all this, the search for security and the act of securing are a fluid constant and a key concern. Individuals are not a tabula rasa canvas for the social to inscribe. Similar to children playing at a local hockey rink or football pitch, sports more structured and rule-governed than dwelling in the world, daily life at Grand Hopes Farm was a "serious game" (Ortner 2006). There were winners, losers, smart players, players who depended on size or speed, exceptional players, "team" players, and egoists. There were players who made foolish choices and players with differing levels of interest in the game. There were those with natural ability who played alongside those who were intensively trained but lacked the knack, and others who longed to play different games.

None of the above should be surprising in general terms. We are all "secured" to one body, one array or suite of changing capabilities, and one life and history of that life—all of which are open to varying interpretations by both ourselves and others. In this sense, individuality is an inescapable physical condition, one that limits or opens past, present, and future experiences of the world. And, given that this universalist notion of a human individual is found to be sound, then it should not be unexpected that many humans, sociocultural milieu notwithstanding, are often individualistic, endowed with an innate conceptualization of individualism—the awareness and agency to think, act, and create apart from others and in agreement, defiance, understanding, misunderstanding, or indifference to the host of social, political, economic, or cultural norms in the many lifeworlds at play: conditions as true outside as inside Gensan.

Working It Out

To introduce all of the individuals on the farm, noting, however briefly, their life histories, impressions of their personality, their jobs on the farm, their skill sets, and so on would be far too cumbersome a project. Nevertheless, the individuals introduced in this book should never be thought of as "ideal" types. They are people, not representatives of categories. Marilyn Strathern notes that "the cultures we find most difficult to place are those whose gatekeeping concepts do not present themselves as candidates for inversion [us and them, that type against this type] . . . within anthropological thought, the concreteness of particular concepts . . . [in Japan and in social anthropology the social self] . . . and their location as self-evident facts about the particularity of places comes from establishing their taken for granted status through comparison with others" (Strathern 1988, 92–94). In this case *ware ware nihonjin, otaku,* or "the Western individual" would serve as easy "us versus them" comparisons. However, she continues: "[These reductive] moves belong to a specific period of anthropological history. . . . The anthropologist, unable to represent one voice completely in terms of the other, would mediate between the two. And in exposing the noncomparability of their voices would cancel any easy assumption about anthropology's own self-sufficiency as a single analytic language" (95). The diversity even under the seemingly limiting rubric of "Tokachi dairy farmer" is substantial.

Previous chapters explained how throughout the farm's short history Otherness and multilevel searches for security have been constant, a point made obvious in the amalgamation of four family farms into one operation. For the farm to function, new workers, new cows, and new technologies arrive daily. Moreover, there is a great deal of overlap and shifting between work spaces and job roles in a constant effort to "secure" (safe-guard or predict) the profitability, and so the future, of the farm. A key analytic issue emerges from such conditions. Explaining how the farm's future is secured in the midst of constant and rapid changes bedevils any attempt to link, in a concrete way, workers with other workers in terms that are a mainstay in the social sciences. For example, given their utterly disparate backgrounds, present concerns, and future aspirations, "class" or even "habitus" would be far too simple and stable a representation of what is, in actuality, a very fluid and flexible lived reality. Before their time on Grand Hopes Farm, many dairy workers, especially younger ones, had never been employed on a farm or worked with animals or even with non-Japanese. As such, the majority of workers were not working-class youth "learning to labor" in the sense of replicating a lasting socioeco-nomic condition, especially through their previous off-farm (university for example) or on-farm education (Willis 2003). Expanded upon in the following chapters, there was little chance that workers would remain at Grand Hopes Farm long term (even including those who hoped to stay in the dairy industry through training or returning to their family farm). Few workers aspired to be long-term farm laborers or saw this as their future and there was a notable lack of workplace or worker solidarity. What *can* be accurately documented is a specific person, doing a specific job, for a specific duration of time, and for a specific purpose, both in functional and personal terms, working to extract milk or to save money for example. Added to this "disassociation" of persons from types, work-ers were often not "familiar" with one another or the work they were engaged in.

Adding to this lack of shared values, goals, and experiences, there was seldom time for prolonged instruction or socialization into job roles as is common in Japan. There are explanations, undoubtedly fit-ting in other areas of work in Japan, whereby an employee goes through a lengthy socialization and training period (Dore and Sako 1989; Plath 1983). Emphasis is put on knowing one's place in the organization and learning by copying senior staff members, similar to learning a martial art or skill through prolonged mimesis (Chiba 2013; Cox 2003, 2008). But this style of lengthy training or learning, and the entrenchment of requisite social structures, is nearly absent on an industrial dairy farm. At Grand Hopes Farm, most workday tasks were learned on the job through briefly being told what to do, watching another worker for a short time (minutes, not hours or days), and then doing—likely poorly at first—the given chore. Workers eventually honed their own methods as they continued working, usually unobserved and unobservable, by others, at least human others. Most jobs did not require a particularly complex skill set. Indeed, as argued in what follows, rural deskilling and alienation are the direct effects of the automated surveillance inherent in new dairy technologies deployed in factorylike settings. Shovel the manure, sweep the barn floor, attach the suction cup to the teat; such tasks do not require extended "social" learning or apprenticeship and learning generally followed a *mite, kite, ima yatte* (watch, come, and now do) model. Workers would be told what needed to be done, asked to briefly watch how to do it with some instruction, and then be prompted to attempt to do it. When they could convincingly respond "un wakatta" (yeah, I get it) to the question "Wakatta?" (Get it?), the "training" was over. Henceforth, they were expected to be able to do the task if they were told to. Such a mode of learning is clearly individualistic; it is largely dependent on the time and the patience of a particular teacher (both usually in short supply as outlined below) and the embodied aptitude of the given worker.

Thus, in contrast with Jean Lave and Étienne Wenger's well-known notion of "legitimate peripheral participation," learning on Grand Hopes Farm clearly *was* a direct link between "learning and intentional instruction" (Lave and Wenger 1991). The authors claim (for good reason in their context of lengthy "career" apprenticeships—midwives, tailors, quartermasters, and butchers) that direct instruction does not fully explain learning. However, the idea that "learning is not merely a condition for membership, but is an evolving form of membership" in a "community of practice" (53) presumes, at the least, that a common "sense" of community exists and that people who come in contact with it, or remain within it, become members "socially." All of these premises are problematic assumptions in what follows. The emphasis on the social indebtedness of learning comes to the fore when the writers go on to say that they "conceive of identities as long-term, living relations between persons and their place and participation in communities of practice. Thus identity, knowing, and social membership entail one another" (53).

To say that practices form a "community" of learning amid an ever-shifting roster of dairy farm workers exaggerates the social elements of mimetic knowledge over the self-determining nature of the individual workers. Most dairy workers are not long-term employees and they seldom relate to each other at work let alone outside of it. In this sense, they are not participating in a "social practice" beyond a short instructive encounter that usually (though not always) was followed by an individual's honing of methods and skills in relative isolation. Moreover, the majority of workers simply did not care about perfecting these particular skills. While a few young dairy farmers did want to learn and enter into the community of Grand Hopes Farm or another area of the industry as a career, for most individuals it was merely a job, a "bullshit job," that paid the bills and bought time (Graeber 2018). Once a task could be done, that was the end of their "work-related" education story. Of course, as will be noted below, there were some jobs, such as catching cows, that required cooperation, and so entailed at least a degree of watching others and increasing one's skill through mimicry. However, in such cases cattle and equipment were often better, and certainly more consistent, at training new employees than humans, a point returned to in the conclusion.

Except to the most ardent of social constructivists, the lack of shared social conditioning and identity should be unsurprising here. The majority of workers labor for nearly the same wages and with nondescript job titles. They come from radically different backgrounds: rural, suburban, and urban, from Hokkaido, Honshu, and increasingly countries outside Japan. While some workers were well traveled, others had never left Japan, and though some came from well-off families, others came from economically marginal backgrounds. Some workers were university graduates, sometimes from prestigious universities like Ritsumeikan or Tohoku University, while others were high school dropouts. And again, none of these usual suspects of social stratification were related to the job itself or any position of responsibility or prestige in their limited "community" of dairy work. Nor, as noted below, and coming as a surprise to me during my time in the field, did such factors relate to the duration of time someone might remain in farmwork. Popular, skilled, and dedicated employees could leave seemingly on a whim, and disliked and incompetent ones might remain on the farm indefinitely. Grand Hopes Farm was a constant site of change but, related to this, it was also very clearly a site of "Otherness," a place where other relatively unknown people were, despite sharing a workday location, constantly coming and going, often with little acknowledgment or ceremony surrounding arrival and departure.

Thus, the notion dairy workers formed a community and not an "assemblage" in social terms is questionable beyond being a convenient label. In sum, various heterogeneous agencies (human and nonhuman) territorialize (come together) and can deterritorialize (fragment momentarily) and reterritorialize (return to a together state or a new state altogether) in meaningful and material (individual or collective) ways (DeLanda 2016). But to claim further that they formed a *community of practice* or habitus would be completely misleading. These identities and embodiments would require time to emerge (certainly beyond a few months of intermittent contact) and at least imply some sense of solidarity. In this regard, Yi-Fu Tuan notes a powerful difference between community and group: "The words differ . . . in their emotional tone—the one is warm and particularistic the other cool and abstract" (Tuan 2002, 311). While dairy farmers can be described as a group, it is clear in what follows that they had little interest or incentive to form a "community." There was no farm "guidebook" to read, though some workers had attended agricultural college and had a "bookish" knowledge of how to accomplish their workday tasks. Such aptitudes as embodied capabilities, whether perceived or real, might, or might not be taken into account by a particular *buchō* when assigning tasks or among workers themselves.

Finally, location and time were often not shared with human Others but with cows and high-technology equipment, and these relations undermine any notion of uniformity, consensus, or "consciousness." Scripted tasks during milking depended on individual prowess, skills, abilities, meanings, and interpretations of these acts. Despite being "the structures of a particular type of environment (e.g., the material conditions of existence characteristic of a class condition)," they did not produce a "habitus, systems of durable transposable dispositions, structured structures predisposed to function as structuring structures . . . as principles of the generation and structuring of practices" (Bourdieu 1977, 72–73). Indeed, the lack of such shared "dispositions" in speech, action, interpretation, past lives, present aspirations, and future goals is made increasingly clear in the ethnographic examples and analysis of the following chapters.

Conclusion

The linking of worker and job should not be thought of as impermeable or longstanding *class*ifying divisions in what follows. In many cases, labels applied to the "type" of person one might be, from life stage to the work they did, were highly contingent. Only a small minority of workers, local or outsider, had settled into their employment permanently. Given the frontier nature of the farm, industry, and region, categories were extremely permeable or pliable depending on the individuals negotiating them. Of course, "distinctions" did exist—workers were part of Japanese society on some level—and some examples of social structures framed as assemblages are outlined in what follows, such as flexible social groupings (locals, lo-siders, outsiders, and no-siders), a gender divide, and local inclusion witnessed in gift-giving and religion. However, I have argued that there is a danger in immediately linking young dairy farmers' lives with other forms of social scientific research on organization or agriculture in Japan, notably the epic discourse surrounding rice agriculture within *nihonjinron* or an overly fragmented identity politics. Research on Japan has, in general, tended to focus on such social structures, the cooperative, the communal, the familial, the traditional or its social inversion, the mirror opposite, one group fighting for distinction among others.

There was an antipathy to such classifications among dairy farmers themselves given self-identification or "liminal" identification, as *furītā* or just doing the job for a "challenge" or as an "adventure" for example. Finally, epic categories were not applicable given the novel history of the area, the farm, and the relatively recent emergence of the mega-farm model. Moreover, such structures were not applicable to some, no-siders such as foreigners on fixed contracts for instance, who literally had no stake or interest in the social order, whether Japanese or local.

Individual jobs were nearly always determined through the day-to-day, even moment-to-moment, needs of the farm and contingency, being at a particular place at (depending on the task) the right or wrong time. The process of dairy farming itself and the need to secure a functioning work environment determined what needed to be done, alongside the workers' real or presumed individual prowess (speed, strength, intellect, tact, finesse) at meeting these needs (among the workers themselves and the owners). In the following chapters, the individual agent and their choices take center stage in the functioning of the farm for owner and worker alike; there are good and bad workers, good and bad jobs, owners' sons, sure successors who choose to quit the farm, and poor workers with little prospect for advancement who opt to remain indefinitely.

Chapter Eight

From Teat to Tot

Following the Flows

Working Bodies

I love this job. I am always working with living things and of course I care for the cows. Those same cows make the milk that my son drinks. I love my son. It is being part of a cycle. There is no better job than being a dairy farmer.

—Interview with a former Hokkaido University agriculture student, now Aso-area dairy farmer

We are building a life. Soon we will buy our own land and have . . . like the American dream. Now we have a house, two cars, a dog, and my son can play outside . . . it's freedom and security . . . I don't worry. There are chances here . . . working for the dairy . . . we can't live like this in Honshu . . . we even named our son Daichi (big land) after Hokkaido.

—Interview with Matsuyama-san, a coworker at Great Hopes Farm

Keeping things flowing, in what follows, is a metaphor that dairy farmers live by (Lakoff and Johnson 2003). Appadurai (1996, 1–19), Castells (2000), and Bauman (2000, 2007) use the metaphor of flows to describe the increasingly "fluid" arrangements of relationships, communications, information, and capital required in global commodities industries with structures that undergo rapid changes internationally and locally. And this sort of metaphoric fluidity is an apt description of dairy farming today, all the more so when keeping in mind that maintaining the flow of a host of liquids is literally central to the industry and any given farm. Cows and humans provide the lifeblood to any functioning dairy farm and the purpose of a dairy farm is to produce milk, another liquid. Milk is produced assisted by or combating yet other liquids, for example, hydraulic oil, rain, or manure slurry, all while keeping an eye on the farm's "liquidity," its ability to keep "afloat" financially. This meshing of animal-human-technology-environment is what dairy farmers (and cows) contend with, day in, day out. And, though it is metaphoric, perhaps the clearest way to initially think about these fluid and complex movements and places is by contemplating them organically, as specific positions, parts, and personnel roles that assemble into a functioning farm much like the organs and processes of a healthy, functioning, living body. In response to the popular "flattening" of actor-network theory (ANT) oriented work, there has been a respectful but rising call by many in social theory circles to return to the idea of unequal, affective, living, agentive, or "vibrant" places and processes (Bennett 2010; Bogost 2012; Grusin 2015; Kohn 2013; Tsing 2015; Wharton 2015 provide examples from architecture to animal bodies that question the flattening of ANT).

Aiding in the use of the body as a metaphoric image, the layout of Great Hopes Farm itself is akin to such a structure. It is skeletal, nervous, and arterial: there are rigidly framed barns, a meshwork of well-worn walkways and flow paths both planned and impromptu, there are numerous networked information relays and collection areas. Workers constantly exert themselves, their blood pumping, as they move about to sustain flows on the farm, such as milk, semen, and excrement, alongside the numerous figurative flows on which these movements depend—human, animal, information, and financial. Like the tempos of a living body, these movements accelerate and decelerate at different times of the day, month, and year and lend themselves to a sort of organic-meets-technological *rhythmanalysis* (Lefebvre 2004). That is to say, akin to the urban physical and temporal flows driving an urban metropolis described by Lefebvre, Great Hopes Farm is also like a living body. It is a deeply integrated assemblage; happenings at one end of the farm, while perhaps seemingly isolated due to location, impact the output or tempo in other areas of the operation. Beings, equipment, and information must flow about the various workplaces within the farm without restriction, like blood or signals through synapses in a body. Akin to a living body, prolonged stasis equates with dysfunction or death. Things must keep flowing to survive. Milk is a highly perishable, organic liquid and the fiscal liquidity of the business depends upon getting it out the doors to flows outside the farm in ceaseless, though hopefully predictable, daily cycles.

The remaining chapters of this book present ethnographic accounts of dairy workers' lives, the Otherness they engage with and themselves inhabit, and the security that many seek from their life in Tokachi, on the farm, and at the center of the various flows. However, to grapple with these complex and shifting assemblages of interrelated places, processes, things, and beings, the farm and the work done on it must first be divided into comprehensible units. This is because attempting to address the biotechnical complexity of an industrial farm holistically would succeed more in confusing than explaining daily life and the relationships among humans, cows, technologies, and place.

Over the next three chapters the farm's workplaces are divided into three general sections. These are separations rooted in a variety of factors: place, function, technology, and work role. They are, obviously given the above description, artificial divisions, but they are not arbitrary. Indeed, they are part and parcel of the vernacular used by workers to refer to locations, tasks, and even particular people and cows based largely on the frequency of the *same employees* doing the *same tasks* in the *same places*. Blanchette (2020), Pachirat (2011), and Porcher (2011) outline remarkably similar divisions of labor on pork and beef production lines. Though ultimately connected, the areas can be separated through general function in the process of producing milk; the head is the *jimusho* (the office), the heart is the *pārā* (the milking parlor), and then there are the various organs and extremities, usually referred to by adding *soto de/no* "X" (the X place outside the heart and head). All are essential for the farm to continue working.

In sum, in the following three chapters the human body is used as a cartographic metaphor as the complex functions of the beings, machinery, and buildings roughly lend themselves to this very familiar, albeit anthropomorphised, analogy in terms of both layout and purpose. This chapter focuses on the place of *head work* where the flow of information and finance emerges. *Heart work* follows in the next chapter, the place where the flow of animals, milk, and humans is most concentrated and closely orchestrated. The final chapter of this trio examines the "external flows," areas outside of the main purpose of producing milk but crucial to keeping the milk flowing and the farm afloat. The three chapters focus on *head work*, *heart work*, and *keeping it working* (office work, parlor work, and work in support of the overall functioning of the farm). They follow the same format: a brief description of job role and purpose, followed by a description of select workers, and then examples of their interactions both inside and outside the workplace. The individual workers introduced here will, along with the previous description of the owners, "snowball"; that is to say, they are referred to with increasing detail in the remaining chapters, along with a lesser developed cast of "characters" from this point until the conclusion.

Head Work: Farm Intelligence

Grand Hopes Farm is located ten minutes by car northwest of Gensan (figure 8.1). Its main office, barns, and milking parlor are located in foothills overlooked by mountains to the north. The "head and heart" of the *bokujō* is situated above open fields utilized for corn silage and a lower

Figure 8.1. An aerial photo of Grand Hopes Farm. Corner left is Mr. Wada's original homestead, across from which are the new apartments. The original parlor, "the head," is in the building above the parking lot. The "arms and legs" radiate out. To the left are the weaning barns, at the top are two automated barns, and the circular shapes are manure lagoons. The large buildings moving out from the center are where cows are housed in groups. Outside the frame is even more cropland and the homesteads of other owners. Photo used with permission of the farm.

barn area to the south used primarily for rearing calves. Beside the lower barns are concrete silage bunkers and the home of the *shachō*, the separate house of his elderly father and mother, and across the road, his former home, the original homestead, that was occupied by Matsuyama-san and his young family during my original stint of fieldwork in 2005–2006. Reflective of the rapid pace of change on the farm, when Matsuyama purchased a small, abandoned farm in 2010, Chinese workers moved into the old house in 2011. By 2014 the house was knocked down and work began erecting a fourteen-room apartment complex for foreign workers. This was completed in 2015. From 2016 this has been home to most of the farm's foreign, originally Chinese and increasingly Vietnamese, staff.

The *kachō*'s house and barn area are approximately half a kilometer east. It is home to three large barns, several concrete silage bunkers, and a large open area set aside for dozens of silage piles covered by blue tarps and earth. The two other original owners live approximately a kilometer to the northwest and northeast respectively. Their land is utilized for growing sweet corn silage and is still leased by Grand Hopes Farm as of 2021.

The structure of the *bokujō* layout and each area's various functions are complex. It takes at least a month to get one's bearings and feel confident in knowing which gates to open or close, where certain tools can be found, navigating shortcuts from one area to another, remembering the intricate order of tasks, or being able to find cattle belonging to a certain *gun* (group). It is an elaborate outlay of animals, machines, and buildings designed to be, although not always working as planned, the most efficient way to get the most milk at the least cost, and the farm's holdings and its complexity increase yearly.

Calling this section and the jobs done in this area *head work* is not meant to imply that tasks conducted in other areas of the farm require less intellect. Simply put, extending the analogy of the human body, the office functions as the "brain" on many levels both literal and metaphoric. First, it is where all of the department *heads* have their desks and it is where decisions regarding the general operation of the farm are made. Second, like the eyes, ears, nose, and mouth of a human body, it is the main entry point for information. All who gain access to the body of the farm come via this portal; for example, it is where hiring is done and it is where other company heads and representatives first call in. It is where workers enter and then leave at the end of their shift. Third, all planning is done through this main office, from fixing the monthly work schedule, to charting attempts at artificial insemination, to plotting what barns cattle ought to reside in. In sum, like a brain information comes in and decisions go out there. Finally, it also acts as the "memory bank," so to speak; all historical documents, paperwork, and computerized information regarding the farm's employees, costs, and cattle are stored here.

Below the job role and the reason why this job is required on the farm is explained. This is followed by an introduction to some of the individuals who perform this role and their interactions with fellow employees, equipment, and the cattle.

JIMUSHO SUTAFU (OFFICE STAFF)

The various *buchō*, *kachō*, and the *shachō* along with the secretary/receptionist had desks in the head office. However, midday the hunter (a job explained below), *shachō*, and secretary were generally the only people there. Others would frequently be glimpsed ducking in to update information or ask a question about daily operations, but generally speaking, most of their daytime work was done elsewhere. It looked indistinguishable from a typical small company office in Japan, cow posters and bovine kitsch aside.

The head office had a wide range of external visitors. The flow of milk from cow to machine, to truck, to factory, and on to stores is all coordinated through the networking of a variety of head offices across Tokachi. At Grand Hopes Farm, the secretary, *shachō*, and hunter were frequently on the phone keeping things flowing from their respective ends. Ordering machine parts, checking milk prices, confirming cattle shipments, casually or eagerly inquiring where a veterinarian might be, or making sure workers were paid and departing workers were replaced; any stoppage in the flow of people, milk, or information was a problem that ultimately returned to and was resolved here.

All visitors, regulars or rarities, checked in. From tour groups to newspaper reporters, from subcontractors to sales and delivery people, and even a prying anthropologist, all have to let go a hearty "sumimasen" (hello/excuse me) from the hallway outside the office to gain access through the main doors. And any of a range of visitors could then pass through the sliding doors upon the bellowed reply of "hai irrashai" (yes, welcome in). Depending on the importance of the visitor, the expectation was that the *shachō* or secretary would contend with whoever dropped by. Traffic (human, financial, and information) in and out of the office is expected and constant and over fifteen-plus years of planned and spontaneous visits I have seldom found it empty between 6 a.m. to 8 p.m. It is a constant hub of activity directing the plans and flows of the farm.

HATSUJŌ HANTĀ (THE "HEAT" HUNTER)

The workday begins at around 3:30 a.m. for the *hatsujō hantā* (hunter of cows in heat). Every morning the cattle are quickly inspected. This is done not only to ascertain if they suffer from obvious signs of sickness, for example, sunken eyes, excessive perspiration, or bloody stool indicative of a range of ailments to be relayed to the veterinarian, but to fulfill the key role ensuring that any cow in heat can be separated from the others for artificial insemination (AI) later in the morning. This task alone makes the hunter a busy role as it is possible that over seventy cows a day might be selected for AI. Moreover, this is a job in which one must possess a considerable amount of specialized knowledge, skill, and often official education than most. Beyond an aptitude for physical mechanics, a strong back, and, if male, the ability to endure colorful taunts regarding one's "hidden desires" to find amorous cows, the hunter possesses a great deal of responsibility in planning, handling, welfare, and profitability regarding cattle. Holsteins are only in heat for a few days every three weeks and common illnesses such as mastitis (an udder infection) can quickly pass through cattle herds in such close quarters, messing up chances at impregnation or having cows too ill to produce milk, which equates with significant losses in production.

The hunter carries a computer printout of numerically identified cattle that includes an impressive array of biographic information ranging from date of purchase, milk production, and attempts at impregnation, including the type and cost of semen used. Catalogued in this highly rational process, all cows—an ever-increasing number, over three thousand head in 2021—are under the sole purview of the *shachō* and *hantā*. Usually they defer to the advice of a partially state-funded veterinarian (outlined below), but this is not always the case. Veterinarians act more as advisors, but owners and hunters ultimately determine the best course of action to take with individual cows.

Thus, the hunter is a *buchō* position that commands considerable respect, prestige, and (usually) higher remuneration when compared with other jobs on the farm. Such kudos are well earned as the hunter, alongside being highly trained and the first at work, frequently puts in overtime and is on call if a cow is injured or, as is sometimes the case, simply "drops" during the milking process. The position also requires the ability to be personable, to knowledgably liaise with a range of people from office staff to veterinarians, pharmaceutical suppliers to coworkers on the farm. Head, heart, body, legs, arms, and beyond—the hunter needs to be thinking, diplomatic, and resourceful, if not a bit crafty, at all times.

Jūi (Veterinarians)

The relationship between the veterinarian and the hunter is outlined above, and so their link to the head office is obvious, despite not working in it. Veterinarians are partially funded through insurance and by the state. Thus, the level of care for cattle—at least in terms of "maintaining" their health to continually produce milk—is high. Many, but by no means all, jūi that service the Gensan region are originally from rural areas. Most have also attended national universities and a high proportion during my time working on the farm came from Hokkaido University (seven out of the nine I met in 2005–2015). Generally, the jūi work in one rural region but change farms in that area through a system of rotation along set routes. Thus, the same farms and cows are not always tended by the same veterinarians. Nevertheless, the veterinarians all know one another and are well acquainted with the owners and department heads of farms in the area.

Working Lives

What follows are ethnographic descriptions of three individuals doing *head work*. In the relaying of *their* stories I am implicated threefold. First, I am directly responsible in the eliciting, recording, interpreting, and relaying of their life stories to you the reader. Second, more times than not, this information was obtained during uncontrolled situations that might well have had an influence on what was done or said, that is, "the context"—of which I was clearly a part—played a key role in what or how something was said. And finally, I often had information relayed to me through informal gossip and not in an interview per se, in which case, I attempted to "triangulate" as best as possible, asking similar questions to several people about the same comment or incident while not revealing where I first heard the information.

MATSUYAMA: AT HOME ON THE RANGE

I met Matsuyama-san my first day in Gensan. As noted in the introduction, Wada-san picked me up in Obihiro, but he had forgotten the keys to my apartment. We arrived at the office at around eight at night and Matsuyama was still at his desk. The *shachō* said that I had had a long journey and asked Matsuyama if he would mind popping by my apartment to teach me how to use the stove, turn on the hot water, and so forth. He added that after this we were to meet him at the local sushi restaurant. Matsuyama agreed, as he always did, and our friendship began. I could not count the number of times I have met with Matsuyama and his family since. He has ceased to be an "informant" and is a longtime friend.

During my first year of fieldwork, I went on a few shopping trips with Matsuyama (then thirty-four), his wife Takako (then twenty-four), and his then-one-year-old son. We went to neighboring *onsen* a few times, at least once a week we talked over dinner or beer, and later as I met more people in the community, we found that we knew some of the same people outside of the farm. As of 2016, his first son was entering junior high and his youngest is the same age as mine. Countless times we have shared a coffee while chatting in his office, a beer at a festival, or a hot chocolate while watching our boys skate on the local outdoor rink.

From the start we had some unique connections. Matsuyama had lived and worked for a year on a horse ranch forty minutes south of Calgary, my hometown, near High River, Alberta, an area world renowned for ranching. Much like my own nomadic twenties, in his twenties, he worked and traveled through Australia, Canada, India, Thailand, and parts of Europe—including a stint as a horse trekking guide in Spain. Matsuyama was raised in rural Akita prefecture in northern Honshu and Takako, his wife, was from rural Hyogo prefecture in central Honshu. Though not from Hokkaido, they were both perfectly at home in a rural setting and in the *shachō*'s old farmhouse.

In the early stages of my research, their home was always in a slight state of disarray. Occasionally affronting the squeamish tendencies of those without the experience of toddlers, live-in dogs, and rural settings—tables and sofas could be curiously sticky. Toys, clothes, bits of furniture that Matsuyama was in the process of building, or the remains of some pet project were always to be found in ad hoc arrangements in the living room. Matsuyama always had interests outside of the dairy farm; handmade bacon, sausages, wine, or cheese and his experiments with Thai-style curries were always shared with enthusiasm. There were photos of the couple's wedding set out. The couple looked happy, dressed in western clothes—very western clothes: cowboy hats, jeans, and belt buckles that he had won at rodeos in Alberta. Daichi kicked around in his own mini cowboy boots too.

When we first met, the couple relayed that their dream was to have a house of their own with space outside for horses. This was realized in 2010, just after I returned from the field for the second time. The *shachō* helped them to buy a small parcel of land with an old house, barn, and machine shop. He did not help them to pay for it. He did not need to. The land was sold at the going rate for bare acreage, an incredible ¥50,000 all included. The important point in brokering such a deal was that the *shachō* vouched for them as good neighbors. On numerous occasions I was told of a local tacit agreement that land was not sold to outsiders easily or cheaply despite rural depopulation and many uninhabited properties. For example, a few years before Matsuyama got this land a wealthy man from Nagoya paid over ¥46,000,000 for a much smaller hobby farm in the area. And before we were married, my wife, a nurse from outside Gensan, had been unsuccessfully searching for property for six years. The few properties that she had found were either well out of her price range or would not be sold to a lone female buyer. In 2012, when asking a local to rent some garden space, we were offered the neighboring house and yard, both admittedly run down, for an incredible ¥20,000. Land was sold to individuals, to particular and particularly scrutinized individuals, that is, who are presumed to stick around and not turn it over for profit. For those who got on with locals, extremely favorable arrangements could be made.

When the Matsuyamas moved out of Wada-san's old homestead, the farm's new Chinese workers moved in. Lacking driver's permits, living there meant that they could walk to work as opposed to being driven by coworkers. Matsuyama was reluctant to spend the money required to repair the old house on his new land. Soon, and somewhat mysteriously, it burned down! Arson or accident? I remain uncertain—but undaunted, perhaps even relieved, they started to build a new house and soon bought some horses. In 2010 their first son got a new brother. Matsuyama and his wife were passionate about Hokkaido, their young family, and their new home, but with these loves also came mounting contradictions and conflicts.

A new house backing onto an expanse of land, two cars, room for a dog, two children involved in a variety of extracurricular activities, not to mention a private barn for horses, would be an impossible lifestyle to maintain in an urban environment and exorbitantly expensive in much of Japan. However, Matsuyama's work and connections made this possible in rural Tokachi. It came at a cost of course. As noted above, few would call a *hantā*'s work easy; going to work at 3:30 a.m. and often working until 7:00 p.m. or later on a four-days-on and one-day-off rotation. Takako's part-time work at the supermarket was of marginal financial importance. She liked working. Matsuyama lamented about his work situation on occasion:

> Grand Hopes no seikatsu wa taihen. tatoeba nagaii hatara-iteiru jikan ga aru shi, tokidoki ningen kankei muzukashii shi . . . demo kore wa shigoto dake ne. shigoto no ato de zen zen kangaenai yo. Shigoto owaru toki iro iro na kyoumi ga aru ne. Shachō wa itsumo shinpai desu yo.

> (Yeah, life [working on the farm] is hard, the long hours, dealing with some of the people, but it's just a job. I don't think about it after hours, I've other interests, but the *shachō* is always worrying you know.)

Matsuyama's big worry was about the future of his sons, Daichi and Kei. Both Matsuyama and Takako felt that life was good for the time being. Their children were in a safe environment and could run around outside and they had the *shachō*'s wife and mother to occasionally look after and dote upon them. But while the local primary school is a two-minute commute, the junior high is a fifteen-minute drive, and their high school of choice is in Obihiro, a considerable daily commute. Both parents thought that the teen years might pose a problem. Although reared in rural areas themselves, or maybe because of that fact, they feared that their sons would become *inakamono* (country bumpkins) and were quietly torn between staying and going.

The Secret Life of Tarō-san

Tarō-san was also in a high-level head work position on the farm. Fittingly, I met Tarō-san on my first official day of work. He loved his job. I was meeting people, handing out my business card, and bumbling through formalized greetings with half-comprehending but widely smiling new coworkers. Tarō-san stood out. With a look of serious reflection, he studied my card, holding it with both hands and, after a moment, he commented favorably on the perceived high rank of my university. He then placed the card under the glass cover on his office desk where it remained for the entirety of my stay at the farm. Tarō-san, and I always called him Tarō-san and not just Tarō, was the *buchō* in charge of the milking parlor and, when not in the office filling out reports on it or reading about it, he was often found eyeing it with a look of unease or pride depending on its state of cleanliness or function. The parlor was undeniably his realm.[1]

While Matsuyama took his job seriously, Tarō-san viewed his more as a spiritual calling. While I was working on the farm, on two occasions, he came into work on his day off because he knew the service technicians were visiting and he wanted to explain the equipment's various operational concerns in person. Tarō-san, like Matsuyama, was in his mid-thirties when we first met. He was slight of build and, in spite of his schoolboy face, had the distinct air of being a generation older. This was not due to a lack of energy. Despite his elevated position he was usually the first one at his milking station. He was also more often than not the last person to leave. He sprang effortlessly from under the *kotatsu* (a heated low table) in the staff room into a dutiful trot to answer the phone or when beckoned by a superior. At ease in his coveralls, though his demeanor made him seem old, he moved with more spritely grace than people over ten years his junior. He was polite when we met, curious about me, and by the time I left we were no longer on speaking terms. We were both happy I was going. Unlike the diplomatic Matsuyama, Tarō-san was not liked by most of his coworkers. One of the smirking subcontractors fittingly always referred to him as *majimesugi-san* (Mr. Overly Serious) behind his back and most were quick to highlight that this comment was a polite understatement.

During milking times Tarō-san was in control of the equipment and workers in the parlor. He would become easily enraged at coworkers and cows. Generally, any parlor worker would suffice, but notably Haruko and Takuto (young contract workers discussed below) were the chosen targets for his outbursts. In these instances, his frustration was often interpretable if not understandable. Undeniably, Haruko was slow and forgetful. Takuto was often more interested in the clock than the work at hand. However, the vehemence of his rage seemed, to all involved, beyond reasonable. If

Tarō-san was working in the final position of the parlor (a system defined in the following chapter) he would constantly demand the speeding up of the equipment, past the comfort level of slower workers. Unlike other managers who ranged from apathetic to engaged and engaging, he would hover around his least favorite workers (again even on his day off at times). He would point out their failings, scream at them, and on more than one occasion I witnessed him strike them or shoulder them away from their task while berating them. Cows were also the frequent recipients of his wrath as he would punch at their legs or hit them with the iodine solution's plastic applicator—breaking it at least twice.

Everybody had an individual and seemingly patented response to Tarō-san's daily fury. Young cattle would become more stressed and generally do whatever had been disturbing him all the more; old cattle were frequently, even shockingly, indifferent; Haruko would weep and Takuto would laugh or make faces when he turned away. However, most would just say, "Hai wakarimashita" with a variance in individual and momentary body language and intonation that expressed a situationally sensitive range of meanings, from a dismissive "Yeah, whatever" to a forthright and apologetic "Yes sir, I understand" acknowledgment of wrongdoing.

Tarō-san was not merely feeling pressure from being in charge of the milking process. He faced all jobs on the farm with incomparable zeal. While scrubbing the parlor floor he would drip with sweat and would let out heavy sighs from time to time. When roping cattle, he preferred to rope them far into the corral and then animatedly grunt and "humph," yanking them across the stall by the halter to be tied up seemingly always the furthest distance from his starting point. Indeed, whether folding summer silage tarps or shoveling snow he made it very clear to those observing that he was working hard. One evening after work he invited me over for a beer. Having spoken to him little beyond work, I arrived at his apartment—a private apartment not affiliated with the farm—expecting it to either have austere bare walls or be rife with instructional cow posters. As it turned out the apartment was filled with dozens of photos.

Tarō-san was a newspaper photographer in Sapporo before starting dairy work at thirty-three years of age. He was also an avid angler, baseball fan, skilled cook, and collector of detective novels. The early evening was spent speaking of our hobbies, but as the empty bottles increased so did the range of topics. Tarō-san had been engaged to a woman. When this relationship ended—"badly" he impressed as emphatically as ambiguously—he sought a new life outside of Sapporo and the bitter memories held within its streets and play places. He expressed that work is hard to find once you have started a career in Japan. He was tired of being a photographer as the pay was poor and it was a stressful lifestyle being "on call" with never-ending deadlines. Photography, his passion at one time, had become no longer enjoyable as a job and he was looking for a change even before his relationship troubles. He claimed that "big money" could be made in dairy farming. Rubbing some dust off with his sleeve, he produced a sepia photo of his grandfather, a dairy farmer near Furano in Hokkaido, a man whom he said he respected more than any other person, due to his being a *shōjiki na hatarakimono* (an honest, hardworking common man). In short, he explained his choice to work at Grand Hopes Farm as a combination of seeking out a new life and the chance to make both money and something of himself as a department head. It was also clear he had a certain nostalgic view of his grandfather and saw dairy farming as a kind of familial succession.

With the toted beer finished we moved on to some *shōchu* from Tarō-san's fridge and the conversation soon became more maudlin. "Ore wa samurai da!" (I am a samurai!), Tarō-san slurred leaning forward on wobbly elbows across the table. Caught off guard by this elucidation, not sure if I was to be taking it literally, my blurry eyes likely widened as I asked what he meant. He went on to explain that the *shachō* had given him a job when others would not and that he would do anything for him. He was outraged that others did not take work seriously or have pride in the company. Moreover, echoing Mr. Wada, but not his optimism, he suggested odds were stacked against Great Hopes Farm and times were increasingly becoming hard because all of the small farmers were getting subsidies and unfairly competing with larger farms and their substantial loans. It would be best if all these small family farms died off and workers from the small dairies moved to work at the larger ones. I expressed *moderate* disagreement. Mega farms have their flaws too, such as high overheads. Recounting some of my ethnographic observations at the time, I also noted that many workers just saw their work at Grand Hopes as a job, a way to make money, a way to see Hokkaido, or a way to take some time out to think about their next step (all brought up below). I added that Wada-san surely all knew this (I had calmly discussed it with the *shachō* before). Tarō-san became furious. Slamming his glass down he yelled, "You are all idiots," this is everyone's "big chance!" He slumped over groaning and it was clearly time for me to go home.

A Shy Girl?

Yukiko arrived at the farm three months after I started. Getting her details from Mr. Wada, I attempted to contact her through email before she arrived. I explained that I was a researcher working at the farm and that I was interested in her impressions of Hokkaido before she came. Despite numerous attempts, there was no response. After she arrived, and we were better acquainted, I asked why she did not reply to my emails. She told me that my emails were *kowai* (scary) because I wasn't Japanese. By this time, however, I realized that nearly everything was scary to Yukiko, let alone Tarō-san. She was from Fukuoka, a large city in Kyushu. She studied sheep breeding at a university in Aomori and wanted some on-farm experience. Although she also told me that she was not particularly interested in this major or even in farming. Her boyfriend found a job at a nearby dairy farm and he had negotiated the same "floating" days off, adapting his work schedule to fit hers.

One afternoon we were assigned the task of scrubbing the floor of the laundry room together, a fairly easy job making prolonged conversation possible. I asked her why she chose to work in Hokkaido. She was conflicted: "Iroiro na dōbutsu dai suki demo inaka wa kirai yo. Kaimono ga naishi, tomodachi mo inai—okashi ne?" (I love all sorts of animals, but I hate the countryside, there's no shopping and I don't see my friends (and so on), it's strange that I chose to live here, isn't it?). What about your boyfriend, I asked, he must like it here? "Zenzen suki ja nai yo X farm wa sugoi hen na hito ga takusan yo" (No way, he hates it there at X farm—his job is full of weird people). Indeed, I later met people who had a host of unpleasant things to say about the owner of that particular farm, ranging from animal abuse to sexual harassment. "So, are you going to stay here?" I asked. "Mada kimemasen ga . . ." (I [we?] haven't decided but . . .) was her reply. My assumption was that she would soon be one of the many who soon quit the farm. However, a few weeks later she was made an assistant to the *hatsujō hantā* and had promised the *shachō* that she would stick around for at least another year.

Head Work: Interactions

I returned to Gensan for a second stint of research in 2008–2009 and despite keeping in contact with people both on and off the farm, I was shocked at the level of change I encountered only a year and a half later, a fact that holds true every time I return to Grand Hopes. Former coworkers, the ones that remained, agreed that change came at a furious pace at the farm. Of the three workers discussed above only Matsuyama was still at the farm. Thus, despite his claims that the dairy was the "big chance" for all of the workers, his commitment to the owners, and a strong desire to remain with the farm, Tarō-san was encouraged to quit by the owners. Encouraged is not meant as a euphemism. He was politely asked by the owners of the farm if he would please consider leaving for the sake of the farm!

At first Tarō-san remained, but eventually seeing that there was no future for him there, he did quit. His frequent altercations with staff and townspeople, outlined in more detail in the following sections and chapters, became a nuisance, even a liability, for the farm owners. Yukiko, uncertain of her desire to stay from the get-go, left the farm despite her promise to stay on for at least a year due to an unplanned pregnancy. Matsuyama was the only worker who remained, and he remained until the time of writing this book. However, his desire to remain as a permanent member of Gensan society is always in question despite his status as a kind of honorary local: his sons are well known and popular local *dosanko* after all. Choices, aptitudes, and contingencies played a key role in these individuals' farm lives. While these three workers were about the same age, Japanese, and linked with the office side of production—united in their engagement with *head work* unlike the other workers on the farm described in the following chapters—they were extremely different individuals.

They did not share similar backgrounds or interests; settling world nomad, former disillusioned salary man, and timid displaced urbanite. They communicated little at work and did not spend time together outside of work. Clearly, they did not share similar future aspirations or possibilities at the farm. Yet, from 2006 to 2008 they represented half of the office staff who were not related to the owners. Yukiko, the only woman beyond the receptionist (a divorced local woman also unrelated to the farm family), was trained at a university in sheep husbandry, but she was from a city and had no practical experience at being a *hantā*. She considered things "un-Japanese" to be unusual to the point of threatening. Initially, she expressed zero interest in being a long-term worker at the farm, seeing the job as a liminal time-out. However, she did commit to a spoken one-year contract in order to learn the pragmatic aspects of the job, and I suspect she likely would have stuck with this obligation if not for her pregnancy. By contrast, Matsuyama, holding the same work position as Yukiko, was raised in rural Akita but had traveled widely. He did not have a university education, but he was very open to foreign things (rodeo, Thai curries, reggae, and so on), and he was ever keen to discuss his views on life or the farm. It was his resourcefulness and practical experience that earned him the position; his skills, his tact, and his *ii hito* status (stable, reliable, not prone to confrontation, seen as likely to remain in the area, having a wife and children) kept him comfortably accepted in his job and the community. While he had no immediate plans to leave, he (quietly) did not discount this option. His family was treated like an extended family by the *shachō*. He was serious, but for him the job was a job; it was important because it afforded a rural lifestyle. In contrast, Tarō-san was extraordinarily eager to remain at the farm; while he had a university education it was in photography and not agriculture. He had very specific ideas of what work life entailed and expected his coworkers to possess a similar "anything for the company" spirit, considering himself a sort of company "samurai" in the service of the farm's *ie*, the futility of which is expanded upon in the following chapter. He was frequently frustrated that his desire for company success and solidarity was not shared by his coworkers. And, despite his strong desire to be part of the farm family, he was not deemed an *ii hito* due to his frequent outbursts of anger and rigid opinions.

Detailed descriptions of other office staff beyond the *shachō* would underscore the same basic point, that very little beyond age, ethnicity, and work itself united these individuals. Each one came from differing backgrounds and interpreted the importance of work and Tokachi as a location in different ways: providing a lifestyle, providing a "big chance," or providing a short-term opportunity. While none of these idiosyncratic office workers were related to the owner by blood, Matsuyama's family shared a "fictive" kinship relationship with the owners. Tarō-san desired such belonging but was kept outside and Yukiko was also an outsider and remained so until her departure to start her own family, but clearly chances of becoming semi-local were opened to her. However, even locals with direct family links such as the aforementioned Kato-san, the farm's daughters, and the *shachō*'s son left the farm permanently or for extended periods. Thus, being "in the family" was not related to having an instant career in *head work* or even having an interest in the daily operations of the farm. Alternatively, being intimately involved in the operation of the farm did not mean one shared a similar trajectory with one's coworkers.

Chapter Nine

Producing and Pumping

Farm Foot Soldiers

The conclusion of this book outlines the parlor system in detail, tying together how human, animal, machine, technology, and production meet in terms of both function and dysfunction on the farm. In short, the parlor and its central role in terms of making milk and money serve as an ideal summary, making an in-depth discussion of how it works here, beyond a broad outline, redundant. But keeping in mind the body and flow metaphor, from head to heart to extremities and back again, the parlor is the central point where the veins and arteries from all over the body lead. In other words, it is where the pathways and collection points that are central to the constant inward and outward flows on the farm meet.

Like the heart, the purpose of the parlor is to maintain a constant circulation. It is a place where humans, bovines, milk, bacteria, and information constantly pass through on the way to or from the body of the operation. When things go as planned, all elements work to get milk from inside the cow to outside the farm as safely and as quickly as possible for the spoilable product, with profits flowing back to keep the farm going.

Heart Work: Producing and Pumping

GYŪNYŪ USHI (DAIRY CATTLE)

Hokkaido's dairy producers have experimented with a variety of different breeds of dairy cattle. Today, far and away the most popular breed, for

169

practical and economic purposes, is the Holstein. An interesting political history of this choice can be found in Russell (2007, 132). Simply, Holsteins produce more milk, though they may not be as hardy as some other breeds. And they produce high-fat-content milk, though not as high as some more delicate breeds. There are small farms that hold other breeds such as Jersey cows, but these are few and far between and are more artisanal, not industrial operations. Grand Hopes Farm dairy cows are all Holsteins, usually black and white, sometimes brown and white, occasionally one of these colors, and rarer still, all three. In functional terms a cow is a number-coded individual unit of production, but they are not only individuated in this macro analytic sense, they are also viewed as individuals, particular and specific, individuated by automated equipment and many are individualized by human workers in daily contact with them. A cow, as will become progressively clear in the following chapters, is not an abstract entity for workers. Cows are idiosyncratic beings one must contend with to do one's job. Any given cow can be skinny, ornery, affectionate; some are surprisingly clever while others are not. And specific cows are remembered by specific workers for personal reasons, a point returned to.

With few exceptions, and leaving out male offspring, industrial dairy cows remain indoors for the entirety of their lives, on average around six productive years, making the daily route from stall to parlor and back to stall two or three times a day. From approximately fourteen months of age cows are impregnated as often as possible; this is accomplished solely through AI. Calves are born, dams are instantly separated, and when possible impregnated again. This increases the output of milk and offspring. Usually after spending a summer season on common community land, male cows are sold as standing meat. Female cows are kept, or less often sold as milking cattle. Smaller cows are inseminated with cheaper semen as it is not expected that they will produce offspring large enough to be highly productive dairy cattle.

SUTŌRU (STALL STAFF)

Stall work is perhaps the most "insular" of the positions on the farm—at least in terms of human contact. The stall workers are essentially responsible for getting the cows to and from the barn areas and to and from the holding area just outside the milking parlor. They maintain bovine bedding and flooring, ensuring that cows have safe and secure mobility and are resting in reasonably sterile environs. Stall workers often drive equipment around the farm for various tasks. For example, they are usually responsible for transporting animals around the various areas of the farm or moving manure to a storage shed or lagoon. Their concern is essentially with the movement of cattle during milking and with the maintenance of the outlying regions of the farm when not assisting with milking. Thus, they have little contact, beyond break-times, with other workers on the farm. And given the nature of the position, even while working with one another verbal communication is limited.

HŌRUDIN (HOLDING AREA STAFF)

In contrast to the closed social work-world of the stall staff, the holding worker is a multispecies go-between. They work between the stall staff and the parlor staff and between the cattle and parlor machine itself, an active liaison between the farm's head and heart. The holding worker's key task is to orchestrate the safe and smooth "flow" of the cattle from the stall area into and out of the automated parlor and then back to the stall area. This requires that the cattle obey the pace of the machine—often a challenge with younger cattle. Occasionally the need also arises to communicate directly with the office staff, but generally cattle that need to be separated after milking are indicated by the hunter via a list of cow numbers and groups on paper. Alternatively, members of the parlor staff make instant decisions regarding the separation of cows based on irregularities or perceived illnesses and these are communicated directly to the holding worker.

Prompting young cows into menacing looking equipment aside, the job is not as demanding physically as some others, but it does require the ability to act quickly and decisively. In this position numerous gambles must be made regarding the movement of cows in and out of the parlor and en route to and from the stalls. Moreover, the worker must select opportune moments to leave their post to tie up sick animals, or, upon seeing a major problem on the horizon—such as broken equipment or missing animals—halt the entire milking process much to the chagrin of other workers keen to see the end of their shift. As such, it is a stressful job with plenty of movement from the stall areas, to the holding areas, to the parlor, and the "catch barn" where separated cows are kept.

PĀRĀ (PARLOR STAFF)

Again, the mechanics and relationships involved in the various parlor jobs are complex and are outlined in the conclusion. However, to the point at hand, the function of the workers and equipment in the parlor is straightforward; first, the extraction of milk from cows as efficiently as possible utilizing a digitized and pneumatic rotary milking machine, and second, the search for any signs of illness that may have been missed by the hunter. During milking, the workers are always within the confines of the parlor and work in four alternating "stations" of varying difficulty and intensity, from applying cleaning solution to teats, to attaching the suction device, to administering injections. Approximately every twenty minutes workers change stations and at the end of the shift they are responsible for cleaning and sterilizing the room and equipment. Thus, while there is a lead worker, the staff share in doing the same tasks for the same duration of time.

Working Lives

Below, two stall workers and six parlor workers are briefly introduced and they reappear along with other workers in the remaining chapters. Like Matsuyama, Yukiko, and Tarō-san, or the owners and their families, these workers also have personal ideas as to what dairy work offers them and how they engage with the work and their position on the farm. They also have differing aspirations, "embodiments," and capabilities. Innate physical speed or coordination, a keen intellect, taking an interest in the work at hand, or viewing such work as a job or lifestyle, all these personal aspects differentiate one worker from another.

Between-san

"Between-san naze kono shigoto wo yamemasen ka?" (Between-san why don't you quit this job?), I asked while we shoveled rows of rice husks out for stall bedding. "Yametain da kedo . . . Grand Hopes de hatarakanai" (I want to quit Grand Hopes but . . . I don't work here). After repeating the question in various forms assuming it was unclear, he assured me that my Japanese language skills were not the issue. As it turned out, one of the farm's best workers, in fact, did not officially work at the farm. I had asked the question because it was clear that he hated the job and had a palpable and, compared to the others, a vocal dislike of the owners. He was not paid the same rate as other workers as he did not receive bonuses, yet he was more knowledgeable and hardworking than most. He was employed by another farm and had been "on loan" at Grand Hopes Farm for over a year. He did not know the details of this arrangement and the owners were not willing to share them with me either. His indentured labor was an accepted mystery. What was certain was the fact that Between-san had worked on three dairy farms since he graduated high school. As months passed, and workers came and went, he would say that next month the owners had promised to let him return to the farm that he had formerly worked on. However, each month another worker would quit, indeed usually one a month did leave, and Between-san would remain in limbo as an overqualified fill-in staff member, unhappy and uncertain.

By all accounts from female staff and my local female friends, he was a stunningly handsome and *otokorashii* (manly) man. He was fit, clever, and meticulous, and these qualities alone made him a valuable stall hand; again, a job with considerable autonomy. I asked him what he disliked about the job. Like all workers his first response was related to the awful hours and rotating shifts, but he insisted that the work itself was OK. What was particularly troubling to him was not that the hours interfered with his hobbies, like Takuto below. It was that he was twenty-eight years old and he wanted a girlfriend. "Shigoto wa mā mā kantan dakedo kanojo ga inai, jikan ga muri dakara" (The job's OK but you have no time to meet a woman). I asked him why he didn't quit both jobs: Grand Hopes Farm and the farm leasing him out. He replied that it is very difficult to find work in Gensan, and all the more difficult if you are seen as lacking *gaman*, the ability to endure. I thought he had endured more than enough. Why don't you move to Obihiro, or Tokyo for that matter? I asked, adding the enticement of there being both more jobs and more women in either place. "Shiranai" (I don't know why) along with a head tilt was always his reply. He was not sure why he was being kept there, he wasn't happy about it, but he wasn't (seemingly) about to do anything to change his lot in life either: as with many workers Between-san was a prime example of someone in the aforementioned state of being *liminally liminal*. He told me his days off were spent sleeping or playing pachinko and dreading the return to work.

TAKUTO, AKA UP, UP, AND AWAY

Takuto was in some ways the counterpoint to Between-san. He worked in the parlor and later in the animal hospital introduced in the following chapter. He was twenty-one years old and sported a few prominent scars, bad teeth, and fake gold chains. Like Between-san he was a local, but he was far from quiet and reserved; rather he was a tough kid from the wrong side of Gensan's unused tracks. He was the quintessence of what Japanese call *Yanīippoi* (Yankee*ish*). In short, he was young, brash, and had an attraction to flashy fashions and customized cars. He would often tote magazines to work and show me car parts he planned to buy with his next paycheck. Politically incorrect, but enlightening all the same, in the UK using a similar level of colloquial slang one might call him a *chav*, in Australia a *bogen*, and in North America a *redneck*.

Takuto had quit a few jobs around town, ranging from a honey distribution truck driver to temporary jobs on other farms. I was told that his constant job shifting made him seem like a poor employee to most prospective employers since he lacked the *gaman* that Between-san had a great store of. He came from a large family, and via small-town gossip it was commonly known that his father was locally infamous as a gambler and drinker. The *shachō* hired him nonetheless and he often seemed to have a soft spot for him, letting whatever infraction slide with a head tilt and hiss, when he might chastise another worker. But for Takuto concern about farmwork was placed far behind concerns with where he would spend his next pay packet or how he could have some fun killing the hours of the workday.

Predictably perhaps, Takuto and Tarō-san were like comic book archenemies. If I was working with one, unfavorable comments about the other were sure to arise. The other was always an idiot, disliked by the others, and hard to work with. Tarō-san bemoaned that it was dangerous that Takuto did not take the job seriously and that this was the problem with Japanese today—*namakemono, bakarashii wakamono* (lazy and foolish youth) and similar derisive comments were common. Takuto told me it was impossible to work with such a *kowarechatta ojisan* (crazy middle-aged man). Both weekly told me that they had reached their *genkai* (limit) with the other.

Foolishly, I would try to reason with both, saying that Takuto was just a kid and likely did not see his future at the farm or that Tarō-san was not such a bad guy outside of work—the general thrust being a combination of "live and let live" and "please don't involve me." After one of my research trips to farms further south I returned to learn that they had gotten into a yelling match during milking and Takuto stormed off before the end of his shift. This was a flouting of workplace authority that couldn't go unpunished and the *shachō* sent Takuto to work in the cow hospital. I was told by Matsuyama that the *shachō* always sent offensive employees to do this rather grim work in hopes that they would quit.

However, this "punishment" actually worked in Takuto's favor. His new job was more flexible in terms of taking time off as he was not responsible for the daily milking of cattle. And his true interest, beyond cars, existed outside of dairy farming. His new schedule enabled him to continue to study to be a balloon pilot. Indeed, for all the lack of interest he had at work he made up in a passion to become a professional pilot on one of the local ballooning teams. His new demotion even enabled him to attend a four-day balloon festival in Honshu. He was overjoyed.

HAIRLESS ICHIRO AND HARMLESS HARU

Ichiro stood apart from the others for various reasons. First, regardless of circumstance he was indefatigably friendly and polite. Second, he was also hard not to notice due to his appearance: he completely lacked hair. Despite interviewing him and talking with him daily I never asked about this. He was clearly self-conscious about his appearance, but beneath his omnipresent hat brim, his smile contagiously beamed and his thin brow-less face gave the impression that he was some sort of timeless Zen master sent to meditate on dairy life. He was an anthropologist's dream: eager to help, patient, good-natured, and generally open to any question. Indeed, he often anticipated the questions that I had before I posed them. Without exaggeration, he was more than bright, more than observant, more than kind; there was something very special—a charisma—that hung about Ichiro.

He came from Nara. His parents worked in real estate. He had attended a private university on scholarship focusing on agribusiness and was keen to pursue a career in industrial cheese making despite not really liking cheese. Only twenty-four years old, Ichiro was deeply concerned about his future and the future of agriculture in Japan. If he were to enter the ongoing debate of local dairy farm owners (Is bigger better?), he saw the move to larger farms as lamentable, but necessary given Japan's population, land base, and world trade position. Ichiro was very clever, articulate, and well informed about the working of the dairy and agricultural businesses in Japan and in general. He knew that there was more of a future, given the aforementioned trends of consumption and his intimate knowledge of them, in milk products rather than in milk production. He wanted to work in agriculture because he disliked cities and crowds and he enjoyed the physicality of farmwork. He was extremely patient and gentle with cows—this was a rare quality among parlor workers, certainly males. On a few occasions we chatted over lunch in the staff room—every day he ate a plain rice ball and the same brand of instant noodles—and although he didn't drink, Ichiro joined me for a beer in my apartment on a few occasions.

One night, chugging back a beer as Ichiro sipped his can of juice, I asked him what he would like to do on his last day of work at the farm. I expected an answer ranging from, "I will never quit" to "go on a vacation," but he caught me completely off guard. He peered directly into my eyes, rare in itself, and he replied, "Ushi zenbu nigeshite agetai" (I would like to set all of the cows free). Two weeks after that rather arresting statement, and without mentioning it to anyone, Ichiro quit. I asked him why, hoping for a long explanation, one that might explain why many workers would just reach an invisible wall and end their time on the farm. "Henna funiki" (bad atmosphere—bad vibes) was as detailed a response as I could get from this usually lucid interlocutor. And, though many asked, and I asked many, nobody could deduce why he quit. As he was usually politely forthcoming with his views, perhaps Ichiro was uncertain himself beyond a vague affective state of unhappiness; and interesting here is that this seemed more related to the life of cows, not work as such. For "Master Ichiro" it was simply time to move on. He promised to keep in touch with everyone. He quietly left the farm without ceremony and nobody heard from him again.

Haruko was also a parlor worker. She was undeniably physically awkward and socially quirky. These are not statements made from my perspective alone—before my arrival she had earned the nickname *uchūjin* (alien) because she would appear from lunch with food all over her shirt, or from cleaning troughs drenched with water and her head covered with cow slobber or dung. She often seemed utterly oblivious to her appearance or often what was going on around her. This, combined with slow movements, uncomfortable linguistic pauses, self-deprecation, and fits of giggling, made her a target for both good-natured and malicious jokes.

"Haru," few called her by her full name, was raised on a small mixed family farm in Nagano. She told me that her family grew apples and persimmons and had a small dairy. When I asked about the size of the dairy herd, she giggled out her reply; they had three cows, all with names, and if she took over the farm her goal was to bump the herd up to ten cows. Despite the surface, Haru was much brighter than many suspected. She had attended a national university to study dairying. She had friends in Obihiro and friends back home who would often call her on her cell phone during the day. Surprisingly, weeks after Ichiro left, she told me that they had been a secret romantic couple—a fact that nobody knew.

All were impressed with Haru's *gaman*-ability. She had made a commitment to stick with this job for a year, and despite daily abuse from Tarō-san—on more than one occasion I found her hiding in the back room literally nose bubbling and convulsing in tears—she lasted her contract and happily moved back to rural Nagano.

"Za" Tokyo Cowboy

The Tokyo Cowboy hated this pseudonym when I told him, but it is too fitting not to use. He started at the farm a month before I did and was well on his way out the door by the first time we met for a beer in my apartment a week after my arrival. He came from an upper-middle-class family. His father owned some buildings in Tokyo and was a salary man, his mother was a homemaker, and his sister had studied ballet in London. He attended a well-known private university in Tokyo to study economics, but he did not finish. Since dropping out he had been a *furītā* in various stores and pubs. At thirty-two years of age he had hoped that dairy farming would be his calling; indeed unlike many workers living in spartan apartments he had shipped a significant amount of furniture and belongings from Tokyo to start his new life . . . which lasted about two months.

We arranged our final meeting the night before he was to return to Tokyo. He was not busy attending goodbye parties. But this was nothing personal, the turnover rate was such that none were ever held. Workers came and left with seemingly few connections to the job or other workers. However, Za Cowboy was an unusual case as nobody at the farm would even talk to him once he announced he was quitting. Communication with him became small talk or instruction alone. He became a workplace pariah and this, perhaps through previous experience, did not bother him in the slightest.

No stranger to vice, he arrived an hour and half late at my door with several drinks already under his belt at the local *sunakku*. Shrouded in a halo of cigarette smoke, he cracked open a new beer and we started in on my poor attempt at green curry.

"Fukinsonovabitchi kaisha" (Fucking son-of-a-bitch company)—"Wakaru?" (Understand—[my English]?)."

I assured him that I understood.

"Hontō ni" (Really?), he chuckled, perhaps pleased that years of English language *juku* torture had at least come to use in this conversation. He disliked nearly everything about Gensan except the librarian.

"Yaritai yo!" (I want to "do" her—[have sex with her]!) "Demo kore kara muri da ne—zannen" (Well, that's not gonna happen now, too bad).

I asked why he had quit Grand Hopes Farm. He replied that his idea of living in Hokkaido was free time, open space, and nature, but as things turned out, the hours were horrible (though he knew the hours before he came) and he hated small-town life. The people, perhaps the librarian aside, were boring and he said he wanted to kill Taro-san every day. "Sankei wakaru?" (Do you know what a 3K job is?)

"Un wakaru yo" (Yeah, I know). And I outlined the meaning in Japanese and added that in English there is a similar description of such employment.[1]

"Nihongo wa sugoinaaaaa Pōru—chyampu iu no?" (Your Japanese is grrrreat [a common lie]—chyampu iu no . . . ?)

"Champu (shampoo?) iu (said), no (is it)? . . .

Thinking this was a Japanese word unknown to me, or an out-of-context reference to shampoo, I shrugged to express my incomprehension.

He thrust his hands in the air, spilling beer on his pants and my floor, "Chyampu ova za worudo, I amu za chyampu . . . Eigo jyanai?" (Champ of the world, I am the champ . . . It's English, isn't it?) I rethought, "Champu, you know?" (Champ—[do] you know [this word]?).

Giggling, I replied that I understood—"Anata no eigo wa sugoi yo. Chotto moto benkyō shitara pera pera ni naru to omou." (Your English is great! With a bit of practice, you'll be fluent I reckon.) We both laughed.

"Glan Hopū is za champu ova San kei, OK. Fukinkaisya" (Grand Hopes is the champion of 3D (crap jobs), OK. Fucking company . . .), he bellowed—cackling himself into a coughing fit.

I asked what the plan was after he got back to Tokyo. After a short trip to Sapporo to hang out with a former university friend, he had landed a job trucking shipping containers between Yokohama and Kobe. He told me that he thought it was going to be a great job. He liked to be alone and to drive.

Tsutomu: Nobody Knows the Troubles I've Seen

Usually Tsutomu worked in the parlor but, much to the frustration of stall coworkers, he would also fill in doing work in the stall area if the need arose. Tsutomu's father was a university professor in Tokyo and Tsutomu had a degree in something—something unknown because he rarely spoke. He was the only nonfamily member to have worked at Grand Hopes Farm for the entirety of its history and the common consensus among workers was that he would continue to work there for the rest of his days. This was not because he excelled at his job. Indeed, he had not moved an inch up the company ladder since starting work at the *kachō*'s farm the year before Grand Hopes was incorporated. He did not enjoy his job like Ichiro. He rarely ever put effort into working like Between-san, and even if he tried, the quality and quantity of work was low. Moreover, his employment longevity was not because the *shachō* wanted him there. Much in the way the *kachō* was dead set against hiring me, I was told the *shachō* intensely disliked Tsutomu. But he came along with the incorporation of the farms and it seemed nobody would take responsibility to fire him. If his name was mentioned around Wada-san, he would let out a low growling "ahhhhhh, Tsutomu na . . ." (ohhhh, that Tsutomu) and quickly change the topic. From the perspective of those along the grapevine, the *shachō*'s contempt was understandable; he had bailed Tsutomu out of debt from gambling and unpaid credit cards (the companies contacted the farm requesting payment) and he was well aware of his lack of work ethic.

Despite an official list of jobs issued during a staff meeting placing Tsutomu in league with the rest of the newer workers, there were times when Tsutomu would take it upon himself to snap the reins of command. If a true *buchō* was around, this never happened. He held very little sway over male staff; he was more or less ignored and unsurprisingly taunted and laughed at by Takuto. But he would often issue commands to female staff. And generally, they would do what he asked of them, though even Haru seemed to follow his commands more out of pity than deference. While this relates in part to gender and status detailed ahead, it must be made clear that such roles were not as determinative as the agency of the individuals who embodied them. In short, while Tsutomu might bully Haru, he never attempted such high-handed persuasion with Yukiko. Her "shy girl" quality aside, she had no problem telling workers, male or female, what she wanted them to do when she began her brief *buchō* role. And it was well known that her very dedicated, rather stocky, and rough-around-the-edges boyfriend was working nearby. Alternatively, Between-san might quietly offer an opinion that his coworkers ought to do X or Y. And on his suggestion, X or Y would soon be done. While Ichiro was a respected and senior male staff member he never, without being told to from above, attempted to take command of other staff members. He was more of a lead-by-example type; rather than say anything he would pick up a shovel and others, myself included, would feel compelled to follow suit.

Tsutomu was twenty-nine years old and passionate about video games—especially *Final Phantasy* (*sic*). He enjoyed reading comics about cyber worlds and collecting figurines. One could consider him the nearest example on the farm to an actual *otaku*. It was rumored that he also enjoyed pachinko and Obihiro's prostitutes on his days off.

THE CHINESE ARE COMING!

"Mō taihen yo" (Sigh, it's difficult), Tarō-san mumbled while forking out new morning straw after I'd asked him about the farm's newest workers. He had been informed that morning that the farm was hiring two new staff members from China through an agency in cooperation with JA (Hansen 2010a further details the lives of these Chinese workers). Tarō-san's initial worry was their complete lack of Japanese language. They read kanji, how hard can it be to communicate "turn the dial" or "spread the straw"? I asked. But this form of radical Otherness was clearly upsetting for many workers while some like Matsuyama were genuinely intrigued to meet them.

Over the next few weeks anticipation grew. Indeed, I was the first *gaijin* that most of my cohorts had ever worked with. Speculation as to what "the Chinese" would be like circulated daily; they will be strong-willed and violent, they are only coming to marry a Japanese man, be careful where you leave your wallet from now on. When workers were told that "the Chinese" had arrived in Japan, this heightened the suspense and chatter. We were told that they needed to be "trained" at a "how-to-live-in-Japan course" with the other Chinese they were arriving with. We were told that there were twelve in all and ten would be placed on different nearby farms. Thus far, all arrangements were made through the JA and a Chinese broker and the owners were largely mute on the subject, only adding to the rampant conjecturing as to what these Others would be like. "I hear that they need to be taught how to use a stove," one worker noted. Tarō-san was moody and anxious (more than usual)—"This is bad, very bad," he frequently grumbled. Observing this, Matsuyama found it comical, slipping me occasional insider joke looks.

As it turned out, both workers arriving at Great Hopes were from Outer Mongolia. For the chance to work in Hokkaido they paid approximately five thousand American dollars in China for their flights, requisite paperwork, and "training." This was to be paid back in installments over their first year as they were promised three years of work if they proved to be good "students." Thus, on paper, they were not officially workers. They were "trainees" in Japan to study dairy farming, though to date I have never met such a trainee, and I have met dozens, who is actually interested in dairy farming as employment upon their return to their home country. The real purpose of this title is that as trainees they could legally be paid half the wages of a regular worker (Hansen 2010a). And as students, they could work a part-time job—an extra twenty hours a week at part-time rates—bringing their income up to three-quarters of a Japanese employee for a third more hours. These work and wage conditions were justified in two ways by staff and owners alike: in China, their Japanese wage represented a lot of money and they had chosen to come, eyes wide open, to the conditions in Tokachi.

When they arrived Tarō-san and equally concerned cohorts were relieved. They could read nearly all the kanji in the parlor and understood their jobs as quickly as a Japanese worker. They treated their work seriously, but they were clearly treated as extreme Others on the farm and in the community of Gensan. They were contract workers and they would leave as soon as their contracts expired.

Heart Work: Interactions

The transient nature and different trajectories of these individuals' lives was made even clearer when I returned to the field in 2008–2009. Between-san had moved to Sapporo to work in a restaurant, returned six months later, and was working at another dairy. Takuto worked in the cow hospital for a few months after I left but then quit. Despite Gensan's small size and wealth of common knowledge, his whereabouts and new work life was unknown by remaining staff members. Nobody had heard a word from Ichiro—he remains a mystery. Haru, however remained in close contact with everyone. In 2009 she was living at home and attending a *senmon gakko* (specialty school) to study persimmon farming while living on her family farm in Nagano. We last spoke in January of 2010. The Tokyo

Cowboy was still, at least as of April 2008—with our last contact being a date that fell through to go drinking in a nightclub area of Tokyo—a truck driver based around Kanto. Tsutomu had remained, by all accounts, unchanged at the farm. "The Chinese" had been deported after Japan Agriculture made mistakes on their visa applications and were replaced by four new Chinese workers.

In sum, one local with a working-class background quit and one worker with an urban privileged background quit—dairy farming was not a chosen occupation for either of them. One worker with a university and family agricultural background quit and returned to school. One worker with a university education in agriculture quit and may or may not be in agricultural employment elsewhere. One local worker with a working-class background quit, moved away to work at another job, and returned to a different Gensan area farm. And one worker with a privileged and university-educated background remained at the farm in the same low-level position. Finally, two foreign workers had been legally forced to leave, for mistakes made by the Japanese officials who hired them in the first place (Hansen 2010a). And, most important of all, the workers who left, Japanese or not, were replaced with a new crop of workers. The farm was a space of rapid change, Otherness, and security seeking at the micro level. As in the previous chapter, there is no simple pattern that emerges from this data, no clear-cut typology of a dairy farm worker type to be found. What is certain is that individuals made choices and acted independently trying to "secure" what they thought was their best personal situation, whether it be a move to a new job, to continue with school, or simply remaining on the farm with no clear plans or goals. To complicate matters, drives and desires are not always expressed or perhaps not even understood. However, no dairy farmer habitus is shared. No specific class of dairy worker is formed. All have differing interpretations of their work and life in Tokachi. Some wished to remain like Ichiro, enjoying the lack of crowds, but mysteriously left nonetheless. Haru had set a clear plan in order to work at the farm for one year, and saw out that commitment. Others like Za Tokyo Cowboy expressed their desire to go as soon as possible, and did. An individual's embodied abilities and capabilities clearly play a key role; while Tarō-san disagreed with Takuto and Haru over work ethics, their responses to him were completely different. While Haru tried as she might, her abilities were such that she could not please him. She was simply a klutz, dropping equipment, tripping while chasing cows, unable to work at high speeds.

Takuto, though quite athletic, had no interest in the job and seemingly even less in pleasing Tarō-san. He was more than capable physically, but he simply did not care and was not interested in the work. For him it was a job like any other. Between-san, dissatisfied with life on the farm, left for the city only to return to dairy farming life less than a year after.

To dismiss the social structural implications and influences upon these relationships such as gender, class, and family connections, for example, is not my point. In the above description Haru is an awkward, young, "outsider" woman. Takuto a cocky, young, tough guy with a "family reputation." Between-san is also a working-class local male with family ties in Gensan, while Za Tokyo Cowboy had no ties to the town and came from a well-heeled background. But these were not determinative distinctions let alone requirements to be involved in dairy farming. People make choices day in and day out and their choices are made in line with idiosyncratic constellations of particular and contingent capabilities, sometimes overtly, as with Takuto's daily "to hell with you, and fire me if you can" attitude, but oftentimes covertly and discretely, as with Haru and her private romantic relations and workplace tears. Social relations and structures surely influence agents, but the point I draw from these ethnographic snippets, and again one frequently overlooked in analyses of social relations, is there is no overarching social role being fulfilled by these individuals.

Chapter Ten

Keeping It All Working

Livelihoods on the Fringe

The work and workers outlined in this chapter are integral for the smooth overall functioning of the farm despite often not being directly related to the production or even distribution of milk. Moreover, while one could walk from the dairy parlor and into the head office in less than a minute and see any of the workers mentioned up to this point—they might have to drive ten minutes to reach some of the silage fields mentioned below, let alone the town of Gensan. Many of the workers in these areas were only sporadically glimpsed by those working in the "head or heart" of the farm. Indeed, workers at one end of the farm may never meet those working at the other end.

Workers in the more distant reaches of the operation were often not employed by the farm directly but worked for the farm through a variety of economic arrangements such as subcontracting or piecework. Many were farmers' wives or older locals who had owned working farms before the shift to industrialized, monocrop agriculture compelled them to stop running a private farm. Still others did not directly work in the dairy industry at all but frequently provided services for dairy farm workers and owners. In this sense, many below are beyond the main scope of this book. Yet, their "cameo appearance" is essential to document because they play essential parts in the working lives of those working on Grand Hopes Farm. Their inclusion completes the overall picture of the operation before drawing together the community distinctions and animal-human-technology relations—the assemblage of work, workers, equipment, and place—in the closing chapters. Like human arms and legs, the areas below progressively radiate out further from the head and heart. And so "flows" both to and through these regions were, in general, less intense or prolonged. For example, working hours were often shorter in these areas, often from eight in the morning until five in the evening. Or, while seasonal work such as silage harvesting required grueling hours, it was only for a few weeks of the year as opposed to the daily pattern of milking experienced in the head and heart of the operation.

Niku ushi (Beef Cattle)

Male, barren, or cows deemed incurably ill (not to say too dangerously ill for human consumption) alongside those too old to keep up with the milking regimen become beef cattle. If a cow looked old or ill the joke would run that the cow would soon be visiting Makku (McDonald's fast-food chain) or made into pet food. And like all jokes, there is some truth behind these comments. All producing dairy cows will either become sick or simply stop producing, usually after around six years, and will meet the inglorious end of becoming middle- or low-grade beef. A cow not part of such a milking regimen can actually live up to twenty years, giving some notion of the intensity of industrial operations and the demands on human and bovine bodies outlined in the following chapters. Unlike the well-known racehorse analogy, that after years of service a horse will get "put out to pasture" to have a life of leisure, for low-producing or high-producing dairy cows it's all the same, their lives end in the abattoir unless they are too ill for humans to consume or they drop dead in the dairy. Indeed, perhaps disappointing to any nonvegan, vegetarian readers, divorcing the beef industry from the industrial dairy industry at present would be impossible. Approximately half of newly born cattle are male. Clearly, they do not produce milk and dairy farmers are dependent upon raising them and then selling them off to become beef and belts. In sum, barring a sudden "natural" death, domestic cows are all eventually rendered into the human consumption chain. In this system of production, idealized and wistful imagination aside, hamburgers, leather coats, and ice cream are all intimately related in terms of industrial production.

There was no facility for slaughter at Grand Hopes Farm. Young, healthy male cattle were shipped out for auction near Obihiro, often after spending spring and summer on a large nationally run and owned cattle range to the north of Gensan in the foothills of Daisetsuzan national park.

There, young Holstein herds grazing in the open are a major tourist attraction, producing a rural idyllic landscape for people to enjoy while eating ice cream, and somewhat disturbingly if thought is given, hamburgers. From auction, young cattle are often shipped to Honshu to be rendered where such facilities, and the market, are larger. Older cattle and the occasional young cow were butchered locally. Nevertheless, young, old, and sick cattle were shipped out of Grand Hopes Farm on a daily basis, sometimes one or two head at a time but more often sold and shipped out by the tractor trailer truckload.

DAINI (SECONDARY AREA WORKERS)

With so many cattle in a confined space, and considering the stress of the daily regimen of milking and impregnation, it is not surprising that the farm has a small, though well-populated and staffed, "hospital" to care for animals that are moderately ill and recovering. The *daini* workers, although not preoccupied with milking as a main task, do need to milk the revolving patient base of around forty head and a fluctuating pregnant herd of around double that number housed in a larger barn across the yard from the hospital. However, the main purpose of the *daini* staff is to clean, feed, and otherwise maintain cattle that have fallen ill, have just given birth, or are just about to. Although, much like the stall staff, the thrust of their job is reasonably self-contained, the hospital *buchō* and two assistant workers do have brief working contact with all other members of the farm. Owners would drop in, veterinarians were of course daily visitors, and the aforementioned workers, less the hunter, might be called upon to help with their chores during slower afternoons.

KO(U)SHI (SHITA) (THE BARN BELOW THE HILL WHERE SMALL COWS ARE KEPT WORKERS)

This area, like that above, is also not attached to the main site. It was the *shachō*'s main barn before incorporating. *Koshi* might seem like awkward phrasing, but it was explained as a combination of "small," "cow," and "below." And this name was used much to the confusion of new staff as the cows were not always small and the location had moved so it was no longer below a hill! *Koshi* was also synonymous with my coworkers as the *obāchan fāmu* (grandma barn). As derogatory and quietly kept as this nomenclature was, it was quite apropos. The workers, with the exception of one young woman, the girlfriend of a stall worker, were all females in their fifties or older. They were the wives and mothers of owners, and in most cases, they were, or were soon to be, grandmothers. In Japan quite often grandparents are left to care for their children's young children when they go to work (Hendry 1989). Here this grandmother role takes on a multispecies twist; while the mothers of the young calves were nursed back to health in the *daini* or are already back to hard work in the milk "factory," the calves were left to the care and guidance of their human "grandmothers." The *koshi* staff clean, feed, and care for the young calves until, at approximately five to six months, they are sent back to the main barns. Here, milk flows from bottles to calves and not the reverse as on the rest of the farm.

"LINKING LIMBS"

Before examining jobs below that are even more removed from the daily operation of milk production, it is essential to note that the *daini* and *koshi* staff like the workers above (the office secretary being the only exception) have daily contact with the cattle, and the duration and shift-ing, embodied and affective quality of this contact is a central issue in the conclusion of this book. However, also of key importance to note is that contact between other human workers in these areas and those working in the head or heart of the farm was seldom a daily occurrence. For example, a couple of times a week, random workers from the main barns would be sent down to the calf barns to assist with loading a trailer, applying skin medicine, or doing more labor-intensive "back and leg" tasks like shoveling out barns to give the "grandmas" a rest. Alternatively, there are times when all the farmworkers pull together. Such a situation occurs during silage season for example. Putting tarps over silage and the subsequent unpleasant job of placing literally hundreds of tires atop the human-made grass and corn mountain requires everybody's participation. As farmers follow the dictates of the sky and not the other way around, overtime was usually required by all workers to finish putting tarps over silage before, or worse during, storms.

Recalling the body metaphor, the "linking of limbs" referred to here underscores the simple fact that in these areas, though human and bovine traffic is surely less hectic than in the work stations covered in the pre-vious sections, animal-human-technology interactions are still essential; for example, cows step on human feet and lick human heads, humans wrestle cows out of stalls or physically bind them, hunters are hired to shoot pigeons and deer, and equipment is used to lift earth to combat the ravages of insects and rodents.

SHITAUKE (SUBCONTRACTORS) AND HOKA (OR BETSU) NO . . . (OTHER WORKERS)

These workers were an eclectic group. There were welders who were contracted to fix gates, build portable metal fences, and so on. There were seasonal workers who farmed crops, thus doing various tasks from spreading manure to putting up silage. Both groups were a perennial feature at the farm and many workers, especially locals, knew them by name as they would occasionally visit the laundry room for a smoke and chat.

While the above workers came at predictable times, workers from other companies would come when called. Farm equipment repair workers came with the near frequency of the subcontractors. At one point, an equipment dealer "lent" Grand Hopes Farm eight of its junior employees for two weeks, couched as a *sābisu* (service) in order for them to get "on-farm" experience. People stalked the vending machines in the laundry room, Tuesdays the "bread man" came to sell his wares, trades people were occasionally required for repairs on the buildings, and one day while walking back from a routine late-morning stall cleaning I was confronted by a troop of middle-aged men toting rifles. Wearing a mix of camouflage and neon, they explained that they were hired to shoot the pigeons that were living in the barns and were paid, not per month, per day, or per hour, but per carcass by the farm. The farm also unofficially gives perks like coffee or the occasional bottle of sake to hunters who shoot a deer, or more rarely a bear. Both deer and bear are problems for farmers in northern Tokachi. Both will rip open hay bales and eat away at corn crops. Deer are more numerous but, for obvious reasons on a livestock operation, bear are more dangerous. (See Hansen 2020b for more on the relationship between local hunters and dairy farms.)

Working Lives

A representative sample of working lives from such diverse groups poses an obvious problem. Again, these jobs are linked by virtue of their "externality" from the head and heart of the farm and highlight a wide range of employees and arrangements: from retired farmer-gentleman hunters to aspiring young farm equipment mechanics. Nevertheless, all are central in keeping the farm functioning smoothly.

THE INVISIBLE LEGACY OF A "NO-GOOD" SON

During an interview with the *shachō* I asked where all of the owners' children were. He first listed off the sons and daughters of the other families. He then mentioned his daughters and noted that none of the owners' daughters chose to work on the farm. He emphatically clarified that he certainly did not want his daughters to work on the farm as, despite his constant and seemingly optimistic expansion, he ironically saw farming as having a dead-end future, at least for women. Daughters could do better to move and marry out of the community as his sister did. Then he paused, waiting for a change of topic. I asked if he had any other children, knowing from a previous conversation with Matsuyama-san that he had a son from a previous marriage. My Japanese friend who came along to see the farm became fidgety, I stared unrelentingly, feigning innocence as best I could, and Mr. Wada haltingly began a short story.

Wada-san confided that he was content working as an independent middle- to large-sized farmer in Tokachi with about 180 head. However, with Japan in a recession and the gradual cutbacks to agricultural subsidies outlined in previous chapters, profits were declining and the future was less certain around the mid-1990s than it had been in his earlier years of dairying. His hope was that his son would be his *kōkeisha* (successor) taking over the farm and he started to search for ways to make the farm more profitable. However, it became clear that his son had other plans.

After high school graduation his son moved to Tokyo and stayed with his uncle, gaining a degree in computer science, but after graduation he decided against that career. He returned to the farm in early 2000 and agreed to be part of the Grand Hopes Farm venture. Unfortunately, he was not a good worker. The consensus seemed to be that he was not a bad fellow—he got on with his coworkers, but he was simply not dedicated to the work. And in his particular case, motivation and interest were important qualities as he was supposed to assist and learn from Matsuyama how to be a *hatsujō hantā*, again, a position requiring relatively light labor but with long hours and important responsibilities. However, after three months he was the first person, and the only one, that his father ever outright fired.

It was clear that these wounds were fresh, and it was equally clear that if I persisted with this line of questioning the interview would come to a halt. I learned that he was living in Sapporo and working as a *furītā* at a restaurant or pub, which his father was not happy about. If he wanted to come back to the farm he would be welcomed—but certainly *not* asked. There was a rumor circulating among the staff that he was going to come back after the summer. However, he never appeared.

THE METAMORPHOSIS OF MASAHIRO

Unlike the "no-good" son, the *kachō's* boy Masahiro was the epitome of the dutiful heir. He worked at the farm nearly every morning and some evenings while finishing his last year of studies at a local agricultural college. He claimed that he enjoyed working at the farm and eventually wanted to take the place of his father. Compared to most workers at the farm this was "outstanding," if not for the earnest and outward show of respect for his father, then for this level of determination and clarity of intention being housed in an energetic and tightly built twenty-one-year-old. Moreover, in Japan it is rare for students to work long hours and attend college. Usually, parents or scholarships pay the way, and while part-time jobs might be held on to for pocket money or for the possibilities of socializing with coworkers, the responsibility and the remuneration attached to this sort of employment are generally low. If one has endured the much commented upon "exam hell" to enter into a college, once there, very little gets done beyond joining various clubs and societies until the crush and panic of final exams, and even more important than any educational pursuit, job hunting. In sum, part-time jobs are for fun, not for education or survival. Of course, this is not true for everyone, but university is a period of life often romantically recounted by some older Japanese as a grace period before the paternalistic responsibilities of marriage and the occasional case of *karōshi* (death from overtime).

Masahiro, despite his laid-back student image of spiky orange hair and flashy T-shirts with illogical English slogans, was very serious about the farm. He wanted to stay on the farm because his father had worked to build it up and his elder brother was uninterested in dairying. He shared his father's pragmatism: in the future, the farm was likely to bring a good profit; for the money that he was going to reap when he took over, short-term sacrifices were worthwhile. However, he did not know why the other workers, such as Ichiro or Haru, stuck around, and unlike his father, he had nothing good to say about Tsutomu; for those who were not members of owners' families he saw it as a dead-end job.

In March of 2005 Masahiro finished his studies and there was a celebratory meal arranged by the owners. It was held in a local *yakiniku* (barbecue) restaurant and was intended to bring in the spring, welcome the new workers, and announce Masahiro's graduation. Despite being informed on the morning of the event, the assumption that nobody had anything to do that night was a sound one as all but one employee came. However, at the party Masahiro was not sitting with his younger farm friends as expected, or with his mother. He sat to the right of his father and the *shachō* at the head of a long table. We each took a turn going around the table making brief introductions, welcoming the new-comers, and thanking our coworkers for assistance. Masahiro earnestly announced, along with requisite bowing, that he would do his best in his new position as stall *buchō*. This sudden promotion was a bit of a shock, with a few hushed "ehh?" uttered among the partygoers, but to me it seemed like a logical progression for the owner's son. In the coming weeks workers witnessed a significant and frequently commented-upon transition as Masahiro made the move from student to manager. The change, unfortunately, was not a smooth one. This is because, though his new position was secure in terms of familial ties, in terms of gaining legitimate authority in the eyes of others Masahiro went through a rough process of the aforementioned *making* and *becoming*. Masahiro did become a new man, but by all accounts, not a better one.

The next workday Masahiro had short and neat black hair and he was smoking, something he had never done in public view at the farm. He sat at the staff room table, not mulling about or joking as usual. Indeed, the room was uncharacteristically quiet. When all the workers arrived, a new trend began. Masahiro called everyone, except me, a shortened name with *kun*, or *chan* as opposed to the more formal *san*; for example, Ichiro-san became Ichiro-kun, odd, but OK. I became a suffix-deficient Pōru, not an issue. But, Kunio-san, a man several years his senior, became Kun'-chan. Several coworkers commented after, in private, that they were appalled at this *shitsurei* (rude) behavior, but it was merely a signpost indicating what lay ahead.

He began poking fun at Haru. Between the daily berating of Tarō-san and Masahiro's new constant haranguing, calling her slow, ugly, poorly dressed, and so on, she began waiting in the corner, or even outside, of the staff room before work. When the Chinese workers came, things, from the perspective of most, became worse. Chinese workers had, at first, nearly no command of Japanese. The *kachō*, unsurprisingly, started the trend of not calling them by their simple-enough single-syllable names, but as *futari* (two people), while his son, although not in front of his father, began to make rude comments, admittedly much to the amusement of some workers. For example, "Chugokū dewa sekken ga aru ka" (I wonder if they have soap in China) to coworkers or, one day to the nineteen-year-old Chinese girl he taunted, "Hentai wakaru, wakaru—wakaranai un ato o oshiete age" (Pervert, understand, understand, no, after I'll teach you). She could do nothing but grin, feel clearly uncomfortable, and say what little Japanese she knew. "Sumimasen. Wakarimasen." (I am sorry. I do not understand.)

Matsuyama-san knew of these situations and suggested that his transformation to empowerment had gone too fast, too far, and not too well. Everyone agreed that calling Kunio-san Kun-chan was disrespectful, and that the workplace was difficult enough for the Chinese workers without being harassed, and that *someone* should do something about it. But, as weeks passed, nothing changed. The needed *someone* never stepped forward. That is, workers nearly unanimously agreed that the situation was bad and felt *kawaiisou* (sorry for) Haruko and the Chinese women, but the response was always *shikata ga nai* (nothing can be done) or *ki ni shinaide* (don't worry about it). Indeed, one could see this "apathy" on a number of accounts. As with other work conditions, if they were unbearable, then why not quit? The group response, even among senior staff, was silence and people generally did comply with Masahiro's demands and suffer his jokes. He had indeed taken on the role of manager, and had secured his position of authority, but at the expense of any respectability.

KUNIO-SAN

Kunio-san has been mentioned several times so far in this book, and though not a young worker he came to play a key role in their lives. He was in his early fifties. He was the oldest hired worker at the farm. He had a family with no sons and a small dairy farm that had stopped production around the time that the incorporated Grand Hopes Farm operation began. He was the most affable of the employees, nearly always speaking with a self-deprecating chuckle attached to his rapid and staccato local dialect. Nonetheless, he was respected, tacitly, by everyone, including the owners. "Kunio san, nani ga ii ka? Kunio san dou shitara ii kana? Anata no iken wa nan desu ka?" etc. (Kunio what do you think is best? Kunio what should we do? What's your opinion Kunio?) were daily questions. If there was a problem, and even despite what a reigning *buchō* might have to say, most eyes strayed to Kunio-san, noting his quiet nodding approval or head tilting "tabun muzukashii," a knowing "it's a bit tricky," disapproval of any plan of action.

He had lived in the area his entire life and confirmed that life in the rural Gensan had changed radically, especially since the 1990s for him. He recalled a time, much like Yūji-san in chapter 5, with no electricity and no automobiles, when all farmwork was done with the power of horses and human hands. Unfortunately, with only a daughter he had no successor to continue his small diary operation. Both he and his brother, who lived on another defunct farm, worked at Grand Hopes Farm.

Blood Brothers

The following workers move progressively further from the body of the farm. They are nevertheless an interesting part of the daily assemblage of individuals who add to its functioning and engage in discussion about the farm, the dairy industry, and Gensan in general. Unlike Masahiro, the "Blood Brothers" were respected by all and they stuck out for several reasons. First, they were brothers and usually found in matching outfits drenched in blood; second, they were, at twenty-three and twenty-nine years of age, very young to be the sole owners of a cow hoof trimming and horn removal business; third, their work ethic was incredible as they would often work from 4:00 a.m. until dark without a break beyond the odd swig of canned coffee; and fourth, they were clearly not of Japanese ethnicity alone. Noting the younger brother's scraggly beard and their combined occupation it seemed a reasonable guess to many that they might be Ainu or *buraku* of some kind (Hankins 2014). I was intrigued by all of the points above and they agreed to meet me in a coffee shop in Obihiro for an interview where I was to be reminded of the adage that "truth is often stranger than fiction."

As it turned out, their mother was from England. She met her husband in the UK in the early 1970s when he, on a work exchange program from Japan, was working in a chicken hatchery. They fell in love and moved to rural Hokkaido where they had brought up their three children; they also had a sister working in Obihiro. Although the mother returned to England on occasion, a small mixed farm in Shimizu, central Tokachi, had always been home for the family.

While the older brother had attended college, school was not an easy time for the younger brother as he was frequently bullied. After he graduated high school the two immediately started their own successful business. At first, they traveled from place to place looking for contracts, but now they only work for larger farms, can thus schedule yearly visits, and in their downtime plan fishing holidays. Grand Hopes Farm paid them very well I was told. The brothers were not paid by the hour—they were paid at a piecework rate by the *shachō* with whom they got on well. They found he was a straightforward man to do business with and he left them to their work, secure in the knowledge that it would be professionally done. For each cow the Blood Brothers were paid 1,500 yen (or 250 yen a hoof or horn) and with the long hours aside and relentless work ethic the brothers were doing very well for themselves.

Dr. Oda and Nurse Kyoko: A Local Eccentric and a Honshu Escapee

Dr. Oda was one of the town's three doctors. He was a Japanese man who was born in China during Japan's occupation, studied in Switzerland, had lived in Asahikawa working in a large hospital, and was semi-retired in Gensan with a private clinic with eclectic hours. He was a member of the "slow food" movement, he vocally protested against auto rally racing in the nearby mountain range and nuclear energy, and had a hobby farm attached to his clinic. His head nurse, Kyoko, a thirty-year-old woman from Kyoto, who it need be added eventually became my wife (Hansen 2018a, 2021b), would recount endless stories of the sensei's "erratic" behavior. For example, he might be in the middle of setting a broken finger when he would notice one of his goats, sheep, cows, pigs, or chickens had gotten free from their various makeshift pens. "Kuso!" (Shit!), he would holler. And turning to the startled patient saying, "Matte, matte ne" (Hold on a minute OK), he would run out the door. After the patient watched the sensei wrestle the goat or chase the chicken back to its place through the window—seemingly unaware how very "unsensei" like his behavior was—Oda sensei would return to the operating room covered with mud or worse and, animatedly recounting his chase scowling or grinning, would continue setting the digit. Truth is, he was well aware of his actions and the local perception of them.

He flaunted his politics by inviting children from Belarus exposed to radiation poisoning, and later Fukushima, to live with him over the summers. He would constantly lament how conservative "typical" Japanese were in dealing with outsiders and how this would have to change. He saw this situation mirrored with the Chinese workers as well. He offered them free medical assistance. One of his "hobbies," and he had many of these, was learning Chinese.

Kyoko said he would see a reserved (likely exhausted) Chinese worker in the waiting room and, ignoring other patients, would sit and chat animatedly in broken Chinese—while Japanese patients tried to look as though they didn't notice this unusual scene. Kyoko spent such moments in the office giggling . . .

> Hen na ojiisan yo, futsū ja nai naa . . . yappari suki da na . . . Kyoto no kangofu no shigoto wa zenzen chigau, jigoku . . . sensei zenbu iya na hito—Gensan wa suki janain demo shigoto wa ii . . . omoshiroi shi, jibun no jikan ga arimasu mo.

> (I like Oda sensei, he's not typical, he's weird . . . In Kyoto working as a nurse is completely different . . . it's like hell . . . and all the doctors are horrible people . . . I don't really care for Gensan, but my job is great . . . it's interesting and I have time for myself.)

Kyoko enjoyed the freedom of Gensan and working for Dr. Oda, who opened his office only five hours a day and paid her the same rate as if she was still working split shifts in Kyoto. She was happy for the time being but was uncertain whether she wanted to stay single in the isolation of Gensan.

Oda sensei and Kyoko claimed that the three main illnesses they saw in the town were directly related to industrial dairy work. Colds from eating poorly and working odd hours, athlete's foot from constantly working in rubber boots, and depression, which was on the rise with patents requesting medication. Both were convinced that what Kyoko coined *nagagutsu raifu* (rubber boot life) was slowly wearing people down and that they knew many of the workers from Grand Hopes Farm by name. They would inform me of their various ailments, somewhat ethically questionable if highly enlightening, but they do corroborate the claims. The upshot was that the hours, the diet, and the physical labor were burning people out and the fiscal strain on some workers and owners was causing a rise in depression and even the occasional suicide.

SUTĀRU: DANCING TO AFRICAN DRUMS UNDER TIBETAN FLAGS AND STARS

"Star" was not a person, but a café. Tibetan prayer flags, wafts of Indian curry, and trance music somehow suited the cabinlike dark wood interior and the two owners, but these elements definitely made the establishment stand apart from the norms of the surrounding area. Their boisterous greeting of "Irasshaimase" (Welcome) was rare in stoic Gensan and appreciated by their regular customers. The proprietors were a couple in their mid-thirties hailing from Nagoya and Osaka, and the café was a regular spot for those from Honshu residing in the area, including the occasional dairy farm worker. They would hold music nights every few months bringing in Japanese African percussionists from Kyushu or folk guitar acts from Hakodate, and these events were followed by a potluck dinner where everyone would first sit around a large table, introduce themselves, and explain why they were in Hokkaido. Hokkaido-born seldom came and never came without an "outsider" partner.

The monthly *tanjōbikai* (birthday meeting) was a similar potluck event with a similar roster of outsiders. It would be held at the houses of those from outside of Hokkaido who volunteered to play host in order to celebrate those who had a birthday that month. Occasionally it was held in the rentable gathering room of the local *onsen*. Similar to the café gatherings, unless one was friends of the host, people from Gensan rarely attended a *tanjōbikai*. Dr. Oda was a frequent guest—an honorary outsider perhaps—and would take command of the kitchen, admonishing others for our unhealthy eating habits while perhaps being the worst offender given his insatiable appetite for wine and cheese.

These occasions all served as conduits for me to hear about what other Japanese people, those not from the area or even involved in farming, thought about Tokachi in general, Grand Hopes Farm in particular, and dairy farm workers who were well known by many like Mr. "In Between"-san or Matsuyama. The group was diverse: nurses, occasional laborers, retired car sales staff, other *bokujō* workers, business people, retired teachers, and public office workers ranging in age from their early twenties to over seventy. One businessman, a former music promoter from Tokyo, uprooted his whole family to move to Gensan in his early thirties. He now ran an internet promotion company and claimed that he could no longer stand office work or life in Tokyo. He was a constant critic of what he saw as "typical Japanese and Japaneseness," an irony outlined below.

Alongside this, professed reasons for coming to Tokachi were remarkably similar. *Hiroi* as noted in the introduction was commonly emphasized. These newcomers enjoyed the spirit of freedom, the love of nature, and the escape from the stress of the city. Sometimes expressed, or sometimes related through gossip, there were other compelling reasons. *Iyashi* (healing) was another constant explanation for being in Hokkaido in general. For example, people needed to get away from their families, commitments, or jobs for a "time-out." In more absolute terms, relationship or career failures (*miyako-ochi*) were also often cited as motivations to enjoy, or for some endure, life in small-town Hokkaido (Hansen 2022)—endure because over time their criticisms of Tokachi and Gensan became as predictable as their stated reasons for coming.

Tokachi locals were often recounted as being boring, rude, simple-minded, conservative, and stubborn. Numerous examples underscoring these perceived traits arose, but perhaps the two most often cited were the lack of respect local people had for the natural environment (for example, littering or the endless and meaningless construction of roads) and their utter reluctance to try anything new (for example, the same foods, drinks, and events at town gatherings). They complained that there was no entertainment in the town and even Obihiro was viewed as an extremely remote backwater. Their reasons for staying in Gensan were always fraught with conscious or unconscious contradictions, and again, a sense of liminal liminality. Leaving was always possible, but not everyone had a plan to leave; indeed, many had no long-term plans at all. While many hated the lack of social life and entertainment in the area, they also enjoyed the distance from the social obligations required of them in other parts of Japan. Though they professed a love for nature, only a handful did not constantly long for cafés or shopping and other joys usually found only on pavement. Assembled together (people, values, environment) they were always betwixt and between, remaining individual and idiosyncratic but forming loose connections highlighted in the following chapters.

Interactions in the Extremities

Jobs found in "the extremities" of the dairy farm outline the extremes of Otherness and the search for security found in the areas surrounding Grand Hopes and Gensan. Long-term changes in the area were often most noted in conversation with older locals like Yūji-san or Kunio-san, people who had seen their community shift over several years. But more immediate change was also clear in the revolving door of Others under the age of thirty who were arriving and departing monthly. Such employees continue to be ever-replenished with fresh blood to keep the dairy pumping and local services in business with new consumers. Thus, Otherness, for local and newcomer alike, is part and parcel of this mode of production as the predominate mode of employment has changed from family farms to family-owned factories. And in this environment, services (medical or commercial for example) try to adjust, try to "secure themselves" in this evolving reality. Given these factors—an increase in different individuals with differing values and ideals, concomitant with internal contradictions in regard to what constituted *ikigai* (the meaning of life) or ontological security rooted in differing views on work and community—life on Grand Hopes Farm was a life of individual negotiations (Mathews 2006). Even among locals these changes were being brokered by people with remarkably similar backgrounds and affiliations. One example, among many, would be the sons of the two main owners of the farm; both the same age, both having been brought up on midsized family farms in Gensan, and both having been invited to play a role in the rapidly changing family operation, they were nevertheless radically different in their "capabilities" (Nussbaum 2006) and desires. One engaged in "crafting himself" from a student into tyrannical manager with honor and money underlying this choice, while the other drifted from student to likeable farmworker to likeable freelance worker with an insecure (financial to be sure) future (Kondo 1990). There have been numerous discussions of such employment and its impact on male security and mobility (Cook 2016; Roberson and Suzuki 2003). Kunio-san had undergone the shift from worker to co-owner—the mirror opposite of the younger former owner Katō-san. The various other positions from farmers' wives, to medical professionals, to biracial hoof trimmers, and alternative café owners underscore the differing interpretations of meaning- and life-making—of work, of belonging, of this location, of what a good life means and, in this frontier place with such a rich history of change, Otherness, and security searching, what being Japanese itself was all about. Grand Hopes Farm and Gensan sit in opposition to the "timeless" or epic image often historically associated with rural life in Japan (Hansen 2018a, 2020b, 2022; Kelly 2006). In the remaining chapters the individuals, their various embodiments and capabilities heretofore considered in the previous chapters, will be analyzed in terms of loose assemblages that they form, broad categories where social cleavages, however transient, can be marked as vibrant and thriving constellations of Otherness and individuated security.

Chapter Eleven

Locals, Lo-siders, Outsiders, and No-siders

Introduction

In the following chapters, the cast of individual characters highlighted to this point are brought together through assemblage theory. The point is not to suggest that individuals do not form lasting social groups, they do of course, but to shed some light on the permeability and contingency of such collectives through the life course of singular agents, human and, in the end, nonhuman. As outlined in chapter 7, one goal of using this sort of theoretical framing is to underscore that these connections *are not descriptions of immutable social orders or groups, long-lasting identities or solidarities,* nor even forming collective "distinctions" or "habitus" to use the ubiquitous language of Bourdieu (1984), but the coming together and pulling apart of permeable heterogeneous agents and things that are all subject to change (DeLanda 2016). They are the confluences of contingency, choice, tempo, and place where *being* is a condition of constant *making* and *becoming* with Otherness—human, nonhuman, material, and ideas or values (cf. Haraway 2016). Put very simply, what follows are captured moments and "partial connections" of idiosyncratic lives coming together and coming apart at particular points, places, and environmental contexts (Strathern 2004). They are interactions in the sociocultural and physical environment of a northern Tokachi dairy farm circa 2000–2020. They are not the interactions of fixed nodes in "networks" but emergent and processual life lines and "meshworks" where change, increasing contact with Otherness, and searches for security, micro to macro, entwine (Ingold 2011; Jackson 2013). If pressed, most of my interlocutors would acknowledge that the various assemblages outlined below existed. However, if pressed further, they would concede that many such social categorizations in the area possessed fuzzy bounds that were constantly morphing in new and often unforeseen directions, a condition whereby the metaphor of an Ingoldian meshwork lends itself to the phenomenological experience of long-term fieldwork more aptly than network (Hansen 2018b).

This framing is not to be elusive or to muddy a clear discussion of social groupings. Quite the opposite, it is to be particular and precise. It is to emphasize that these groupings were malleable, constantly negotiated and interpreted, and contingent upon a variety of factors seen and unseen. For example, I see no problem with calling Gensan a community. As noted in previous chapters some individuals had resided and interacted in this particular location for the entirety of their lives. They knew and grew with one another and shared innumerable ties in terms experience, biology, ecology, and history. But what is interesting is how the conceptualization of community—what it means to an individual or who was included or excluded—was not constant. There was the passing of elderly residents, the departure and occasional return of young locals, an ever-increasing number of diverse newcomers, alongside their idiosyncratic ideas, demands, and their own conceptualizations of the area and their place within it, and of course, newborn children who could be a mix of local and nonlocal.[1] Being a *small* community means that, eagerly or begrudgingly, locals and nonlocals met and meshed. Unlike a larger community, say an urban center where anonymity is possible, people had no choice but to interact even if only through superficial niceties in passing. There is a resonance here with other livestock areas undergoing similar rapid social, economic, and cultural changes and exchanges (Blanchette 2020; Pachirat 2011; Weiss 2016).

There was a tension between the community of "locals" and the wider, often discordant social values held by those considered to be "no-siders" (as seen below, individuals with no local connections and no interest in having any or no possibility of gaining any beyond the pragmatics of daily life). These are two poles with the former more stratified, coded, or territorialized than the latter (Deleuze and Guattari 1987; Hansen 2022). In short locals had the "tightest" assemblage. They were more likely to have shared notions of place, shared codes of language or conduct, and the strictest boundaries on who belongs and who does not. No-siders, on the other hand, were the polar opposite, they simply had very limited interest in the location or even with others within the very "loose" assemblages to which they themselves contingently belonged. But as these final chapters emphasize, the entwining of inside and outside, self and other, went beyond this. Few live in a world determined by such easily reducible binary distinctions (Weller and Wu 2020). Many individuals were liminally liminal, caught between being in the local community and being outside it. They were in a position of ever negotiating—making and becoming—their individual situation (Kato 2009; Klien 2020; Sugimoto 2022; Traphagan 2019). As outlined in the previous chapters, people frequently and freely left and returned, while others from outside Gensan could remain in the area, treated as "new" arrivals seemingly indefinitely. Moreover, wanting to belong or attempting to "buy" one's way in was not enough to be seen as being a part of the local or even farm community.

Taking Matsuyama's case as an example of this complexity is telling. Again, he had to become part of the farm community through *making* a role for himself there and being accepted as a kind of faux family member of Wada-san. And in so doing he was *becoming* accepted as a "good sort" by locals on and off the farm. This enabled him to buy an affordable house, to give a concrete example. Thus, his belonging was not dependent only upon himself, his desires, and actions alone, but a constellation of other relationships. In short, to become a community member one had to not just live "in" the community: one had to live "with" the community, playing a part in, if they wished to fit, an ever-tightening physical, ideological, social, human, and other-than-human assemblage that was always adapting to changes. Matsuyama's house was a home, but it also was also interpreted as a material symbol of belonging to the community. Moreover, his wife worked in a local store and he was father to two *dosanko* sons, but despite all this *he* was still not considered a local. His sons clearly are, however. This chapter describes and theorizes such connections of shifting belonging and community.

The Enigmatic Art of Becoming Local

Industrial dairy farmers can be seen as forming four distinguishable yet permeable groupings in the community of Gensan. They can be viewed as locals, lo-siders, outsiders, and no-siders. One could say, again borrowing the language of assemblage theory, that locals are the most stratified and territorialized of these groupings. That is to say, they were the most secure and secured, theirs the hardest associations to enter or to leave and the least open to Otherness and change. But as noted in what follows all of these distinctions are transient, based not only on social factors, but a given person's desire to be part of the community alongside an individual's particular embodiment: physical strength, temperament, intellect, physical coordination, among other qualities. Individual capa-bilities often enabled or disabled becoming, making, and so belonging (Nussbaum 2006, 273–315). But belonging is also influenced by both the material and ideological environment, how an individual fit, or could be made to fit, within an assemblage. Moreover, an individual could be seen as being between these groups, perhaps moving toward acceptance in one while remaining part of another. People were always susceptible to changing and influencing changes.

Locals, as they largely defined themselves, were people born in the Gensan area. The members of the four families who originally owned Grand Hopes Dairy Farm were all at least second-generation locals. Kunio-san and his brother were also clearly locals. They were born in the area, they owned land, and when I met them they had been dairy farmers in the recent past. But many who had never owned farms had family members, usually young adult males, who worked or had worked on local farms; for example, Between-san and Takuto were both born and raised in the Gensan area and are absolutely considered locals. But importantly, there were locals working in industries not related to farming and still other locals who owned shops, worked for shops, or commuted to work to one of the larger centers such as Otofuke or Obihiro. Yūji-san, my friend and tatami maker, was considered a local for example. There were also, in essence and as awkward as it sounds, locals no longer living locally: people who lived elsewhere but would return for sporadic visits. They were still considered part of the community even if their spouses or children were not.

Thus, what was important in being considered local was not static or "locational" at a given moment. It was the fact that one was raised there and known by other locals. Belonging was a condition of shared history, of both being *and* becoming with other people and knowing the place, being a "part of the location" so to speak. The agricultural areas outlying Gensan were further stratified—families intimately knew other families and had for generations. Grandfathers had worked alongside other grand-fathers, their sons had grown up alongside their friends' sons, and some home-grown high school attractions had become marriages, divorces, and remarriages. When people coming from outside this area meet locals, they are quick to realize that locals are already along their journey of being lifelong friends and foes with other locals. They have gone to the same small and isolated schools together from elementary school.[2] Beyond schooling, teenagers and young adults are frequently involved in various clubs in town such as *minibori* (beach volleyball less the beach). These histories formed a base of common knowledge and connection that was difficult to penetrate even for relatively young outsiders. Again, in terms of long-standing residents, from the late 1950s until the mid-2000s it was more common to see local sons and daughters go to the big cities than to see new people arrive.

Beyond birth, becoming a local was an active process accomplished through acts of making, that is, of ever-continuing to *be* and *become*, a local. There were a large number of unofficial local groups ranging from the ballooning teams mentioned in previous chapters to the retiree cross-country ski club to a club learning the Chinese language. For residents with children being an active PTA (Parent Teacher Association) member at a local school is a parental expectation. As in Honshu, Gensan had *chōnaikai* (neighborhood associations) and being a member was another expectation, albeit there were those who were eager participants and others like Wada-san who saw it as a chore to be delegated to others if possible. These associations come together both in times of need and for celebrations. For example, when Between-san's grandfather passed away the *chōnaikai* organized the reception, and when Grand Hopes Farm erected a *chikukonhi* plaque (a Buddhist monument dedicated to the souls of livestock) and a *batō kannon* statue (a horse-headed incarnation of a savior Bodhisattva) members of the association, and of course clergy from the temple performing the dedication service, were invited to a lunch in the conference room at the farm. Workers at the farm were not invited to attend either the event or the lunch despite their daily role in the operation or contact with the cows. This ritual interaction was a decidedly local affair like most of the above means of meeting, making, and sustaining relationships in the area.

This not to say local life was without discord. Beyond the relatively inclusive participation in associations and clubs, there are clear local-only divisions as well, stratifications within an already highly stratified assemblage. While the residents of the outlying areas consider themselves to be part of the broader Gensan community, those living within the limits of the town of Gensan usually separate themselves as *machi no hito* (townspeople) from *yama no hito* (mountain people) to the north. This is a distinction particularly interesting when talking with outsiders, or even most "lo-siders" (described below, but in essence long-term residents not considered local) who do not make this distinction. They refer to all of Gensan and the surrounding area (and for some all of Hokkaido) as *inaka* (countryside) and residents as *inakamono* (country folk but also having a pejorative meaning akin to "hick" or backward). In a very tangible way, one could view the residue of a Meiji-era "Honshu-centric" perception of *bunmei* (civilization or progress) in the way these people expressed their belonging within Gensan (Morris-Suzuki 1998, 24–25). For example, the outlying areas did not have harvest festivals despite being farmers, while the town did. In this sense, the town was seen as superior by many of its residents. If asked why there were no festivals on the outskirts, people from town would claim that the outer reaches of Gensan were too poor or too sparsely populated to hold their own festivals. However, when the agriculturalists on the margins were asked the same question, they responded that they were uninterested or too busy to organize such gatherings. As far as many were concerned, agricultural festivals were not for agriculturalists but townspeople! That is, these rituals were for townsfolk trying to belong, to fit, into this largely agricultural place. To add to this complexity, outsiders from Honshu would often scoff at what a poor excuse for festivals Gensan locals had. Townspeople focused on the act of meeting and less the aesthetics of presentation. So, for any given gathering the same costumes, beer tents, and omnipresent fried chicken were on offer. Moreover, instead of calling the chicken *karaage* in "proper" Japanese, locals spoke in the Hokkaido dialect, proudly rendering the food *zangi*. Yet, this term, among others, was often emphasized by some outsiders in a dismissive way to affect their small-town disdain: *minna ZANGI wo tabeteiru—tanoshii ne* meaning something akin to (everyone is eating "HILLBILLY" chicken, what fun) sarcastically stated.

Outsiders can be defined as those people who are not from Gensan and who clearly do not plan to remain. For example, Haru was decidedly an outsider. From the start, her plan was to stay at the farm to gain experience for a year and to return to her family farm in Nagano. She clearly enjoyed being in Gensan and interacting with locals, but her stay in town and at the farm was viewed as a time-out by both parties. The Tokyo Cowboy prided himself on being an outsider and escape could not come quickly enough for him. By necessity being an outsider can only be defined in a way more fluid, less stratified, than being a local as some outsiders gradually become lo-siders over time.

Lo-siders (local outsiders) were outsiders who chose to make Gen-san a permanent home, or at least home for the currently foreseeable future. Matsuyama and his wife are good examples, though their two sons obviously complicate a simple definition. Both boys were born in the area and, having a wide pantheon of local friends, they were clearly seen as locals, certainly by those involved with the Great Hopes operation who even saw them as akin to the *shachō*'s family. But again, desiring to be a lo-sider is not enough to become labeled one. Some were unable to secure this identity, such as Tarō-san. Intersectional contradictions were common among members of this collection of people. Matsuyama, like nurse Kyoko, viewed local life as stable "for now." In general, *lo*-siders had *low* interest in local politics and as a sort of feedback loop were allowed a *low* level of participation in these largely local social activities. Again, Matsuyama and Takako had reservations about their sons attending the local high school in the future. They did not participate in the neighborhood association beyond its minimal expectation of contributing funds and occasionally collecting signatures, although Matsuyama sometimes attended meetings and joined in the celebrations they organized such as *bōnenkai* and *shinnenkai* parties (year end and new year gatherings). In addition, they did not belong to any local clubs. It was commonly known that Matsuyama-san worked odd and long hours at Grand Hopes Farm and this likely allowed him a bit of participatory leeway. However, Matsuyama's wife Takako was more involved. She and the aforementioned businessman who chose to move with his family from Tokyo were very active members in the PTA. On the other hand, the owners of the Sutaru café were lo-siders who shunned local politics. Nevertheless, they were very "worldly," accepting, and unlike many lo-siders could count several locals as friends, or at least acquaintances. In part this was surely related to being in the service industry. Yet, most outsiders, and many lo-siders had few, if any, local friends; their friends consisted of the "revolving door" outsiders and fellow lo-siders, such as those attending the aforementioned monthly collective birthday party, or links maintained with relatives and friends living in Honshu who would occasionally visit (see also Klien 2020 and Traphagan 2019). None of these long-term lo-siders had concrete plans to leave the area. But while outsiders could disappear at any time, there still lingered an air of impermanence regardless how long any lo-sider had been in the area.

But by far the most transitory assemblage, those with the lowest stratification and territorialization, are the final collection of individuals I call no-siders. They clearly view their farmwork as a job alone, for example, foreign workers (Hansen 2010a)—a group that is growing nationwide and one that quadrupled at Grand Hopes from 2006 to 2016. These are essentially exploited economic migrants on fixed contracts and visas who have no stake in Japanese society and thus seldom care about local or family politics of the household business they work for as long as they are paid. It is possible that in the future such workers might move on to become lo-siders or even locals, but at the time of writing (2019–2022) there are no examples of this kind of inclusion in Gensan. They are carefully kept on the periphery economically, politically, culturally, and socially.

Tied to the notion of contingency is a point of connection shared by *young* locals, lo-siders, outsiders, and no-siders, individuals roughly from their twenties to mid-thirties. Regardless of their residential status, many young people self-identified as *furītā*. Both Takuto and the Tokyo Cowboy claimed this first and foremost as a self-distinction. Nearly all workers conform to two of the three *furītā* "types" as outlined by the sociologist Kosugi Reiko: "the moratorium type" (choosing to put off getting a full-time job), "the under duress type" (those between jobs or in the midst of a life crisis), and "the dream seeker type" (those who are employed to make ends meet while pursuing some other, often artistic, interest) (Kosugi 2008, 11–14).

There were no "dream seeker types" on the farm and I met none in the Gensan area. Some preferred a relatively solitary life, such as shy Ichiro and the loner Tsutomu. Others enjoyed the nearby mountain sports as recreation, but these were thought of as hobbies, not potential careers. A few outsiders, and indeed some lo-siders, did loosely fall into the moratorium type. They had university degrees and could not find related suitable employment. Often, they were working at the farm while weighing other options. However, the majority of workers, both lo-sider and outsider, were between this type and the "under duress" type. Unable to find other work or wanting a challenge, these workers would often have a set time, for example, one year, to work and think about their next step in life before returning home. However, many would surpass a year and continue, as discussed above, in a kind of liminal liminality. A few would make the concrete choice to stay for a longer term, often taking an offered position as Yukiko did in becoming a department head. But as noted in the previous chapters, planning to stay and staying are two different things. Life takes its own contingent twists and turns.

Thus, the shift from outsider to lo-sider is not a permanent one or a move easy to predict or map. It is a movement rooted in chance and

contingency, or simply, luck (Rapport 2012). Yukiko's unplanned pregnancy ended her job and the couple moved back to Honshu. Though
Tarō-san wished to remain in Gensan, due to his temper outbursts he was
essentially driven out of the job when it became obvious that he would
never get a promotion and, as it sadly turned out, mental health issues
took a greater hold on his life. There were also those who embodied a
"pioneering spirit." One young man from Tokyo, unmentioned thus far,
arrived on a Harley-Davidson motorcycle in 2005. He worked temporarily
on a variety of dairy farms and spent the rest of his time building a log
house with the timber coming off the marginal land he had purchased
and cleared himself. But by 2018, though he was still doing this freelance
farmwork, he had been gradually "domesticated" or progressively stratified, territorialized, and coded. Like Matsuyama he became a lo-sider with
local children. He settled into a larger modular home with his expanding
family: a wife, three daughters, and two dogs. He has no plans to leave,
but he never planned to stay. Though cliché, "life happens," and nowhere
is this contingent nature of assemblage more apparent than in the shifting
categories of outsider and lo-sider.

Life after the *Ie*: Assembling Otherness and Security

As noted, there is a long-standing trend of framing Japanese people, and
especially rural Japanese, in terms of an "epic" notion of Japaneseness
perhaps exemplified in *nihonjinron* studies, but also present in the use
of numerous binaries to describe Japanese social structures. Taking one
example to task here, the above-noted fluid urbanite immigration and
local outmigration and the constant circulation of people in and out of
the Gensan area sheds light on changes in the classic conception of the *ie*
(corporate household structure) at least on industrializing Tokachi dairy
farms.[3] By and large, the *ie* was not viewed as important by the lion's share
of dairy farmers, especially those under the age of forty, and while owners viewed it as important enough to make a list of job roles with family
members in symbolic roles of authority, most were unconcerned with its
replication in reality as long as the fiscal security of the farm and its daily
operations were not threatened. When I asked farmers direct questions
about the influence of the *ie* on daily affairs, the reply was usually *imi ga
nai* or *kankei nai* (there is no meaning, no connection). Given the neoliberal present and the particular history of place this is understandable.

Francis Hsu, describing essential characteristics of *iemoto*, notes the importance of a master–disciple relationship, an interlinking hierarchy, the wide acceptance of the supreme authority of the master, and resemblance of a real or fictional family structure (Hsu 1975, 62–68). No dairy farm worker would accept this as an explanation of their working relationship, Tarō-san's somewhat disturbing dedication being an outlier perhaps. Moreover, though the owners may have felt secure in their power over their workers, they did not depend on their reliability or respect in the way a master would demand. The *ie* structure is further weakened in contemporary Gensan through the necessity of employing a great number of outsiders and no-siders as part and parcel of the change from mixed family farms to the industrial and mega-farm mode of production. Other than locals are frequently unable, uninterested, or unwilling to partake in more traditional forms of local community or regional identity building and this also includes adherence to the authority of an *ie* structure. They thought of themselves as freelance employees and would switch farms or move on as opportunities emerged. Likewise, farms were individual family-owned homesteads in the early process of *becoming* independent family businesses. The relationships fostered under such circumstances, as noted in chapters 2 and 7, are not synonymous with centralized villages and cooperative rice production.

Beyond the mode of production, there are many additional reasons for a decline in the influence of the *ie* structure somewhat specific to Tokachi. The Japanese *ie*, ideal or real being a separate issue, was made illegal in the postwar Occupation period under the new civil code. Again, this was a time when many pioneer families were settling in Tokachi. New area, and so new structures, at least not the replication of illegal and archaic notions of hegemonic power, seems a reasonable course for new settler families to take, especially given the best part of these people were "escaping," attempting a break from their past (Irish 2009; Mock 1999). Aside from Hokkaido's particularly independent history of escape and exile, in many areas of Japan the structure has also diminished in importance—though its imagery and imaginary have remained strong. Anthropologist Theodore Bestor, in his study of a family-owned business in Tokyo's Tsukiji fish market, has remarked that while thinking of the business in terms of *ie* remains important for the owners and senior staff, younger workers are not usually concerned with its continuation (Bestor 2004). Sunhee Lee outlines that in rural Tohoku, there is a shift in the conceptualization of the *ie* structure in that it has moved away from a model based on an extended vertical family to a nuclear model and anthropologist John Traphagan highlights how traditional gender roles are in tension with women taking leading roles in family businesses (Lee 2007; Traphagan 2017, 77–94, and 2019). In sum, Tokachi is not alone in having independent farm women. In rural Tohoku there has been a steady movement of women from the traditional role of homemaker to wage earner. Due to this shift the decrease in familial ties and an increase in childcare facilities have led to a weakening of lateral support systems such as the *ie*. In short, as workers move out of the extended family home they tend to work away from home and utilize facilities for childcare or the elderly (Lee 2007; Rosenberger 2001). Through such economic and temporal distancing, familial links, for example, between grandparent and grandchild, are rapidly being weakened. Moreover, there are urban similarities to this nuclear shift throughout the 1970s, 1980s, and 1990s. So given neoliberalism, illegality, neolocal kinship, and a popular and general desire to move from the past to the present, the *ie* in its classic formulation as a vertical structure seems to be in decline in overall, but as noted above, specifically in Gensan and its mega farms given the more fluid assemblages of local and outsider cum lo-sider that are emerging.

More to the point, while local social standing was in some part inherited, being born "made" as it were, belonging came down to a process of self-making. That is to say, for outsiders and lo-siders local identity building was a very individualized and individualistic process, seen in the contrast between Tarō-san and Matsuyama for example. Personalities and skills played a central role in career aspirations and local acceptance. And as the cases of outsider Tsutomu or local Takuto bring to light, progression up the "company ladder" was far from inevitable regardless of time spent in its service or one's place of birth. Moreover, the desire to continue the *ie* line was not always adhered to even in economic terms by kin members. For example, while the *kachō*'s son worked long hours and keenly entered the family business as a young department head, the *shachō*'s son had no interest in the farm and moved away to the city. And in contrast, Kato-san, whose father had passed away and left him his share in the farm—indeed a double stake in the classic vertical *ie* (familial and financial)—quit. Moreover, though remaining in the family business, the reasoning of the *kachō*'s son was not merely of fulfilling obligation, duty, or following of a familial role. Though he respected his father, he clearly noted that his motives were individual and economic. As he said, there was good money to be made if he stuck around. Tarō-san and Matsuyama, on the other hand, both desired to move up within the company and competed for the familial favor of the *shachō* through long hours and dedication. Leaving blood or arranged marriage completely out of the picture, it was abundantly clear, to everyone except Tarō-san perhaps, that Wada-san favored Matsuyama, not only because he was clever, congenial, and did not have conflicts with workers, but also because—and I suggest importantly—he was perceived as a good sort by locals by making himself part of the community, including having children, or put another way, *making* two locals. And, the family had settled in the area on their own property near the farm, further tightening, in this sense quite literally, territorialization, further stratifying his position in the location. In short, the *ie* concept is not dead as an ideal, but it clearly has adapted if not weakened in practice. It has significantly changed to incorporate a diversity of Otherness and to secure the community status of those seen as making a life for themselves in the community through becoming individuals who belong.

Thus, *ie* belonging is (or perhaps has always been) far more "personalized" and process oriented rather than being the fulfillment of roles or social givens. The point here is that any continuing assemblage adapts to fit place and highly specific and individual situations, further stratifying and territorializing, or coming apart and ending relations. For example, while they were not "adopted" into the *ie* in any official sense (they were not registered in Hokkaido as a family or *koseki* for example) Matsuyama, his wife, and sons are treated as family members by the *shachō* and his wife. Their personal ties grow ever closer and Matsuyama's dedication (though not obsession) to work and the will of Wada-san as a "master" was strong. In return, Matsuyama was well paid and Wada-san had intervened in the local community to secure a house for this "fictive" son, even hinting that he might be a potential successor by saying things such as "when I retire Matsuyama will still be around." Tarō-san was simply out of the picture—*dis*assembled as it were.

Moreover, even direct family members (such as the farm's daughters and many absent sons) do not view their work primarily in terms of familial obligation or as a central source of identity, community, or pride. If solidarity among owners was weak, then among workers it was virtually nonexistent. Moreover, the owners made no real effort to promote or enforce general feelings of the workplace as family, positive or negative. What remained was a loosely adhered to idea of a familial power structure on the farm, an *ie*-like ideal type structure with the owners at the top, *buchō* beneath, and a fluid roster of underlings at the base. As noted, a hierarchy chart of sorts, identifying who was in charge of what and whom, was circulated by the owners. But beyond deference to the owners, the chart was ignored. The capable took charge and the least capable, despite rank, were ignored or somehow placated into thinking they held sway until their backs were turned and someone took over.

One could frame changes perpetuated through these novel assemblages of becoming and making as follows: the familial aspects of the *ie*, less its vertical and authoritative elements, plus the inclusion of heterogeneous otherness, are still seen as important and maintain a powerful influence on how these industrial family farms function. All of the farm owners that I encountered, small, medium, large, or mega, were local people. They were not professional managers hired by an outside party. They considered their farm, even if it was shared with other owners, to be a local family business. There were both locals and lo-siders who worked in *buchō* positions within these farms, but the proportion of farm family members in positions of authority was clearly higher and not related to experience or age. In short, the child of an owner may well be younger, have less work experience, less natural ability, and less education than those who work under them. Outsiders were not in positions of authority although, in specific work situations, they might covertly or overtly be placed in a role of "team leader." No-siders were perennially expendable.

Farm owners, like business owners elsewhere in Japan, were usually elder males and similar in status to lower- or middle-level salarymen depending on the size and profitability of their holdings. Lo-siders were most often like *kaishain* (salaried workers) with slightly higher wages than other workers, who received bonuses, company perks such as housing, and possessed a reasonably high level of job security (and so other forms of security). Outsiders, as noted above, were often precarious *furītā*. Although they held temporary *kaishain* status, they generally did not remain with the company long enough for their wages to increase, nor were they offered *buchō* positions unless they were first deemed good workers and second expressed a willingness to stay in the area, on the farm, and out of trouble with others. If these requirements were fulfilled, then positions emerged or were "made" for them. Through the choice to take a *buchō* position, one essentially became a lo-sider, a member of the work community if not the broader Gensan community. No-siders were, sadly and simply, migrant workers exploited by both the state and the farms. While there were exceptions, such as workers who quit for personal reasons (such as Yukiko) or who were let go (such as Tarō-san) or workers who endlessly lingered despite remaining outsiders and were unlikely to be offered superior positions (such as Tsutomu), for the most part, owners and workers fit the above pattern of local, lo-sider, outsider, and no-sider.

Finally, on a slightly broader scale, familial intercompany "parent and child relations" were common. One of the largest nearby farms was in fact the *kogaisha* (child company) of a large construction firm, and in fact the parent–child relationship was also literal in this case, as the father ran the construction company and the son ran the farm. Beyond this revamped *ie*, relationships of reciprocity existed with a range of Gen-san subcontractors. Welders, hoof trimmers, and silage harvest helpers all offered the owners of the farm *o-seibo* (year-end gifts) and in return Grand Hopes Farm offered the milk company and equipment dealers similar gifts (Hendry 1993). This exchange symbolized the hopes of the smaller companies that the previous year's cycle of patronage would continue. The gifts were always rather uncreative and functional—office grade coffee, boxes of work gloves, laundry detergent—but so was their intent. When asked why they exchanged such mundane gifts, responses clearly underscored the meaning, "Rainen minna to isshō ni hatarakitai node" (Because everyone wants to work together next year). And all knew that the next year would exclude a large number of outsiders and no-siders.

Thus, the exchange of *o-seibo*, much like religion explained in the following chapter, was a local affair. Lo-siders might be included, but no-siders and outsiders were not a part of the exchange or ritual cycle. Such individuals found their identity in their own ways—through being financially, politically, and/or socially independent or often forging links with people of their own choosing outside of work or inside the broader rural community of like-minded Hokkaido-dwelling others. Otherness and self-security searching were central features for them within the ever-shifting community of Gensan. For the "chosen" lo-siders and locals however, though their gifts may have lacked "individuality," the purpose did not. The exchange represented individual aspirations for security in the face of uncertainty and contingency both in the industry and community. The gift exchange cemented their part in fluid assemblages laying bare their hopes of continued financial cooperation, continued each otherness, and the continued securing of a place in the community of Hokkaido dairy farmers, a bastion of macro-level alterity.

Conclusion

Early in fieldwork I asked Kunio-san if he was disappointed in not having a successor for his own family farm. He tilted his head, "Watashi no bokujō wa chisai kara. Unn, sore wa muzukashii to omou naa" (My farm is very small so [a successor] well, hum, it's difficult I reckon). A local, he planned to continue life as a worker at Grand Hopes Farm. He was resigned to his farm being sold off or leased out after his retirement or passing. However, by the middle of my second stint of fieldwork this had unexpectedly changed. Kunio-san reacted to Kato-san's absence in the way he thought best. He offered to join his lands to the farm and had become a new co-owner, throwing his lot in with the "bigger is better" camp. I met him driving to the farm one morning and I congratulated him on his being a new owner. Kunio-san replied that he was pleased with this lucky twist of fate. Through this choice his interest in the mega farm changed. It became an economic and familial one with his security, his livelihood, and income linked with other owners of the farm and its future. Moreover, he became further entrenched in the assemblages of relations in the loose *ie* structure of the farm. Will he now try to find a successor, an outsider or lo-sider to take under his wing and continue reciprocal relations in the community?

In the context of contemporary Tokachi dairying, the *ie* might best be thought of as a flexible assemblage of relationships based not on blood or hierarchical power as much as place and individual capabilities concomitant with one's ability and desire to make oneself belong at a given time. It consisted of people choosing to stay in the area, apply themselves to work, be able to get along with others, and in so doing relate to a certain set of values in terms of place and politics. Importantly, as Kunio's case so well represents, contingency also plays a key role in all this—call it luck, fate, or chance. The notion of being from company A or B or being part of one *ie* or another is of less importance for contemporary dairy workers than Nakane depicts in her classic model of Japanese rural structure (1967). Though Nakane and Hsu (1975) do note that there are regional variations, the largest being between East and West Japan, there is unsurprisingly no mention of Hokkaido.

While there is tension in Gensan between small family dairy farms and the new burgeoning mega farms, most farms in the area had congenial, even cooperative, relationships. Relationships went beyond farms to

216 | Hokkaido Dairy Farm

a meshwork of related businesses. Owners and locals are very conscious of where farms fit in the continuum of large to small operations, but nonetheless they would occasionally lend equipment and visit one another without any obvious animosity. They are not perceived as competing corporate households, just *Other* households. For example, the search for the no-sider Chinese workers was carried out by a group of large independent farms cooperating with each other. Mutual farm communication was obvious in other ways. For example, information about me spread quickly. Large farms in the area were often prepared for my "impromptu" visits and occasionally, and disconcertingly at times, the *shachō* would ask me how my visit to X or Y farm went despite my not mentioning visiting. Of course, no-siders, outsiders, and even the majority of lo-siders were not concerned about distinctions between farms. They had a job and their working conditions and wages were of more interest than any sort of local ranking system.

Bokujō hours of employment and fluctuating days off hampered any attempts at a predictable social life for workers and owners alike. But this atmosphere was less stratified, more relaxed, and perhaps more "worldly" among the outsiders and lo-siders than with the locals. Again Between-san, despite his attractiveness and competence, never dreamed of moving to Sapporo early in fieldwork. He merely wanted a good local job and a girlfriend. However, many outsiders and lo-siders had traveled in Japan, and some had traveled more extensively, before they found their way into Hokkaido employment. Others were in Hokkaido buying time for their next career or education move outside of Gensan. Some outsiders had postsecondary education, not infrequently from rather prestigious universities. It was common and unsurprising if someone decided to return home, leaving the world of farming behind, and gossip frequently circulated about who was leaving or on the cusp.

Nevertheless, though outsiders and lo-siders might view local people as the epitome of conservative "typical" Japanese, they felt free from these derided "average" ways within their loose assemblages (Hansen 2018a). As noted, lo-siders and outsiders often expressed their desire to escape *futsū no nihonjin no kangaekata* (typical Japanese thinking) as a motivation for being in Hokkaido. This expression, or similar variants of it, constantly surfaced as derogatory comments. For example, talk about failures in the world of Tokachi business would be met with "Kono hen no hito wa futsū no nihon no kangaekata dakara" (Because [locals] think like typical Japanese), a somewhat ironic claim given the fact that most people saying this would be from Honshu, and Tokachi, as I have argued, is far from any Honshu-centric notion of average. Tarō-san was seen among female friends as a "futsū no nihon no ojisan" (typical Japanese middle-aged man), a statement usually accompanied by a scowl, emphatic headshake, and topped with "iya na hito" (disagreeable fellow). In these ever-morphing assemblages of local, lo-sider, and outsider, people lived with such contradictions. Here, the "open landscape" of Tokachi with the loose social relationships it availed was a central aspect of making and becoming. To a large degree, at least to a degree larger than they felt was possible in their former lives outside Tokachi, they were making their own meanings and their own lives—feeling free from the constraints of essentialist Japaneseness. *Senpai–kōhai* (junior–senior), *soto–uchi* (outside group and inside group) relations were extremely fluid among outsiders and lo-siders (Hansen 2021a). As a result, the expectation to *become* "typically," or to follow a set path with requisite social expectations, was low in Gensan. Many existed in a state of extended liminality with the expectation that they would—eventually—return to Honshu, to family, to a career, to social relations viewed as typical. However, a mirroring ironic perspective emerges here. Locals did not feel themselves to be "typical" Japanese at all. As noted in the introduction, locals considered Honshu to be a distant place, historically and culturally.

Chapter Twelve

Assembling Communities

Two Genders and One Religion

Introduction

Thus far, this book has focused on differences. I have been attentive to
Otherness in an ever-narrowing scope from Hokkaido, to Tokachi, to the
northern Tokachi town of Gensan, and finally on to Grand Hopes Farm
as locations of alterity. I have outlined the particularity of these places and
of dairy farming itself, and notably industrialized dairy work, as a distinct
way of life linked to local ecologies and social-political economies rooted
in individuation and, in large part, individualism. I highlighted how this
stands in opposition to epic agrarian ideas and Japanese identity, such as
mixed family farms or seasonal crop farming, such as rice cultivation,
as found in much of Japan. The main argument forwarded is that Tokachi and livelihoods like dairy farming support particular security projects (national, community, and personal) and that social and economic
changes fostered by the present condition of neoliberal industrialization
have led to numerous and rapid sociocultural changes, such as the inclusion of lo-siders, outsiders, and to a growing degree no-siders along with
the outmigration of young locals.

However, before concluding this book it is essential to reinforce
a key point that is perhaps easy to overlook in highlighting opposi-
tions. These places and people remain very much part of contemporary
Japan. The previous chapter noted there is a wide divide between local
and no-sider with looser assemblages of Others who can be labeled as

outsiders and lo-siders found in Gensan. This is a common situation in Japanese society even if it is perhaps somewhat more flexible in Hokkaido given the history of the region and the circumstances of agricultural industrialization. For example, similar societal divisions can be seen in Tokyo neighborhoods (Bestor 1989) and suburbs (Guarné 2018; Robertson 1994) whereby "locals" engage with rapid change and the halting, but often inevitable, acceptance of new social actors, their ideas, and their material culture. Japan is diverse and ever-changing. This chapter continues along these lines of "similar . . . but not quite the same" by focusing on two more examples that tend to assemble people into loose groups: a general compliance with gender roles seen as normative and religious praxis that reifies local making and becoming.

Gendered expectations and divisions of labor found in rural Tokachi are unsurprising if compared with Honshu. However, the ways in which young women resist traditional categorizations and young men view their masculinity as challenged—not by their inability to become "salarymen" (recent research highlights uncertainty as to how consistently interpreted this category is itself) (Cook 2016; Dasgupta 2013), but by changing social structures and the individual self-making and becoming it demands—differs from prior generations. These young men and women are not nostalgic, wishing they could more easily transition to the role of housewife or salaryman circa 1970, but as noted in previous chapters many are anxious about their liminally liminal future, with some bucking tradition to ambitiously make their own way while others drift from day to day uncertain of what to do beyond what they currently do.

As outlined in chapter 3, religion in Japan has long held a place for bovine and human relations and in Tokachi dairy farmers have religious practices particular to the area. What is more, local interpretations of common Japanese religious practices are, and can only be by definition given the place and its pioneering past, a product of modernity. That is, in Tokachi at least, novel religious practices can only harken back to the late Meiji period for any claim to "local" authenticity. As such, local religious praxis helps to track contemporary Otherness and security concerns. Religious practices or rituals, even leaving the complexity of idiosyncratic personal beliefs aside, underscore the particularity of both people and of place. They highlight adaption to new conditions, Otherness, in their relation to both their human and nonhuman elements, and like all religious practices they grapple with ontological security and what constitutes individual and collective "insecurities" and, indeed, belonging.

The gender norms and religious forms found on Tokachi dairy farms are not alien in the context of Japan. That is not the point. The argument is that while clearly remaining *of* Japan they stand out, they are identities and ideologies that both secure people and make them feel secure as "Others" within a long-marginalized place and industry that continues to change influenced by Japanese trends and through its own particular influences, physical and ideological. Tokachi, Hokkaido, its dairy industry, and Grand Hopes Farm are home to novel ways of being and becoming.

Farm Women

For women from outside of Gensan, failed romantic relationships were often cited as a reason to escape to Hokkaido for a new start and such uprooting and solo voyages are not decisions taken lightly in Japan (Hansen 2018a; 2022). If one takes this base observation alone, the stereotype of the demure and submissive female, an image commonly associated with urban and urbane Japanese femininity, is a difficult one to maintain on the margins of rural employment in Hokkaido as elsewhere (Allison 1994; Carbert 1995; Martinez 2004). Moreover, as opposed to "typical" working women in Japan—such as those anthropologist Dorinne Kondo both encountered and found herself to be "crafting" into—the women on Grand Hopes Farm and other local farms, young and old and in differing ways, were often highly independent, competent, and confident people (Kondo 1990). And in being on the periphery of Japan's increasing conditions of precarity perhaps they need to be (Allison 2013).

Unlike the image of the young female *furītā* in relatively low-paying, low-ceiling, temporary positions, the often slightly older but equally underpaid Japanese "OL" (office lady) buying time until marriage, or even the middle-class, young homemaker engaged in part-time work (Kimoto 2003; Kosugi 2008; Rosenberger 2001), women who *chose* to work at the farm—and aside from locals, for these women it was *always* by choice— were doing the same jobs as their male coworkers for the same recompense. It is undeniable that there was a clear gendered bias for some tasks. For example, males were favored for jobs requiring greater physical strength such as penning calves and females were often given more "bookish" work like documenting those same cows. Nevertheless, workers, male or female, were not excluded from either sort of work if bodies were needed. Not a single job on the farm was only done by women or men in absolute terms. However, if less demanding tasks on the body were required it was inevitably the female employees who were sent to do them. Given the unpredictable ebb and flow of farmwork, such designations of labor are not as simple and straightforward as they first sound. Indeed, the flexibility of how work is doled out is dependent upon who is present at any given time. Work is frequently not comprised of only routine roles but often reactions to moment-to-moment contingent conditions: situations like a cow dropping during the milking process and the need to remove its dead body now entangled in the equipment or the need to round up cows that have broken free and are meandering into the silage. This immediacy of need is a clear indicator of how a combination of individuated embodiment and interpretations play a central role in daily life on the farm: if any woman proved that she was physically able, there was little stopping her from being assigned, or doing, any particular job. The majority of men were perceived to be physically stronger, but there was, to my knowledge, never any conflict over these interpretations. It was a shared "common knowledge" that men would tend to do the lifting, women would tend to do the sorting, and given this "understanding" any particular *buchō* was liable to make split-second decisions regarding work responsibilities as they were required. If a cow needed to be penned, the *buchō* would size up the workforce—say a fifty-kilogram woman and a seventy-kilogram man—and unapologetically opt for the bulkier worker to do the task. The point here is that gender played a role, but beyond physicality, it did not determine one's on-farm position. As noted in chapter 8, Yukiko was chosen over senior male cohorts to train as a hunter as she was viewed as clever, hardworking, and indeed physically able to do the work required. And on several occasions Takuto or other workers perceived as less than competent would be passed over even having the rather awkward Haru do work because it was assumed that she would (somehow) get the job done.

Wives and mothers of the farm families tended to focus their attention on the calves and on their human families. As such, their working hours were usually not doled out in split shifts; they nearly always worked a morning to early evening shift. Here too there is traditional gender-role division made. The older farm women had all raised children and this division of labor, between homemaker and farmer, was viewed as normative and perhaps, given embodiment again, functional. Kimoto (2003, 154–158) and Sugimoto (2022) make similar observations. In essence being a farm owner equates with being its "top" employee. One can certainly make a gender-oriented argument in terms of women not being in ownership/top management positions as in Japanese corporate structures (Nemoto 2016). However, women working on the farm did not want to be "at the top." Hypothetically, if they did and acted on this, I cannot comment whether there would be resistance from surrounding farmers. My suspicion is there would not be resistance but perhaps surprise and likely some level of enthusiastic support. And here, Traphagan (2017, 2019) makes similar observations about successful entrepreneurial, rural women. However, in line with the examples outlined above, during the more demanding seasons such as silage harvesting, it was common for the older women, again the vast majority of them farm family members, to fill in doing any task that was required of the men, from driving trucks to humping tires on top of silage bunkers. On occasion the women teased men about how easy such work was. They would exclaim how nice it was that their sons and husbands would have to take them out for dinner because there was no time to prepare a meal that day, all done with smiling and reassuring *ne?* and *sou da ne!* (isn't that right, yes that's right) batted around across the gender divide for a combination of emphasis and comedic effect. It is essential to note again that there were also wives and mothers who did not choose to work on the farm at all; indeed, the *shachō*'s wife did not work on the farm, though she did eventually manage a café linked to it. And Takako, their aforementioned fictive daughter and wife of Matsumoto, chose to work at the local supermarket despite living a stone's throw from the aforementioned female domain of the *koushi* care area.

Though I asked, I was not privy to any complaints relating to these work roles, sexism, or gender bias in my time at the farm. This may have to do with my own embodiment as a male and the potential reticence of female workers to discuss such issues with me. This is not my impression, however. My interlocutors were rather open with far more personal and controversial topics than these rather obvious and observable local life course expectations. More to the point, women who came from outside of the farm were treated as any other employee. They received the same wages for the same hours, with the same benefits for engaging in nearly the same tasks. The Chinese workers, clear no-siders, were a notable exception (Hansen 2010a). But any alternative treatment they received seems more an issue of legality, prejudice, ethnicity, and not a gender issue primarily. A woman working at Grand Hopes Farm, another at a neighboring dairy farm, and a good female friend on a nearby beef farm were all nonlocals (lo-siders as outlined in the previous chapter) and all were promoted to the position of *buchō* in charge of males and females alike. These positions and statuses were earned. In two cases they held this position despite being younger and working at the farm for a shorter term than many of their male coworkers. Although often covered over with the requisite Japanese downplaying, it was their individual skill, education, or savvy that got them the *buchō* position—gender was seemingly not at issue for them or their employer.

Of course, one obvious and important factor related to this sort of independence is age. All of the young women at the farm were without children at the start of my fieldwork. However, by the end of my second fieldwork term two of the women I had worked with and interviewed were pregnant and both had quit the farm. No young mothers, even those in farm families, engaged in farmwork. Whether a gendered "glass ceiling" exists in the dairy industry, at least to the degree it clearly does in other forms of Japanese employment, is doubtful as very few women (or men for that matter as noted below) want to continue in farming. Yet, the few who do are often concomitantly encouraged by local owners and successful in their careers. However, similar to female *furītā* or OL in Japan, the expectations of and for both males and females was clear if tacit. The assumption was that young women would eventually want to leave farms by opting to get married and return to urban life or in a minority of cases choose to play a new role through getting married to a farmer, having children, and (likely) playing the dual role of homemaker and flexible family farm worker much as farm wives do now. In accord with arguments made by Traphagan, such traditional expectations of gender roles can indeed "block" women from moving up the dairy farm employment ladder, but this is more a matter of personal choice and desire than strict gender discrimination (Traphagan 2017). This was certainly the case at Grand Hopes Farm and neighboring farms. The women I met seemed happy with this arrangement. I have never met a *bokujō* owner in Hokkaido who was female and outside of Hokkaido I have only met one, an indomitable eighty-odd-year-old widow in Kumamoto, Kyushu, who had no plans to retire. Nevertheless, this situation was a continuation of a long-held lifestyle, not a decision to start farming anew.

As noted in previous chapters, it was common for some male members of staff to curtly order female members of staff to do certain tasks or even berate them into tears. At first, I presumed that this was an entrenched power structure with gender as its base. In short, it initially appeared that the female employees were considered lesser, weaker, and subservient to their male coworkers. However, I soon learned that such a simple reading needed to be interrogated. Usually, these bullying males were in senior employment positions. This is an important issue in traditional Japanese power hierarchies, even taking the issues of gender into account. And many of these senior employees, including the *kachō*, acted the same way in relation to male staff members. Much like the selection of work tasks, there was clearly an element of individual embodiment and perception at play here as well as, perhaps (culturally speaking), women being socialized to avoid conflict from a young age (Adis Tahhan 2014; Ben-Ari 2003; Cave 2007). This is not to downplay gender as a factor, nor the abuse that some young women like Haru endured, but angering them likely posed less of a physical danger to the verbal aggressor than brandishing the same "bravado" toward a similar or larger proportioned male, although this happened as well with results varying as noted, from fistfights to walking off the job.

Of the three males on staff at Grand Hopes who frequently engaged in this sort of bullying toward the female staff, two were widely (on and off the farm) regarded as having social or mental problems, a theme I will return to below. The other was simply regarded as a *warui hito* (bad guy) or *baka* (idiot) depending on who was asked about him. However, while some female workers clearly found the bullying difficult to contend with (and some men did as well, though their usual response was to quit), "woman as victim" is not an accurate portrayal of these situations or these women.

On one occasion off the farm, Kyoko, the aforementioned nurse from Honshu, complained first to the housing authorities and then directly to the *shachō* about the threatening behavior of Tarō-san. He was soon evicted because of this. And later, after Tarō-san began berating a new female employee (in the manner to which he had grown accustomed with some of the other female staff such as Haru), he was quick to find out that this newcomer would not silently bow and bear it. I was not witness to the exchange but was told that colorful language was used by both parties and when the shift was over the new female worker stormed into the office and demanded: "Either he goes or I go." The *shachō* heard their stories with the result being that, despite gender and senior status, she stayed and he went, sent off to the conflict resolution exile of the hospital barn where he, in essence, had Takuto sent after their earlier conflict. And so, the "weak and meek" Haru, who was brought to tears nearly daily by the insults of bullies, not only finished out her yearlong and self-appointed stint by doggedly refusing to quit, but she was also given the satisfaction (and she told me later that she was pleased) of seeing one of her tormentors demoted from *buchō* to stable hand to eventually being "asked" to leave the farm, in part through the actions of an outside woman and a junior, female, staff member.

In sum, while being a woman played an observable role, it did not play a decisive role, especially for women from outside the local community. These women had chosen a difficult lifestyle and were determined, for an assortment of personal reasons, to make their Gensan and farm lives work. Indeed when it came to simpering and complaining about the heat, cold, or the task at hand it was seldom a woman doing it. Oftentimes farm women proved mentally and socially "stronger" and more stoic and determined than many male workers, for example, finishing out their contracts or resolving conflicts without fisticuffs. And as for the older local women, while their choice to engage or not to engage in farmwork might be more limited, entwined in the assemblage of place, family livelihoods and the cheap flexible labor they provided, three out of the four wives chose to work on Grand Hopes. Thus, the wife-mother-coworker was a common triad of experience on other local farms both large and small. The crunchy and smooth of daily life considered, farm women, the rare times I could have a leisurely talk with them, told me that they were happy with life on the farm. At least, if there was any form of gender-oriented coercion to work, they did not betray it. However, interestingly, while many young women originally from outside the area chose to work on the farm alongside most of the owners' wives, *none* of the owners' female children chose to. Indeed, not one worked in an industry related to agriculture and no owner or mother was encouraging them to change their minds.

Farm Men

Like their female counterparts, men were brought to farmwork through troubled romantic relationships. But in addition, problems in their former work environment were also common motivations. Tarō-san had a history of both. If the stereotype of the submissive urban Japanese woman does not hold, neither does the image of the privileged salaryman or the effeminate urbanite hold in the world of dairy farm workers or working-class laborers in general. Masculinity in Japan is complex and has increasingly become the focus of social scientists, from relations with alcohol (Christensen 2015), to work life (Cook 2016; Hidaka 2010; Roberson 1998; Roberson and Suzuki 2003), to sexuality and gender roles (Darling-Wolf 2003, 2004; Dasgupta 2000, 2013; Ito and Yanase 2001). Anthropologist Gordon Mathews, who has also done fieldwork in Hokkaido, quotes numerous conversations held with his middle-aged Japanese informants who are confused by the current state of Japanese masculinity; perhaps the most telling is that one wanted to "drag youth from their cars and put Judo holds on them" (Mathews 2006, 10). To be clear, what follows is not a full account of masculinity in Japan but a partial, and surely not impartial, account of it on Grand Hopes Farm.

Popular media may depict young male farmworkers in Hokkaido as fashionable heartthrobs of a sensitively sensual ilk (nurturers and outdoorsmen) and numerous part-time employment magazines depict these precariats as vibrant happy-go-lucky youth, but most of the male workers I encountered were "Suzuki-sans," that is, Mr. Smiths, average guys. For example, Between-san was by most accounts *kakkō ii* (cool), but he was no salaryman and not cultivating the image or actions of a tough guy or urban hair stylist. He was attractive to women, a point ceaselessly brought to my attention by female friends, but he was unlike the many media representations of men combining bookend stereotypes into an *ikumen* (sensitive guy), *ikemen* (cool guy), nor "an androgynous hybrid" (Darling-Wolf 2003). Between-san was simply a handsome guy who was, in addition, clever, softspoken, hard-working, and friendly. Perhaps he sounds like "a catch" for many a single woman. However, herein lies the problem for many male farmworkers. Despite desperately wanting a girlfriend, having the looks and personality to attract would-be suitors, and being open about his desire to settle down, he was stuck in dairy farming. He was perpetually single, with little economic security or control over work conditions, putting in long and unusual hours at a low-profile and essentially dead-end job that intensified feelings of alienation inside and outside of the workplace.

Ikigai (life's meaning) played a large role in the lives of male informants and this preoccupation was intimately linked with Otherness and security. While work, family, and following one's dreams are noted as the main sources of *ikigai* for many Japanese males (Hasegawa et al. 2003, 2020; Hidaka 2010), dairy work, especially in the context of a mega farm, offers such satisfactions to very few. To all involved, work pressures made

family life difficult to start or maintain and free time to pursue other interests scarce. To most from outside of the community the work was viewed
as a temporary job, and given the turnover rate, it was a disagreeable one.
For those few outsiders like Tarō-san who sought satisfaction from work
as a self-professed *kigyō senshi* (corporate warrior), their expectations
that others would "display the qualities of loyalty, diligence, dedication,
self-sacrifice, hard work; qualities which in an earlier era had been associated with another influential discourse of masculinity—the *bushidō* of the
samurai" (Dasgupta 2000, 195), would be met with mockery by coworkers
and disinterest from senior staff. In this sense, males are perhaps in a more
difficult position, more trapped in the state of (in)security (the relation
of being secured to a job that makes other aspects of life insecure), than
females, at least in the context of dairy farm work. Simply, they cannot
live up to the hybrid images expected by many contemporary Japanese
women. An important point to mention here is the normative acceptance
of heterosexuality, and especially male heterosexuality. I met two women
at different farms who were in same-sex relationships. However, I never
met a man who proclaimed to be gay or one that seemed outwardly interested in finding a male partner. It also seems reasonable that this "private"
aspect of life would be repressed in order to fit the deeply entrenched
gendered norms outlined in this chapter.

While many single women in Gensan told me that they wanted
a partner (and among Kyoko and her female friends this subject was
pursued tirelessly) they would not consider dating a farmer let alone a
farmworker. Bestor has noted a similar pattern of female reluctance to
date young male fishmongers in Tokyo by women outside the industry
(Bestor 2004). But there are some key differences: Gensan is not Tokyo
and a metropolitan market is not a settlement of agriculturalists. One's
local life is public knowledge as the social world is a small and closed
one. The pool of single people with similar schedules, let alone interests, is
minuscule. While the workers in Tokyo's Tsukiji market start work at 3:00
a.m., they are finished work by noon and have every Sunday and regular
holidays off. Bestor notes that often the young workers had dreams and
interests that they pursued outside of working hours, one could try to
pursue one's *ikigai* being a rock musician for example. Such a schedule is
radically different from having no vacations, no set day off, and working
split shifts starting at 4:00 a.m. and often continuing until 8:00 p.m. or
later in a rural, very rural, location.

Thus, unable to live up to the "dream seeker" or sensitive urbanite image and unable to provide the security that a "salaryman" lifestyle
could provide, male dairy workers, even handsome and cool ones, are a
hard sell to available women. One might even say that dairy work is an
extreme example of what underpins the already well-documented popularity of "arranged" foreign brides in rural Japan (Chen 2008; Faier 2008;
Yamashita 2008). While women are expected to eventually quit working
on the farm, men were expected to continue working and earning. They
were expected to make themselves fit into the stages of becoming, belonging, and so being: from marriage, to children, progressing one hopes,
to being a respected community member. But such success stories for
dairy-farm-working males were few and far between. Indeed, many saw
these stages as unattainable, and the banality of their interests (sleep,
video games, cars, or pachinko) was augmented by their irregular hours,
the exhausting nature of the work, and their poor pay. They were trapped
in a Catch-22 cycle.

Among males these conditions lead to alienation and violence per-
petrated on both humans and cows, discussed in the following chapter.
Tarō-san clearly had a problem controlling his temper. Fistfights were not
uncommon. There were three at Grand Hopes Farm over my first year of
research, including one of my own as outlined below, all involving males.
Kicking or punching cows was common among men as well. This was
not only the case at Grand Hopes Farm. A worker on a nearby beef farm
was dismissed for severely beating a young cow.

Kyoko and Dr. Oda commented on this information. Both suspected
that there were many such cases. Indeed, the doctor mused that many men
on farms preferred to work away from humans but still desire "skinship"
(a common term in Japan denoting a physical and emotional connection
with living things—often mother and son) (Doi 2007). Such workers, he
concluded, are attracted to work in remote locations with little human
contact yet still long for living contact that they hope to foster with nonhuman others, cows for example. Consciously or not the doctor was building from Doi Takeo's work on dependency, which has become common
Japanese pop psychology. Put another way, the workers, troubled in the
human realm, were perhaps seeking the "unconditional love" of animals.
Whether this is the case in all (or any) I am uncertain, but the nurse and
doctor recounted stories of some extraordinarily emotionally distraught
and socially inept patients, some of whom indeed had worked at Grand

Hopes Farm, and as the conclusion highlights a dairy farm is not a place well designed to foster intimate relationships human or nonhuman.

As a brief but poignant personal note on the issue of male violence, I had a conflict-ridden relationship with the *kachō*'s son. The reasons for this conflict could be numerous. Masahiro was in a new position of power at a young age, under stress, and moreover, he was not trained in the "human management" aspects of presiding over dozens of employees, many of whom were his senior in both age and experience. Also, he was surely aware that his father was against hiring me for the job (and it's safe to say neither of them were fans of foreigners, be they Chinese or Canadian). Let me also clarify for the reader, as an ex-ice hockey agitator, I was no stranger to quick tempered escalations, verbal or physical. Moreover, I was feeling the strains and stresses of a very long tour of duty as an ethnographer and was increasingly flustered by the *shikata ga nai* stance of male coworkers in the face of a person who I viewed, 'at the time' noted in the Epilogue of the book, as a bully and tyrant. These reasons all seem probable causes for our discord, and eventual farmyard fistfight, and it is clear how Otherness and security could be seen as central to this situation. Pointed and personal insults were exchanged, a push, a return shove, and punches started flying with co-workers diving in to pull us apart. Social scientists generally do not get into brawls with their informants unless that is their said intention (studies of boxing, for example Wacquant 2000). I was sure that I would be sacked due to our conflict. But fights among males were common as was the institutionalized violence against nonhumans noted in the final chapter. Insofar as senior workers were concerned, "it happens," nothing was ever mentioned about our altercation. In lieu of being fired there was just silence. Given the rapid introduction of Otherness experienced by all on the farm, such conflicts were inherent and expected (even by outside observers like Kyoko and Dr. Oda). These issues are obviously linked to both stresses and the physical, social, and economic security of individuals and for the farm itself. However, the ontological security of knowing one's self, one's reactions, or temperament in the face of Otherness or contingencies for example, or one's position as "owner's son" or as "detached social science observer" were constantly under question and strained; again, a certain liminality ruled. And people, but most notably males, were well aware that such positions—social, economic, physical—were not fixed but in flux.

In terms of the economic security of the farm, the *shachō* frequently interviewed hopeful employees on the phone. Sometimes he would think that the applicant was strange, but his better hiring judgment was occasionally outweighed by the desperate need for workers in the face of the shift to industrial production. When I explained, admittedly dodging naming people at the farm, that I thought many staff were *chotto kowareteiru* (a bit broken), pointing at my head due to not knowing a polite way to call somebody crazy in Japanese, and so sheepishly continuing, "Ma, byōki, tokidoki kurutteiru mitai kana?" (Ahm well, sick, sometimes crazy I guess?).

The *shachō* leaned back and burst out laughing: "Hontō ni, takusan ga imasu yo!" (Honestly, many are crazy, you better believe it!). And, knowing a bit about my research by then, with a devious smirk he added: "Honshūno hito dakara hokkaidō jin wa daijōbu da yo" (It's because they come from Honshu—people from Hokkaido are fine).

I replied: "Tarō-san wa dou?" (What about Taro-san?), knowing that he was from Hokkaido. The *shachō* merely tilted his head and hissed; this was essentially a pan-male staff issue not linked to place of origin, class, or on-farm status.

We discussed a few workers who had come and gone, for example, one who would stop coming to work for days on end and then simply appear as though everything was normal, and another who simply went *pan* (an onomatopoeic expression meaning snapped) one day and started punching the aforementioned saintly Ichiro-san who, turtling, had no idea what brought this on. We discussed a few remaining workers that both of us clearly thought belonged in the *okashii* (odd) category. We ended in agreement, but I suspect not completely jokingly, that I too was of questionable sanity for wanting to do the research I selected.

Making the claim that there exists a high percentage of mentally ill in a given population is controversial. The local backlash surrounding anthropologist Nancy Scheper-Hughes's fieldwork on rural Irish male farmworkers, *Saints, Scholars, and Schizophrenics*, is one prominent example of how claiming mental health issues are rampant can cause problems for individuals and communities under study (Scheper-Hughes 1979). This section is one reason why pseudonyms for Gensan and its people are used in this book. My claim is not as extreme as the one Scheper-Hughes made in regard to the rural Irish, especially young, rural Irish men, as I lack the statistical data or hospitalization records, and so on, to back it up. Nevertheless, there were many suicides in the area (seven from 2004 to 2010) and most of them were males related to farmwork—including the *shachō*'s cousin. Yūji-san was also saddened by the suicide of his daughter's husband in 2013. Approximately 70 percent of suicide victims are male in Japan and though the suicide rate has dropped from its peak in 2003, Japan is ranked number nine in the world (well above other developed nations) in suicides per capita as of 2017. Since Durkheim's pioneering study of suicide, the notion that rural area suicide rates are higher due to "geographic clustering," from "alienation and poverty," for example, has been a popular theoretic claim (Baller and Richardson 2002). In comparative terms, around the same period of my research due to financial pressures brought on by a change in different technology and insecurity (for example, the control over GM crops), there has been a spike in suicide rates among Indian farm owners as well (Roberts 2008, 2–5). As noted above, workers involved in industrial monoculture farming are in a demanding and unstable job with their physical security at risk. They are often eating poorly, lacking sleep, lacking holidays, performing repetitive tasks at a fast pace with a myriad of uncooperative elements, including the weather, other workers, or cows, animals that are also under stress: the result is what I would call an cosmopolitical assemblage of suffering. Added to this, they lack contact with family and friends, sometimes by choice, but often due to the requirements of their work.

These conditions were trying and shared in varying degrees by male and female staff cutting across the shifting rubrics of local, outsider, lo-sider, and no-sider. However, males did have additional stresses and strains related to the ideal masculine images outlined above: neither sensitive *ikemen* nor *ikumen*, lacking the stability of a salaryman or the free time to follow their desires. Moreover, many male locals, like Katō-san and the *shachō*'s son, were placed in a position of being successors to farms they did not want (not unlike the aforementioned young Irish farmers in Scheper-Hughes's study [1979]). Katō-san quit and in the latter case the son left Gensan. Although I was not told directly, as in Ireland, some sons remain in the industry against their inclination out of obligation and through believing that they lack alternative employment skills. As expanded upon in the conclusion of this book, even those who wish to continue dairy farming face innumerable insecurities—continual rural deskilling, an uncertain future, inheriting an industry with massive overheads and a volatile market, along with overseeing a product that must be maintained daily (cows) and a by-product that lacks the ability to be stored for more than a day (milk). Even those wanting to remain in the industry are aware of the rural deskilling that the shift to high-tech equipment has brought; anyone could be trained to milk or care for a cow despite their knowledge or skill and the scale of the new equipment also necessitated the importation of cheap labor from outside of the local area and increasingly from outside Japan. The family farm is going the way of the dinosaur as the family factory is taking hold. Yet perhaps the most difficult situation faced by male dairy workers, certainly locals but many others as well, is their exclusion—their outsider status, local or not, as forced Otherness from epic Japanese expectations ranging from family connections right down to state holidays.

While some male workers, usually those from outside of the community of Gensan, claimed that exclusion from societal expectations could be a boon—an escape from "typical" Japanese society, albeit an open and liminal one—for many individuals born in Gensan or to those individuals hoping to remain, their employment was often seen as a source of economic, social, and cultural alienation. Blocked from becoming and belonging without colossal efforts toward making themselves what *they viewed* as "normative" Japanese young adults—being in a relationship or, better, married with kids, and middle class. Other dairy workers were classically liminal, this was a set time-out, a time of self-proving or self-discovery and they would return to life in university or at some other career. Still others were liminally liminal; living month to month with no goal or end in sight, they simply lacked the qualities of "self-making" that the job required of them and were in effectively precarious, *san K*, dead-end jobs. For them becoming and belonging were also seemingly impossible. While this impacted the lives of both men and women—I suggest it impacted the lives of men more profoundly—and this relates back to the epic discourse of Japan.

One key reason for this pressure on men is rooted in traditional gender expectations found across Japan. *Uchi*, the home, the inside, the family, and its management are conventionally seen as a feminine realm. At the same time, *soto*, the outside, the workplace, and community are the spaces where masculinity has traditionally been expressed and confirmed. As noted above, all over Japan this view is increasingly being challenged by micro challenges, novel stories. And mainstream gender identity and related social expectations are one such battleground of Otherness and security in Gensan. For dairy farm workers employment is not seasonal, their hours are consistently both long and irregular, holidays nonexistent, and the likelihood of marriage remains low for any choosing to stay in the industry. Remaining a dairy employee, their ability to "become" part of the social fabric of even the greater Gensan community is hampered. This is true of women and men. However, given traditional roles, socially acceptable femininity can be attained by leaving the dairy farm and settling down, albeit usually in an area distant from agriculture, while men, inside or outside dairy farming, are often compelled to be the main providers. As for dairy workers, most do not partake in village festivals, most do not belong to community organizations such as the *chōnaikai* or PTA, and their leisure, by necessity, is often in the form of noncommunal pursuits. Similar to "the corrosion of character" in the modern, mobile, "teamwork"-oriented workplace (Sennett 1998, 15–31; and more recently Stiegler 2016), there is nowhere to turn for support, there is no workers' union, many are far from family connections, there is no romantic partner or much of a promise of finding one, and often there are no friends beyond bovine ones. There is work and work alone, singular, insecure, and alienating.

Batō San, Not Sama: Local Protection from Life's Insecurities

Religion is one final way to demonstrate the above shifting assemblage of individual and group Otherness, a way of expressing the distinctions between townspeople, rural people, individuals employed in the livestock industry, and locals, lo-siders, outsiders, and no-siders. There is a common expression: "Born Shinto—die Buddhist" (Reader 1991). Shinto is native to Japan, and taking great license, is comparable to Daoism or animism. Buddhism in Japan follows, for the most part, the East Asian Mahayana (Great Vehicle) tradition though there are native "new" religions and representative factions of all world religions in Japan (Kasahara 2001). By and large, however, Japanese identify as Buddhist at least post-humously as funerals are predominately a Buddhist affair. However, there are some distinctions that mark rural religion in Tokachi, and among livestock farmers in particular, that underscore social change, their Otherness even in Hokkaido, and a multivalent search for security.

A statue of Jizō-sama (a *kami* [deity] of travelers and the dead) sits at the crossroads leading to Grand Hopes Farm. Somebody would continually upkeep the icon. The statue would be cleaned and the surrounding grass or snow would be dealt with. In this respect, little differentiated Jizō-sama's care from that of a swing set in a public park or a fountain. This care went beyond aesthetics alone, however. Jizō-sama had a steady flow of drinks, snacks, and cigarettes. He had a matching red ski cap, vest, and scarf to shield him from biting Tokachi winter winds and a straw hat to shade his concrete head in the summer. In return for looking after his mundane existence he drew attention to the two flags placed in front of him "Supīdo-daun" (slow down) and comforted those whose loved one had been lost on that stretch of road. However, unlike some sort of spiritual superhero, Jizō-sama did not just miraculously appear here in an appropriate space and at a time of need. Pictured in figure 12.1, "he" was placed here by human agency and with significant costs and planning. Over fifteen years I have had interesting and conflicting answers to my questions about the origin of the statue despite it only being three years old at the time I started research. At first, I heard Katō-san's family had paid for it after the loss of his father in a car crash. Several coworkers agreed with this story. Then a *buchō* claimed that the *chōnaikai* erected it in response to a rise in farm traffic brought about by increasing industrialization and this was the *shachō*'s recounting as well. Bringing the story up in passing to a local Buddhist cleric a couple years later, I was told the statue was paid for by a local temple and this story was supported by others from outside the farm. Oddly, the cost for erecting it, about ¥2,000,000, was agreed upon by all.

Religious studies scholars Ian Reader and George Tanabe have, wittily, called the Japanese "practically religious" (Reader and Tanabe 1998). There is a two-pronged meaning at play here: practically meaning pragmatically and practically meaning almost or sort of. During the Tokugawa

Figure 12.1. An ever-vigilant and well-maintained Jizō-sama statue offering his message of "Slow down," about two kilometers from the farm. Photo by the author.

period (1603–1867) Buddhist temples (which were in reality combined nearly seamlessly with Shinto shrines) were the pragmatic organizational site of the military government's administration of common people (Ketelaar 1993). Japanese (less those completely outside the system, for example, *burakumin* outcasts) were registered with a temple and there existed strict laws curtailing mobility (both temporal and social) within the largely closed, feudal, ad hoc nation. This led to a brief but vicious persecution of Buddhism and the promotion of "nationalist" Shinto during the first few years of "revolutionary" modernism and unification during Meiji rule (Victoria 2001). But Buddhism soon recovered some of its former prestige in part though proving its worth to the new Meiji state apparatus—ironically emulating Christian aid societies such as the Red Cross—and in part through the complete inability of Shinto clerics to replace the well-organized and educated Buddhists as community builders and leaders. Japan's militarism has always been supported by certain strands and strains of Buddhism and charismatic leaders (for example, Rinzai Zen and Nichirenshū) and the modern era was no exception to this historical trend (Heisig and Maraldo 1995).

Nonetheless, with the Japanese defeat and Occupation (1945–1952) two key changes developed in Japanese religious culture. The emperor was no longer the divine sovereign of Japan, indeed many called for his persecution as a war criminal (Bix 2001), and the new constitution enshrined the freedom of religion (Dower 1999), giving legal sanction to an already flourishing current of new religions, a "rush hour of the gods" (McFarland 1967). Some new religions eagerly sought converts and in turn became substantial political powers within civil society and abroad, notably Sōka Gakkai established in 1930, formed the Kōmeitō national political party in 1962, and was part of a national government coalition as the "new" Kōmeitō party in 1999 (Fisker-Nielsen 2012). Indeed, many Japanese will fervently claim they are not religious while engaging in overtly religious acts or belonging to numerous religious organizations. Reader claims that religious practices can be seen simply as part of a pleasurable experience, such as a day trip to a famous temple or stopping by the grounds of a jinja on the way to lunch. Religious practice is often a celebration of culture or even Japanese ethnicity and not tied to overtly spiritual beliefs.

To underscore religious "practicality" over and above doctrine for many Japanese, when I visited Haru after her tenure at Grand Hopes Farm at her family farm in Nagano she insisted that we visit a shrine the night before I left. We climbed a few stairs, tossed our coins into the offering box, rang the tin bell, clapped twice, and bowed our heads toward the closed doors of the shrine. Nothing more was said. Pressing on home toward her parents' farm I asked Haru why she was so keen to do this ritual the night before I left. "Was she religious—a believer?" (*Shūkyō o shinjiteimasu ka*), I queried. She replied that she was not, but that this was, "well, Japanese culture" (*iya . . . Nihon no bunka . . . kana*). She paused, perhaps knowing after my year and a half of odd, irksome, and ill-worded questions that this was not going to please me, and added, "Ma, anshin dakara" (It's for ease of mind or safety), or a feeling of security. I expected this response as I have heard similar ones from Japanese friends, countless times, while engaging in "nonreligious" religion with them.

For many Japanese people religion is equated with a security (or the securing) of identity via tradition, becoming, belonging, and so being Japanese—what Ama Toshimaro terms (if, given the above history, in somewhat essentialist terms) Japanese "natural religion" as opposed to "revealed religion" (Ama 2005, 1–11). Religion is often associated with culture and ritual, not *necessarily* metaphysical beliefs or a devout faith. As opposed to many other forms of religious belief, Japanese religion has always been (even from the early oracle bone readings pointed out earlier in this book) practical or pragmatic—praxis concerned with "this-worldly" benefits such as the curing of ailments, protection from life's unknown fates, and even the passing of exams, or indeed, traveling home safely. These are practical desires aimed at making life more secure through managing risks or perhaps safely hedging metaphysical bets. These goals are accomplished through supporting religious performances by experts (examples are given below), or by oneself through maintaining a statue as noted at the beginning of this section, going on pilgrimages, or simply by purchasing an amulet. This may well be motivated through the desire to engage in a shared culture or community with or without the baggage of metaphysics. A pilgrimage may concomitantly appeal to intense adherents and those simply seeking something fun and cultural (Ackermann et al. 2007, 175–176). Religion buffers individuals from the ups and downs of existing in, or coping with, the mundane world, in short, the fostering and securing of communities (us and them) alongside the more individuated and individualized support that religious communities offer in terms of identity and "ontological security" (Giddens 1991, 35–70) or even more tangible support systems such as childcare services or the organization of funeral arrangements. For the case at hand, this covers some of the scope of security and securing that religion potentially provides. What follows explains how practical religion is marked by Otherness in the face of insecurity in Tokachi.

The remains of Tokachi's first dairy farm lie at the mouth of the Tok-achi river delta. Between two deep gullies, the site of former silos, there is a tilting memorial stone erected in 1916. The stone, now worn with time and ravaged by moss, was meticulously carved by hand. The marker morns the passing of cattle during a particularly harsh winter storm, when the settlers, overcome by snow, could not feed their livestock. The monument prays for the rest of the animals' potentially vengeful souls. Such more-than-human recognition is not uncommon. There are similar monuments and similar reasoning among contemporary fishmongers in Tokyo—notably those who flay live eels in Tsukiji (Bestor 2004, 172–174) and funeral rites for pets as protection from their possibly vengeful ghosts (Ambros 2010, 2012). As outlined in previous chapters, in some ways cows and humans shared a symbiotic relationship at least until the 1960s. While the farmers protected and cared for these nonhumans, they also utilized their bodies for power, drank their milk, and occasionally ate their flesh to survive. It might seem easy to dismiss this monument offhand as a relic of a past era. But I sought it out after noting the numerous similar monuments in front of many if not most contemporary dairy and beef farms. It is but once instance highlighting the importance of multispecies, indeed cosmopolit-ical, connections on the Tokachi frontiers of place and more-than-human personhood that bring the environment, technology and spiritual belief into the conversation, past and present, of human and cow connections.

Batōkannon (horse-[headed] Kannon) or *chiku(san)konhi* (livestock [holder's] monument) have early Indic roots. *Batōkannon* usually has eight arms and a crown of horse heads. Kannon is the Japanese interpretation of the Chinese bodhisattva of compassion Guan-yin, and so, also of India's Avalokiteśvara. Its essential purpose, in the guise of the horse-headed Kannon, is to guide the spirits of departed animals to the Pure Land, as well as to alleviate suffering, and in so doing rid human adherents from being plagued by vengeful or "hungry ghosts." In essence, the deity pro-vides protection, a feeling of security, from the bad luck that the animals' spirits might encounter on the postmortem travels and the ill luck they might in turn bring upon the farmers who used their lives, perhaps too cavalierly on occasion, toward financial ends.

A *chikukonhi* monument is similar to a gravestone. Generally inscribed is a thanks and an apology offered to the *tamashī* (soul) of numerous animals. Usually on the one plaque the names of the farm own-ers are also added. Given the rational, progressive, and modern nature of the Grand Hopes Farm, when a coworker informed me that the farm was in the process of installing a new *chikukonhi* monument I was surprised;

but not as surprised as I was to be by the reasoning behind it. When I asked the *shachō* about the monument his reply, as usual, was direct and it clearly underscored the point that the worlds of environment, animal, and human are still far from separate in modern Tokachi. He was being haunted by the *tamashī* of cows in his dreams. He hoped that by erecting the monument he would feel *anshin* (relieved, safe, or secure) (Hansen 2018b). I assumed that this was all metaphoric. Surely if pressed he would be unable to "rationally" explain this search for security, to underscore any causal "actual" links between his business, the cows, their souls, his dreams, and the promise of salvation the statue was intended to provide. However, he could.

He flatly told me, in the way he might relay the procedures for hiring a worker or buying feed, that a cow that dies emits a ball of blue light. This was the soul of the cow and its energy would cause harm to the farm if not allowed a place to peacefully and securely reside. This misfortune was a cause of waking anxiety and sleep-robbing stress, and the ¥1,400,000 he put out for the plaque was, to his mind, a small price to pay if the farm was protected and he could rest securely. The monument was both a form of apology to the cows and a show of respect for their assistance in the farm's profitability. I nodded, took notes, and then promptly raced off to the aforementioned lo-sider oasis of the Sutaru café, convinced he was having me on.

One of the café owners was interested in world religions. To my stunned amazement she agreed that this was the reasoning of many livestock owners including some that she knew well. She was quite knowledgeable about religion in the area and had a keen curiosity about global strands of Buddhism and Hinduism. She explained that there was a recent trend in Tokachi of installing a *gyūkannon* (cow-headed Kannon) in areas related to livestock. Cows are often featured in Japanese temple grounds, especially those related to trade and transportation. In this sense *gyūkannon* may or may not be particular to Hokkaido, though I have never heard of this incarnation appearing elsewhere. I asked if there were any of these monuments nearby and she jotted down a map of where I could visit the rather large statue seen in figure 12.2.

Intrigued that there could be a common anthropomorphic, metaphysical, and cosmopolitical view of cows among "hardened" dairy owners, I visited some of the local farms where I previously interviewed dairy workers. Now curious and aware, I noted that nearly all had *chikukonhi* monuments tucked away somewhere on their respective farms. Moreover, all agreed with the *shachō*'s more-than-human description and explanation

Figure 12.2. A statue of Tokachi's divine bovine: Kannon with a cow perched on its head rather than the more common horse head. Near Shimizu town, Hokkaido. Photo by the author.

of blue lights, souls, and salvation. All had paid a considerable amount of money for the monuments. All had yearly rites performed, usually in May or June. And nobody gave any indication that this was a superstition or simply viewed as a cost of doing business as some workers, including myself, had mused. However, stories of empathy and anthropomorphism went beyond this animal-human link.

All new to me, at that point I confused *batōkannon* and *chikukonhi*. Standing in a farmer's yard I insisted that he tell me about his statue of *batōkannon*. He insisted he did not have one nor did he have a clue what a *batōkannon* was or why I should be bothering him about it. As my arm-waving and partially coherent babble continued, he proved himself to be a patient man. Nodding and head tilting, he walked down his driveway with me and I pointed out the plaque, immediately realizing my mistake. "Ahh, gomenasai ne, machigaimashita. batōkannon jya arimasen . . . asoko wa chikukonhi desune" (Oh, sorry my mistake, that isn't *batōkannon* . . . that is a *chikukonhi* isn't it?), I said. And with this admission he realized what I had been blathering about up in his yard. Chuckling he replied deleting the cumbersome religious baggage of "Kannon." "Ahhh, wakaru, wakaru, *batō san* ne" (Ohh, I get it, you meant *Mr. Batō*), he replied.

Like a local friend or an acquaintance, "Batō san" was not seen in the same way as Kannon (a lofty and distant bodhisattva) nor was he even an honorable *sama*; he was, like any member of the community, simply *san*. Batō san was there as a "practically religious" reminder of security and posthuman or cosmopolitan connections, or that cows, humans, the environment, and the fates had to work in concert even for contemporary industrial farms to continue functioning smoothly. Mr. Batō brought the Tokachi dairy community together, not only in terms of tacit shared knowledge (as no no-siders, outsiders, and only one lo-sider had ever heard of *batōkannon*, let alone Mr. Batō as a local "incarnation"), but also by providing *anshin* and *anzen* (safety, security, and peace of mind), alongside security in terms of identity and continuity through rituals such as cleaning and keeping the lines of connection open for salvation of animal souls at the monument and human souls at the temple. In sum, *batōkannon* and *chikukonhi* were a local affair—those outside had few ideas about their meaning or the rituals surrounding them, those inside were, quite literally, familiar: seen with intimate family connections.

However, the contemporary and costly mass-produced statues are distant from the original hand-carved monuments mentioned above. Perhaps the apologies have become less "heartfelt" for many today. The relatively new parlor systems at the heart of the contemporary dairy business may lead to "disenchantment" caused by the "iron cage of technology" (Maley 2004). That is to say, as with tractors and electricity in the past, alongside artificial insemination, medicated feed, and the parlor system in the present, such changes have weakened the magic, reduced the scope of the mysteries of farming, nature, and fate, all points addressed in the final chapter. Nonetheless, the division between human, cow, and the religious remains a somewhat hazy one for locals. As mega farms grow so do the size and costs of the religious icons and their upkeep. Dairy farmers pay a hefty price to maintain ties with Mr. Batō, and other religious markers, and unabashedly proclaim the belief that "he" and other icons are doing their job of providing security while unintentionally, perhaps, securing a novel local identity.

Conclusion

A final point regarding religion in Tokachi and becoming, belonging, and security draws the themes from this chapter together. There are few *butsudan* (a Buddhist altar used to memorialize the dead) and a great many multi-*shūkyō* (denomination) *hakaba* (cemeteries) in Tokachi. This is unlike the densely populated regions of Honshu, where *butsudan* seem to far outnumber *kamidana* (a Shinto spirit shelf). Simply put, Tokachi is home to more new beginnings than old stories for Japanese settlers, or even the descendants of Japanese settlers.[1] The nondenominational mixed graves in the area indicate that individuals from varying *shūkyō* (affiliated with community and location on Honshu) historically came to live in Tokachi—again in what could be seen as internal Japanese exile or even "ex-patriot" communities—bringing their own regional traditions and eventually dying together on the "frontier" of each Otherness in this north central periphery.

Both Gensan's *kannushi* and Matsuyama discussed these topics with me after the *kannushi* performed rituals installing a *kamidana* in Matsuyama's new home. The *kannushi* said that all Japanese were "shintoists" (his term) before Buddhists. He performed such religious rites for the purpose of promoting security and safety at the behest of many locals. After he left, the lo-sider Matsuyama hesitated: "Tabun, kamisama o shinjiteinai" (Maybe, I don't believe in animistic spirits), "demo boku wa nihonjin soshite taisetsu da to omoimasu" (but, I am Japanese [that's] why it is important). First, installing the *kamidana* in his new home was not done out of a select metaphysical faith but a faith in belonging. And second, as there had been a fire in the previous home on the site, the rites provided a feeling of *anshin* (safety and security). Again, like offering gifts to larger companies or having one's friend clap their hands at a Shinto shrine, there is a practical and individual hedging of bets involved here alongside a sense of belonging. In short, it seemed to him that it was the right thing to do. This act underscored a trinity of concerns: change, the start of a new life and home; Otherness, marking himself and his family's Japaneseness; and security, securing the home and family in place and from harm. This also served to establish his lo-sider, perhaps even through his son's *becoming* local, household by actively *making* it a part of the Gensan community. However, the majority of Gensan outsiders and dairy farmers do not have *kamidana*. They remain outsiders, male or female, and have a *butsudan* "back home"—wherever that home may be or be found.

Conclusion

On the Frontiers of Animal-Human-Technology

Introduction

The scope of this book has moved from the past to the present, and through macro, meso, and micro levels of analysis. From the history of *Ezo ga shima* imagined by its colonizers as an unsettled frontier, to the location being violently secured, "domesticated" as the north sea route, and internalized into the contemporary Japanese nation-state through a process of settler colonialism mirroring and even mimicking processes found, for example, in North America or Australia, Japan has had a history with many internal buffer zones and peripheries from Okinawa to Tohoku, but only one has been and popularly continues to be imagined as an Americanesque, "New World" frontier.

Hokkaido has thus long been viewed as a place of novel alterity, from wild Ezo to the settler-tamed north. In so becoming, it has been and continues to be a popular bulwark against an invented discourse of epic homogeneity. Hokkaido, more specifically northern Tokachi, is a place where people who did or do not fit this homogenizing discourse go or end up. Those hoping to stay and fit in must mesh with a *specific* Otherness rooted in a *specific* frontier imaginary. I have argued that dairy farming is a livelihood that well encapsulates both of these elements. This regional history has led to particular economic, political, military, and food security concerns long associated with Hokkaido. This came to its first modern culmination point with *wajin* settlers forming mixed farms with a largely symbiotic, now iconic, relationship to livestock, notably dairy cattle, in their attempts to secure lives on this island. Northern

243

Tokachi is at the center of this story, literally in topographic terms and figuratively being defined as "Milkland," the core of Hokkaido's dairy industry today. Thus, shifting notions of Otherness have always played a role in the history of Tokachi in terms of its geography, climate, and its human and nonhuman populations, a point well represented by the dairy industry and the policies and products associated with it. Underpinned by its past, I have highlighted ethnographically how rapid changes have happened over the last two decades in the Tokachi town of Gensan and on Grand Hopes Dairy Farm in terms of the shift to mega farming and its impacts. What remains to be discussed are two emergent "frontiers": technological frontiers and frontiers of living bodies. This shift to the micro and interpersonal (the personal also being bovine) underscores how dairy farmers secure, and become secure with, Other bodies, human and nonhuman.

Rotary parlor systems are the most popular shift from previous milking technologies in the area. While robotic milking technologies are even more advanced (Holloway 2007), at present this is not a popular adaptation in Tokachi, mainly due to the prohibitive cost and the large scale of existing farms. Developments in the area have built off of earlier systems like hand or herringbone milking systems (Dempster 1966). The increasingly wide adoption of rotary parlor milking systems has spurred the emergence of a host of interactions with Otherness in the workplace and community, including the escalation of human and bovine numbers to meet the demands of an industrializing dairy system. As in other regions and agricultural industries, this has meant a rise in the use of related technologies such as automated medical surveillance and artificial insemination (AI) (Blanchette 2020; Holloway 2005; Pachirat 2011; Novek 2012). This conclusion addresses this "change of heart" in the Tokachi dairy industry and how an assemblage of cow-human-technology is currently impacting, and may impact in the future, Otherness, posthuman cosmopolitics, and security in the region.

For the dairy owners the shift to a rotary parlor system is a high-stakes gamble on a high-tech solution. It involves taking on crushing debt, hired laborers, related technologies—from antibiotics to AI—and radically increased herd sizes in order for the system to be workable and, if lucky, pay off. This often requires legal partnerships with neighboring individuals in the community who might have radically differing notions of what is desirable in dairy farming as a livelihood or in the meaning of life full stop, a move beyond economic risks alone. It is the cause for numerous and competing individual searches for security, financial sure, but also physical, social, ontological, emotional, encompassing quests for personal identity, happiness, or meaning—in a word, *ikigai* (Hasegawa et al. 2020).

Below I assess how rotary parlor systems divorce owners and their families from daily embodied relations with their cows and their local human community. Dairy farmers are increasingly pushed from a former way of life and pulled toward being industrial surveyors and managers of "stock": technology, bovines, and humans. Concomitantly, the many nonrural outsiders, lo-siders, and no-siders they employ are now the ones in the daily "contact zone . . . a space of becoming with" radical Other bovine bodies (Haraway 2008, 35–36; Nancy 2000). Links between the panoptic gaze and animal husbandry have been examined by many researchers (cf. Blanchette 2020; Grasseni 2005; Holloway 2005; Novek 2012; Shukin 2009), focusing on the sectioning of animal bodies into functional parts or the progressive "disassociation" of the whole animal or whole processes into desired parts, images, and outcomes. Similar to Sarah Franklin's well-known work on sheep cloning, the focus is on how husbandry technology "pulls bodies apart," so to speak, and reconstructs them through aesthetic or scientific judgment, ways of seeing related to ways of rationalizing (Franklin 2008). Such a process of functional individuation is important in what follows, but its application is different. I argue that the rotary parlor system is *itself* an individuating regime (Gillespie 2018; Porcher 2011) designed to be clinically, and I conclude chronically, rationalizing. This system is part of a larger assemblage of panoptic power (Foucault 1977). The panopticon was a prison design first envisioned in 1791 by philosopher Jeremy Bentham to surveil and discipline in order to cost-effectively reform criminals—the bodies and minds of social Others. Herein, the logic remains the same, but the subject has shifted from criminals to the bodies of workers, both human and bovine.

I draw upon Gilles Deleuze and Félix Guattari (and others influenced by their work) to better explain the micro linkages between human and nonhuman animal in this technological environment, an environment of "becoming-animal" wherein the blurring of embodiments and identities across species' lines, or lines of flight (beings as constant becomings), are not genealogical (Deleuze and Guattari 1987; Hansen 2014b). Instead, these are

> like an abstract immense Abstract Machine, abstract yet real
> and individual; its pieces are the various assemblages and

individuals, each of which groups together an infinity of particles entering into an infinity of more or less interconnected relations . . . [technology and its rational ordering are] . . . a fixed plane, upon which things are distinguished from one another only by speed and slowness . . . not a unity of substance but the infinity of the modifications . . . [becomings] . . . that are part of one another. (Deleuze and Guattari 1987, 254)

Such a notion of interconnection best represents the workings at the contemporary heart of dairy farming, the rotary parlor and its many dependent and interrelated flows of information, macro and micro biology, and finance: it is, I contend, an "animal-human-machine" assemblage, an apparatus wherein taken-for-granted ontologies, and so ontological security, are under question; for example, in terms of socially constructed identities, such as owner and worker or outsider and lo-sider, but its functioning also complicates, meshes *and* flattens, what divides human, cow, and machine. Such embodied frontiers are made slippery, contextual, and contingent by the functioning and logic of the rotary parlor milking system.

Much as Bentham's drive was utilitarian, to bring the greatest good to the public via prison reform, the rationale of rotary parlor construction is to simplify the burden of getting the most milk efficiently and safely. Yet, outlined below, add to such noble intentions a general neoliberal climate of acquisitive progress and unintended consequences emerge. As noted, today, the skills to be a dairy farm worker are generally not learned through human social practices or ethical guidance. The notion of apprenticeship or collegiality is absent; there is no esprit de corps to speak of. For most workers industrial dairy farming is not a long-term employment option and few seek to perfect their skills through carefully observed practice as an artisan or craftsperson might. Moreover, work time is spent "around" and not "with" people. Time is largely spent with the Otherness of machines and sentient nonhumans. And in many cases, but especially during the process of milking as outlined below, technology determines the quality and quantity of time a given worker spends with both humans and bovines.

Similar shifts of industrialization and deskilling in animal–human relationships are witnessed in other "live-stock" (or bio-capital to invoke Shukin [2009]) industries. Vialles documents changes in French abattoirs, where the focus of prolonged training to produce individuals skilled in the practice of producing the best cuts of meat has, through progressive industrialization, led to a situation where "the logic of the craftsman has ceased to exist . . . except in the smallest abattoirs" (Vialles 1994, 69). This is also the case in terms of genetics in bovine husbandry, wherein the former focus on understanding the visual and tactile aesthetics of animal bodies, as a link to their reproductive or meat-productive capabilities, is shifting to an internal scientific gaze of understanding and manipulating genetic codes (Holloway 2005). Animal behaviorist Temple Grandin documents the industrialization of livestock handling in America—including the concomitant shift from knowledgeable handlers to underpaid high-turnover workers—and the impact on animal safety, security, and even productivity: interesting and controversial is the fact that she is a high-functioning autistic who claims that this particular embodiment allows her to affectively understand nonhuman suffering more acutely and accurately than other researchers (Grandin 2009, 141–172). Reliance on undertrained staff and technology unsettles—makes insecure—human identities related to hard-earned employment skills in such industries, a point similarly made in Sennett's work on automation in bakeries and IBM corporate downsizing (Sennett 1998). An excellent example of this human devaluation in relation to animals, not objects, can be found in English champion horse breeding. Rebecca Cassidy concludes that artificial insemination is seen as a threat to the constructed identities of those at the core of the industry, such as expert breeders (Cassidy 2002, 169–170).

What follows underscores how industrial dairy farming in Gensan is undergoing both similar and dissimilar transitions. One interesting outcome of the change to rotary parlor systems is that while owners and farm families are ever-increasingly divorced from contact with their cows—Others they know very well—they are faced with a new "frontier" of human Others they often have a hard time understanding: workers from outside the community. Simultaneously, while many temporary workers are perhaps more comfortable than some older farmers in high-tech surroundings, they are confronted with cows as a new "frontier" of embodiment and agency. Often this presents itself in moments of human-bovine suffering and recognition, daily shared intervals of disenchantment and reenchantment where a nonhuman becomes a more empathetic agent than humans (Blanchette 2020; Gillespie 2018; Pachirat 2011; Porcher

2011). This presents a final notion of the frontier well beyond geopolitics or novel cultural products, it is the micro frontier of the embodied human interface with cows and technology.

Inside the Animal-Human-Machine

Rotary parlors are increasingly common on industrial dairy farms in Tokachi. The American designed BouMatic Daytona rotary dairy parlor found at Grand Hopes Farm was at the cutting edge of such milking technology when installed.[1] It is the centerpiece, again the heart, of its operation. What follows is a brief explanation of how the rotary parlor functions followed by an in-depth description of the individual relationships shared among people and cows related to this technology. Importantly, it is via engagement with the parlor that the central function of dairy farming is achieved, the extraction of milk. There is no avoiding this process. It is also the site of the most singular embodied engagement with posthuman or more-than-human cosmopolitics, Otherness and insecurity. Whether working the morning, afternoon, or evening milking shift, a wide range of humans and hundreds of individual, and highly individuated, bovine Others enter the system. For approximately three hours two or three times a day all encounter a technologically integrated building designed for maximum efficiency and rationality in producing entwined flows of liquid, lives, and capital.

In one sense, the rotary machine and its accompanying advanced technology can be viewed as a great equalizer, albeit an ultimately negative one. On any given shift the *shachō* might be working alongside, literally doing the exact same work as, any of the parlor workers past, present, and into the foreseeable future. For example, Takuto, Ichiro, Tsutomu, Haru, and the Tokyo Cowboy were all regular workers in the parlor. The Chinese staff nearly exclusively worked in parlor positions. And while Tarō-san was the *buchō* in charge of the parlor at my time of employment, Kunio-san took over his role and, if needed, other department heads, even Yukiko or Matsuyama, could fill in. But what workers became equal partners in, as will be shown, was not a sense of shared workplace solidarity but an even more intense sense of individual alienation. Humans were effectively (and affectively) separated from each other. And, in addition to being codified, cattle were individuated from their herds, from their offspring, even from their body parts, all to fit the logic of this "abstract machine" to return to the framing of Deleuze and Guattari above (1987). Abstract here is not to be understood as somehow "unreal," but in the sense of abstract*ing* or making life purely numerical (Hansen 2018b, 2020a). Their information was collected by equipment, stored by equipment, and equipment was often a key agent governing the life of a particular cow, from insemination to extermination.

Upon first sight (see figure C.1), this rotary parlor looks more at home in a science fiction film than in a rural barn.[2] Made of metal,

Figure C.1. A view of the fully loaded rotary parlor. Cattle enter at twelve o'clock and exit by backing out of the apparatus at eleven o'clock (the gate seen to the left). The space between 11:00 and 12:00 is where the holding worker stands above the other workers able to view the full rotation of the equipment. Photo used with permission of the farm.

plastic hoses, and blinking digital readouts, the parlor steadily rotates clockwise. It is designed to milk, in a constant flow, fifty cows. Holstein cows are generally 680 kilograms (1,500 pounds) and 1.45 meters (four and a half feet) at the shoulder that produce an average of 27.3 liters (six-odd gallons) of milk per day. The equipment fills a twenty by twenty meter (approximately sixty square foot) room. The machine and these mammals are massive. When combined they become an impressive and somewhat intimidating sight.

The milking process functions as follows. A holding worker first guides the cows into the rotating parlor. As cows enter a Chromalloy stall on the parlor platform, a worker standing on a concrete floor below the platform, at approximate udder to eye level, cleans each teat with an iodine solution excreted from a pneumatic wand. Parlor workers do not actually touch cows as all contact between human and cow is mediated by equipment during the milking process. The next pair of workers are "milkers" and they function in tandem. They adjust the pneumatic suction head that automatically rises from the base of the machine to udder level and attach the four suction hoses to each teat while checking for any leg bands that indicate sickness or dysfunctional udders. After attaching four hoses they push a button that, from a sensor attached to each animal's collar, sends the sort number, group number, and a record of each animal's daily milk output to a central computer (as seen in figure C.2). During this stage of the milking process human and animal contact averages less than eighteen seconds. The cattle cannot see the workers and workers only encounter cow and machine as segmented: as bovine legs, udders, suction equipment, and a digital readout of cattle numbers. For a third of a minute each cow becomes an unpredictable and frustrating part of the equipment, possibly standing on inattentive workers hands or releasing their formidable bowels overhead (see figure C.3).

In this relentlessly repetitive process, the boundary between "it" the machine and "it" as an animal, a living, thinking, feeling creature is blurred by their merging into joined parts of a massive moving techno-human-bovine assemblage. Barring cattle kicking off the suction head, the device is set to automatically release when the flow speed of milk reaches a threshold set in common for all cows, much in the way the parlor's rotational speed is set in common for all workers. When the threshold is reached it automatically drops below the parlor floor again ready for the next cow.

Figure C.4 is a diagram of how a parlor functions and a description of work station roles. The third job is the "runner." They act as a fast-

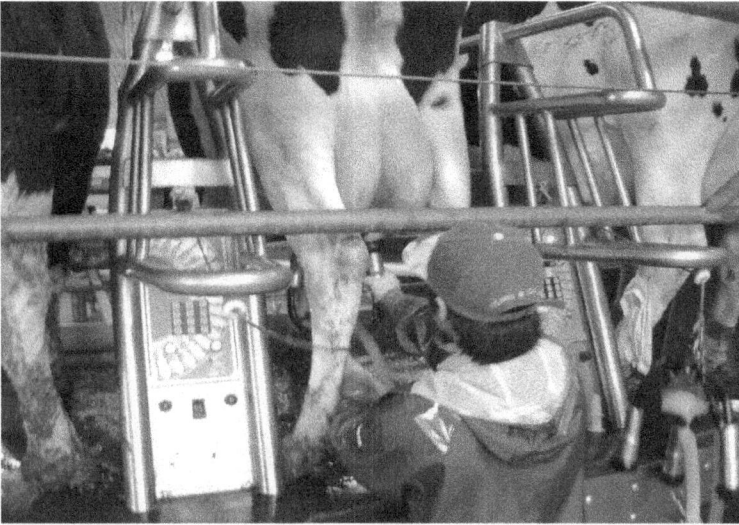

Figure C.2. A gloved and rain-suited worker attaching the pneumatic milking head. The digital readout, detached milking head, and a green leg band can be seen in the stall to the right. Photo by the author.

Figure C.3. Haru cleaning an unloaded parlor stall. She was infamous at the farm for being a poor judge of when a cow might defecate. This photo shows the eye-level view of the parlor floor, the aforementioned equipment, and rather graphically underscores the obvious link between bodies, fluids, and flows—human, animal, and machine. Photo by the author.

Cow's exit point to inner holding area. This is the route to return to stalls or move on to medical care. Disinfecting teats and communication with holding worker

Cow entry point having come from the stall area to the outer holding area. Selecting speed and cleaning of teats.

Parlour

The runner reattaching equipment and listening for workers requesting help.

Two workers applying the pneumatic devices to the teats.

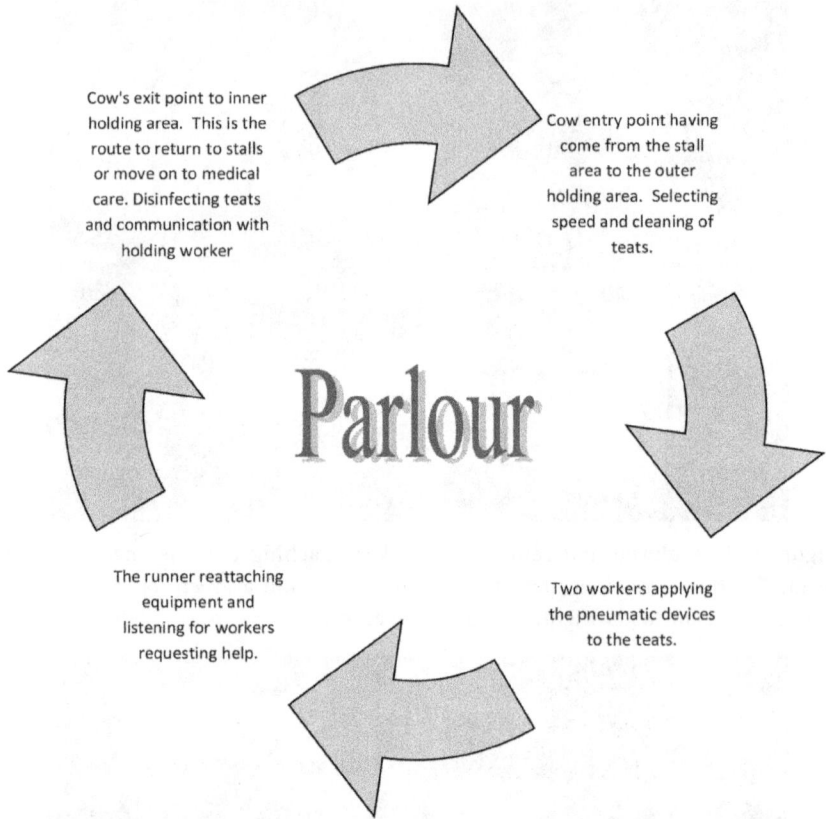

Figure C.4. A model of parlor workers' stations and roles. Diagram created by the author.

paced troubleshooter reattaching equipment that the animals kick free, administering antibiotic injections, or assisting coworkers falling behind who yell for their help over the loud pneumatic staccato of *thuck, thuck, thuck* and the constant gushing flow of hundreds of liters of milk flowing into stainless steel holding tanks. The last parlor worker applies a final iodine solution to combat infection and liaises with the holding worker standing above. Communication is short and functional, for example, they may shout out "owari" (done) indicating the last cow of a group or call out the number of a single animal in need of medical attention, mastitis, lesions, and lameness being the most common ailments discovered during milking.

When the cows are milked, ideally in under one revolution (as slow milking cows retard the efficiency by needing a second turn) they exit the parlor. They back out of the stall and move past the aforementioned holding area worker, whose purpose is to maintain a steady flow of cattle into and out of the system. The holding worker generally acts as an observer, only intermittently called into action with exiting cows. They are generally most concerned with the cattle entering the parlor with the aid of a twenty-meter-long (sixty foot) automated gate (as seen in figure C.5).

The gate electronically senses the lack of cattle body weight impeding its forward progress and pushes ahead until it contacts an animal. Cattle in such cramped conditions naturally move to where there is more space, specifically, the space ahead where cows have already entered the parlor access chute. However, more reluctant cows, often young cattle fearful of the noise and bright lights of the parlor, are manually, often violently, prodded along—usually through twisting their tails or hitting them with a taped aluminum baton, a section of ski pole—so as to keep

Figure C.5. One automatic gate and one cattle group (actually stretching to the right farther than one can make out from this vantage point) waiting for afternoon milking. Photo by the author.

pace with the machine and allow as few "free stalls" as possible. Again, in most cases this "hinge" between the parlor and stall area was the author's work station.

On their return from being milked in the parlor the cattle pass through holding on route to the stall area where, for the purpose of efficient collection and cleaning, groups of around two hundred cattle are housed in rows of concrete and metal stalls with rubber and rice chaff covered floors. At the entrance to the stall return chute each cow's sensor is read a final time by the equipment. And at this point a holding worker can choose to separate cow or an automated gate may have been set to separate cattle whose numbers are entered earlier into the central computer by the office staff, for instance cows known to be ill or cattle moving to another group due to the stage of pregnancy. But these animals can also automatically be separated without human intervention. Determined by fluctuations in individual milk output the machine has recorded, the system itself separates cows it deems to be irregular or due to be inseminated.

Liquid materials and motions were central to everything on the farm. Indeed, even the rotary engine of the machine itself was run off of hydraulics. Cattle and humans would flow in and out through this machine three times a day. Milk would be extracted while cattle would urinate or defecate on workers and equipment, which would then be cleaned with gallons of water to prepare for the next flow of cattle.

Being a Cow, Becoming Cattle

Putting parlor technology aside for the moment, one ought to consider contemporary dairy cows as a product of human technology. For hundreds of years cows have been strategically bred, and more recently engineered, to increase both milk production and docility. The Holstein is widely accepted as the greatest milk producer in the world. But, of course, they are not *just* equipment, not mere units of production, "cattle are social animals in the fullest sense of the word, with complex communication channels and alleomimicry exhibited in many behaviors" (Phillips 2002, 84). This can also be noted with other domesticated animals, common companions such as cats or dogs (Haraway 2003; Oliver 2003), or horses, pigs, and chickens (Grandin 2009). The complete range of these behaviors and their individualistic expression is well beyond the scope of these final pages, but in short, through strong matrilineal ties (for example, cow and calf separated by a fence will fight to remain in visual contact), through voice and through rational thought (Hurley and Nudds 2006) and through their particular embodiment—especially mimicry, head, and tail expression:

> Cattle live in hierarchically ranked groups and begin to order themselves within the group at a young age. . . . Physical communication and grooming help to establish this social ranking. What may appear to be a game, such as head-butting or shoving, is actually a method of determining which animals within the group are dominant. Interestingly, the strongest or most dominant animals do not necessarily become the leaders. . . . Cattle in a small herd, for instance, will join with up to three other animals to form a small group of friends. The animals in the group will spend most of their time together, frequently grooming and licking each other. . . . And, like most animals, cattle also experience strong emotions such as pain, fear, and anxiety. (US Humane Society 2003)

As a thought experiment in anthropomorphism, I ask the reader to remove the word *cattle* in the above text and replace it with *the Japanese* and extract the word *animal* replacing it with *person, exchange head-butting and shoving* with *bowing,* and remove *licking.* Now, reread the description. It sounds remarkably similar to older conceptions of "the Japanese" discussed in previous chapters: communicative, socialized or "groomed" to respect groups and hierarchy, forming tight-knit friendships among similar-aged cohorts. I am not, I hope obviously, making the claim that Japanese are akin to cows! The point is that comparisons between human and animal social relationships *can and ought to be made.* Anthropomorphism is not anthropocentrism. With some comedic license, this description mirrors an essentialist vision of a human community for good reason; cows are a lot more like humans than humans often consider them to be. At a minimum, they are sensitive and sentient creatures. And essential in what follows, they were often the only living beings that many human workers were regularly able to spend time with at Grand Hopes Farm.

Milking, as noted above, is a particular process in terms of contact and certainly the most dependent on technological prosthesis. Within this system both cows and humans become like chattel, property, the etymological root of the word *cattle*. Below I outline how both were harmed, mentally, socially, and physically by the systematic abuses and individuation of the rotary parlor system, a system that separates living beings from their ascribed status, but also their physical and social needs. Mega dairy farming in Hokkaido is not alone in such abuses. Conducting a discourse analysis of South African ranching communities, Les Mitchell concludes that modern mega ranching practices lead to a language (found in farm and science journals and magazines for example) of production, science, enslavement, and achievement and concludes "that in all these discourses animals are objectified—treated as production machines, objects for scientific study or manipulation, or personal property. There is an attempt to create distance between human and animal, thereby preventing the drawing of parallels or any relation of empathy" (Mitchell 2006, 55). If positioned outside such a discourse and machine, and kept in pasture conditions, cows form close ties with other beings. This includes sheep or donkeys with which they can graze without conflict. Due to their daily contact with human handlers, dairy cows view stockholders as herd leaders. They come when called, remember different handlers, and engage in affective behaviors, such as licking or nudging, with humans much as they do with other cattle. However, the life of a cow in the rotary parlor system differs considerably from these pastoral descriptions.

So as not to be caught up in the parlor equipment or injure themselves at play in the close quarters or on the concrete floors required by this mode of production, horns are cut off, tails are docked, and occasionally hind legs are bound to prevent splaying on the many slippery surfaces they encounter that their hooves are not designed to tread upon.

Thus, adult "play" and mimicry, along with the animal's instinctive ability to "swish" flies away or express emotive states with their tail is restricted or abolished to become more "machine" friendly. Upon birth calves are separated and weaned in pens where they not only lose contact with their mother but also are unable to play with their cohorts. The reason is threefold: calves consume their mother's milk (the end goal of the parlor), diseases can quickly be isolated, and if need be, their lives terminated, and calves cannot enter the spatially individuated system with their dams. At four or five months of age calves do begin to associate with other calves, but not with adult cattle. This reduces their ability to mimic appropriate adult behaviors or understand their roles within the hierarchy of a herd. This leads to inter-cow violence that follows them into their adult life as the parlor system requires, for the sake of efficiency, that groups determined by milk output and stage of impregnation be shifted almost daily. However, even "minor changes [in herd composition] result in an approximate doubling of aggression activity for about 24 hours, longer if dominant cattle are introduced to a stable group when cattle may continue fighting for 30 to 45 days as they create a new social order" (Phillips 2002, 118). Thus, despite attention to maintaining their productive capacities, stress is an obvious by-product of the parlor system and tangibly seen in the many badly scarred animals from excessive mounting displays in cramped quarters to determine dominance. Finally, to accord with mass scale efficiency, female cattle, shortly after a year of life, are artificially inseminated and kept in a constant cycle of impregnation until their premature deaths: on average after six years. Barren cattle are rendered after three attempts at impregnation. Male cattle usually spend a year "fattening" on or near the farm before being shipped and rendered elsewhere. For both bovine sexes, a high-protein feed of mixed corn silage—not grass or hay—causes painful bloating in the stomachs of ruminants, occasionally causing one of their four stomachs to rise agonizingly, killing the cow. But space is at a premium and collecting cows to milk must keep pace with the parlor. Given these demands, natural grazing is seldom an option.

Bovine Lessons in Becoming Human

As alluded to above, what follows underscores some similarities between cows and humans in regard to their relationships with contemporary rotary parlor milking technology. The human ability to imagine another's "being and becoming," human or cow, is an empathetic or affective endeavor and these concepts will be expanded upon in the final section.

The rotary parlor system bears more than a passing resemblance to the aforementioned panopticon prison design. Indeed, it can be thought of as a cross-species or posthuman reading of panoptic control and discipline. In both systems each "inmate" is codified, numbered, and individuated, with their individual progress mapped and stored in a central repository. Relations between kept and keeper are, ideally, dehumanized—distant, cold, and clinical. Understanding how the system functions underscores that human designers have learned about bovine bodies in a highly enlightenment-oriented way: the scientific gaze. These are systems of control, or literally in both cases, systems of securing, wherein the keepers watch and regulate the kept with the inability of the latter to witness or resist the surveillance. Beyond *Discipline and Punish* (1977) one can see this mode of thinking about the play of "to be secure" and "securing" in other works by Foucault, for example in "Society Must Be Defended" (1976) or *Herculine Barbin* (1980). The purpose, in all cases, is to produce re-formed "docile bodies"—normative bodies useful to society. Finally, in both systems there is dissolution of hierarchies beyond the distant one of keeper and kept. Jailers like prisoners—and workers like cattle—could be replaced with no effect on the functioning of the system.

Taxonomic species' separations are, of course, enforced and negotiated by humans but anthropomorphizing is an equally common human trait. Cows are not human, but they are comparable to humans (Asquith and Kalland 1997; Calarco 2008, 144–148; Wolfe in Cavell et al. 2008, 1–41). This is unsurprising as throughout history nonhuman animals have lived alongside humans, and indeed historically some people on what were considered "frontiers" by people from outside those locations have been considered less than human, for example, the First Nations people of Canada or the Ainu in Japan. Cows, as noted in the previous section, form lifelong social groups, they play, they are mammalian, and they clearly feel and express pleasure and pain. Cows have "personalities" and like human individuals they have distinctive and often memorable individual endowments (capabilities) and embodiments (Hansen 2014b, 2018b). Such facts have been clearly articulated in research focused on companion animals, which need not be "pets," more than research on livestock (deVedas 2002, 535; Fudge 2008; Kete 1994). However, this focus is changing (Gillespie 2018; Weiss 2016). At the least, human and cow do share affective resonances (Porcher 2011).

Tim Ingold rightly points out: "Both humans and animals . . . can be virtually reduced to a machine existence through the systematic repression of their powers of autonomous action," their freedom to act and play (Ingold 2000, 307). He concludes that "machines have not so much made as been made *by* history, one in which human beings, to an ever-increasing extent, have become the authors of their own dehumanization" (311, emphasis Ingold's). The rotary parlor provides an excellent example of this. The shift to rotary system technology at Great Hopes Farm among others, and by extension the impact of this technology on the town of Gensan, is at the heart of more-than-human social hierarchies being called into question. I have outlined "docilization" effects of the parlor process of production on bovine bodies, but it is similar for human workers. Due to the increasing prevalence of parlor systems, human inter-actions with Others have numerically increased. But human interactions are increasingly superficial. Due to the demands of the parlor, the long and irregular hours for example, as noted in this book most workers remain peripheral in each other's lives, with only a select few integrating into the local community. Dairy work was what people at Grand Hopes Farm had in common, and what was increasingly commonplace was the individualizing nature of such work from human social practices. Thus, both human and bovine were forced to contend with rapid changes in their social community and increasing interactions with Otherness both within and across species demarcations. Put plainly, shifting herds, like shift-working humans, were pushed together, making their former social hierarchies uncertain and violence common. And this is not "particular" to Gensan, it has been witnessed in other areas where industrial farming and community hollowing have taken hold, with perhaps the US being the depressing vanguard (cf. Blanchette 2020; Porcher 2011).

Through the attempt to keep pace in the daily ritual dance with the parlor, stress and violence are produced by the system itself. For example, natural embodied processes are hindered and in the case of both cows and humans, nutrition and sleep are compromised. Workers' capabilities, two or four legged, were strained to keep pace with the equipment. As noted above, cows fare poorly in this situation, their bodies altered and abused to fit the logic of the machine and not the logic of their being. However, one can make a lesser but similar argument about repetitive motion inju-ries in the human element of the animal-human-machine assemblage. In discussing human ailments with Dr. Oda, he told me that nerve and tendon damage in arms and necks were regular complaints for rotary parlor workers, alongside the occasional broken bone, depression, and exhaustion. Again, the doctor was convinced that many outside workers suffered from mental problems before arriving in Hokkaido, and that their initial desire to work on a dairy was guided by a romantic pastoral image of Hokkaido, a yearning for a more-than-human animal bond. The rotary system promotes very different more-than-human contact, however. Indeed, it is the antithesis to sentient connection. Through the isolating ritual dance of this machine-human-bovine assemblage, a daily presence, workers quickly became disillusioned with their rural dreams of pastoral romance. A place often initially seen as an escape from "typical" Japan soon left them socially isolated with arduous, meaningless, and poorly paid work. Their depression, alienation, and any problems with physical well-being were surely exacerbated and not aided. This is because during the *actual* functioning of the parlor system there is no need for humans to skillfully observe, record, or consider bovine bodies or human coworkers beyond a basic question: Are they doing what they should in accord with their idealized role in the milking process? During milking there is little human or animal control over the pace of the dance. Avenues of resistance are minimal and there is no immediate responsibility for animal or coworker. The technology functions in terms of its programmed norms of size and speed. Living elements are attached as though they are animate prosthesis to this equipment, not the reverse, and are forced to adjust their "shared" biological needs—the need for sleep, food, or free movement—to preset mechanical rhythms: the pneumatic and hydraulic "heartbeat" of BouMatic.

Thus, problems and irregularities while milking cannot easily be compensated for. The process is rooted in overlapping levels of standardization including the model size or speed of its living components. To stop the machine is to stop the ritual dance, to halt the entire highly stratified and territorialized process of milking. One's responsibility, imposed on humans, and in turn often violently imposed on cows, is to keep the machine moving at the expense of the sentient. A few brave workers, often those who had come from smaller family farms, would refuse to violently force animals to comply, despite the pace of the equipment and despite the anger and taunts of fellow workers who were keen to just get the milking over with. Most workers became somewhat indifferent, complicit slaves to the pace determined by the parlor technology. Like many of my coworkers, while forcing cattle to move I too twisted tails until I felt them break in my hand, I cut and cauterized horns, and I hit panicking cattle to conform to the logic of the parlor system. Such embodied actions had affective consequences, again what I would call an assemblage of cosmopolitical suffering. Personally, I was not made insecure by the metaphysical haunting of bovine souls like the aforementioned farm owners, but I had gory and disturbing nightmares of tails breaking off in my hands and, though a lover of beef and dairy, I was unable to drink milk even months after fieldwork. This posthuman triad of cow-human-technology left its physical and psychological imprint on me, and as noted below, on other coworkers as well. Many have commented on the similarities between concentration camps and industrial agriculture (Wolfe in Cavell et al. 2008, 43–90; Esposito 2008). However, in terms of industrial dairy farming one is not "forced" to be abusive through "just following human orders" per se, but being hypnotized into a particular tempo of place, the techno-rhythm and shared dance of rational production, hour after hour and day after day and, for some, year after year.

Of course, local owners are not unaware or indifferent. They are insecure about their economic futures. They are led to believe that agriculture is ever in crisis (Hansen 2014a) and trapped in what Terry Maley, building off Weber's iron cage of rationality, calls the "iron cage of technology" (Maley 2004): in essence, the belief that problems stemming from technological advancements can only be checked by advancing increasingly complex technological solutions that cause further problems. Take, for example, the catch-22 crisis of not being able to produce enough feed, the need to import feed, leading to the then imported post-cow crisis of having too much manure to spread on the land that, ipso facto, is not large enough to produce enough feed. Existing in the political, social, ecological, and economically insecure industry and environment highlighted in this book, owners are foremost entranced in a form of speed politics—what Paul Virilio has called dromocratic progress—the belief that increased speed itself equals progress (Virilio 2007, 70). And the ever-increasing pace is mechanically forced upon their workers two and four legged.

Industrial farm life was a daily drama with an ever-shifting cast of unknown Others. And each individual had their own individual history, desires, projects, and projections for the future. Each was a unique constellation impossible to reduce into a concrete or meaningful "type" without doing significant violence to each individuated ethnographic "reality." However, while the logic of the parlor divorced human and cow alike during milking, its logic brought them together in daily contact outside of the parlor in other areas of the farm. And often specific cows played a key role in a particular dairy worker's life. As seen below, in the face of the relentless rational logic at the frontier of dairy technology, there was resistance. Outside the parlor anomie shifts. Outside the parlor the daily dance is not a tightly controlled courtly ritual, but a negotiated and affect saturated sharing of movements and moments across a species frontier.

Unlikely Enchantments: Dancing Outside the Panoptic Gaze

Dancing might seem an odd description for human–cow relations, but in fact one had to learn to read the body movements of bovine partners.

Failure to do so could occasionally result in embarrassment or minor inju-ries. Like all awkward dance partners, this usually only meant stepped-on toes or bruised egos from misreading a cue in front of others. But severity could escalate; being urinated on, bruises, having the wind knocked out of you, and sprains were common occurrences and grossly misjudging the movement of a cow could potentially be lethal. However, the movements of their massive bodies soon became predictable for most workers previ-ously unfamiliar with these animals. Their first weeks of skittish cringing and proclamations of *kowai kowai* (scary), gave way to silent movements and knowledgeable expectations. Workers would learn to "read" their nonhuman dance partners and soon understood that moving slowly to the left would cause a cow to veer right. Catching them required a similar knack, and much of this was the ability to predict, to *read*, bodies rather than futilely try to outmuscle or outthink them. For new workers, cows were the best teachers, certainly the most consistent. Cows generally knew where they ought to be in their daily dance and they knew where a given worker should be as well. For example, clearing them from stalls was easy. They often began exiting a stall when they saw a worker with a shovel but would remain still if no shovel was in sight. If one was late spreading out silage in the morning, a line of fifty cattle would face that worker with big brown eyes that seemed to imply, "Hey, glad you didn't forget."

More to the point, most socially well-adjusted humans know that understandings can be shared and communicated, including with peo-ple who may look different and perhaps cannot communicate through a shared language. What is shared is pathos. "The biopolitics of otherness must here be understood as an extreme reduction of the social to the biological; the body appears to be the ultimate refuge of humanity" (Fassin 2001, 5). Ichiro, Haruko, and even the rather brash Takuto all confided that they saw similarities between themselves and cows. They "under-stood" them and could "regard the pain" of these bovine others as their own (Sontag 2003). These daily workmates were not tourist brochure cows beckoning one to buy ice cream, they were warm bodies with methane smells, distinctive calls, and distinctive individual traits. They were, in a word, real.

Recall that, just before mysteriously quitting the farm, Ichiro claimed that his greatest desire on his last day would be, if possible, directed toward the majority of others he worked with. He wished that he could set all the cattle free. Outside the hyperrationality of the rotary system, becoming bovine meant crossing a species boundary—if only occasionally, incompletely, and affectively. In an interesting contrast to Blanchette's work, whereby seeing oneself as the animal other was a form of self-deprecation as an animal-like outsider (2020, 80–85) or the fulfillment of masculine or feminine ideals (91–103). At Grand Hopes Farm, and outside its mechanical heart, it was to commiserate in shared alienation, understanding that the world of the farm was, in a tangible and embodied sense, a place of common suffering for creatures that were perhaps not so very different after all, human, cow, Japanese, Chinese, local, or newcomer (Gillespie 2018; Porcher 2011).

Nearing, the end of my research, and hoping to somehow qualify my own feelings and quantify those of others, I began to ask what coworkers thought of particular cows. I sought to produce a kind of posthuman, cosmopolitical, or multispecies ethnographic record, to produce single numbers and narratives out of over 1,700 four-legged and nonverbal candidates. I baited coworkers with information about specific cows that had somehow "entered my life"—moved beyond the epiphenomena of "bare life"—on the farm (Esposito 2008). For example, taking a cow that I thought looked unique or a cow that had given me a playful nudge on a rough day, I would ask, "347 no bango ushi wa dou desu ka" (How about that cow number 347?) or, "Tokubetsu na ushi ga imasu ne" (She's a special cow hey?). For some coworkers these were very odd questions indeed and the reply was a tilted head and "Ehh, dou iu imi?" (What on earth do you mean?) or "ma, nai desuyo" (ahm . . . no) with a facial expression underscoring curiosity, not about a particular cow but my state of mind. Yet, despite the distancing technology of the rotary parlor, the sheer quantity of cattle on the farm, the limited time workers were able to spend with any particular cow, and the use of random numbers to identify them, a surprising number of cows, for a surprising variety of reasons, were remembered and discussed by farmworkers.

This is interesting in and of itself, but more interesting were the reasons why one particular cow might be memorable and another not. Of course, some were known to most of the workers. Many workers remembered the numbers or physical features of some animals—cow 138 was very large, cow 614 was tricolored—or recalled specific cows for practical reasons—cow 1028 was a slow-milking cow—but many remembered cows that others did not, ones "standing out from the herd" for them. Such selections were often highly individual and personal; cows that the workers had "shared a moment with," a moment of becoming animal, of crossing an ontic boundary, becoming memorably "touched" physically and/or affectively. For me, 603 would insist on being the last cow to enter the parlor and would always rest her heavy head on my shoulder while waiting. A bit uncomfortable at first, I grew to enjoy, even look forward to, her cud-chewing sour mash breath, power, and decisive knowledge, daily choosing the exact moment to leave me, walk ten meters down the chute to the entrance of the parlor while rarely missing an open stall as the last cow. Workers had cows that would follow *only* them, or others that they just liked the look of, or the first cow they caught, and so on. There was, in short, a very "personal," a very individual link with significant nonhuman others outside the parlor. And in some cases, this surely seemed to be a two-way link. These were not "pets," but nor were they distant machinelike creatures.

In essence, while the parlor was the locus of speed politics and disenchantment, other areas of the farm were places for possible reenchantment—of seeing individual animals, like people, animated with identities and "person"-alities. Did these random connections offer the "skinship" that Dr. Oda claimed the young workers were searching for? Did it aid with their individual voyages of *iyashi* (healing)? I cannot say with certainty, but on more than one occasion, coworkers claimed that they preferred to be with cows over the humans that they shared their days with. Again, these human relationships were often difficult. When I left the farm on my final day of work, I did not say goodbye to many of my coworkers—this was not rude but a common practice among distant no-siders, outsiders, and even lo-siders—yet, I did go out of my way to pat 603's neck one last time.

Conclusion

The rotary parlor system can be viewed as a collection point in examining how a more-than-human, posthuman, or cosmopolitical sense of Otherness and each otherness emerges in searches for security that conjoin from the macro level to the community and micro level through expanding the concept of "the frontier" to include the porous frontiers of and boundaries of individual bodies and their engagement with personal cross-species histories and with technology. Aspects of the rotary parlor system can be seen as panoptic emphasizing how this technology enhances the individuation of animal and human bodies. Simultaneously, it underscores how this alienating technology also draws humans and cows into empathetic or affective "each Otherness" relationships based on embodied encounters and understandings outside the parlor.

Rotary parlor technology is symbolic of the chronic chrono-logic of rationalization that besets not just Hokkaido's dairy industry and agricultural policy in Japan but industrializing agriculture in other frontier zones outlined above. Fear of Otherness on a macro or national scale is reflected in the quest for security, the "need" to secure human and animal to a series of standardizing regimes that physically, technically, socially, and in terms of policy, nationally refuse to allow for novelty or Otherness that has been ever-present, and is indeed increasingly present, at the micro, meso, and macro levels. In Hokkaido the image of symbiotic production remains a popular nostalgic relic. Dairy products, dairy cattle, and dairy farmers become nostalgia saturated standardized images and are fetishized as consumable commodities. Such imaginings are central in Tokachi's pantheon of symbols: a local epic story perhaps. When driving in the area one is constantly reminded with fiberglass ice cream cones, cartoon cattle issuing invitations, and signs for tourist milk farms that they are in "Milkland Hokkaido," a particular place of internal alterity. But I wish more would pause and ask a simple question that has been at the core of this book: Where are the *actual* cows and dairy farmers? The mural depicted in figure C.6 begs this question much in the way that the artist's rendition of the photo seen in figure I.2 interrogates the actual Hokkaido dairy farm. Are dairy farms and farmers found in the idealized rural imaginary, the reality of the parlor floor, or somewhere in between, with the livelihoods of particular individuals always becoming and negotiating the cosmopolitical connections of frontiers from the imagined geopolitical to the embodied cross-species and interpersonal?

First, dairy farmers are diverse. Within the local agricultural community there is a growing divide, and animosity, between pro- and anti-industrialization farmers and townspeople. There is a split between farm owners who are and who are not able (or indeed willing or not willing) to industrialize. The smallest farm I encountered with a rotary parlor system in Tokachi had over three hundred head, dwarfed by Grand Hopes Farm obviously, but nevertheless it is a scale that would be impossible for a single family to milk using other forms of technology.

Second, the overall population of farm owners has been declining and ageing. Those opting out of running their own farm find other employment, sometimes working for the mega farm outfits that drove them out of business, and their children (especially female children)

Figure C.6. A Japan Agriculture–sponsored billboard. The caption reads, "Delicious! You ought to drink milk!" This sign is one of a multitude of similar ones. In this case it is painted on the side of the cattle shed wherein cattle, and many farmers, spend the majority of their lives. Photo by the author.

frequently move to larger urban centers. This situation leads to problems for younger local males as there are few employment opportunities for the sons and daughters who choose to remain at home to care for their ageing parents or inherit the family homestead, and in a vicious cycle of dysfunction, there are few local females left for eligible men to partner with. So, many young rural Japanese men find themselves working on large industrial farms in essentially dead-end labor jobs and are often unable to enter the traditional community hierarchies through marriage and children.

Third, as the local labor pool decreases through ageing and outmigration, there remains an insatiable need for rotary parlor workers and this operational need has often drawn employers to be less selective when they seek employees. Incoming workers fill the need, but like owners, they too are an extremely diverse group. As noted, beyond a propensity for many to be in a state of liminal liminality, it is difficult to typify an outsider or even lo-sider worker. Traditional relationships, for instance between senior and junior, often become confused as employees of differing ages, backgrounds, and knowledge of dairying work together at the same repetitive low-skill tasks. Unlike locals, these workers tend to view their work relationships, status, and performance as merit based, not hereditary. In short, individualistic ability takes precedence over having a "set" place in the social order.

Fourth, most view their job as temporary and not as a source of social or self-identity. They are also, generally speaking, not concerned with the longevity or productivity of the farm. These extended "tourist" workers, like cattle, are thus important but exchangeable—when one leaves, and again, on average one a month did leave, a new one could arrive without any effect to the functioning of the parlor system. They are replaceable parts in a larger assemblage of posthuman relations. This precarity was not freedom but ultimately insecurity.

Fifth, the predominant feelings of dairy farm owners contrast with the lion's share of contracted dairy farm workers. While the former do not seek freedom from "traditional" Japaneseness, both experience alienation as a result from the deskilling function of industrialization. Owners were insecure because they no longer felt in control. As marginalized, national Others, they were controlled by debt and governmental production targets and a logic of crisis and speed politics. Even in the parlor, the heart of their own operation, they were reduced to the same labor as transient workers lacking their past daily embodied relationship with personally known cows. The very functioning of the rotary system they depend upon is a technological attack on their former identities.

Mr. Wada will likely be the last in his family to be a dairy farmer; Matsuyama, may or may not, remain in the industry; and as for the legions of outsiders and no-siders I met over the course of an almost twenty-year-long research project, countless have left while only a handful have remained. How can dairy farming survive? There must be a shift from a search for the impossible to achieve political, ideological, food, and so on, macro security goals alongside the attendant discourse of permanent crisis that support them. These macro level imperatives only result in making the day-to-day individual lives of dairy workers, human and bovine alike, increasingly insecure, increasingly caught up in panoptic regimes and dead-end drives from dromocratic progress. What is needed is community and individual openness to the flourishing of individual Otherness, a rethinking of cosmopolitical frontiers, and an acceptance of novel thinking and novel beginnings in lieu of epic notions of national, regional, or individual identity.

Epilogue

Akita

The hardest part in writing this book was the blessing and curse of remaining deeply entrenched in this field site as a resident, both of Hokkaido and, nearly every weekend, of the town of Gensan for eighteen years (detailed in Hansen 2021a). So, unlike many ethnographers who pack up their fieldnotes and go home after a year, their chronicles perhaps punctuated with follow-up research stints, there was, to my mind and in my experience no "natural" break in this history-ethnography until I moved to Akita in 2023. At the risk of sounding trite, life happens. While in Hokkaido, nearly every week I had occasion to meet up with or just run into a number of the locals and lo-siders discussed in this book. New news constantly came my way. Negotiations of each Otherness continue, outsiders and lo-siders, cows and technologies come and go, and security concerns, individual, group, and national, are always emerging, negotiated, and ever-shifting.

As highlighted in this book and elsewhere, municipal and agricultural policy are never stagnant internationally or locally and are a meshing of security concerns (Jentzsch 2021; MacLachlan and Shimizu 2022; Odagiri 2021). Taking one example, the role of the US in the TPP was of central concern for the Abe cabinet in 2015, US participation off the table in 2017, and in 2018 the partnership was ratified without the US. In 2021 the Biden cabinet opted to reopen trade dialogue through Quad, a four-way security alliance including Japan, India, America, and Australia, to inaugurate the Indo-Pacific Economic Framework (IPEF) in 2022 as an economic means to counter the security threats posed by Russia and China. However, by 2022 Japan had already joined the

Regional Comprehensive Economic Partnership (RECP), including South Korea, China, India, New Zealand, and Australia in conjunction with the Association of Southeast Asian Nations (ASEAN). These are major shifts in trade and security partnerships over the span of less than a decade: what the future holds for dairy farmers is always uncertain. Again, as this book would have it, they are ever part of the "(in)secure" relations of *being* through constantly shifting processes of *becoming* as an inescapable part of dealing and dwelling with Others, human and nonhuman, from the creation of governmental policy to how such policies become implemented (and enlivened) on any particular farm. The global COVID-19 pandemic and the war in Ukraine are also excellent cases in point as to how macro security concerns influence micro level frontiers and relations. Taking one collateral impact as an example, the yearly flow of foreign laborers, largely from China and Vietnam, that industrial dairy farming had become increasingly dependent upon from 2006, stopped overnight in 2020 due to coronavirus-influenced visa restrictions; this was a major rift, but by 2022 "trainees" started to trickle back in. Dairy farming, as explained in this book, is a deeply Othered industry dependent on a wide range of imported inputs—from fuel to feed—and these are under unprecedented pressure from the rapid depreciation of the Japanese currency and the Ukraine/Russia conflict, the latter a geopolitical neighbor with which Japan continues to have tense security relations. Crises, real and imagined, will continue to come and go.

Through all this macro change, Grand Hopes Farm has relentlessly expanded. By 2022 it had over three thousand head of milking cows. Today there are two rotary parlors at either end of the operation working on three-times-a-day shifts. The lack of foreign workers caused by COVID inaugurated more robust experiments with fully automated barns in the area. As of 2022, Grand Hopes Farm has two four-hundred-cow "robotic" barns. Robotic milking, driven by bovine agency and not an industrialized pneumatic heartbeat, allows for more natural biological tempos to flourish and is an improvement in the health conditions for both 2 and 4 legged workers. Squarely facing another insecurity, the dairy constructed a multimillion-dollar methane energy plant that runs on the overabundance of manure slurry that it produces. This system now powers some of the dairy, and perhaps most interestingly, an onsite, year-round, greenhouse project that grows, among other agricultural experiments and oddities, delicious strawberries in the depths of the Tokachi winter. These berries are used at the dairy farm's café, which opened in Gensan in 2018, another victory over JA for Mr. Wada.

Indefatigable Mr. Wada "retired" in 2020. He still has shares in the operation, but he constructed an enormous home in the center of Gensan, complete with a five-car garage, home to a variety of luxury cars, and of course a new Toyota Crown. He only visits the farm occasionally. Matsuyama-san has continued on in his role as a "heat hunter." His latest culinary experiment is a wood-fired pizza oven constructed in his horse barn, making for a unique mixture of aromas. The concerns that he and Takako had about the education of their children was solved for at least for one boy. Bookish by nature, independent, and interested in learning English, their eldest son sought out information about schools and asked his parents to let him attend high school in Fiji. He began his studies in 2018 and graduated in 2022. Masahiro, my past pugilistic nemesis, has become a polite and pleasant acquaintance. Until my family moved to Sapporo in 2019, my son and his daughter attended the same elementary school class. We often met. He remains working on his father's farm, intending to take over. Far from an insecure bully, he is a dedicated father, a leading member of the PTA, and immensely proud of his daughter becoming the regional speed skating champion in her age group. Finally, in 2019 the "no good son" returned. Now married with a managerial role at the farm, it seems likely that he will remain there now that Mr. Wada has pulled back. One hundred years ago, ten years ago, as today, rural Tokachi remains a macro, meso, and micro frontier of Otherness, cosmopolitics, and security seeking with an evolving dairy industry at its core. What the future holds on the frontiers of individuated bodies or socio-spatial geopolitics, is always open to speculation. But I suspect that, despite the potential liberation offered through increased automation, and even if—as needed as unexpected—Japan opens its borders to more egalitarian and inclusive immigration rather than essentially government abetted human trafficking in the guise of trainee programs, extreme intersectionality and liminal liminality will long continue in this very particular location of animal-human-technology security searching.

Notes

Introduction

1. The notion of Hokkaido, and certainly Tokachi, "looking like" a foreign country is not my impression alone. It is promoted as such: "Gaikoku ni kita-mitai to omou darō" (You will think you are in a foreign country). Variations on this theme are ceaselessly stated in tourist pamphlets such as *Tokachi de asobu: kurukuru hando bukku* (Have Fun in Tokachi Tourist Handbook) updated yearly and given out at prefectural information centers.

2. Examples critiquing social constructivist thought within anthropology in general can be found in Candea (2010), Ingold (2011), Jackson (2013), Kohn (2013), Rabinow et al. (2008), Rabinow (2011), or Rapport (2012). All offer contemporary critique. See DeLanda (2006, 2016) and Latour (2005, 2013) for more theory/philosophy-oriented attacks on social constructivism.

3. See Bourdieu (1984), as a cornerstone text alongside Bourdieu with Gisele Sapiro and Brian McHale's (1991, 627–638), and the outstanding documentary film *La Sociologie est un Sport de Combat* (Sociology Is a Martial Art), directed by Pierre Carles (2002). Bourdieu's ubiquitous influence in social studies of Japan can be seen in Kosugi's *Escape from Work: Freelancing Youth and the Challenge to Corporate Japan* (2008) or Roberson's *Japanese Working-Class Lives: An Ethnographic Study of Factory Workers* (1998), among other examples. The argument here is not "against" these fine social studies, it is only to highlight that this book comes from a differing theoretical perspective and tradition with less reverence given to neo-Marxist/Bourdieuesque influences.

4. For example, key linkages are made with regard to Haraway's work (Haraway 1995, 2003, 2008, 2016) and other key posthumanist theorists such as Connolly (2011), Kohn (2013), and Cary Wolfe (2010) are all essential and extraordinarily diverse sources utilized in the latter half of this book. In terms of cosmopolitan theory, the main tensions discussed herein can be seen as those between Appiah's notion of "rooted cosmopolitanism" (2005, 213–272) and the late Ulrich Beck's idea of "forced cosmopolitanism" (2009). The "capabilities approach" is from Nussbaum (2006).

5. For example, schools in Hokkaido have a longer winter holiday and a shorter summer holiday stemming from an agrarian past and the cost of keeping school services running in the winter. Or the fact that every school north of Obihiro has an outdoor speed skating oval could be another way to mark the Otherness of area.

6. Gensan and proper human names related to the ethnography of this book are pseudonyms.

7. Takata notes that Hokkaido is populated in a "Scattered Modern" pattern, not a "clustered village" pattern as in Honshu in "Formation and Characteristics of a Farming Village in Eastern Hokkaido" (Takata 2004, 146) and (Soda 2006). They, as do others, compare Hokkaido settlement to that found in North America or the north of Europe.

8. Communication was carried out in Japanese, not poetic, melodic, or even grammatically correct, but Japanese.

Chapter One. A Conceptual Scaffolding

1. Social anthropology traditionally favored social explanations seen as distinct from cultural anthropology's "interpretations" (Kuper 1994, 541) and deeply influenced by functionalist, structuralist, and Marxist thought (Ingold 2000, 157–171). Rapport has accused contemporary anthropology, notably of a Bourdieuan ilk, of viewing humans as having little agency "trapped" in social structures, a point with which this book wholeheartedly agrees (Rapport 1997, 1–12); for representative examples, see Bourdieu (1977, 1984). Rapport is an ardent critic but he is far from alone. See King (2000) or Ortner (2006, 16–18, 108–112) for similar critiques of the ubiquitous work of Bourdieu. Overing and Rapport contend that "social structures produce culture which, in turn, generates practices which, finally, reproduce social structures. . . . [This theorization of agency] . . . ends up being a structurally causal model based on reified abstractions and materialist determinations" (Overing and Rapport 2000, 2–3); the individual and autobiographical thus becomes a neglected focus in anthropology. Latour makes a similar point through Actor Network Theory and later iterations of it but sees focusing on the individual over the social as no better (Latour 2005, 2013). DeLanda also offers similar critiques via an Assemblage Theory perspective (DeLanda 2006, 2016).

2. Search word "secure" at *Ask Oxford Online Dictionary*, http://www.askoxford.com/concise_oed/secure?view=uk, accessed June 20, 2017.

Chapter Two. Toward Modernity:
The Forming and Reforming of a Northern Frontier

1. It could well be that the Dutch greatly exaggerated Russian power in order to increase their own leverage with the *bakufu* (personal communication

with Professor Richard Siddle on February 18, 2016). The point here is the perception of power and the fact that the *bakufu* had little of it outside their borders.

2. See http://www.lib.hokudai.ac.jp/en/northern-studies/, accessed August 23, 2019. This is truly an outstanding facility and I am indebted to the staff for kind and patient assistance.

3. Many examples of such images can be seen in advertising but a good place to start is the Milkland-Hokkaido promotional website: http://www.milkland-hokkaido.com, accessed February 21, 2019.

Chapter Three. From Traction to *Teishoku*: Tracing the Human-Bovine Trajectory

1. I am greatly condensing a complex history for the sake of brevity. Buddhist thought tends to be separated into distinctive schools and time periods for the sake of explanatory simplicity. But older schools existed alongside newer ones and Shinto was often intermeshed with Buddhism ideologically and spatially. By the end of the feudal period new "charismatic" religions—the first wave of the so-called "new religions"—developed widely in Japan. In the feudal period temples acted as de facto regional powers—employing armies and waging wars. But by the late Tokugawa, temple power had deteriorated to the degree that temples were essentially viewed as administrative centers, tax collectors, and extensions of *bakufu* power, opening the road for new religions and the persecution of early Meiji Buddhist centers. For more detail consult Fujiwara (2021), Ketelaar (1993), and Victoria (2001).

2. This is prone to exaggeration. It is clear clandestine trade did continue with Asian and, to a lesser extent, Western merchants and pirates as well. Shipwrecked fishers occasionally appeared on Japanese shores filtering information outside of Dutch influence. Such information was likely patchy as late Tokugawa scholars were shocked that Dutch was not the global lingua franca. See also Cullen (2017).

Chapter Four. Problems Protecting the Japanese Dairy Industry

1. American lobby groups pointed to a Canadian cow, Canada pointed to its being shipped from "down south," raising jingoistic rhetoric on both sides of this North American border. Mexican officials claimed there was no link with *their* beef. American officials then hinted that a crackdown on illegal workers in the livestock industry was overdue. In the end, all agreed that given NAFTA tracking systems and laws BSE could evolve in any member nation.

2. The Holstein Association of Hokkaido (June 2013) claims there are no part-time dairy farms registered in Hokkaido. Moreover, the number of full-time

dairy farms in Hokkaido radically surpasses any other region of Japan, home to approximately half of Japan's dairy cows at 779,400 head with 6,310 full-time dairy households, next to Iwate with 963. Tokachi is the undeniable epicenter of dairy farm industrialization (MAFF 2017).

Chapter Five. Farm Structures

1. Rice was by no means the staple food of Japanese in Hokkaido. It was prohibitively expensive and often used for trade with Ainu. Hybrid varieties in the 1970s made rice production possible but still not profitable in Tokachi. See Takahashi Man'emon's "The History and Future of Rice Cultivation in Hokkaido" (1980) for an early modern history of Hokkaido rice alongside the dates and the regions it was attempted in.

2. See Hansen (2010a) "Milked for All They're Worth: Hokkaido Dairies and Chinese Workers." Also, Assmann (2016).

3. This was the first college to offer degrees based on an American model in Japan and it was to morph into Hokkaido University. The importance of Clark's (*Kurāku-san*) image is hard to miss at Hokkaido University today with "Boys be ambitious" in roman script (non-katakana) English everywhere in Japan. There can be little doubt as to the significance of Clark and other American pioneers/teachers in Hokkaido's past and present.

Chapter Seven. Dairy Farmers: Being, Becoming, and Making

1. This opens a Pandora's box of issues. The "anthropologist" and "ethnographer" are often conflated but are often conflicting roles. See also Ingold's *Being Alive* (2011).

2. For key examples consult Benedict (1934, 1946), Geertz (1973, 1983, 1988, 2000), and Weber (2003).

3. For key examples see Bourdieu (1977, 1984), Durkheim (2008), or Radcliffe-Brown (1965).

4. I am not alone in this call. See Cohen (1994), Ingold (2000, 2011), Jackson (1995, 2005, 2013), Rapport (1997, 2003, 2012), and Stoller (2009) for resonant ideas in anthropology. In terms of Japanese studies see Amos (2011), Guarné (2018), or Willis and Murphy-Shigematsu (2008) as a samples of defenders of the need for agentive individuals in social scientific research in a Japanese context.

5. A sampling of such "commonsense" generalizations can be found in numerous classic studies of Japan. See Dore (1978), Fukutake (1976), Reischauer (1977), Smith (1959), Suzuki (1970). *Nihonjinron* is rife with such ideas and sound criticisms can be found in Befu (2001), Kuwayama (2007, 2009), and Morris-Suzuki (1998).

6. Japanese "uniqueness" cannot be derived from rice cultivation as globally there are an astounding number of people who, like Japanese, were feudal peasants, traditionally lived in paternally organized villages, fished, and cultivated wet rice. Yet texts such as Doi (2007), Lebra (2004), or Tsunoda (1985), and a host of popular work influenced by such research, still underscores how Japanese hierarchies and value systems—ergo, social and cultural relationships—stem, uniquely, from this system of food production or some presumed union with "nature." More nuanced studies that are largely ignored today even predate this work, such as Bellah's *Tokugawa Religion* (1957), focused on ideological history, value development, and social stratification.

7. See Ertl and Hansen (2015, 1–28) for a detailed discussion. But a representative sample might include: Doi (1973, 2007), Hsu (1975), Kato (2005), Lebra (1976, 2004), Wagatsuma and DeVos (1984), and the list could continue on. Of course, research climates change. Doi in the 2007 reissue of his classic *Amae no kozō* significantly backpedals, declaring that his earlier work does not account for today's young people (2007, foreword). Attachment theorist John Bowlby underscores how dependency is a need for security that is shared by *all* humans (1988, 12–17). In other words, dependency is a human trait and not a uniquely Japanese one.

Chapter Eight. From Teat to Tot: Following Flows

1. Workspaces must be separated but should not be thought of as rigid. As a hunter, Matsuyama would wander through the body of the farm inspecting cows, but he occasionally filled in as a parlor worker. Similarly, Tarō-san worked in the office as well and was somewhat removed from a "regular" parlor worker. Most jobs were interconnected to some degree.

Chapter Nine. Producing and Pumping

1. *Sankei* means 3K—similar to 3D jobs in English—*kitanai, kitsui, to kiken* (dirty, difficult, and dangerous). I have also heard *kusai* (smelly), *kane ga nai* (poor paying), *kibishii* (strict), and even *kuroi* ("black" or exploitative work). All workers I asked, including the owners, told me that dairy work was considered some form of *sankei* employment. This might have been tongue-in-cheek for owners (sure, *your* job is some form of 3K, but I own the place, mate).

Chapter Eleven. Locals, Lo-siders, Outsiders, and No-siders

1. Community could be seen as the long-standing embodied and affective interactions of locals while outsiders saw their relationships with one another and the local community as largely impersonal and pragmatic.

2. In 2006 the primary school nearest to Grand Hopes Farm had eleven students ranging from six to twelve years of age and three teachers (one of whom was the father of two students).

3. Perhaps the best-known explanation of the rural and corporate *ie* structure is provided by Nakane (1967) and commented upon later in detail by Hsu (1975) and Lebra (2004). Nakane offers a three-hundred-year history of the *ie* as the ideal household, not to be confused with kinship despite both being highly region- and situation-specific in Japan (Nakane 1967, 1–40). *Ie* are often linked with other *ie* through what she describes as "local corporate groups," which are not based, at least essentially, on kinship but arise out of economic necessity. She outlines three such groups, however only one concept out of the three, *oyako* (parent–child) *kankei* (relations), played a role at Grand Hopes.

12. Assembling Communities: Two Genders and One Religion

1. Of course, discussion of the entire issue of Ainu ritual and spiritual practices is lacking in this book. There were no references made by my interlocuters in regard to Ainu and I did not encounter any self-proclaimed Ainu dairy workers or owners. However, Ainu more-than-human cosmopolitical and posthuman connections is a topic in need of research well beyond the scope of this book.

Conclusion: On the Frontiers of Animal-Human-Technology

1. Exact specifications of a range of BouMatic rotary systems can be found at http://www.boumatic.com/ accessed March 15, 2019. DeLaval, another maker, has a useful online PDF to accurately plan the ideal rotary parlor at http://www3.delaval.com/ImageVaultFiles/id_22320/cf_5/PR2100_Planning_Guide_Brochure_PREVIEW_LOW_RES.PDF, accessed March 20, 2019.

2. A similar account of this section can be found in Hansen (2014b).

References

Ackerman, Peter, Dolores Martinez, and Maria Rodriguez. (2007). *Pilgrimages and Spiritual Quests in Japan*. London: Routledge.

Adis Tahhan, Diana. (2014). *The Japanese Family: Touch, Intimacy and Feeling*. London: Routledge.

Akamatsu, Paul. (1972). *Meiji 1868: Revolution and Counter Revolution in Japan*. Translated by Miriam Kochan. New York: Harper & Row.

Allen, Matthew. (2002). *Identity and Resistance in Okinawa*. Oxford: Rowman & Littlefield.

Allison, Anne. (1994). *Nightwork: Sexuality, Pleasure, and Corporate Masculinity in a Tokyo Hostess Club*. Chicago: University of Chicago Press.

———. (2013). *Precarious Japan*. Durham, NC: Duke University Press.

Ama, Toshimaro. (2005). *Why Are the Japanese Non-religious? Japanese Spirituality: Being Religious in a Non-Religious Culture*. Lanham, MD: University Press of America.

Ambros, Barbara. (2010). "Vengeful Spirits or Loving Companions? Changing Views of Animal Spirits in Contemporary Japan." *Asian Ethnography* 69 (1): 35–67.

———. (2012). *Bones of Contention: Animals and Religion in Contemporary Japan*. Honolulu: University of Hawai'i Press.

Amos, Timothy. (2011). *Embodying Difference: The Making of Burakumin in Modern Japan*. New Delhi: Navayana.

Anderson, Benedict. (1991 [1983]). *Imagined Communities: Reflections on the Origin and Spread of Nationalism*, revised ed. London: Verso.

Appadurai, Arjun. (1996). *Modernity at Large: Cultural Dimensions of Globalization*. Minneapolis: University of Minnesota Press.

Appiah, Kwame, A. (2005). *The Ethics of Identity*. Princeton, NJ: Princeton University Press.

Arai, Andrea. (2006). "The 'Wild Child' of 1990s Japan." In *Japan after Japan: Social and Cultural Life from the Recessionary 1990s to the Present*, edited by Harry Harootunian and Tomiko Yoda, 216–238. Durham, NC: Duke University Press.

Arendt, Hannah. (1998). *The Human Condition*. Chicago: University of Chicago Press.

Arudou, Debito. (2006). *Japanese Only: The Otaru Hot Springs Case and Racial Discrimination in Japan*. Tokyo: Akashi Shoten.

Ashkenazi, Michael, and Jeanne Jacob. (2000). *The Essence of Japanese Cuisine: An Essay on Food and Culture*. Surrey, UK: Curzon.

———, and Jeanne Jacob. (2003). *Food Culture in Japan*. Westport, CT: Greenwood Press.

Asquith, Pamela J., and Arne Kalland, eds. (1997). *Japanese Images of Nature: Cultural Perspectives*. Surrey, UK: Curzon.

Assmann, Stephanie. (2015). "The Remaking of a National Cuisine: The Food Education Campaign in Japan." In *The Globalization of Asian Cuisines: Transnational Networks and Culinary Contact Zones*, edited by James Farrer, 165–186. New York: Palgrave Macmillan.

———, ed. (2016). *Sustainability in Contemporary Rural Japan: Challenges and Changes*. London: Routledge.

Azuma, Echiro. (2019). *In Search of Our Frontier: Japanese America and Settler Colonialism in the Construction of Japan's Borderless Empire*. Oakland: University of California Press.

Bachnik, Jane. (1994). "Uchi and Soto: Authority and Intimacy, Hierarchy and Solidarity in Japan." In *Situated Meanings: Inside and Outside in Japanese Self, Society, and Language*, edited by Jane Bachnik and Charles Quinn, 221–243. Princeton, NJ: Princeton University Press.

Bakhtin, Mikhail. (1981). *The Dialogic Imagination: Four Essays*. Translated by Michael Holquist and Vadim Liapunov. Austin: University of Texas Press.

Baller, Rob, and Kelly Richardson. (2002). "Social Integration, Imitation, and the Geographic Patterning of Suicide." *American Sociological Review* 67 (6): 873–888.

Barth, Fredrik. (1959). *Political Leadership among Swat Pushtuns*. London: Athlone Press.

———, ed. (1969). *Ethnic Groups and Boundaries: The Social Organization of Culture Difference*. Prospect Heights, IL: Waveland Press.

Bauman, Zygmunt. (2000). *Liquid Modernity*. Cambridge, UK: Polity.

———. (2007). *Liquid Times: Living in an Age of Uncertainty*. Cambridge, UK: Polity.

Bay, Alexander. (2005). "The Swift Horses of Nukanobu: Bridging the Frontiers of Medieval Japan." In *JAPANimals: History and Culture in Japan's Animal Life*, edited by Brett Walker and Gregory M. Pflugfelder, 91–124. Ann Arbor: Center for Japanese Studies, University of Michigan.

Beck, Ulrich. (1992). *Risk Society: Towards a New Modernity*. Translated by Mark Ritter. London: Sage.

————. (2002). "The Terrorist Threat: World Risk Society Revisited." *Theory, Culture and Society* 19 (4): 39–55.

————. (2009). *World at Risk*. London: Polity Press.

Beghin, John C. (2006). "Evolving Dairy Markets in Asia: Recent Findings and Implications." *Food Policy* 31: 195–200.

————, and Isabelle Schluep Campo. (2005). "Dairy Food Consumption, Production, and Policy in Japan." Working Paper 05-wp-401, August 2005, Center for Agriculture and Rural Development University of Iowa. beghin@iastate.edu.

Befu, Harumi. (2001). *Hegemony of Homogeneity: An Anthropological Analysis of Nihonjinron*. Melbourne: Trans Pacific Press.

————. (2015). "Epilogue: 'Inclusion' as a Moving Target." In *Reframing Diversity in the Anthropology of Japan*, edited by John Ertl, John Mock, John McCreery, and Gregory Poole, 247–253. Kanazawa: Kanazawa University Center for Cultural Resource Studies.

Bellah, Robert. (1957). *Tokugawa Religion: The Values of Pre-Industrial Japan*. Glencoe, IL: Free Press.

Ben-Ari, Eyal. (2003). "State, Standardization and 'Normal' Children: An Anthropological Study of a Preschool." In *Family and Social Policy in Japan: Anthropological Approaches*, 111–130 Cambridge: Cambridge University Press.

Benedict, Ruth. (1934). *Patterns of Culture*. Boston: Houghton Mifflin.

————. (1946). *The Chrysanthemum and the Sword: Patterns of Japanese Culture*. Boston, MA: Houghton Mifflin.

Bennett, Jane. (2010). *Vibrant Matter: A Political Ecology of Things*. Durham, NC: Duke University Press

Berger, Peter. (1963). *An Invitation to Sociology: A Humanistic Perspective*. New York: Doubleday.

Berry, Wendell. (1996). *The Unsettling of America: Culture and Agriculture*. San Francisco, CA: Sierra Club Books.

————. (2005). *The Way of Ignorance and Other Essays*. Berkeley, CA: Counterpoint Press.

Bestor, Theodore C. (1989). *Neighborhood Tokyo*. Stanford, CA: Stanford University Press.

————. (2004). *Tsukiji: The Fish Market at the Center of the World*. Berkeley: University of California Press.

Bix, Herbert. (1986). *Peasant Protest in Japan, 1590–1884*. New Haven, CT: Yale University Press.

————. (2001). *Hirohito and the Making of Modern Japan*. New York: HarperCollins.

BizVibe. (2021). "Biggest Dairy Companies in the World." https://blog.bizvibe.com/blog/top-dairy-companies. Accessed May 16, 2021.

Blanchette, Alex. (2020). *Porkopolis: American Animality, Standardized Life, and the Factory Farm*. Durham, NC: Duke University Press.

Blaxell, Vivian. (2009). "Designs of Power: The 'Japanization' of Urban and Rural Space in Colonial Hokkaido." *Japan Focus* (August 31): 1–18.

Boas, Franz. (1996 [1887]). "The Study of Geography." In *Volksgeist as Method and Ethic: Essays on Boasian Ethnography and the German Anthropological Tradition*, edited by G. W. Stocking, 9–16. Madison: University of Wisconsin Press.

Bogost, Ian. (2012). *Alien Phenomenology: Or What It's Like to Be a Thing*. Minneapolis: University of Minnesota Press.

Bourdieu, Pierre. (1977). *The Logic of Practice*. Translated by Richard Nice. Oxford, UK: Polity Press.

———. (1984). *Distinction: A Social Critique of the Judgment of Taste*. Translated by Richard Nice. London: Routledge.

———. (2002). *La Sociologie est un Sport de Combat* [Sociology Is a Martial Art]. Directed by Pierre Carles, 219 minutes. V-P Productions and VF Films, France.

———, with Gisele Sapiro and Brian McHale. (1991). "First Lecture. Social Space and Symbolic Space: Introduction to a Japanese Reading of Distinction." *Poetics Today* 12 (4): 627–638.

Bowlby, John. (1988). *A Secure Base: Clinical Applications of Attachment Theory*. London: Routledge.

Brennan, Brian. (2002). *Scoundrels and Scallywags: Characters from Alberta's Past*. Calgary, AB: Fifth House.

Bresner, Katie. (2009) "The Ainu as 'Other': Representations of the Ainu and Japanese Identity Before 1905." *PlatFourm*, Vol. 10, 31–44. Victoria: University of Victoria.

Buckley, Helen. (1992). *From Wooden Ploughs to Welfare: Why Indian Policy Failed in the Prairie Provinces*. Montreal, QC: McGill-Queens University Press.

Calarco, Matthew. (2008). *Zoographies: The Question of the Animal from Heidegger to Derrida*. New York: Columbia University Press.

Candea, Matei. (2010). *Corsican Fragments: Difference, Knowledge, and Fieldwork*. Bloomington: University of Indiana Press.

Carbert, Louise. (1995). *Agrarian Feminism: The Politics of Ontario Farm Women*. Toronto: University of Toronto Press.

Carrithers, Michael. (1992). *Why Humans Have Culture: Explaining Anthropology and Social Diversity*. Oxford: Oxford University Press.

Cassidy, Rebecca. (2002). *The Sport of Kings: Kinship, Class, and Thoroughbred Breeding in Newmarket*. Cambridge: Cambridge University Press.

Castells, Manuel. (2000). "Grassrooting the Space of Flows." In *Cities in the Telecommunications Age: The Fracturing of Geographies*, edited by James O. Wheeler, Yuko Aoyama, and Barney L. Warf, 18–27. London: Routledge.

Cave, Peter. (2007). *Primary School in Japan: Self, Individuality, and Learning in Elementary Education*. London: Routledge.

———. (2013). "Japanese Colonialism and the Asia-Pacific War in Japan's History Textbooks: Changing Representations and Their Causes." *Modern Asian Studies* 47 (2): 542–580.

Cavell, Stanley, Cora Diamond, John McDowell, Ian Hacking, and Cary Wolfe. (2008). *Philosophy and Animal Life*. New York: Columbia University Press.

Chapman, David. (2008). *Zainichi Korean Identity and Ethnicity*. London: Routledge.

Charlesworth, Simon. (2000). *A Phenomenology of Working-Class Experience*. Cambridge: Cambridge University Press.

Chen, Tien-Shi. (2008). "The Increasing Presence of Chinese Migrants in Japan." In *Transnational Migration in East Asia: Japan in a Comparative Focus*, edited by Shinji Yamashita, Makito Minami, David W. Haines, and Jerry S. Eades, 39–52. Senri Ethnological Reports 77. Osaka: National Museum of Ethnology.

Chiba, Kaeko. (2013). *Japanese Women, Class, and the Tea Ceremony: The Voices of Tea Practitioners in Northern Japan*. London: Routledge.

Chomsky, Noam, and Edward Herman. (1988). *Manufacturing Consent: The Political Economy of the Mass Media*. London: Vintage Books.

Christensen, Paul. (2015). *Japan, Alcoholism, and Masculinity: Suffering Sobriety in Tokyo*. London: Lexington Books.

Christy, Alan. (2012). *A Discipline of Foot: Inventing Japanese Native Ethnography, 1910–1945*. Lanham, MD: Rowman & Littlefield.

Clammer, John. (2001) *Japan and Its Others: Globalization Difference and the Critique of Modernity*. Melbourne: Trans Pacific Press.

Clifford, James. (1997). *Travel and Translation in the Late Twentieth Century*. Cambridge, MA: Harvard University Press.

Cohen, Anthony. (1994). *Self Consciousness: An Alternative Anthropology of Identity*. London: Routledge.

Connolly, William. (2011). *A World of Becoming*. Durham, NC: Duke University Press.

Cook, Emma. (2016). *Reconstructing Adult Masculinities: Part-Time Work in Contemporary Japan*. London: Routledge.

Cox, Rupert. (2003). *Zen Arts: An Anthropological Study of the Culture of Aesthetic Form in Japan*. London: RoutledgeCurzon.

———, ed. (2008). *The Culture of Copying in Japan: Critical and Historical Perspectives*. London: Routledge.

Crenshaw, Kimberlé. (1989). "Demarginalizing the Intersection of Race and Sex: A Black Feminist Critique of Antidiscrimination Doctrine, Feminist Theory and Antiracist Politics." *University of Chicago Legal Forum* 140: 139–167.

Cullen, Louis M. (2003). *A History of Japan, 1582–1941: Internal and External Worlds*. Cambridge: Cambridge University Press.

———. (2017). "The Nagasaki Trade of the Tokugawa Era: Archives, Statistics, and Management." *Japan Review* 31: 69–104.

Cwiertka, Katarzyna. (2006). *Modern Japanese Cuisine: Food, Power and National Identity*. London: Reaktion Books.

Dale, Peter. (1986). *The Myth of Japanese Uniqueness*. London: Croom Helm and Nissan Institute for Japanese Studies, University of Oxford.

Darling-Wolf, Fabienne. (2003). "Male Bonding and Female Pleasure: Refining Masculinity in Japanese Popular Cultural Texts." *Popular Communication* 1 (2): 73–88.

———. (2004). "Women and New Men: Negotiating Masculinity in the Japanese Media." *Communication Review* 7 (3): 231–248.

Dasgupta, Romit. (2000). "Performing Masculinities? The 'Salaryman' at Work and Play." *Japanese Studies* 20 (2): 189–200.

———. (2013). *Re-Reading the Salaryman in Japan: Crafting Masculinities*. New York: Routledge.

Davies, Roger, and Osamu Ikeno, eds. (2002). *The Japanese Mind: Understanding Contemporary Japanese Culture*. Tokyo: Tuttle.

DeLanda, Manuel. (2006). *A New Philosophy of Society: Assemblage Theory and Social Complexity*. London: Continuum.

———. (2016). *Assemblage Theory*. Edinburgh: Edinburgh University Press.

Deleuze, Gilles, and Félix Guattari. (1987). *A Thousand Plateaus: Capitalism and Schizophrenia*. Minneapolis: University of Minnesota Press.

Dempster, Prue. (1966). "Obihiro, a Farmer in Hokkaido: Yoichi Nakamura, a Farmer." In *How People Live: Japan*, 79–88. Toronto: Saunders.

Derrida, Jacques. (2008). *The Animal That Therefore I Am*. New York: Fordham University Press.

deVedas, Anath. (2002). "A Dog's Life among Teenek Indians (Mexico): Animals' Participation in the Classification of Self and Other." *Journal of the Royal Anthropological Institute* 8 (3): 531–550.

Dickin, Janice. (2004). "Roughing It in the West, or, Whose Frontier, Whose History?" In *Challenging Frontiers: The Canadian West*, edited by Lorry Felske and Beverly Rasporich, 97–116. Calgary, AB: University of Calgary Press.

Dillon, Michael. (1996). *Politics of Security: Towards a Political Philosophy of Continental Thought*. London: Routledge.

———. (2015). *Biopolitics of Security: A Political Analytic of Finitude*. New York: Routledge.

Doi, Takeo. (1973). *The Anatomy of Dependence*. Translated by John Bester. Tokyo: Kodansha International.

———. (2007). *Amae no kōzō* [The Structure of Dependence]. Tokyo: Konbundō.

Dore, Ronald. (1978). *Shinohata: A Portrait of a Japanese Village*. New York: Pantheon.

———, and Mari Sako. (1989). *How the Japanese Learn to Work*. New York: Routledge.

Dorst, John. (1999). *Looking West*. Philadelphia: University of Pennsylvania Press.

Dower, John. (1999). *Embracing Defeat: Japan in the Aftermath of World War II*. London: Penguin Books.

———. (2014). *Ways of Forgetting, Ways of Remembering: Japan in the Modern World*. New York: New Press.

Draper, Alizon, and Judith Green. (2003). "Food Safety and Consumers: Constructions of Choice and Risk." In *The Welfare of Food: Rights and Responsibilities in a Changing World*, edited by Elizabeth Dowler and Catherine Finer, 54–69. Oxford: Blackwell.

Durkheim, Émile. (2008 [1915]). *The Elementary Forms of Religious Life*. Edited by Mark Cladis and translated by Carol Cosman. Oxford: Oxford Paperbacks.

Ertl, John, and Paul Hansen. (2015). "Moving Beyond Multiculturalism as a Framework for Diversity in Japan." In *Reframing Diversity in the Anthropology of Japan*, edited by John Ertl, John McCrery, John Mock, and Greg Poole, 1–28. Kanazawa: Kanazawa Center for Cultural Resource Studies.

Esposito, Roberto. (2008). *Bios: Biopolitics and Philosophy*. Translated by Timothy Campbell. Minneapolis: University of Minnesota Press.

Faier, Liebra. (2007). "Filipina Migrants in Rural Japan and Their Professions of Love." *American Ethnologist* 34 (1): 148–162.

———. (2008). "Runaway Stories: The Underground Micromoments of Filipina *Oyomesan* in Rural Japan." *Cultural Anthropology* 23 (4): 630–659.

Fassin, Didier. (2001). "The Biopolitics of Otherness: Undocumented Foreigners and Radical Discrimination in French Public Debate." *Anthropology Today* 17 (1): 3–7.

Felske, Lorry, and Beverly Rasporich, eds. (2004). *Challenging Frontiers: The Canadian West*. Calgary, AB: University of Calgary Press.

Figal, Gerald. (2000). *Civilization and Monsters: Spirits of Modernity in Meiji Japan*. Durham, NC: Duke University Press.

Firstpost. (2021, December 24). "Japanese Officials Are Practically Begging Public to Drink Milk, Here's Why." https://www.firstpost.com/world/japanese-officials-are-practically-begging-public-to-drink-milk-heres-why-10232261.html. Accessed January 3, 2022.

Fisker-Nielsen, Anne Mette. (2012). *Religion and Politics in Contemporary Japan: Soka Gakkai Youth and Komeito*. London: Routledge.

Forero-Montoya, Betsy. (2020). "Representation of a Foreign Woman in Contemporary Japan." *Asian Journal of Social Science* 48 (5–6): 513–534.

Foucault, Michel. (1970/1994). *The Order of Things: An Archaeology of the Human Sciences*. New York: Vintage Books.

———. (1976/1997). *"Society Must Be Defended" Lectures at the College De France*. Edited Mauro Bertani and Alessandro Fontana, translated by David Macey. London: Allen Lane/Penguin Press.

———. (1977). *Discipline and Punish: The Birth of the Prison*. Translated by Alan Sheridan. New York: Vintage Books.

———. (1980). *Herculine Barbin (Being the Recently Discovered Memoirs of a Nineteenth-Century French Hermaphrodite)*. Translated by Richard McDougal. London: Pantheon Books.

Franklin, Sarah. (2008). *Dolly Mixtures: The Remaking of Genealogy*. Durham, NC: Duke University Press.

Freidberg, Susanne. (2004). *French Beans and Food Scares: Culture and Commerce in an Anxious Age*. Oxford: Oxford University Press.

Fudge, Erica. (2008). *Pets*. Stocksfield, UK: Acumen.

Fujita Fumiko. (1994). *American Pioneers and the Japanese Frontier: American Experts in Nineteenth-Century Japan*. London: Greenwood Press.

Fujiwara, Gideon. (2021). *From Country to Nation: Ethnographic Studies, Kokugaku, and Spirits in Nineteenth-Century Japan*. Ithaca, NY: Cornell University Press.

Fukuoka Yasunori. (2000). *Lives of Young Koreans in Japan*. Melbourne: Trans Pacific Press.

Fukutake Tadashi. (1967). *Japanese Rural Society*. Translated by R. P. Dore. Ithaca, NY: Cornell University Press.

Funabashi Yoichi. (2007, December 13). "Kanji for 'Fake' Takes '07 Cake." *Japan Times*, https://www.japantimes.co.jp/news/2007/12/13/national/kanji-for-fake-takes-the-07-cake/. Accessed January 15, 2021.

Furuki Toshiaki. (2003) "Considering Okinawa as a Frontier." In *Japan and Okinawa: Structure and Subjectivity*, edited by Glenn Hook and Richard Siddle, 21–38. London: RoutledgeCurzon.

Geertz, Clifford, ed. (1973/2000). *The Interpretation of Cultures: Selected Essays by Clifford Geertz*. New York: Basic Books.

———. (1983). *Local Knowledge: Further Essays in Interpretive Anthropology*. New York: Basic Books.

———. (1988). *Works and Lives: Anthropologist as Author*. Cambridge, UK: Polity.

———. (2000). *Available Light: Anthropological Reflections on Philosophical Topics*. Princeton, NJ: Princeton University Press.

Genda, Yūji. (2005). *A Nagging Sense of Job Insecurity: The New Reality Facing Japanese Youth*. LTCB International Library Trust. Tokyo: International House of Japan.

———. (2009). *Hataraku Kajyō: Otona no tame no Wakamono Dokuhon* [Too Much Working: A Book for Adults about Young Readers]. Tokyo: NTT Syuppan.

Giddens, Anthony. (1984). *The Constitution of Society: Outline of a Theory of Structuration*. Berkeley: University of California Press.

———. (1991). *Modernity and Self-Identity: Self and Society in the Late Modern Age*. Stanford, CA: Stanford University Press.

Gill, Tom. (2001). *Men of Uncertainty: The Social Organization of Day Laborers in Contemporary Japan*. Albany: State University of New York Press.

Gillespie, Kathryn. (2018). *The Cow with Ear Tag #1389*. Chicago: University of Chicago Press.

Gluck, Carol. (1985). *Japan's Modern Myths*. Princeton: Princeton University Press.

———. (1998). "The Invention of Edo." In *Mirror of Modernity: Invented Traditions of Modern Japan*, edited by Stephen Vlastos, 262–284. Berkeley: University of California Press.

Goodman, Roger. (2008). "Afterword: Marginals, Minorities, Majorities and Migrants—Studying the Japanese Borderlands in Contemporary Japan." In *Transcultural Japan: At the Borderlands of Race, Gender, and Identity*, edited by David Blake Willis and Stephen Murphy-Shigematsu, 325–334. London: Routledge.

Gore, Albert. (2007). *An Inconvenient Truth: The Planetary Emergency of Global Warming and What We Can Do about It*. New York: Rodale Books.

Goto, Akira, and Odagiri Hiroyuki. (1997). *Innovation in Japan*. Oxford, UK: Clarendon Press.

Graeber, David. (2018). *Bullshit Jobs: A Theory*. New York: Simon & Schuster.

Grandin, Temple. (2009). *Animals Make Us Human: Creating the Best Life for Animals*. New York: Houghton Mifflin Harcourt.

Grasseni, Cristina. (2005). "Designer Cows: The Practice of Cattle Breeding between Skill and Standardization." *Society and Animals* 13 (1): 33–49.

Groemer, Gerald. (2001). "Creation of the Edo Outcast Order." *Journal of Japanese Studies* 27 (2): 263–293.

Grusin, Richard, ed. (2015). *The Nonhuman Turn*. Minneapolis: University of Minnesota Press.

Guarné, Blai. (2018). "Escaping through Words: Memory and Oblivion in the Japanese Urban Landscape." In *Escaping Japan: Reflections on Estrangement and Exile in the Twenty-First Century*, edited by Blain Guarné and Paul Hansen, 90–121. London: Routledge.

———, and Paul Hansen. 2018. "Escaping Inside and Outside." In *Escaping Japan: Reflections on Estrangement and Exile in the Twenty-First Century*, edited by Blain Guarné and Paul Hansen, 1–25. London: Routledge.

Guo, Nanyan, ed. (2005). *Tsugaru: Regional Identity on Japan's Northern Periphery*. Otago: University of New Zealand Press.

Hamabata, Mathews Masayuki. (1986). "Ethnographic Boundaries: Culture, Class, and Sexuality in Tokyo." *Qualitative Sociology* 9 (4): 354–371.

Hane, Mikiso. (1992). *Modern Japan: A Historical Survey*. Boulder, CO: Westview Press.

Hankins, Joseph. (2014). *Working Skin: Making Leather, Making a Multicultural Japan*. Berkeley: University of California Press.

Hansen, Paul. (2010a). "Milked for All They're Worth: Hokkaido Dairies and Chinese Workers." *Culture and Agriculture* 32 (2): 78–97.

———. (2010b). *Hokkaido Dairy Farm: Change, Otherness, and the Search for Security*. PhD Thesis, University of London SOAS.

———. (2013). "Urban Japan's 'Fuzzy' New Families: Affect and Embodiment in Dog–Human Relationships." *Asian Anthropology* 12 (2): 83–103.

———. (2014a). "Culturing and Agricultural Crisis in Hokkaido." *Asian Anthropology* 13 (1): 52–71.

———. (2014b). "Becoming Bovine: Mechanics and Metamorphosis in Hokkaido's Animal-Human-Machine." *Journal of Rural Studies* 33 (January): 119–130.

———. (2015). "The Manufacture of Descent, Dissent, and Decent in the Anthropology of Japan." In *Reframing Diversity in the Anthropology of Japan*, edited by John Ertl, John McCrery, John Mock, and Greg Poole, 1–28. Kanazawa: Kanazawa Center for Cultural Resource Studies.

———. (2016). "Betwixt and Between JA: Japan, Jamaica, Agriculture, Education and the Will to Employment." In *The Impact of Internationalization of Japanese Higher Education: Is Japanese Education Really Changing?*, edited by Kawamura Hiroaki, John Mock, and Naganuma Naeko, 159–175. Rotterdam, NL: Sense.

———. (2018a). "Kyoko's Assemblage: Escaping '*futsū no nihonjin*' in Hokkaido." In *Escaping Japan: Reflections on Estrangement and Exile in the Twenty-First Century*, edited by Blai Guarné and Paul Hansen, 152–178. London: Routledge.

———. (2018b). "Fuzzy Bounds: Doing Ethnography at the Limits of the Network and Animal Metaphor." *Humanimalia: A Journal of Human/Animal Interface Studies* 10 (1). https://www.depauw.edu/humanimalia/issue%2019/hansen.html.

———. (2020a). "Linking Cosmopolitan and Multispecies Touch in Contemporary Japan." *Japan Forum* 32 (4): 484–510.

———. (2020b). "From Agribusiness to Deer Hunter: Locating Food Industrialization and Multispecies Health in Tokachi, Hokkaido." In *Japan's New Ruralities: Coping with Decline in the Periphery*, edited by Wolfram Manzenreiter, 27–47. London: Routledge.

———. (2021a). " 'We Have Always Been Cosmopolitan': Towards Anthropologies of Contemporary Complexity in Japan." In *Methods, Moments, and Ethnographic Spaces in Asia*, edited by Nayantara Sheoran Appleton and Caroline Bennett, 171–194. Lanham, MD: Rowman & Littlefield.

———. (2021b). "Rur-bane Relations: Assemblage and Cosmopolitics in Central Hokkaido." In *Rethinking Locality in Japan*, Sonja Ganseforth Hanno Jentzsch, 52–68. London: Routledge.

———. (2022). "Rural Emplacements: Linking Heterotopia, One Health and Ikigai in Central Hokkaido." *Asian Anthropology* 21 (1): 66–79.

Haraway, Donna. (1995). "A Manifesto for Cyborgs: Science, Technology, and Socialist Feminism in the 1980s." In *The Postmodern Turn: New Perspectives on Social Theory*, edited by Steven Seidman, 82–116. Cambridge: University of Cambridge Press.

———. (2003). *The Companion Species Manifesto: Dogs, People, and Significant Otherness*. Chicago: Prickly Paradigm Press.

———. (2008). *When Species Meet*. Minneapolis: University of Minnesota Press.

———. (2016). *Staying with the Trouble: Making Kin in the Chthulucene*. Durham, NC: Duke University Press.

Hardacre, Helen. (1989). *Shinto and the State 1868–1988*. Princeton, NJ: Princeton University Press.

Harootunian, Harry D. (1989). "Visible Discourses/Invisible Ideologies." In *Postmodernism and Japan*, edited by Masao Miyoshi and Harry Harootunian, 63–92. Durham, NC: Duke University Press.

———. (2019). *Uneven Moments: Reflections on Japan's Modern History*. New York: Columbia University Press.

———, and Tomiko Yoda, eds. (2006). *Japan after Japan: Social and Cultural Life from the Recessionary 1990s to the Present*. Durham, NC: Duke University Press.

Harper, Douglas. (2001). *Changing Works: Visions of Lost Agriculture*. Chicago: University of Chicago Press.

Harrison, John A. (1953). *Japan's Northern Frontier: A Preliminary Study in Colonization and Expansion with Special Reference to the Relations of Japan and Russia*. Gainesville: University of Florida Press.

Hasegawa Akihiro, Fujiwara Yoshinori, Hoshi Tanji, and Shinkai Shoji. (2003). "Kōrei-sha ni okeru 'ikigai' no chiiki-sa: kazoku kōsei, karada jōkyō narabini seikatsu kinō to no kanren" [Regional Differences in *Ikigai* among Elderly People: The Relationship between *Ikigai* and Family Structure, Physiological State, and Functional Capacity]. *Nichirouishi* [Geriatrics] 40: 390–396.

———. (2020). "Saishin no 'ikigai' [Japanese] narabini 'ikigai' [Romanji] kenkyū no dōkō: kongo no ikigai kenkyū wa genten kaiki ga mikoma reru" [Recent Trends in Japanese *Ikigai* and Non-Japanese *Ikigai* Research: Expecting a Return to the Origins in Future Research]. Japan Foundation of Health and Aging Net. https://www.tyojyu.or.jp/net/topics/tokushu/kenkochoju-ikigai/Ikigai-research-doko.html. Accessed February 12, 2021.

Hashimoto, Mitsuru. (1998). "Chihō: Yanagita Kunio's 'Japan.'" In *Mirror of Modernity: Invented Traditions of Modern Japan*, edited by Stephen Vlastos, 133–143. Berkeley: University of California Press.

Heidegger, Martin. (1988 [1975]). *The Basic Problems of Phenomenology*. Translated by Albert Hofstadter. Bloomington: Indiana University Press.

Heisig, James, and John Maraldo, eds. (1995). *Rude Awakenings: Zen, the Kyoto School, and the Question of Nationalism*. Honolulu: University of Hawai'i Press.

Hendry, Joy. (1989). *Becoming Japanese: The World of the Pre-school Child*. Honolulu: University of Hawai'i Press.

———. (1992). "Individualism and Individuality: Entry into a Social World." In *Ideology and Practice in Modern Japan*, edited by Roger Goodman and Kirsten Refsing, 55–71. London: Routledge.

———. (1993). *Wrapping Culture: Politeness, Presentation, and Power in Japan and Other Societies*. Oxford, UK: Clarendon Press.

———. (2000). *The Orient Strikes Back: A Global View of Cultural Display*. London: Routledge.

Hidaka Tomoko. (2010). *Salaryman Masculinity: The Continuity of and Change in the Hegemonic Masculinity in Japan*. Leiden, NL: Brill.

Hobsbawm, Eric, and Terence Ranger, eds. (1983). *The Invention of Tradition*. Cambridge: Cambridge University Press.

Holloway, Lewis. (2005). "Aesthetics, Genetics, and Evaluating Animal Bodies: Locating and Displacing Cattle on Show and in Figures." *Environment and Planning D: Society and Space* (23): 883–902.

———. (2007). "Subjecting Cows to Robots: Farming Technologies and the Making of Animal Subjects." *Environment and Planning D: Society and Space* (25): 1041–1060.

Hook, Glen, and Richard Siddle, eds. (2003). *Japan and Okinawa: Structure and Subjectivity*. London: RoutledgeCurzon.

Horikawa Makoto. (2006). *Hokkaido wakuku chizu ehon* [An Exciting Hokkaido Picture Map]. Sapporo: Hokkaido Shinbunsha.

Howell, David L. (1994). "Ainu Ethnicity and the Boundaries of the Early Modern Japanese State." *Past and Present* (142): 69–93.

———. (2005). *Geographies of Identity in Nineteenth-Century Japan*. Berkeley: University of California Press.

Hsu, Francis. (1975). *Iemoto: The Heart of Japan*. New York: Schenkman.

Hudson, Mark J. (1999). *Ruins of Identity: Ethnogenesis in the Japanese Islands*. Honolulu: University of Hawai'i Press.

———, Ann-Elise Lewallen, and Mark Watson, eds. (2014). *Beyond Ainu Studies: Changing Academic and Public Perspectives*. Honolulu: University of Hawai'i Press.

Humphrey, John. (2002). *The Great Food Gamble*. London: Hodder Press.

Hurley, Susan, and Matthew Nudds, eds. (2006). *Rational Animals?* Oxford: Oxford University Press.

Ichijo Atsuko, Venetia Johannes, and Ronald Ranta, eds. (2019). *The Emergence of National Food: The Dynamics of Food and Nationalism*. London: Bloomsbury Academic.

Ingold, Tim. (2000). *The Perception of the Environment: Essays in Livelihood, Dwelling and Skill*. New York: Routledge.

———. (2011). *Being Alive: Essays on Movement, Knowledge and Description*. New York: Routledge.

Irish, Ann. (2009). *Hokkaido: A History of Ethnic Transition and Development on Japan's Northern Island*. Jefferson, NC: McFarland.

Ishige Naomichi. (2001). *The History and Culture of Japanese Food*. London: Paul Kegan.

Ito Satoru, and Ryuta Anase. (2001). *Coming Out in Japan: The Story of Satoru and Ryuta*. Melbourne: Trans Pacific Press.

Ivy, Marilyn. (1995). *Discourses of the Vanishing: Modernity Phantasm Japan*. Chicago: University of Chicago Press.

Jackson, Michael. (1995). *At Home in the World*. Durham: Duke University Press.

————, ed. (1996). *Things as They Are: New Directions in Phenomenological Anthropology*. Bloomington: Indiana University Press.

————. (2005). *Existential Anthropology: Events, Exigencies, and Effects*. New York: Berghahn Books.

————. (2013). *Lifeworlds: Essays in Existential Anthropology*. Chicago: University of Chicago Press.

Jentzsch, Hanno. (2021). *Harvesting State Support: Institutional Change and Local Agency in Japanese Agriculture*. Toronto, ON: University of Toronto Press.

Jussaume, Raymond. (1991). *Japanese Part-Time Farming: Evolution and Impacts*. Ames: University of Iowa State Press.

Kamishihoro Yakuba choushihen inkai. (1992). *Kamishishihoro chou shi: hotsuiban* [Kamishihoro's History: New Edition]. Kamishihoro: Kamishihorochou yakuba.

Kasahara Kazuo, ed. (2001). *A History of Japanese Religion*. Translated by Paul McCarthy and Gaynor Sekimori. Tokyo: Kosei.

Kato Etsuko. (2009). *Jibunsagashi no imintachi—kanada, bankūbā, samayou nihon no wakamono* [Self-Searching Migrants: Young Japanese Searching in Vancouver, Canada]. Tokyo: Sairyūsha.

Kato Kazuo. (2005). *Functions and Structure of Amae: Personality-Social, Cognitive, and Cultural Psychological Approaches*. Fukuoka: Kyushu University Press.

Kelly, William W. (2006). "Rice Revolutions and Farm Families in Tōhoku: Why Is Farming Culturally Central and Economically Marginal?" In *Wearing Cultural Styles in Japan: Concepts of Tradition and Modernity in Practice*, edited by Christopher Thompson and John Traphagan, 47–71. Albany: State University of New York Press.

Kerr, George. (2000 [1958]). *Okinawa: The History of an Island People*. Singapore: Tuttle.

Kete, Kathleen. (1994). *The Beast in the Boudoir: Petkeeping in Nineteenth-Century Paris*. Berkeley: University of California Press.

Ketelaar, Edward James. (1993). *Of Heretics and Martyrs in Meiji Japan: Buddhism and Its Persecution*. Princeton, NJ: Princeton University Press.

Kimoto, Kimiko. (2003). *Gender and Japanese Management*. Translated by Teresa Castelvetre. Melbourne: Trans Pacific Press.

Kimura, Aya. (2018). "Hungry in Japan: Food Insecurity and Ethical Citizenship." *Journal of Asian Studies* 77 (2): 475–493. DOI: https://doi.org/10.1017/S0021911818000037.

King, Anthony. (2000). "Thinking with Bourdieu against Bourdieu: A 'Practical' Critique of the Habitus." *Sociological Theory* 18 (3): 417–433.

Kingston, Jeff. (2018). "Watchdog Journalism in Japan Rebounds but Still Compromised." *Journal of Asian Studies* 77 (4): 881–893. DOI: https://doi.org/10.1017/S002191181800253X.

Kitano, Shu. (2009). *Space, Planning and Rurality: Uneven Rural Development in Japan*. Victoria, BC: Trafford.

Klien, Susanne. (2020). *Urban Migrants in Rural Japan: Between Agency and Anomie in a Post-growth Society*. Albany: State University of New York Press.

Knight, John. (2003). *Waiting for Wolves in Japan: An Anthropological Study of People–Wildlife Relations*. New York: Oxford University Press.

Kohn, Eduardo. (2013). *How Forests Think: Toward an Anthropology beyond the Human*. Berkeley: University of California Press.

Kondo, Dorinne K. (1990). *Crafting Selves: Power, Gender, and Discourses of Identity in a Japanese Workplace*. Chicago: University of Chicago Press.

Kondo Shiaki and Yoshida Mariko, eds. (2021). *Kuu, kuwareru, kui au maruchi-supīshīzu minzoku-shi no shikō* [Eat, Consume, Symbiose: Exploring Food Systems From the Perspective of Multispecies Ethnography]. Tokyo: Seidosha.

König, Tilman, and Daniel Kremers, dirs. (2008). *Sour Strawberries: Japan's Hidden "Guest Workers."* DVD Ger, 60 minutes, Leipzig/Tokyo.

Kosugi, Reiko. (2008). *Escape from Work: Freelancing Youth and the Challenge to Corporate Japan*. Translated by Ross Mouer. Melbourne: Trans Pacific Press.

Kuper, Adam. (1994). "Culture, Identity, and the Project of Cosmopolitan Anthropology." *Man*, New Series 29 (3): 537–554.

Kuwayama, Takami. (2004). *Native Anthropology: The Japanese Challenge to Western Academic Hegemony*. Melbourne: Trans Pacific Press.

———. (2007). "Looking Beyond Culture." *Journal of Education for International Understanding* (3): 26–40.

———. (2009). "Japan's Emic Conceptions" in Yoshio Sugimoto ed. *The Cambridge Companion to Modern Japanese Culture*. Cambridge: Cambridge University Press.

———. (2012). "The Ainu in the Ethnographic Triad: From the Described to the Describer." In *Anthropologists, Indigenous Scholars, and the Research Endeavour: Seeking Bridges Towards Mutual Respect*, edited by Joy Hendry and Laara Fitznor, 44–54. London: Routledge.

Kuwabara Masako and Kawagami Jun. (2018). *Hokkaido no rekishi ga wakaru hon* [A Book to Understand Hokkaido History]. Sapporo: Ansusha.

Kuwayama, Takami, with Tsuneo Ayaba. (2006). *Yoku wakaru bunka jinruigaku* [A Good Understanding of Cultural Anthropology]. Kyoto: Minerva.

Kyodo News. (2005). "Snow Brand Exec Faces Fraud Charge." *Japan Times*, May 19, 2005.

———. (2007). "Scandal-Stung Meat Hope Fires Staff, Packs It In." *Japan Times Online*. http://www.japantimes.co.jp/news/2007/06/26/national/scandal-stung-meat-hope-fires-staff-packs-it-in/#.VrlrBdDrd_l. Accessed February 10, 2019.

Lakoff, George. (1999). *Philosophy in the Flesh: The Embodied Mind and Its Challenge to Western Thought*. New York: Basic Books.

————, and Mark Johnson. (2003 [1980]). *Metaphors We Live By*. Chicago: University of Chicago Press.

Latour, Bruno. (2005). *Reassembling the Social: An Introduction to Actor-Network Theory*. Oxford: Oxford University Press.

————. (2013). *An Inquiry into Modes of Existence: An Anthropology of the Moderns*. Translated by Catherine Porter. Cambridge, MA: Harvard University Press.

Lave, Jean, and Étienne Wenger. (1991). *Situated Learning: Legitimate Peripheral Learning*. Cambridge: Cambridge University Press.

Lebra, Takie Sugiyama. (1976). *Japanese Patterns of Behavior*. Honolulu: University of Hawai'i Press.

————. (1985). "Is Japan an *Ie* Society, and *Ie* Society a Civilization?" *Journal of Japanese Studies* 11 (1): 57–64.

————. (2004). *The Japanese Self in Cultural Logic*. Honolulu: University of Hawai'i Press.

Lee, Sunhee. (2007). "Women's Lives in Family and Local Communities: The Tohoku Region." In *Gender & Law in Japan*, edited by Miyoko Tsujimura and Emi Yano, 157–170. Sendai: Tohoku University Press.

Lefebvre, Henri. (2004). *Rhythmanalysis: Space, Time and Everyday Life*. Translated by Stuart Elden and Gerald Moore. New York: Continuum.

Leheny, David. (2006). *Think Global, Fear Local: Sex, Violence, and Anxiety in Contemporary Japan*. Ithaca, NY: Cornell University Press.

Lesser, Jeffery. (2003). *Searching for Home Abroad: Japanese Brazilians and Transnationalism*. Durham, NC: Duke University Press.

Lewallen, Ann-Elise. (2016). *The Fabric of Indigeneity: Ainu Identity, Gender, and Settler Colonialism in Japan*. Albuquerque: University of New Mexico University Press.

Long, Susan Oprett. (1999). "Shikata ga nai: Resignation, Control, and Self-Identity." In *Lives in Motion: Composing Circles of Self and Community in Japan*, edited by Susan Orpett Long, 11–25. Ithaca, NY: Cornell University Press.

MacLachlan, Ian. (2001). *Kill and Chill: Restructuring Canada's Beef Commodity Chain*. Toronto, ON: University of Toronto Press.

MacLachlan, Patricia, and Kay Shimizu. (2022). *Betting on the Farm: Institutional Change in Japanese Agriculture*. Ithaca, NY: Cornell University Press.

MAFF (Japanese Ministry of Agriculture, Forestry and Fisheries). (2004). *Annual Report on Food, Agriculture and Rural Areas in Japan*, FY 2004. http://www.maff.go.jp/e/pdf/fy2004_rep.pdf. Accessed February 2, 2019.

————. (2017). "Production of Raw and Drinking Milk." *92nd Statistical Yearbook* (2017). http://www.maff.go.jp/e/data/stat/92nd/index.html. Accessed February 13, 2019.

————. (2020). "Food Action Nippon." https://syokuryo.maff.go.jp/. Accessed April 3, 2021.

Maki, John M. (1996). *William Smith Clark: A Yankee in Hokkaido.* Sapporo: Hokkaido University Press.

Maley, Terry. (2004). "Max Weber and the Iron Cage of Technology." *Bulletin of Science, Technology and Society* 24 (1): 69–86.

Martin, Kylie. (2018). "'Escaping' the Hokkaido Homelands: Ainu Heteroglossia and the Performance of Ainu Urban Indigeneity in the Kanto Region." In *Escaping Japan: Reflections on Estrangement and Exile in the Twenty-First Century,* edited by Blai Guarné and Paul Hansen, 122–151. London: Routledge

Martinez, Dolores P. (1992). "NHK Comes to Kuzaki: Ideology, Mythology, and Documentary Film Making." In *Ideology and Practice in Modern Japan,* edited by Roger Goodman and Kirsten Refsing, 150–170. London: Routledge.

———, ed. (1998). *The Worlds of Japanese Popular Culture: Gender, Shifting Boundaries, and Global Cultures.* Cambridge: Cambridge University Press.

———. (2004). *Identity and Ritual in a Japanese Diving Village: The Making and Becoming of Person and Place.* Honolulu: University of Hawai'i Press.

Mason, Michele. (2012). *Dominant Narratives of Colonial Hokkaido and Imperial Japan: Envisioning the Periphery and the Modern Nation-State.* New York: Palgrave Macmillan.

———. (2017). "Dishing Out Silver Spoon: Agricultural Tourism in the Tokachi-Obihiro Area of Hokkaido." *International Journal of Contents Tourism* 1: 31–43.

Mason, R. H. P., and J. G. Craiger. (1997). *The History of Japan.* London: Tuttle.

Matanle, Peter, Anthony Rausch, and the Shrinking Regions Research Group. (2011). *Japan's Shrinking Regions in the 21st Century: Contemporary Responses to Depopulation and Socioeconomic Decline.* New York: Cambria Press.

Mathews, Gordon. (1996). "The Stuff of Dreams, Fading: *Ikigai* and 'the Japanese Self.'" *Ethos* 24 (4): 718–747.

———. (2006). "Can 'A Real Man' Live for His Family? *Ikigai* and Masculinity in Today's Japan." In *Men and Masculinities: Global Masculinities,* edited by Steven Whitehead, 109–125. Routledge: London.

———, and Bruce White, eds. (2004). *Japan's Changing Generations: Are Young People Creating a New Society?* London: RoutledgeCurzon.

McFarland, Neil. (1967). *Rush Hour of the Gods: A Study of New Religious Movements in Japan.* London: Macmillan.

Meyer, Gary. (2018). "Japan Grants Preferential Dairy Access in New Agreements." *USDA Gain Reports.* Last modified April 25, 2018. https://gain.fas.usda.gov/Recent%20GAIN%20Publications/Japan%20Grants%20Preferential%20Dairy%20Access%20in%20New%20Agreements_Tokyo_Japan_4-25-2018.pdf. Accessed July 10, 2023.

Miller, Andrew. (1982). *Japan's Modern Myth.* Boulder, CO: Weatherhill Press.

Millstone, Eric, and Patrick van Zwanenberg. (2003). "The Evolution of Food Safety Policy-Making Institutions in the UK, EU, and Codex Alimentarius."

In *The Welfare of Food: Rights and Responsibilities in a Changing World*, edited by Elizabeth Dowler and Catherine Finer, 38–53. Oxford: Blackwell.

Mitchell, Les. (2006). "Animals and the Discourse of Farming in Southern Africa." *Society and Animals* 14 (1): 39–59.

Miyajima, Toshimitsu. (1998). *Land of Elms: The History, Culture, and Present-Day Situation of the Ainu People.* Toronto, ON: United Church.

Miyoshi Masao. (2000). "Japan Is Not Interesting." In *Re-mapping Japanese Culture*, edited by Vera Mackie, Alina Skoutarides, and Alison Tokita, 11–24. Melbourne: Monash Asia Institute.

Mock, John. (1999). *Culture, Community and Change in a Sapporo Neighborhood, 1925–1988: Hanayama.* Lampeter, Wales: Edwin Mellen Press.

———. (2014). "Hidden Behind Tokyo: Observations on the Rest of Japan." In *Critical Issues in Contemporary Japan*, edited by Jeff Kingston, 246–262. New York: Routledge.

———, with Kawamura Hiroaki, and Naganuma Naeko, eds. (2016). *The Impact of Internationalization on Japanese Higher Education: Is Japanese Education Really Changing?* Rotterdam, NL: Sense.

Moore, Richard. (1990). *Japanese Agriculture: Patterns of Rural Development.* Boulder, CO: Westview Press.

Morasukii Maiku (2017). *Nihon no jyazu bunka* [Postwar Japanese Jazz Culture]. Tokyo: Iwanami Shoten.

Morris-Suzuki, Tessa. (1996). "A Descent into the Past: The Frontier in the Construction of Japanese History." In *Multicultural Japan: Paleolithic to Postmodern*, edited by Donald Denoon, Mark Hudson, Gavin McCormack, and Tessa Morris-Suzuki, 81–94. Cambridge: University of Cambridge Press.

———. (1998). *Re-inventing Japan: Time, Space, Nation.* London: An East Gate Book / M. E. Sharpe.

———. (2000). "Roads to Otherness: Ainu and Identity Politics in Twentieth-Century Japan." In *Re-mapping Japanese Culture*, edited by Vera Mackie, Alina Skoutarides, and Alison Tokita, 35–60. Melbourne: Monash Asia Institute.

———. (2011). *Borderline Japan: Foreigners and Frontier Controls in the Postwar Era.* Cambridge: Cambridge University Press.

Mulgan, Aurelia George. (2006). *Japan's Agricultural Policy Regime.* London: Routledge.

———. (2015a). "What Does the TPP Mean for Japan's Agricultural Sector?" *East Asia Forum: Economics, Politics and Public Policy in East Asia and the Pacific*, last modified November 19, 2015. http://www.eastasiaforum.org/author/aureliageorgemulgan/page/2/. Accessed February 10, 2019.

———. (2015b). "Japan's Agricultural Reforms Watered Down but Still Significant." *East Asia Forum: Economics, Politics and Public Policy in East Asia and the Pacific*, last modified May 7, 2015. http://www.eastasiaforum.org/author/aureliageorgemulgan/page/2/. Accessed February 10, 2019.

———. (2017). "What Does the TPP Mean for Japan's Agricultural Sector?" *East Asia Forum: Economics, Politics and Public Policy in East Asia and the Pacific*, last modified November 19, 2015. http://www.eastasiaforum.org/author/aureliageorgemulgan/page/2/. Accessed February 10, 2019.

Murakami, Haruki. (1997). *Underground: The Tokyo Gas Attack and the Japanese Psyche*. Translated by Alfred Birnbaum and Philip Gabriel. New York: Vintage.

Nakane, Chie. (1967). *Kinship and Economic Organization in Rural Japan*. London: Athlone Press.

———. (1973). *Japanese Society*. Middlesex, UK: Penguin.

Nancy, Jean-Luc. (2000). *Being Singular Plural*. Translated by Robert Richardson and Anne O'Byrne. Stanford, CA: Stanford University Press.

Nelson, John K. (2000). *Enduring Identities: The Guise of Shinto in Contemporary Japan*. Honolulu: University of Hawai'i Press.

Nemoto, Kumiko. (2016). *Too Few Women at the Top: The Persistence of Inequality in Japan*. Ithaca, NY: Cornell University Press.

Nikkei Asia. (2016, March 11). "Milk Distribution Becomes Focus in Japan's Butter Shortage." https://asia.nikkei.com/Politics/Milk-distribution-becomes-focus-in-Japan-s-butter-shortage. Accessed July 3, 2018.

Nishizaki, Kunio. (2002). "Status and Prospects of Manure Management in Japan—Composting Approaches." In *Greenhouse Gasses and Animal Agriculture: Proceedings from the First Annual Conference on Greenhouse Gasses and Animal Agriculture, Obihiro, Japan, 7–11 November 2001*, edited by Junichi Takahashi and Bruce Young, 297–301. Tokyo: Elsevier.

———. (2009). "Current Status and Prospects of Biomass Technologies in Japan: For Successfully Using Biofuels." *Engineering in Agriculture Environment and Food* 2 (4): 156–159.

Novek, Joel. (2012). "Disciplining and Distancing: Confined Pigs in the Factory Farm Gulag." In *Animals and the Human Imagination: A Companion to Animal Studies*, edited by Aaron Gross and Anne Valley, 121–151. New York: Columbia University Press.

Nussbaum, Martha. (2006). *Frontiers of Justice: Disability, Nationality, Species Membership*. London: Belknap Press.

Obara, Kakuyu, John. H. Dyck, and Jim Stout (2005). "Dairy Policies in Japan." *Economic Research Service USDA*, LDP-M-134-01: 1–27.

Obe, Mitsuru. (2018, January 26). "Asia Puzzles Over Trump's TPP Remark." *Nikkei Asian Review Online*. https://asia.nikkei.com/Politics/International-Relations/Asia-puzzles-over-Trump-s-TPP-remark. Accessed April 23, 2018.

Odagiri Tokumi. (2014). *Nōsanson wa shōmetsu shinai* [Farming and Mountain Villages Will Not Vanish]. Tokyo: Iwanami shoten.

———. (2021). *Nōsan seisaku no henbō—sono kiseki to arata na kōsō* [The Change of Farming Policy: Miracles and New Plans]. Tokyo: Nisan gyoson bunka kyokai.

Oguma, Eiji. (2002). *A Genealogy of Japanese Self-Images*. Melbourne: Trans Pacific Press.

Ohnuki-Tierney, Emiko. (1993). *Rice as Self: Japanese Identities through Time*. Princeton, NJ: Princeton University Press.

———. (2002). *Kamikaze, Cherry Blossoms, and Nationalisms: The Militarization of Aesthetics in Japanese History*. Chicago: University of Chicago Press.

———. (2006). "McDonald's in Japan: Changing Manners and Etiquette." In *Golden Arches East: McDonald's in East Asia*, 2nd ed., edited by James Watson, 161–182. Stanford, CA: Stanford University Press.

Oliver, Elizabeth. (2003). *Dog Tails: Home Sweet Home*. Osaka: Animal Rescue Kansai (ARK).

Ortner, Sherry. (2006). *Anthropology and Social Theory: Culture, Power, and the Acting Subject*. Durham, NC: Duke University Press.

Overing, Joann, and Nigel Rapport. (2000). *Social and Cultural Anthropology: The Key Concepts*. London: Routledge.

Ōyama, Shiro. (2000). *A Man with No Talent: Memoirs of a Tokyo Day Laborer*. Translated by Edward Fowler. Ithaca, NY: Cornell University Press.

Ozawa, Takeyuki, Nicolas Lopez-Villalobos, and Hugh T. Blair. (2005). "Dairy Farming Financial Structures in Hokkaido, Japan, and New Zealand." *Animal Science Journal* 76: 391–400.

Pachirat, Timothy. (2011). *Every Twelve Seconds: Industrialized Slaughter and the Politics of Sight*. New Haven, CT: Yale University Press.

Pawlick, Thomas. (2006). *The End of Food: How the Food Industry Is Destroying Our Food Supply—And What You Can Do about It*. Vancouver, BC: Greystone Books.

Pedlar, Neil. (1990). *The Imported Pioneers: Westerners Who Helped Build Modern Japan*. Sandgate: Japan Library.

Peng Tingjun and Thomas Cox. (2005). "An Economic Analysis of the Impacts of Trade Liberalization on the Asian Dairy Market." Staff Paper 490, 1–25. University of Wisconsin–Madison Department of Agricultural and Applied Economics.

Perez, Louis. (1997). "Revision of the Unequal Treaties and Abolition of Extraterritoriality." In *New Directions in the Study of Meiji Japan*, edited by Helen Hardacre and Adam Kern, 320–334. Leiden, NL: Brill.

Pflugfelder, Gregory, and Brett Walker, eds. (2005). *JAPANimals: History and Culture in Japan's Animal Life*. Ann Arbor, MI: Center for Japanese Studies, University of Michigan.

Phillips, Clive. (2002). *Cattle Behaviour and Welfare*. Oxford: Blackwell.

Pickering, Andrew. (1995). *The Mangle of Practice: Time, Agency, and Science*. Chicago: University of Chicago Press.

Plath, David. (1980). *Long Engagements: Maturity in Modern Japan*. Stanford, CA: Stanford University Press.

————, ed. (1983). *Work and Lifecourse in Japan*. Albany: State University of New York Press.

Pollack, David. (1992). *Reading against Culture: Ideology and Narrative in the Japanese Novel*. Ithaca, NY: Cornell University Press.

Pollan, Michael. (2006). *The Omnivore's Dilemma: A Natural History of Four Meals*. London: Penguin Books.

Porcher, Jocelyne. (2011). "The Relationship between Workers and Animals in the Pork Industry: A Shared Suffering." *Journal of Agriculture and Environmental Ethics* 24: 3–17.

Pottier, Johan. (1999). *Anthropology of Food: The Social Dynamics of Food Security*. Cambridge: Polity Press.

Povinelli, Elizabeth. (2016). *Geontologies: A Requiem to Late Liberalism*. Durham, NC: Duke University Press.

Rabinow, Paul, George Marcus, James Faubion, and Tobias Rees. (2008). *Designs for an Anthropology of the Contemporary*. Durham, NC: Duke University Press.

————. (2011). *The Accompaniment: Assembling the Contemporary*. Chicago: University of Chicago Press.

Radcliffe-Brown, A. R. (1965). *Structure and Function in Primitive Society*. London: Free Press.

Ram, Kalpana, and Christopher Houston, eds. (2015). *Phenomenology in Anthropology: A Sense of Perspective*. Bloomington: Indiana University Press.

Rapport, Nigel. (1997). *Transcendental Individual: Towards a Literary and Liberal Anthropology*. London: Routledge.

————. (2003). *I Am Dynamite: An Alternative Anthropology of Power*. London: Routledge.

————. (2012). *Anyone: The Cosmopolitan Subject of Anthropology*. New York: Berghahn Books.

Reader, Ian. (1991). *Religion in Contemporary Japan*. London: Macmillan Press.

————. (1996). *A Poisonous Cocktail? Aum Shinrikyo's Path to Violence*. Copenhagen: NIAS Books.

————. (2000). *Religious Violence in Contemporary Japan: The Case of Aum Shinrikyo*. Honolulu: University of Hawai'i Press.

————. (2001). "Consensus Shattered: Japanese Paradigm Shift and Moral Panic in the Post-Aum Era." *Nova Religio* 2 (4): 225–234.

————, with George Tanabe Jr. (1998). *Practically Religious: Worldly Benefits and the Common Religion of Japan*. Honolulu: University of Hawai'i Press.

Reischhauer, Edwin. (1977). *The Japanese*. Cambridge, MA: Harvard University Press.

Richie, Donald. (1982). *Different People: Pictures of Some Japanese*. Tokyo: Kodansha International.

————. (2003). *The Image Factory: Fads and Fashions in Japan*. London: Reaktion Books.

Roberson, James. (1998). *Japanese Working-Class Lives: An Ethnographic Study of Factory Workers*. London: Routledge.

————, and Nobue Suzuki, eds. (2003). *Men and Masculinities in Contemporary Japan: Dislocating the Salaryman Doxa*. London: RoutledgeCurzon.

Roberts, David. (2008). *Human Insecurity: Global Structures of Violence*. London: Zed Books.

Robertson, Jennifer. (1994). *Native and Newcomer: Making and Remaking a Japanese City*. Berkeley: University of California Press.

————. (1998a). *Takarazuka: Sexual Politics and Popular Culture in Modern Japan*. Berkeley: University of California Press.

————. (1998b). "It Takes a Village: Internationalization and Nostalgia in Postwar Japan." In *Mirror of Modernity: Invented Traditions of Modern Japan*, edited by Stephen Vlastos, 110–129. Berkeley: University of California Press.

Robson, L. L. (1965). *The Convict Settlers of Australia*. Melbourne: University of Melbourne Press.

Rosenberger, Nancy, ed. (2001). *Gambling with Virtue: Japanese Women and the Search for Self in a Changing Nation*. Honolulu: University of Hawai'i Press.

————. (2016). "Japanese Organic Farmers: Strategies of Uncertainty after the Fukushima Disaster." *Ethnos* 81 (1): 1–24. DOI: 10.1080/00141844.2014.900101.

Roth, Joshua Hotaka. (2002). *Brokered Homeland: Japanese Brazilian Migrants in Japan*. Ithaca, NY: Cornell University Press.

Runge, C. Ford, Benjamin Senauer, Philip G. Pardey, and Mark W. Rosegrant. (2003). *Ending Hunger in Our Lifetime: Food Security and Globalization*. Baltimore, MD: Johns Hopkins University Press.

Russell, Harold. (2007). *Time to Become a Barbarian: The Extraordinary Life of General Horace Capron*. New York: University Press of America.

Ryang, Sonia, ed. (2000). *Koreans in Japan: Critical Voices from the Margin*. New York: Routledge.

————. (2004). *Japan and National Anthropology: A Critique*. New York: Routledge.

Saunavaara, Juha. (2018). "Reconstructing and Redefining Hokkaido during the Post-war Period." *International Journal of Asia Pacific Studies* 14 (1): 27–55. https://doi.org/10.21315/ijaps2018.14.1.2.

Scheper-Hughes, Nancy. (1979). *Saints, Scholars and Schizophrenics: Mental Illness in Rural Ireland*. Berkeley: University of California Press.

Seki Hideshi, Masato Kuwabara, Yukio Ōba, and Akio Takahashi. (2006). *Shinban— Hokkaidō no rekishi ge: kindai-gendai* [New Edition—The History of Hokkaido: From Modern [Times] to Today). Sapporo: Hokkaidō Shinbunshya.

Seki, Keigo. (1963). *Folktales of Japan*. Translated by Robert Adams. Chicago: University of Chicago Press.

Sennett, Richard. (1998). *The Corrosion of Character: The Personal Consequences of Work in the New Capitalism*. New York: W. W. Norton.

Shapiro, Michael. (1997). *Violent Cartographies: Mapping the Cultures of War*. Minneapolis: University of Minnesota Press.

Shigematsu Kazuyoshi. (2004). *Shiryou Hokkaidō kangoku no rekishi* [Prison Data: The History of Hokkaido]. Tokyo: Shinzansya.

Shukin, Nicole. (2009). *Animal Capital: Rendering Life in Biopolitical Times*. Minneapolis: University of Minnesota Press.

Siddle, Richard. (1996). *Race, Resistance, and the Ainu of Japan*. London: Routledge.

———. (1998). "Colonialism and Identity in Okinawa before 1945." *Japanese Studies* 18 (2): 117–133.

———, ed. (2013). *Critical Readings on Ethnic Minorities and Multiculturalism in Japan*. Leiden: Brill.

Sjöberg, Katarina. (1993). *The Return of the Ainu: Cultural Mobilization and the Practice of Ethnicity in Japan*. Chur, Switzerland: Harwood Academic.

———. (2008). "Positioning Oneself in the Japanese Nation-State: The Hokkaido and Ainu Case." In *Transcultural Japan: At the Borderlands of Race, Gender, and Identity*, edited by David Blake Willis and Stephen Murphy-Shigematsu, 197–216. London: Routledge.

Smith, Thomas C. (1959). *The Agrarian Origins of Modern Japan*. Stanford, CA: Stanford University Press.

Soda, Osamu. (2006). *Philosophy of Agricultural Science: A Japanese Perspective*. Melbourne: Trans Pacific Press.

Sontag, Susan. (2003). *Regarding the Pain of Others*. New York: Picador.

Sternsdorff-Cisterna, Nicolas. (2019). *Food Safety after Fukushima: Scientific Citizenship and the Politics of Risk*. Honolulu: University of Hawai'i Press.

Stiegler, Bernard. (2016). *Automatic Society: Volume One, the Future of Work*. Translated by Daniel Ross. Cambridge: Polity Press.

Stockwin, Arthur. (2017). "Press Freedom and Politics in Japan." *East Asia Forum*. https://www.eastasiaforum.org/2017/09/29/press-freedom-and-politics-in-japan/. Accessed September 29, 2017.

Stoller, Paul. (1997). *Sensuous Scholarship*. Philadelphia: University of Pennsylvania Press.

———. (2009). *The Power of Between: An Anthropological Odyssey*. Chicago: University of Chicago Press.

Storey, Kenton. (2018). *Settler Anxiety at the Outposts of Empire: Colonial Relations, Humanitarian Discourses, and the Imperial Press*. Vancouver: University of British Columbia Press.

Strathern, Marilyn. (1988). "Concrete Topographies." *Cultural Anthropology* 3 (1): 88–96.

———. (2004). *Partial Connections*. Walnut Creek, CA: AltaMira Press.

Sugimoto, Ayumi. (2022). "Success and Succession: Agritourism, Heterotopia and Two Generations of Rural Japanese Female Entrepreneurs." *Asian Anthropology* 21 (1): 39–52.

Sugimoto, Yoshio. (1997). *An Introduction to Japanese Society*. Cambridge: University of Cambridge Press.

Suzuki, D. T. (1970). *Zen and Japanese Culture*. Princeton, NJ: Princeton University Press.

Takahashi Man'emon. (1980). "The History and Future of Rice Cultivation in Hokkaido." Working paper for United Nations University Japan, 1–15. Tokyo: United Nations University. https://d-arch.ide.go.jp/je_archive/pdf/workingpaper/je_unu22.pdf. Accessed February 13, 2019.

Takata Wakizo. (2003). "The Present State of Green Tourism in Eastern Hokkaido." *Regional Research* (12): 103–119.

———. (2004). "Formation and Characteristics of a Farming Village in Eastern Hokkaido: A Case Study in the Kushiro Area." *Regional Research* (13): 89–106.

———. (2007). "Development of Green Tourism and Characteristics of a Farming Village in Hokkaido: A Case Study in the Nemuro Area." Paper presented November 17–18, 2007, at the 2007 AJJ Conference, 139–155. Tokyo: Temple University.

Tanimura Issa. (1922). *Live Stock Economics*. Tokyo: S. Kawade Seibido.

Thompson, Niobe. (2008). *Settlers of the Edge: Identity and Modernization on Russia's Arctic Frontier*. Vancouver: University of British Columbia Press.

Tipton, Elise K. (2002). *Modern Japan: A Social and Political History*. London: Routledge.

Toby, Ronald. (1984). *State and Diplomacy in Early Modern Japan: Asia in the Development of the Tokugawa Bakufu*. Princeton, NJ: Princeton University Press.

———. (1998). "Imagining and Imaging: 'Anthropos' in Early-Modern Japan." *Visual Anthropology Review* 14 (1): 19–44.

Tokachi kyōdo kenkyōkai: Shin tokachishi kankyushaīnkai. (2001). *Shin tokachi shi* [A New Tokachi History]. Obihiro: Tokachi Mainichi Shinbun.

Totman, Conrad. (2000). *A History of Japan*. Oxford: Blackwell.

Traphagan, John. (2019). *Cosmopolitan Rurality, Depopulation, and Entrepreneurial Ecosystems in 21st-Century Japan*. New York: Cambria Press.

———. (2017). "Entrepreneurs in Rural Japan: Gender, Blockage, and the Pursuit of Existential Meaning." *Asian Anthropology* 16 (2): 77–94.

———, ed. (2006). *Wearing Cultural Styles in Japan: Concepts of Tradition and Modernity in Practice*. Albany: State University of New York Press.

Tsing, Anna Lowenhaupt. (2015). *The Mushroom at the End of the World: On the Possibility of Life in Capitalist Ruins*. Princeton, NJ: Princeton University Press.

Tsuda Takeyuki. (2003). *Strangers Inside the Ethnic Homeland*. New York: Columbia University Press.

Tsunoda Tadanobu. (1985). *The Japanese Brain: Uniqueness and Universality*. Translated by Oiwa Yoshinori. Tokyo: Taishukan.

Tuan, Yi-Fu. (2002). "Community, Society, and the Individual." *Geographical Review* 92 (3): 307–318.

Turner, Victor. (1969). *The Ritual Process: Structure and Anti-structure*. New York: Transaction.

———. (1987). *The Anthropology of Performance*. New York: PAJ.

Umesao, Tadao. (2003). *An Ecological View of History: Japanese Civilization in the World Context*. Edited by Harumi Befu and translated by Beth Cary. Melbourne: Trans Pacific Press.

Ueunten, Wesley. (2008). "Okinawan Diasporic Identities: Between Being a Buffer and a Bridge." In *Transcultural Japan: At the Borderlands of Race, Gender, and Identity*, edited by David Blake Willis and Stephen Murphy-Shigematsu, 159–178. London: Routledge.

US Humane Society. (2003). "Cows." http://www.humanesociety.org/animals/cows/. Accessed June 3, 2020.

van Herk, Aritha. (2007). *Audacious and Adamant: The Story of Maverick Alberta*. Toronto, ON: Key Porter Books.

———. (2001). *Mavericks: An Incorrigible History of Alberta*. Toronto, ON: Penguin Books Canada.

Vialles, Noilie. (1994). *Animal to Edible*. Translated by J. A. Underwood. Cambridge: Cambridge University Press.

Victoria, Brian. (2001). *Zen at War*. New York: Weatherhill.

Virilio, Paul. (2007 [1977]). *Speed and Politics*. Translated by Benjamin Bratton. New York: Semiotext(e).

Vlastos, Stephen. (1986). *Peasant Protests and Uprisings in Tokugawa Japan*. Berkeley: University of California Press.

———. (1998). *Mirror of Modernity: Invented Traditions of Modern Japan*. Berkeley: University of California Press.

Vogel, Ezra. (1979). *Japan as Number One: Lessons for America*. Lincoln, NE: iUniverse.

Wacquant, Loic. (2000). *Body and Soul: Notebooks of an Apprentice Boxer*. Oxford: Oxford University Press.

Wagatsuma, Hiroshi, and George A. DeVos. (1984). *Heritage of Endurance: Family Patterns and Delinquency Formation in Urban Japan*. Berkeley: University of California Press.

Walker, Brett L. (2001). *The Conquest of Ainu Lands: Ecology and Culture in Japanese Expansion, 1500–1800*. Berkeley: University of California Press.

———. (2010). *Toxic Archipelago: A History of Industrial Disease in Japan*. Seattle: University of Washington Press.

Walthall, Anne. (1991). *Peasant Uprisings in Japan*. Chicago: University of Chicago Press.

Watanabe Hiroaki. (2018). "The Case against Abe's Constitutional Amendment." *East Asia Forum: Economics, Politics and Public Policy in East Asia and the Pacific*. http://www.eastasiaforum.org/2018/04/05/the-case-against-abes-constitutional-amendment/. Accessed February 10, 2019.

Watanabe Hitoshi. (1998 [1972]). *The Ainu Ecosystem and Group Structure*. Seattle: University of Washington Press.

Watanabe, Shōichi. (1989). *The Peasant Soul of Japan*. Toronto, ON: Palgrave Macmillan.

Watanabe Zenjiro. (2019). "The Meat-Eating Culture of Japan at the Beginning of Westernization." https://www.kikkoman.co.jp/kiifc/foodculture/pdf_09/e_002_008.pdf. Accessed February 10, 2019.

Watson, Mark K. (2014). *Japan's Ainu Minority in Tokyo: Diasporic Identity and Urban Politics*. London: Routledge.

Watsuji Tetsurō. (1996). *Watsuji Tetsurō's* Rinrigaku: *Ethics in Japan*. Edited and translated by Robert Carter and Seisaku Yamamoto. Albany: State University of New York Press.

Weber, Max. (2003). *The Protestant Ethic and the Spirit of Capitalism*. Translated by Talcott Parsons. New York: Dover.

Weiss, Brad. (2016). *Real Pigs: Shifting Values in the Field of Local Pork*. Durham, NC: Duke University Press.

Weller, Robert, and Keping Wu. (2020). *It Happens among People: Resonances and Extensions of the Work of Fredrik Barth*. New York: Berghahn Books.

Wenger, Étienne. (1998). *Communities of Practice: Learning, Meaning, and Identity*. Cambridge: Cambridge University Press.

Wharton, Annabel. (2015). *Architectural Agents: The Delusional, Abusive, Addictive Lives of Buildings*. Minneapolis: University of Minnesota Press.

White, Daniel. (2015). "How the Center Holds: Administering Soft Power and Cute Culture in Japan." In *Reframing Diversity in the Anthropology of Japan*, edited by John Ertl, John McCrery, John Mock, and Greg Poole, 99–120. Kanazawa: Kanazawa Center for Cultural Resource Studies.

Wigen, Karen. (1995). *The Making of a Japanese Periphery 1750–1920*. Berkeley: University of California Press.

Willis, David Blake, and Stephen Murphy-Shigematsu, eds. (2008). *Transcultural Japan: At the Borderlands of Race, Gender, and Identity*. London: Routledge.

Willis, Paul. (2003 [1977]). *Learning to Labour: How Working-Class Kids Get Working-Class Jobs*. Surrey, UK: Ashgate.

Wittgenstein, Ludwig. (2001 [1953]). *Philosophical Investigations*. Translated by G. E. M. Anscombe. Oxford, UK: Blackwell.

Wolfe, Cary. (2010). *What Is Posthumanism?* Minneapolis: University of Minnesota.

Wood, Donald. (2012) *Ogata-Mura: Sowing Dissent and Reclaiming Identity in a Japanese Farming Village*. New York: Berghahn Books.

Wu, Keping, and Robert Weller, eds. (2020). *It Happens among People: Resonances and Extensions of the Work of Fredrik Barth*. New York: Berghahn Books.

Yamashita, Shinji. (2008). "Transnational Migration of Women: Changing Boundaries of Contemporary Japan." in Nelson Graburn, John Ertl, and Kenji Tierney ed. *Multiculturalism in the New Japan: Crossing the Boundaries Within*, edited by Nelson Graburn, John Ertl, and Kenji Tierney, 101–116. New York: Berghahn Books.

Yamashita Yūsuke. (2015). *Chihō shōmetsu no wana—Masuda repōto to jinkō genshō shakai no shōtai* [The Disappearing Regions Trap: The Health of Depopulating Communities in the Masuda Report]. Tokyo: Chikuma Shinsho.

Yamazaki, Masakazu. (2000). *Individualism and the Japanese: An Alternative Approach to Cultural Comparison*. Translated by Barbara Sugihara. Tokyo: Japan Echo.

Yoda, Tomiko. (2006). "A Roadmap to Millennial Japan." In *Japan after Japan: Social and Cultural Life from the Recessionary 1990s to the Present*, edited by Tomiko Yoda and Harry Harootunian, 16–53. Durham, NC: Duke University Press.

Yonekura Masahiro. (2018). *Hokkaido 150 nen no shashin kiroku—ehagaki ko shashin ko chizu de yomigaeru kaikyū no jidai* [150 Years of Hokkaido Photographs: Looking at the Age of Nostalgia through Postcards, Old Photographs, and Old Maps]. Tokyo: Foto.

Yuji, Genda (2005). *A Nagging Sense of Job Insecurity: The New Reality Facing Japanese Youth*. Translated by Jean Connell Hoff. Tokyo: International House Japan.

———. (2009). *Hataraku kaijyō: otona no tame no wakamono dokuhon* [Too Much Work: A Young Reader's Book for Adults]. Tokyo: NTT Syuppan.

Zammito, John. (2003). *Kant, Herder, and the Birth of Anthropology*. Chicago: University of Chicago Press.

Zandanhōjin Hokkaido Shinchōson Shinkō Kyōkai. (2004). *Hokkaido 212 infōmeshi-yon hozonban* [Hokkaido 212 Information File]. Sapporo: Kouhoushya.

Ziomek, Kristen. (2019). *Lost Histories: Recovering the Lives of Japan's Colonial Peoples*. Cambridge, MA: Harvard University Press.

Zuehlke, Mark. (2001). *Scoundrels, Dreamers and Second Sons: British Remittance Men in the Canadian West*. Toronto, ON: Dundurn Group.

Index